D1175655

Strategic Unionism and Partnership

Strategic Unionism and Partnership

Boxing or Dancing?

Edited by

Tony Huzzard
National Institute for Working Life, Malmö and Lund University, Sweden

Denis Gregory
Ruskin College, Oxford, United Kingdom

Regan Scott
Labour and European Research Consultancy, London, United Kingdom

Selection and editorial matter © Tony Huzzard, Denis Gregory, Regan Scott
Individual chapters © Contributors 2004

All rights reserved. No reproduction, copy or transmission of this
publication may be made without written permission.

No paragraph of this publication may be reproduced, copied or transmitted
save with written permission or in accordance with the provisions of the
Copyright, Designs and Patents Act 1988, or under the terms of any licence
permitting limited copying issued by the Copyright Licensing Agency, 90
Tottenham Court Road, London W1T 4LP.

Any person who does any unauthorised act in relations to this publication
may be liable to criminal prosecution and civil claims for damages.

The authors have asserted their rights to be identified
as the authors of this work in accordance with the Copyright,
Designs and Patents Act 1988.

First published in 2004 by
PALGRAVE MACMILLAN
Houndmills, Basingstoke, Hampshire RG21 6XS and
175 Fifth Avenue, New York, N.Y. 10010
Companies and representatives throughout the world

PALGRAVE MACMILLAN is the global academic imprint of the Palgrave
Macmillan division of St. Martin's Press, LLC and of Palgrave Macmillan Ltd.
Macmillan® is a registered trademark in the United States, United Kingdom
and other countries. Palgrave is a registered trademark in the European
Union and other countries.

ISBN 1–4039–1756–6

This book is printed on paper suitable for recycling and made from fully
managed and sustained forest sources.

A catalogue record for this book is available from the British Library.

Library of Congress Cataloging-in-Publication Data

Strategic unionism and partnership : boxing or dancing? / edited by Tony
Huzzard, Denis Gregory, Regan Scott.
p. cm.
Includes bibliographical references and index.
ISBN 1–4039–1756–6
1. Industrial relations – Europe. 2. Industrial relations – United States.
3. Labor unions – Europe. 4. Labor unions – United States. 5. Cooperativeness.
I. Huzzard, Tony, 1957– II. Gregory, Denis. III. Scott, Regan.
HD8374.S77 2004
331′.094—dc22   2004046703

10 9 8 7 6 5 4 3 2 1
13 12 11 10 09 08 07 06 05 04

Printed and bound in Great Britain by
Antony Rowe Ltd, Chippenham and Eastbourne.

Contents

List of Tables, Figures and Exhibits

List of Abbreviations

AB	aktiebolag (public limited company, Sweden)
ACTU	Australian Council of Trade Unions
ADAPT	Adaptation of the workforce to industrial change (EU fifth framework project)
AFL-CIO	American Federation of Labor – Congress of Industrial Organizations
AG	joint-stock company (Germany)
AIB	Allied Irish Banks
AMICUS	acronym for engineering and electrical union, UK
AT&T	American Telephone and Telegraph Company
AWG	Anglian Water Group
AWS	Anglian Water Services
AWVN	National Employers' Service Institute (Netherlands)
B and D	boxing and dancing
CAE	European company representatives (Italy)
CB	collective bargaining
CBI	Confederation of British Industry
CEECs	Central and Eastern European Countries
CEEP	European Centre of Enterprises with Public Participation and of Enterprises of General Economic Interest
CEO	Chief Executive Officer
CF	Swedish Association of Graduate Engineers
CGB	Christlicher Gewerkschaftsbund Deutschlands (Christian Trade Union Federation, Germany)
CGIL	Confederazione Generale Italiana del Lavoro (The General Confederation of Italian Workers)
CGT	Confédération Générale du Travail (General Confederation of Unions, France)
CISL	Confederazione Italiana Sindacati Lavoratori (The Italian Confederation of Workers' Unions)
CNSRL	Confederatia Nationala a Sindicatelor Romane Libere (The National Free Trade Union Confederation of Romania)
CNV	Christelijk Nationaal Vakverbond (Christian National Trade Union Confederation, the Netherlands)
CSE	Comhlucht Siúicre Éireann Teoranta (former state owned sugar producer, Ireland)
CWA	Communications Workers Union (USA)

DAG	Deutsche Angestellten-Gewerkschaft (German White-Collar Trade Union)
DBB	Deutscher Beamtenbund (German Public Servants Federation)
DG5	Office of the Director General for Employment and Social Affairs (EU)
DGB	Deutscher Gewerkschaftsbund (German Trade Union Federation)
DPG	Deutsche Postgewerkschaft (Postal Trade Union, Germany)
DSM	Current name and former abbreviation for De Staatsmijnen (Dutch state mines that later developed into a leading player in the chemical industry)
EDC	European Distribution Centre
EEC	European Economic Community
EFTA	European Free Trade Area
EIRO	European Industrial Relations Observatory
EJIR	European Journal of Industrial Relations
EMF	European Metalworkers Federation
EMU	European Monetary Union
ESOP	employee share ownership plan
ETUC	European Trades Union Confederation
ETUI	ETUC Research Institute
EU	European Union
EUR	area of Rome where the CGIL Congress has taken place, Italy
EVC	Communist Trade Union Confederation (Netherlands)
EWC	European Works Councils
EWON	European Work Organisation Network
FEMCA	Federazione energia, moda, chimica e affini (Federation of Energy, Fashion, Chemical and Allied Workers, Italy)
FIE	see IBEC
FILCEA	Federazione Italiana Lavoratori Chimici (Italian Federation of Chemical Workers)
FIM-CISL	Federazione italiana metalmeccanici (Italian Federation of Metalworkers)
FIOM	CGIL Federazione italiana operai metallurgici (Italian Federation of Manual Metalworkers)
FNV	Federatie Nederlandse Vakbeweging (Confederation of Netherlands Trade Unions)
GDP	gross domestic product
GEW	Gewerkschaft Erziehung und Wissenschaft (Education and Science Trade Union, Germany)
GHR	Rotterdam Port Authority
GMB	General, Municipal and Boilermakers Union, UK

GNP	gross national product
GSO	Government Stationery Office (Ireland)
GWC	Global Works Council
HBV	Gewerkschaft Handel, Banken und Versicherungen (Trade, Banking and Insurance Trade Union, Germany)
HRM	human resource management
IBEC	Irish Business and Employers Confederation
IBOA	Irish Bank Officials' Association
ICFTU	International Congress of Free Trade Unions
ICI	Imperial Chemicals Industries
ICT	information and communications technology
ICTU	Irish Congress of Trade Unions
IG BAU	Industriegewerkschaft Bauen-Agrar-Umwelt (Construction, Agriculture and Environment Industrial Union, Germany)
IG BCE	Industriegewerkschaft Bergbau, Chemie, Energie (Mining, Chemicals and Energy Industrial Union, Germany)
IMF	International Monetary Fund
ILO	International Labour Organisation
IOD	Institute of Directors (UK)
IPA	Institute of Public Administration (Ireland)
IR	industrial relations
IT	information technology
IWU	Industrifacket (Swedish Industrial Workers Union)
LF	Lärarförbundet (The Swedish Union of Teachers)
LO	Landsorganisationen (Swedish blue-collar union confederation)
LR	Lärarnas Riksförbund (The National Union of Teachers in Sweden)
MBL	Medbestämmandelagen (Swedish Co-determination Act)
ME	Law on Mandatory Extension (Netherlands)
MHP	Vakcentrale voor Middengroepen en Hoger Personeel – (Trade Union Confederation for White Collar Groups, the Netherlands)
MNC	multinational company
MST	modern socio-technical approach
NAPs	National Action Plans for Jobs
NCPP	National Centre for Partnership and Performance (Ireland)
NER	Non-union Employee Relations
NET	Nítrigin Éireann Teoranta (former state owned fertiliser manufacturer, Ireland)
NGG	Gewerkschaft Nahrung-Genuss-Gaststätten (Food, Beverages and Catering Trade Union, Germany)
NGOs	non-governmental organisations

NKV	Nederlands Katholiek Vakverbond (Netherlands CatholicTrade Union Confederation)
NRC	Current name and former abbreviation for Nieuwe Rotterdamse Courant (New Rotterdams Newspaper)
NS	Dutch Railways
NVV	Nederlands Verbond van Vakverenigingen (Netherlands Confederation of Trade Unions)
OECD	Organisation for Economic Co-operation and Development
OFWAT	Office of Water Regulation (UK)
OMC	open method of co-ordination
OPEC	Organization of the Petroleum Exporting countries
OPEL	group work agreements (Germany)
OT	organisation theory
ÖTV	Gewerkschaft Öffentliche Dienste, Transport und Verkehr (Public Services, Transport and Traffic Trade Union, Germany)
PCW	Programme for Competitiveness and Work (Ireland)
PESP	Programme for Social and Economic Progress (Ireland)
PNR	Programme for National Recovery (Ireland)
PPF	Programme for Prosperity and Fairness (Ireland)
QWL	quality of working life
R & D	research and development
RIL	Rotterdam Internal Logistics
RSU	Rappresentanze sindacali unitarie (Union unitary representatives – Italy)
RUD	The Union Role in Workplace Development (LO, Sweden)
SACO	Sveriges Akademikers Centralorganisation (The Swedish Confederation of Professional Associations)
SAF	Svenska Arbetsgivareförening (Swedish Employers Confederation)
SAP	Svenska Arbetarnas Partiet (Swedish Social Democratic Party)
SAYE	Save-as-you-Earn
SEK	Swedish Kronor
SER	Social-Economic Council (Netherlands)
SIF	Sif (Swedish Association for Professional and Technical Workers in Industry)
SIPTU	Services, Industrial, Professional and Technical Union (Ireland)
SME	small and medium sized enterprise
STAR	Foundation of Labour (Netherlands)
SVZ	Port Employers Federation (Rotterdam)
TCO	Tjänstemannens Centralorganisation (the Swedish Confederation of Professional Employees)
TGWU	Transport and General Workers Union, UK
TUAC	Trade Union Advisory Committee (ILO)
TUC	Trades Union Congress (UK)

TUPE	Transfer of Undertakings Protection of Employment (UK)
UAW	United Automobile Workers Union (USA)
UIL	Unione Italiana del Lavoro (The Union of Italian Workers)
UILM-UIL	Unione Italiana Lavoratori Metalmeccanici (Italian Union of Metalworkers)
UK	United Kingdom
UNICE	Union of Industrial and Employers' Confederations of Europe
UNISON	acronym for public service union, UK
US	United States
USCC	union strategic choice curve
VAL	value added logistics
ver.di	Vereinte Dienstleistungsgewerkschaft (United Services Trade Union, Germany)
VMBO	Dutch school system
VVMC	a young non-confederation union of NS drivers (Netherlands)

Notes on the Contributors

Mirella Baglioni is Professor of Industrial Relations at the University of Parma (Faculty of Economics). From 1995 to 2000 she taught Comparative Industrial Relations at the University of Florence. Her recent fields of research are European Industrial Relations, Social Dialogue and European Works Councils. She has worked on public policies and industrial relations and interest representation: among the various articles produced in this field, publications in English include 'Public policy, territorial agreements and socio-economic regulation', in Széll G. and G.P. Cella (2002), *The Injustice at Work*, Frankfurt, Peter Lang and (together with S. Vicari); *Two Models of Local Development Politics*, 'Government and Policy' (1995, vol. 13).
E-mail: mirella.baglioni@ipruniv.cce.unipr.it

Steven Deutsch is Professor Emeritus, Labor Education and Research Center, University of Oregon. His career over four decades focused upon labour participation at work and in the economy. He introduced union training on worker participation in union and university labour education curricula in the US, the AFL-CIO training curricula, and in work with many national unions in the US and internationally (Canada, Australia, New Zealand, Norway, Sweden). He has written widely on industrial democracy, work restructuring, work environment and strategic unionism.
E-mail: sdeutsch@uoregon.edu

Erling Forsman graduated with a degree from the Stockholm College of Journalism in 1973. Since the beginning of the 1980s he has worked as a journalist for a number of trade union newspapers and journals in Sweden. His particular areas of interest include work organisation, payments systems and trade union strategic choices. He currently works as Chief Editor for *TCO-tidningen*, the newspaper of the Swedish Confederation of Professional Employees (TCO) in Stockholm.
E-mail: erling.forsman@tco.se

Denis Gregory teaches Labour Relations and Labour Economics at Ruskin College Oxford. He has been a consultant to the Trade Union Research Unit at Ruskin for more than 30 years. During this time he has supported a wide range of UK trade unions as a consultant and trainer. He has recently been heavily involved in developing and delivering joint training programmes for unions and companies looking to achieve high performance labour relations. Since 2001 he has been an Associate Consultant to the TUC Partnership Institute.
E-mail: dgregory@ruskin.ac.uk

Tony Huzzard holds a PhD in Business Administration from Umeå University. His research interests are organisational learning and change as well as critical perspectives on management and organising. He is currently a senior lecturer at the Department of Business Administration, Lund University and is also a Research Fellow at the National Institute for Working Life in Malmö. His research activities have included organisational development and the quality of working life in a regional health authority as well as studies of social partnership and European Works Councils. Recent publications include: *Labouring to Learn: Union Renewal in Swedish Manufacturing* (Boréa, 2000) as well as a number of journal articles on trade union organisation and learning.
E-mail: tony.huzzard@arbetslivsinstitutet.se or tony.huzzard@fek.lu.se

Karl Koch is Emeritus Professor of Modern Languages at London South Bank University and Visiting Professor in the Graduate School of Management, Assumption University, Bangkok, Thailand. He has held Visiting Professorships at the University of New South Wales, Sydney, Aristotle University, Thessaloniki, University Sorbonne IV, Paris and Luis Vives (CEU) San Pablo University, Madrid. He is a past Chair of the Association for the Study of German Politics. He has published widely on German and Comparative Industrial Relations and German Area Studies. He is currently researching on European models of employee participation and cultural diversity in management.
E-mail: karl.koch@eidosnet.co.uk

Martin Kuhlmann holds a Dr. disc. pol. from Göttingen University as a sociologist. He works at the Soziologisches Forschungsinstitut (SOFI) [sociological research institute] at the University of Göttingen covering different areas of industrial sociology. He has worked on the impact of new production technologies and management concepts on working structures in different industries such as cars, chemicals and pharmaceuticals *Trendreport Rationalisierung* (Berlin, 1994), on new concepts of work organisation such as group work and continuous improvement and their impact on workers, and on a broad range of work-related issues including reorganisation, shop floor management and pay systems *Konzepte innovativer Arbeitspolitik* [concepts of innovative work policy] (Berlin, 2004); *Arbeit im Umbruch?* [Work in transition?] (Berlin, 2004).
E-mail: mkuhlma1@gwdg.de

Aldo Marchetti holds a degree in History and Philosophy from the State University of Milan and a post-degree diploma in Sociology from the COSPOS School of Sociology. He has worked as a researcher at CISL (Italian Confederation of Workers Unions) and he currently works as senior researcher at the Pietro Seveso Foundation. He also works at the Industrial and Labour Sociology Department of the State University of Milan as

Temporary Contract Professor. His research interests are working time and working conditions, industrial relations and vocational training. Recent publications include *La crisi dei ceti medi* (Guerini, 2000), *Sistemi territoriali della produzione automobilistica* (F. Angeli, 2002).
E-mail: marchetti.aldo@tiscali.it

Tommy Nilsson holds a PhD in Sociology from Lund University, Sweden, and is an Associate Professor in Sociology at Stockholm University. He works at the Swedish National Institute for Working Life in Stockholm, and his research is mainly in the fields of work organisation, modern production systems, payment systems and local industrial relations. He has published books and articles on individual wage setting for blue-collar workers, and on shop floor workers' participation in continuous improvement, and industrial relations in Sweden. He is now finishing a critically oriented book about networking for competence development, which Swedish unions have used as a method in order to support local union representatives in their work on work organisation issues.
E-mail: tommy.nilsson@niwl.se

Kevin O'Kelly was a research manager at the European Foundation for the Improvement of Living and Working Conditions, Dublin, until 2003, working on a range of research projects on industrial relations and work organisation. He represented the Foundation on the European Commission's Work Organisation Network (EWON). He also works with the Council of Europe, Strasbourg, the International Labour Office Training Centre, Turin, and the European Trade Union Institute, Brussels, on a wide range of workplace related issues, including work organisation, employment and social dialogue, in particular in the Central and Eastern European and Balkan countries. He is currently a visiting research fellow with the University of Limerick.
E-mail: okellykp@eircom.net

Regan Scott spent 34 years working in various capacities in the head office of the UK's leading multi-industrial union, the Transport and General Workers Union. Originally in economic research, he became managing editor of the union's newspaper and media, was appointed National Secretary for Research, Education and Parliamentary Affairs in 1979, and took up a newly created post of National European Coordinator in 1992. This involved the start of EWC development in the UK, liaison with the Brussels Commission and European Parliament and sectoral work notably with the European Metalworkers and Foodworkers Federations and the European TUC. He is now a freelance researcher.
E-mail: reganscottlondon@excite.com

Wim Sprenger studied Social Sciences at Amsterdam University. Until his pre-retirement in 2001 he was a paid officer for the largest Dutch Confederation

of Trade Unions, FNV, and its predecessor NVV. In between he lectured industrial relations at the Hogeschool van Amsterdam. At NVV and FNV he was responsible for trade union education and has served as a research manager, policy officer and project organiser. Since 2001 he has been an independent researcher and project organiser, specialising in trade union innovations. Among his publications are a comparative study on unions and their educational work in four European countries, educational leave in Germany, Italy and the Netherlands, industrial relations in professional soccer and horse racing, trade unions and outsourcing, as well as descriptions of participation projects within unions.
E-mail: wim.sprenger@xs4all.nl

Aurora Trif is currently completing a PhD at London South Bank University. The PhD is titled 'The Transfer of a Market Economy Model of Industrial Relations at Plant Level to Eastern Europe: Case Study – Romania.' Her main research interest is in the transformation of industrial relations in different economic and political contexts. She has worked on a project for the European Commission on 'Industrial Relations in the Construction Sector of Central and Eastern European States' and has been teaching HRM and Employment Relations at London South Bank University. Recent publications include: *The Transformation of Industrial Relations at the Micro-level in Romania* (2000) and *Trade Union Rights in Romania* (2001).
E-mail: a.trif@lycos.com

Maarten van Klaveren is an economist and consultant at STZ Consultancy & Research, Eindhoven, the Netherlands. He worked in the Research Department of the main Dutch trade union confederation FNV and its predecessor NVV (1969–86), researching and developing union policies on industrial democracy, work organisation and new technology. As an STZ workers' consultant, he has been involved in a number of large projects on organisational and technological change, especially in the port of Rotterdam, in the food industry, and in banking and insurance. He has researched and published widely on employment and the quality of work in these and other sectors, and on the methodology of working life research. Current research focuses on labour market segmentation, industrial relations and trade union innovation, teleworking and call centre work.
E-mail: K.G.Tijdens@uva.nl or stzhq@planet.nl

Editors' Foreword
The SALTSA Project 'The New Trade Union – Boxing and Dancing'

This book is the major output of a project called 'The New Trade Union – Boxing and Dancing' which took its first steps in 1998. It was one of many other projects within the framework of the Swedish 'SALTSA' research programme. 'SALTSA' is the acronym for the four Swedish actors involved, namely, the three top union confederations of LO (the blue collar confederation), TCO (white collar and professionals) and SACO (professionals) together with the National Institute for Working Life, which also finances the programme. The SALTSA projects have focused on various aspects of working life covering the areas of 'work environment', 'labour market' and 'work organisation'. The project presented here was performed within the area of work organisation.

The New Trade Union project was unique within the SALTSA programme in the way that both researchers and union activists from a range of countries were involved. These individuals constituted a network that met twice a year to exchange experience and engage in discussion on union and industrial relations 'futures'. This type of international exchange generated a knowledge base that was valuable both for the unionists and for the academic participants. The project started with participants from Germany, the UK, The Netherlands, Ireland, Italy and Sweden, representing the EU, and Hungary and US as two countries outside EU. For various reasons the participants from Hungary could not participate in the project to the end and that country's experience is therefore not represented in this book. At a late stage, however, we were able to include a contribution on Romania. The US was included as a counterbalance to what would otherwise have been an entirely euro-centric view of trade union futures. Moreover, it was felt necessary to have at least some reference to the many 'experiments' on co-operation at company level that have taken place in recent years in the US.

Context of the project

The research project was initiated in a contextual backdrop marked by two major influences. The first of these was the general international trend towards the decentralisation of industrial relations that has been observed from the 1980s. The fact that bargaining and other key industrial relations activities were increasingly taking place at enterprise or workplace level, called for a development of new or additional forms of co-operation between organised labour and capital at various levels. These emerging forms of co-operation have been seen by some as a sort of renaissance of what Schmitter has called 'Neo-Corporatism' (see Traxler, 1996 and Elvander, 2002). Others have described these new developments as 'managerial corporatism' (see Brulin and Nilsson, 1991), 'micro-corporatism' (Ferner and Hyman, 1998) and 'competitive corporatism'. The dominant use of the word 'corporatism' rather implies that the independence of unions was somehow at risk from the particular type of co-operation that has emerged. In later chapters we attempt to shed some empirical light on this contention.

The second source of inspiration for this project was the Green Paper 'Partnership – for a New Organisation of Work', published by the European Commission in 1997 (European Commission, 1997). The message in the Green Paper was that in order to improve competitiveness in the EU and increase employment, employers and worker representatives (whether through trade unions or works councils) had to develop more efficient forms of work organisation through greater dialogue and participation at the workplace. The Green Paper was, in effect, an important alternative to both the neo-liberal, economic orthodoxy espoused by the EU's earlier 1993 White Paper: 'Growth, Competitiveness and Employment.' It also challenged the view that 'lean production' as exemplified by the Japanese auto industry, was set to be the dominant form of (neo-Taylorist) work organisation in all developed economies. The message of the Green Paper, were it to be taken seriously, had major implications on trade union roles, identities and strategies.

The core terms of the book

The book is aimed at both practitioner and academic audiences with all the compromises that implies in both form and substance. From the points of departure outlined above, it explores the relationship between *social partnership* and *trade union renewal* in a comparative context with a view to informing and stimulating debate among industrial relations practitioners and researchers. By way of introduction to the text, however, a brief presentation of the key terms in the book is called for. As we explain in the book, the notion of 'social partnership' is conceptually troublesome, not least because of varying national and industrial relations cultures. To get round such difficulties we have used the terms *'boxing'* and *'dancing'* throughout the project and this book as metaphors for denoting adversarial and co-operative modes of industrial relations engagement respectively.

We have found that the terms 'boxing' and 'dancing' are usable for both practitioners and researchers as generic metaphors that cut across the problems of international diversity and provide us with a common language for the dialogue from which the book is a product. We also explore the issue of partnership or 'dancing' as a trade union strategy. In this connection, we draw on and develop the concept of *strategic choice* from the industrial relations literature (Kochan *et al.*, 1984). In our view this offers a conceptual bridge between *social partnership* and *trade union renewal* in that both of these can be seen as strategic choices; the question, however, is the extent to which they are related and conditional on one another.

References

Brulin, G. and Nilsson, T. (1991) 'From Societal to Managerial Corporatism: New Forms of Work Organization as a Transformation Vehicle', *Economic and Industrial Democracy* 12(3): 327–46.

Elvander, N. (2002) *Industrial Relations – A Short Story of Ideas and Learning*, Stockholm: National Institute for Working Life, Work Life in Transition, 2002: 3.

European Commission (1997) *Partnership for a New Organisation of Work*. Green Paper COM 97: 128.

Ferner, A. and Hyman, R. (eds) (1998) *Changing Industrial Relations in Europe*. Oxford: Blackwell Publishers.

Kochan, T. A., McKersie, R. B. and Capelli, P. (1984) 'Strategic Choice and Industrial Relations Theory', *Industrial Relations* 23(1): 16–39.

Traxler, F. (1996) 'Collective Bargaining and Industrial Change – A Case of Disorganization? A Comparative Analysis of Eighteen OECD Countries', *European Sociological Review* 12: 271–87.

A Brief Note on Method

We elaborate further on our core terms – social partnership, boxing and dancing, strategic choice, trade union renewal – at appropriate places in the book. Before proceeding, however, a brief note is required on our methodology. The book contains country overview chapters from eight countries that aim to tell the basic recent storyline on boxing and dancing in the country concerned. These are supplemented and supported by a number of case studies undertaken by the researchers and practitioners active in the project. The cases are selected to illustrate aspects of the national story in each case, yet cannot be considered to be necessarily representative of what are hugely complex and diverse phenomena.

Accordingly, there was no systematic design for precise choices on fieldwork, but the final selection of cases included in the Appendices and from which the country chapters draw do represent a broad diversity of focus, both in terms of industrial sector and level of union activity.[1] Moreover, two cases of trade union innovation are included, the RUD Project and Industribution, from Sweden and the Netherlands respectively. One aim of the cases has been to generate dialogue between researchers and practitioners within the course of the project. It is also our hope that the material will also stimulate further dialogue within and between these two communities elsewhere.

Note

1. An important industrial relations arena emergent at the transnational level is that of European Works Councils (EWCs). Extensive treatment of these, however, is beyond the scope of the current study given its focus on a comparative perspective across countries. Two members of the research team contributing to this book have, however, been actively engaged in research on EWCs, findings from which will be reported elsewhere, notably the online facilities of the European Foundation for the improvement of Living and Working Conditions.

Acknowledgements

By way of an acknowledgement, we would like to express our thanks to all who participated in the project and the rich dialogue to which they contributed and without which this book would not have materialised. A full list of the participants is as follows:

Mirella Baglioni	University of Parma, Italy
Steven Deutsch	University of Oregon, Eugene, USA
Erling Forsman	The Swedish Confederation of Professional Employees, Stockholm, Sweden
Denis Gregory	Ruskin College, Oxford, UK
Jörg Hofmann	IG Metall, Germany
Tony Huzzard	The National Institute for Working Life, Malmö, Sweden
Martin Kuhlmann	University of Göttingen, Germany
Aldo Marchetti	Pietro Seveso Foundation, Milan, Italy
Jack Nash	SIPTU, Dublin, Ireland
Tommy Nilsson	The National Institute for Working Life, Stockholm, Sweden
Claes Norrhede	The Union of Service and Communication Employees, Stockholm, Sweden
Regan Scott	Labour and European Research Consultancy, London, UK and formerly the TGWU Head Office, London
Wim Sprenger	Formerly of FNV, Amsterdam, The Netherlands
Maarten van Klaveren	STZ Consultancy & Research, Eindhoven, The Netherlands

We would also like to thank Karl Koch (London South Bank University) and Per-Olof Bergström (formerly of the Swedish Trade Union Confederation) for their valuable critical commentaries on early drafts of the text at a seminar in Parma, Italy, in June 2003. Thanks are also due to Karl Koch, Aurora Trif (London South Bank University) and Kevin O'Kelly (University of Limerick) for agreeing to contribute to the book in the closing stages. Finally, we would like to thank all involved with the SALTSA Programme, without whose support the book would not have been possible.

1
Seconds Away: Naming and Framing the Book

Denis Gregory and Tommy Nilsson

Aims of the book

The main questions addressed in this book concern how unions in a number of European countries and the US have handled the challenges raised by the need to develop structures and practices of social partnership. How far has union management co-operation extended when it comes to issues that are beyond wages and working conditions, such as economic growth, competitiveness and work organisation development? Has social partnership changed the level and nature of union management engagement at workplace, company, sectoral, regional or national level? Have unions compromised their independence through social partnership? Finally, does partnership work in the sense that it delivers measurable business and social benefits that are sufficient to sustain this new form of co-operation?

Linked to the specific issues raised above is the more general question of the importance of social partnership as a distinctive approach to industrial relations and the challenges it poses for the key actors involved. From a national or an EU perspective it is plain that the particularities of industrial relations systems have a direct role in delivering or constraining work organisation and competence development at the micro level with consequent effects at a macro level on competitiveness, economic growth, employment and welfare development. This was the perspective and linkage explored in the 1997 Green Paper 'Partnership – for a New Organisation of Work' (European Commission, 1997). The singular message in that text was that a social partnership approach at the micro level could, if sufficiently diffused, generate significant macro-economic benefits at national and EU level.

From an employer point of view social partnership tends to be framed in the micro-economic context of increased competitiveness and profits. The initial research questions here concern whether the promise of social partnership has proved sufficient to overcome the well-known reluctance of some employers to engage with unions at all and the extent to which it has encouraged others to widen their existing engagement beyond the narrow confines of pay bargaining and grievance handling. At a practical level, all employers, whether reluctant or willing participants in social partnership are interested in the results. As our case studies show, this interest is not wholly confined to 'bottom line' profits and productivity expectations. Employers have also recognised that social partnership can be a powerful mechanism in designing and delivering change processes at the workplace. The question here concerns the degree to which employers who invite unions and workers to participate in organisational change gain durable competitive advantage over rivals who impose change in a more unilateral fashion.

As far as unions are concerned, it has been claimed, not least in texts published by union confederations in both the UK and US, that social partnership holds out a number of possibilities. Most obviously at enterprise level it could provide the potential for unions to extend their influence and with it their ability to defend and advance their members' interests (Nilsson, 1999). Moreover, extending and applying the concept of social partnership at sectoral and national level can arguably boost union influence and credibility within the framework of bi- or tri-partite agreements. Attractive though these possibilities are, they are not risk-free for the unions involved. The key union actors in partnership development tend to be acutely conscious of the charge that partnership inevitably leads to 'corporatism' and the compromising of union independence. There is a tension between extending union influence over decision making and 'being in bed with management' (with all the consequences that such a position traditionally implies) which ensures that partnership is never an easy option for trade unionists. Nevertheless, union density and influence has declined considerably in many developed countries in the last two decades compelling unions to search for new strategies to demonstrate their value and legitimacy. In this context, the chances of a revival for the European union movement might depend upon unions' ability to develop partnership approaches that combine the capacity for both bargaining (and using the conflict weapon) and co-operation to protect the employees' short-term and long-term interests. Streeck (1987), for example, has argued that it is important for unions to choose a 'productionist strategy' and not the alternative of 'optimistic conservatism'. One of the purposes of this book is to assess the effectiveness of social partnership as a dynamic strategy for union renewal. In doing this we develop and apply the concept of strategic choice initially introduced into the industrial relations vocabulary in the mid-1980s by Thomas Kochan and colleagues in the US (Kochan *et al.*, 1986).

We are acutely aware that the debates around social partnership have proved, ideologically, to be a highly contested terrain within most, if not all, European trade union movements. Some practitioners, inspired by Marxist positions, are instinctively suspicious of partnership and argue that almost by definition it is an act of collusion with the adversary and must inevitably undermine the capacity of unions to perform their basic function: that of looking after members' interests. Others, however, would argue that if unions are to exist as legitimate actors in working life they also have to 'add value' to employers and that co-operation is perfectly natural where joint interests of survival and prosperity can be discerned in an increasingly competitive and globalised environment. So where do we stand? Our aim is neither to embrace partnership as a union strategy nor to debunk it. Rather, the approach adopted here is to evaluate partnership in practice with a view to stimulating discussion and debate on trade union futures. If we provoke either side in the debate, or better still both, then we will have succeeded in our aims.

The 'boxing and dancing' metaphor

In the 'New Trade Union' project the metaphor 'boxing and dancing' has been used to convey the range and type of engagement that typifies an industrial relations system. The adversarial approach ('boxing') to joint regulation normally associated with collective bargaining is contrasted with approaches where employers and unions seek to co-operate and work together ('dancing') to find common ground for mutual gains (Kochan and Osterman, 1994). To put this a little more incisively, collective bargaining is frequently caricatured as a process whereby 'excessive' union demands for higher pay collide with 'derisory' offers and 'unrealistic' expectations from management. From these unpromising beginnings a negotiation, sometimes punctuated with bouts of industrial action, takes place until a 'shabby' compromise is reached. At the end of the bargaining process the parties leave the table with a signed agreement but with suspicious minds. Rarely is either of the sides fully satisfied with the result. Nonetheless, the outcome of the negotiations tends to be easy to administer, the employees get more money and the employers settle back to running the business. The two parties' *mutual* work is finished until the next bargaining round begins.

However, compared to wage bargaining, issues like work organisation, skills development and the introduction of new technology require important differences in the nature and timing of any union–management engagement. The successful implementation of these issues depends upon the promotion of a far higher degree of consensus at the workplace based on continuous dialogue, in other words the *dancing* of mutual exploration. In collective bargaining (boxing) the respective roles of the partners are clear-cut and familiar. Not so when the unions accept the employer's invitation to the dance – the roles are much less familiar: what happens on the dance floor? Who is leading whom in the dance of workplace development?

It is hardly surprising, then, that uncertainties abound on the dance floor. For example, unions can either be reactive or proactive here. They can be passive and wait for the employers to make the first move before revealing their own moves. This reactive strategy has, for example, often been deployed at Swedish workplaces when the Co-determination Act has been used. By contrast, unions can independently take the initiative in solving problems and putting important issues on the table. A proactive union approach is normally based on well-developed local knowledge and competence concerning issues like work organisation and change processes. In Sweden, for instance, this has materialised in the LO (Landsorganisationen) project 'The Union Role in Workplace Development', which is presented in this book as Appendix 15.

There are also a variety of 'dance floors' from workplace level through to national level where dancing generally involves three partners: organised labour, capital and the state. Recently, the development of trans-national European Works Councils (EWCs) has significantly expanded the variety of trade union partners as well as extending the location of the union–management engagement. However, it should be noted here that the limited roles adopted by most EWCs have tended to restrict both the frequency and potency of the dance at this level.

It is plain that the incidence and influence of industrial relations 'dancing' varies between countries. In some, such as France and Italy, dancing appears to be relatively weakly developed at the company level. In others, for example, Sweden, dancing has taken place for some years at national and sectoral levels as well as at company level. It is worth noting, however, that at national level the once-powerful centralised Swedish model has declined during the last 20 years (Hammarström *et al.*, 2004). In Ireland dancing has been well-developed at the national level through the 'Partnership 2000 for Inclusion, Employment and Competitiveness' programme. In countries where works councils exist, a type of dancing activity is inherent in the concept itself. Management and workers' representatives are supposed to work together within the framework of information and consultation. This may partly explain why unions sometimes appear (e.g., in Germany) to be more reluctant to try new forms of dancing. However, Dutch unions, who up to now have not hesitated to be involved in various types of dancing, do not seem to be constrained by their lengthy exposure to works councils. The extent to which the existence of a works council may impose a constraint on 'dancing', for example, by overformalising the union–management engagement (a bit like Texas-line dancing: lots of movement (discourse) but all of it agreed and rehearsed in advance) is of course a highly pertinent question given the implementation of the EU's Directive on Participation and Consultation due to come into force in 2005.

We elaborate further on our metaphors of 'boxing and dancing' in Chapter 2, but before moving on it is perhaps worthwhile explaining why metaphors are useful at all. The distinction between adversarial and co-operative modes of engagement is of course nothing new in industrial relations. Accordingly, readers of this book may well ask 'why bother' to deploy new metaphors for well-established phenomena. Our reply to this is to draw attention to the potential that metaphors have of opening up new ways of seeing and understanding. We use metaphors not just because they are effective representations of what we are thinking (Lakoff and Johnson, 1980), but also because of their simplicity and their capacity to relate our experiences to what we already believe. Their power as linguistic artefacts has been acknowledged in the retrospective sensemaking that is ongoing both in the empirical settings we study and in our own engagements with our settings as researchers (Weick, 1995). The more directly a metaphor can translate something into a context we are familiar with – that is, the semantic field that the metaphor constructs – the easier it becomes for us to make sense of that something. But metaphors have a double-bind: they contain representations of phenomena that are known yet at the same time they open up possibilities for innovation as they also give shape and meaning to the unknown.

Throughout the project on which the current book is based we have consistently used the 'boxing' and 'dancing' metaphors in our dialogues with practitioners from various countries. We have also found that practitioners in the field have used them, often without prompting, in our empirical investigations, for example, during interviews. Moreover, during the course of the project we have discovered that the terms 'boxing' and 'dancing' have set up two rich semantic fields for exploring the complexities of contemporary industrial relations. We know that unions will rarely, if ever, engage with employers on either a wholly co-operative or a wholly adversarial basis (Haynes and Allen, 2001). Some elements of both will co-exist to greater or lesser degrees. But where collective bargaining is dominant, we can evoke images of the boxer Muhammad Ali 'floating like a butterfly and stinging like a bee', doing 'the Ali shuffle'. Alternatively, in a situation of comprehensive partnership a Morris dance or the dance at a Ceilidh may be better images than the shared interests and movement of a waltz as even in the most enduring partnerships there can indeed be moments of aggressive disagreement.

The difficulties of the 'dance'

During the last two decades unions in Western Europe and the US have been facing a range of problems and challenges. At a general macro-economic level the trend towards what Margaret Thatcher once called 'rolling back the state' has been prominent across most of the developed nations of the world. The US and the UK may have begun the neo-liberal strategies of deregulation and privatisation but most EU member states facing similar budgetary pressures soon followed their lead. This rupture in the post-war social democratic consensus, together with the abandonment of Keynesian economic management for the harsher rigours of market forces represented not so much a change of tune, as the arrival of a completely new orchestra with different instruments. The tempo of industrial restructuring with heavy job losses in the manufacturing sectors and major upheavals (privatisation) in the public sector made dancing very difficult for many unions throughout the 1980s and well into the 1990s.

Notwithstanding these constraints, dancing did survive in the 1990s at the national level in certain country contexts. In some, tripartite employment pacts in fact added to the existing structures of dialogue and participation. Moreover, the development of sectoral tripartite dialogues within the EU further extended the dance floor at the European level. The EU Green Paper on 'Partnership for a New Organisation of Work' can be read as a logical extension of the Commission's dialogue strategy but it was also a highly significant signal for labour and capital to start dancing again at enterprise and workplace level.

Boxing and dancing as modes of industrial relations engagement require contrasting mindsets, discursive techniques and skills. Yet a trade union official or shop steward may necessarily be obliged to switch from a boxing mindset with the employer over salary negotiations before lunch to a dancing mindset in a workplace development project after lunch. This may conceivably be followed by a further role – that of competent consultant on, say, work organisation at a union branch meeting in the evening as a means of buying a ticket for subsequent admission to the dance floor. Union or works councils representatives will thus often be required to shift between conflictual and co-operative practices even on a daily basis, albeit within a culture that is predominantly conflictual or predominantly co-operative.

Globalisation and transnational union responses

Considerable debate has waged in recent years on the contention that a process of globalisation is underway marking profound shifts in economic structures, the organisation of work and institutional arrangements. Evidence of this is typically presented in the form of increasing competitive pressure, global outsourcing, developments in communications technology, a reduction in tariffs and a homogenisation of consumer tastes and branding (Klein, 2000). Bartlett and Ghoshal (1989), for example, argue that the world economy is becoming dominated by three trading blocs: Europe, North America and the Pacific Rim with multinational companies operating across borders within each bloc and transnational companies active in all three. Moreover, what particularly marks out the current trend is the expanded role of world financial markets, 'increasingly operating on a real-time basis' (Giddens, 1998: 30). Although transnational business operations have a long history (Hirst and Thompson, 1996), what is indisputably new is the codification of financial information in electronic databases and its instantaneous electronic transmission (Zuboff, 1988; Blackler, 1995).

The upshot of globalisation is that international factors outside the control of European firms and governments are dictating their competitive environments and thereby the terms on which employment is created and maintained on the continent. Moreover, the impact of these factors is profound not just on firms and states, but also on trade unions. In the context of global competition in manufacturing and the downward pressure on wages from newly available labour markets in places such as Eastern Europe, unions in the EU will find it increasingly difficult to simultaneously improve the pay and conditions of their members and deliver job security (Klein, 2000). This has even been seen as presaging a collision course between the haves and have-nots (Stiglitz, 2003). A further consequence is the impact of technology on the labour process in service industries. In many cases, services no longer need to be produced and consumed simultaneously in time and space. Many call centres, for example, are now being outsourced from Europe to Asia as firms seek to add value through cost reductions. In sum, labour has to find new ways in which to compete if jobs are to remain in Europe.

These trends pose a considerable challenge to unions. Strategic responses have included, for example, the setting up of European Works Councils, an ongoing process that has been made possible not least by political strategies of labour movements in Europe that have sought to pursue legislative underpinning for transnational organising. Yet in many respects, infant though EWCs are, there is little likelihood that they will suffice as a strategy for keeping multinational capital in check, not least because the true arena of capital is the global marketplace – well beyond the EU's legislative reach (Hardt and Negri, 2001). A further difficulty is that many unions still work cognitively and behaviourally within the assumptions and limitations of nation-based institutional formations. The problem here is that strategies relying on such formations are about closing the stable door of the nation state long after the horse of global capital has bolted. The need for exploring new strategic options has therefore become an urgent requirement for EU unions, particularly as the union itself – and thereby its market – has been enlarged to include countries with radically different union traditions and cost bases that make it hard for established EU workplaces to compete.

Drum and base rate

Currently, the macro-economic dance floor, in the EU at least, is reverberating to the drumbeat of the European Central Bank as it seeks to enforce the fiscal harmony (convergence criteria and stability pact) required of the members of the European Monetary Union (EMU). The consequences of this are measured in continued and in some cases increasing pressures to cut public expenditure thus further straining relationships with significant sections of the trade union movement right across the EU. As the EMU gears up to enable the EU to compete globally, unions are being encouraged to partake in yet another dance to improve 'workforce flexibility and skills' which may also include work organisation development (Casey and Gold 2000: 122). In the meantime, whilst inflation has been reduced to manageable levels within most of the EU, unemployment remains high in some member states. In addition, the enlargement of the EU has introduced further fears of social dumping and raised the prospect of significant relocation of productive capacity to the new entrants at the expense of employment opportunities in Northern and Western Europe. With no real signs of any slackening in the grip of neo-liberal economics on the governments of the EU, the potential for dancing at the macro-economic level remains severely constrained from a trade union standpoint although, paradoxically, the need for such engagement has, if anything, grown more urgent.

At the micro-economic (enterprise) level there are two contradictory trends. One is related to the traditional management pursuit of organisational efficiency through cost reductions and increased labour productivity. The favoured strategy to achieve this remains the widespread implementation of 'lean production/lean manning', with a strong emphasis on team working, continuous improvements and quality enhancement. From a work organisation perspective, lean production has been criticised as being highly 'Tayloristic' and oppressive to the workforce (Parker and Slaughter, 1988; Berggren, 1995). It has, in addition, been shown to be at odds with the more participative approach to work organisation favoured by the developers and practitioners of socio-technical systems theory who dominated much of the European debate until the early 1980s (Huzzard, 2003).

To an extent, the shift to lean production effectively killed off what had been a fairly productive dance on work organisation (the closure of Volvo's Uddevalla plant was perhaps the most significant example of this). The other, somewhat contradictory, trend concerns the management focus on skills improvements and organisational learning to optimise customer adaptation and ensure high quality in products and processes. Teamwork and continuous improvements are also crucial here but are achieved through much greater delegation of authority and responsibility to the teams on the shop floor. This may be an EU adaptation of lean production or it could be a genuine alternative to it. Either way, it cannot be both. As Keenoy (1985) has pointed out, the 'empowerment' of the latter strategy offers more prospects for a productive dance in the manner favoured by Streeck (1987) but it stands in direct contrast to the one-way dialogue favoured by the proponents of lean production.

Where have all the dancers gone?

A seemingly popular theme in industrial relations is that trade unions are in secular decline. Even in the minority of occupations where they will continue to have a presence, it is argued, collectivist ideologies need to be jettisoned and roles and identities recast around individual service provision (Phelps Brown, 1990; Bassett and Cave, 1993). The argument is that we now live in postmodern times – unions, as organisations representing labour, enjoyed their heyday when labour processes were more collective in character such as production lines and white-collar bureaucracies. Work has now become individualised (Allvin and Sverke, 2000). Identities are now shaped more by one's role as a consumer than a producer (Giddens, 1991; Lyon, 1999).

The 'secular decline' thesis certainly finds support on union membership trends in certain countries in the last 20 years. For Western Europe as a whole, union membership density dropped from 44% down to 32% between 1980 and 1998 (Beori *et al.*, 2001, Table 2.1). The same decline holds true for unions in the USA. In countries such as France, trade union membership has fallen to very low levels, in France's case around 10% of the workforce. The exceptions appear to be those countries where the trade unions play a key role in distributing state benefits. Thus, membership is much higher and more robust in Sweden, Denmark and Belgium. Whatever the reasons for the decline and many have been put forward including high unemployment, structural changes in the economy and compositional change in the labour market, the fact remains that it plainly affects the ability of unions to both 'dance' and 'box'. As one Irish union leader expressed it: how can the unions be strong and effective during a period of 'enormous economic, legal, political, technological and social change'? (SIPTU 2000: 3).

In our view, however, despite the apparent level of membership decline, pessimism about the prospects for union futures is based on weak foundations. As has been argued elsewhere, claims that we are in a new 'postmodern' epoch incorrectly stereotype the nature, stability and uniformity of 'modernism' rendering the modern–postmodern division artificial at best (Thompson, 1993; Kelly, 1998). Indeed, many newer occupations such as call centres, retail and fast food outlets share many of the same basic features of the Tayloristic factories that dominated work in the first half of the twentieth century and provided fertile territory for union organising.

This is not to deny, however, that there have been recent changes in labour processes that have posed major challenges to unionism. Teamworking, in its various formats, comprises a different means of social interaction at work than that of the production line. New managerial ideologies abound such as employee involvement, empowerment and organisational culture as well as technologies such as lean production, total quality management – even Human Resources Management (HRM) itself. Although these often promise more than they deliver (Willmott, 1993; Thompson and McHugh, 2002), they nonetheless impact significantly on employee subjectivity and have the potential to undermine the commitment of employees to their union and thereby the capacity of the latter to mobilise. On the other hand, an increased focus on changes in work organisation has prompted many unions to extend their focus beyond distributional matters such as pay and conditions and onto production issues (Sandberg *et al.*, 1992). Scandinavian unions in particular have developed new agendas around proactive engagement on the organisation of work (Huzzard, 2000).

The growth in insecure and atypical employment modes in effect creating a three-tiered workforce of relatively secure, relatively insecure and totally insecure jobs together with the increased mobility of capital are further indications of the complexity of the challenge facing modern trade unions. Some commentators have drawn attention to the sharp fall in union militancy as a sign that unions are in retreat pointing to the 90% fall in days lost through strikes in Western Europe between 1979 and 1996 (Beori *et al.*, 2001: 8). Such reports of the death of trade unionism (as a fighting force), in the light of the recent rise in trade union militancy in Germany, Italy, the UK and France, appear to be exaggerated, however. Nonetheless, the combination of lower levels of membership, higher levels of unemployment and the three-tiered workforce has, seemingly, reduced the propensity to strike across most of the EU. The chapters that follow attempt to shed some light changes in the relationship between militancy and co-operation at enterprise and country level.

New traits in industrial relations

In sharp contrast to the differences in structures and practice which characterise the relations between organised labour and capital at national level, a more or less universal trait can be observed, namely, the decentralisation of industrial relations. In a review of the industrial relations tendencies in ten industrial countries, Bamber and Lansbury (1998) contended that in most countries the enterprise level has become more important as the critical locus for HRM strategies aimed at promoting co-operation between employees (team working) or between unions and management (social dialogue). This is due to the increased need for enterprise competitiveness and collaboration between managers and workers/unions to maximise the productive use of capital and labour. According to recent studies, the then 12 EU member states were characterised by a decentralisation of their bargaining systems. Ireland, the Netherlands and Portugal were exceptions (Beori *et al.*, 2001: 72–4; see also Ferner and Hyman, 1998).

The trend towards decentralised industrial relations is, however, not totally straightforward or simple. For example, the decline of the old centralised Swedish model has not precluded a new strongly co-ordinated, bipartite agreement at national level on wage formation based on price stability. Significantly, this agreement includes procedures that, with help of the Mediation Office, make it more difficult to initiate conflicts. This type of constrained 'social pact' can also be found in Finland and Ireland (Beori *et al.*, 2001: 70–5). As Ferner and Hyman (1998) have noted, some other countries have gone in the direction of a higher level of co-ordination, for instance Spain and Italy. Moreover in Germany and the Netherlands, industrial relations could be typified as 'centrally co-ordinated decentralisation' with the UK and the USA perhaps warranting the label 'disorganised decentralisation'. The country overviews and case studies presented in this book reflect on and explore these differences.

Alongside the decentralisation of industrial relations activity there is also evidence of a widening of the scope of co-operation at the enterprise level. This can be seen in Sweden (Nilsson, 1999; Hammarstöm *et al.*, 2004), Ireland (von Prondzynski, 1998), Austria (Traxler, 1998), Italy and Spain (Elvander, 2002), to give some European examples. This can also be observed in the USA to some extent (Deutsch, 1994; see also Chapter 11 by Deutsch in this book), where as early as the beginning of the 1990s Appelbaum and Batt (1994) pointed out that American unions tended to 'recognise the need to represent members' interests by taking a proactive rather than a reactive stance on corporate decisions that affect the ability of a company to remain profitable in an increasingly competitive environment'. In the case of the US, this might be seen as a more palatable alternative to the concession bargaining that high unemployment foisted on many US unions in the 1980s. On the other hand, in Europe the willingness of unions to widen the industrial relations agenda probably also owed something to union 'realism' shaped by the experience of high unemployment and buttressed by the continued uncertainties linked with deregulation, privatisation and general economic restructuring. Be that as it may, the outcome has seen various unions developing proactively a wider co-operative agenda that has moved beyond the traditional focus on wage bargaining and job-saving activities.

Union arguments for widening participation have differed between countries and have also changed over time. For example, in Sweden the argument for greater co-operation at company level was, in the 1980s, based on the notion that workers' empowerment would improve workers' positions in their immediate workplace environments. In the course of the 1990s unions extended the empowerment framework to secure greater worker 'voice' in the drive for increased (total) productivity, competitiveness and high quality in products, services and processes (Nilsson, 1999). The same tendencies are to be found in other developed countries as the more extreme unitarist forms of HRM have given way to the pluralism of 'learning organisations' where the intellectual capacity of the workplace is recognised as the source of competitive advantage. The best way to release the potential of the accumulated knowledge and experience of the workplace is, it is argued, through more frequent and more inclusive dialogue at the workplace. The fact that this has enabled certain unions to take on more responsibility for work organisation and longer-term company development is a key aspect of the 'dance' that has accompanied the development and application of learning organisation strategies (Huzzard, 2000; van Klaveren, 2002). As the case studies presented in this book illustrate, it has also provided opportunities for unions and management to co-operate to achieve mutual gains ('win-win') at the workplace as opposed to the 'zero sum' outcomes that have frequently characterised the outcomes of more conflictual industrial relations engagement.

Social partnership and economic outcomes

In the Green Paper there was an assumption that social partnership could be of importance for economic growth and increased competitiveness. It was argued that the interaction of the social partners could play a key role in developing forms of new work organisation and new production systems at enterprise level. The theoretical support for this assertion is rooted in the proposition that enterprises that make optimum use of their full range of intellectual resources at workplace level also make better judgements and are more effective at change management. The empirical evidence for this is harder to adduce and appears to be inconclusive (see Casey and Gold, 2000). At the beginning of the 1980s, Freeman and Medoff could provide some evidence, from American studies, of a positive relationship between unionised companies and economic performance. However, from studies of the relationship between unionised and non-unionised companies and productivity, Freeman and Medoff also showed there were no major differences comparing unionised and non-unionised companies. The authors pointed out that 'unionisation is neither positive nor negative to the productivity in the companies' (Freeman and Medoff, 1984: 179). Of vital importance, though, is the nature of the relationship between the union and management at the workplace.

According to Freeman and Medoff (ibid.), management and unions must have the capacity to co-operate. More recently, Pfeffer has argued that it requires that 'union leadership understands the elements and the importance of high performance work arrangements for both the companies and the union members' (Pfeffer 1998: 250). Whilst from a European perspective Casey and Gold (2000: 80) in their study of social partnership and economic performance in Europe observed: 'Overall, it has to be concluded that whether or not partnership produces benefits depends on the form it takes and its context.' However, where the capacity to co-operate has existed, some results have been promising. For example, in a study of the North Italian textile industry, Locke (1996) shows that companies characterised by co-operation and mutual trust were more efficient and more able to adapt to new market conditions, compared to those companies in which only traditional wage bargaining and conflicts had taken place. Moreover, Mishel and Voss (1992) contend that unions could be a supportive force in facilitating a secure, motivated and participative workforce, in other words, the key ingredients of the high-performance business systems thought to be essential for corporate viability. Evidence of unions as a 'supportive force' for improved performance and productivity has been found in studies of partnership in the UK carried out by Guest *et al.* (1998), Knell (1999) and more recently by Guest and Peccei (2001).

A common feature of the empirical studies of co-operation and partnership at the workplace (Locke 1996 and the case studies presented in this book) is the centrality of the need to develop a level of mutual trust that goes beyond the norms that have hitherto existed even in the more progressive forms of industrial relations. The empirical evidence presented here shows that mutual trust whilst essential is, nonetheless, a fragile commodity that requires careful nurturing. This raises the question of whether the mutual trust so necessary for 'dancing' can survive disagreements ending in disputes and 'boxing'?

The 1997 EU Green Paper

The EU White Paper 'Growth, Competitiveness and Employment' had all but ignored the importance of work organisation in the competitiveness equation. In contrast, the 1997 Green Paper, by stressing that there ought to be a will and an ability 'to take initiatives, to improve the quality of goods and services, to make innovations and to develop the production process and customer relations', drew policy makers' attention to the changes in industrial relations that were taking place in several EU countries and their links with improved competitiveness. Crucially, though, the Green Paper held out the prospect that by developing dialogue-based, participative forms of work organisation, the nations of the EU could gain competitive advantage over those competitor nations that lacked the essential traditions and social infrastructure for such an approach.

The social partners, politicians and academics are all interested in how the EU bureaucracy, in particular the Commission, views the idea of social partnership. Does the relevant Director General see unions or other forms of worker representation (works councils) as important actors in the development of modern production systems? Director General 5 (DG5), which has the task of handling issues such as work organisation, employment and work environment, started well in the mid-1990s with the publication of the Green Paper. This document made it clear that unions, as one of two parties on the labour market, have a key role at the workplace in developing new forms of work organisation and new production apparatuses. The Green Paper's positive attitude to union engagement in corporate affairs was partly due to the fact that the head of DG5 at the time was a Swede, Allan Larsson, who was once a researcher at the Swedish Metalworkers Union, Metall. Whilst with the union, Larsson was one of the officers involved in the discussions that set up the Co-determination Act of 1977 and was quite plainly familiar with co-operative practices.

After its publication, responses to the Green Paper were rather discouraging. Academics, not least in Sweden, judged the content as both deficient and unscientific. Employers had tended to take a negative attitude from the beginning, reflecting their traditional fear of Commission recommendations that could end up in legislation or in other types of binding regulations. They need not have worried, as in many other cases, this Green Paper was not followed by a White Paper, or any specific recommendations. Instead, DG5 issued a communiqué that in its reassertion of the employers' prerogative within the area of work organisation was widely interpreted as an appeasement of the employers' position. It should be added, too, that the Green Paper was greeted with a distinctly lukewarm response in certain union quarters, notably in France.

From being an issue of some importance with the Commission in the mid-1990s, social partnership and work organisation development latterly seem to have been downgraded to a rather minor question. Some of the Green Paper's political resonance was lost when the Swedish Presidency of the commission elapsed later in 1997. Furthermore, in 1999 a new commissioner was installed at DG5 who soon showed that her main priority was the issue of employment generation. The Commission's interest in promoting and researching the whole issue of work organisation tended to be hived off to the European Work Organisation Network (EWON), whose members struggled to fulfil its brief, ending up as a reference group within the ambit of the EU's Dublin Foundation in 2003. One explanation for the demise of work organisation and social partnership as key EU labour market issues relates to the composition of the main actors within the Commission and DG5. When Allan Larsson left DG5 in 2000, the Commissioner and the persons responsible for work organisation came from southern Europe (Greece, France and Spain), countries which have relatively little experience of co-operation between employers and unions. At the same time, the employment issue has been of considerable importance in these countries, particularly in Greece and Spain.

The Green Paper can thus be seen as an alternative discourse on the organisation of work in Europe (see e.g. Hague *et al.*, 2003 and Chapter 3 of this volume). Yet a central argument developed in the Green Paper was that new conditions would also usher in the need for social partnership as a new means of industrial relations engagement. Such a view, were it to be taken up seriously, had wide-ranging implications for trade union roles, capacities and identities. In both retrospect and prospect, then, to what extent is the alternative discourse on work organisation, as set out in the Green Paper, also a new discourse for underpinning trade union renewal?

Unions have to make a choice: 'do you wanna dance?'

With or without support from the state or supranational state bodies such as the EU, unions have to make a choice. They can stick to the traditional strategies of wage bargaining and job security, leaving production issues to management. Or, they can choose to engage in the development of new types of workplaces and new competencies. According to Bamber and Lansbury (1998), the introduction and development of 'integrated flexible production systems' can be made in three ways: a restoration of managerial prerogative without union participation (the 'neo-liberal model'), through direct co-operation between management and employees (the unitarist HRM model), or between unions and management (the pluralist model).

Faced with the emergence (or re-emergence) of the first two models in many workplaces, progressive union leaders at all levels have increasingly opted for Streeck's 'productionist strategy' since the 'optimistic conservatism' of sitting tight and doing nothing has been recognised as one of the reasons why unions who followed this line in the 1980s saw their credibility fall and with it their influence and membership levels. Adoption of a more proactive strategy is one way of avoiding marginalisation and a decline of union membership (Streeck, 1987). It also puts unions back at the heart of the profound changes taking place in society and at the workplace.

In this book we show some of the ways that unions are trying to assist employers develop a co-operative and committed workforce in order to meet the varied demands of the marketplace. We also explore how this activity co-exists with the continued use of orthodox, wage bargaining practices. The country overviews and case studies support the contention that the variety and degree of influence unions can have in the various countries depend upon '… their strategic choice, institutional opportunities and the historical, political, social and economic context' (Bamber and Lansbury, 1998: 20). The main trend we identify seems to be that unions are not only using the boxing ring but are also learning how to behave on the dance floor.

We can only speculate how the relations between employers and unions will look in the future. One thing is sure, though: if partnership is to develop at company level, it depends on how the employers think and act. As long as the employers stick to short-term interests, that is securing the fastest and greatest return on capital, then the room for social partnership is limited, if not to say nil. On the other hand, there has to be two to tango; if unions follow their traditional path of wage maximising bargaining supported by the threat of industrial action, again this will limit the action on the dance floor. Maybe the Irish union leader was right when he said that there has to be a change in unions, a change 'from a reactive to a proactive organisation – a union with the capacity not only to defend but also to anticipate, to initiate and to influence the nature of change' (SIPTU, 2000: 3).

Evaluating the dance

We recognise that choices on social partnership are a contested terrain across trade union movements. Our response to this has been to subject experiences of partnership in practice to empirical scrutiny. Making sense of partnership in a comparative context, however, is far from easy, not least because of the wide variation in what appears to be subsumed within the 'partnership' label in practice. For example, there is a considerable difference between, say, the choice to enter a partnership agreement with a view to establishing a presence at a firm and legitimacy in the eyes of the employer and the choice to co-operate with employers with a view to proactive advance on developmental agendas. The term social partnership, it seems, is used in diverse ways – hence our preference for using the generic metaphor 'dancing' to denote co-operative industrial relations. Nevertheless, we have sought to evaluate codified 'dancing' arrangements in each case study by relating to a set of clear auditing principles for informing trade union practice. These are as follows:

- gains in information and consultation rights and procedures
- structural improvements in trade unionism
- gains (and scope) in joint problem solving
- advances in substance of collective agreements
- measurability of gains
- improvements in target setting and aspiration management
- preservation of union independence
- advances in the quality of working life and/or work organisation

Although any level of generalisability from the cases here must be considered to be low, we have nevertheless thought it fruitful to throw light onto experiences of social partnership in practice and identify lessons for trade unions.

One of the outcomes of our project has thus been the formulation of a simple-to-use audit of social partnership arrangements. These are appended to our case studies and while we would not wish to aggregate them into any sort of database – they would hold that potential in a bigger project, of course – we suggest that this approach may recommend itself as a possible approach to the search in academia for evaluative criteria on social partnership. It is, of course, not just an academic matter: unions, to our knowledge, have so far approached these issues as matters of either doctrine or membership choice. We appreciate the initial comparative approach formulated by Kelly (2004) in respect of UK data, but have hoped that using boxing and dancing as a background reference might serve as an indicator of the balances of power and the inherited 'positional' choices of the trade union actors and their influence on outcomes. Interestingly, Kelly's data concern comprehensive wage, condition and process agreements at company/enterprise level: our own data on partnerships and innovatory projects by unions are typically less unitary (of boxing and dancing) and our audits look at positional and qualitative gains for unions and workers in the dancing arena. It is early days in this area of understanding co-operative industrial relations at the level of bargained agreements, and we can only hope our approach makes a useful contribution.

Organisation of the book

The theoretical foundation of the book is set out in Chapter 2 wherein the metaphors of boxing and dancing are explored and the concept of strategic choice at the core of our work is introduced and developed. The book then proceeds in Chapter 3 with a discussion on recent developments in the European-level institutional context in which our evaluation of social partnership and union renewal is embedded. Chapters 4 to 11 present the storylines of boxing and dancing in each of the countries participating in our project dialogue – the UK, Sweden, the Netherlands, Germany, Italy, Ireland, Romania and the USA. Each chapter attempts to analyse both boxing and dancing at various levels of industrial relations processes as well as discuss possible future trends.

The main findings of the book are then analysed in comparative perspective in Chapter 12 wherein the varieties, politics, processes and outcomes of the dance are reflected upon. Thereafter the book concludes with a chapter containing a reflective and comparative discussion that draws general conclusions for trade unions from our findings on the implications of the strategic choice to take to the dance floor. We end the chapter by speculating on European industrial relations futures.

In the appendix to the book we set out a number of case studies. As stated in our 'Editors' Foreword', these are selected as being illustrative of certain aspects of the country storylines rather than being truly representative. We intend them to be used as discussion material, particularly but not solely for undergraduates on comparative HRM/IR (Industrial Relations) courses. We hope they will also be of interest to practitioners from both union and management quarters, and that they will stimulate both reflection and debate.

References

Allvin, M. and Sverke, M. (2000) 'Do New Generations Imply the End of Solidarity? Swedish Unionism in the Era of Individualization', *Economic and Industrial Democracy* 21: 71–95.

Appelbaum, E. and Batt, R. (1994) *The New American Workplace*. Ithaca, New York: ILR Press.

Bamber, G. J. and Lansbury, R. D. (eds) (1998) *International and Comparative Employment Relations* (3rd edn). St Leonards, Australia: Allen & Unwin.

Bassett, P. and Cave, A. (1993) *All for One: the Future of the Unions*. London: Fabian Society.

Beori, T., Brugiavini, A. and Calmfors, L. (eds) (2001) *The Role of the Unions in the Twentieth Century*. Oxford: Oxford University Press.

Berggren, C. (1995) 'The Fate of the Branch Plants – Performance Versus Power' in Sandberg, Å. (ed) *Enriching Production*. Aldershot: Avebury.

Blackler, F. (1995) 'Knowledge, Knowledge Work and Organisations: An Overview and Interpretation', *Organisation Studies* 16(5).

Casey, B. and Gold, M. (2000) *Social Partnership and Economic Performance – The Case of Europe*. Cheltenham: Edward Elgar.

Deutsch, S. (1994) 'New Union Initiatives on Technological Change and Work Organization', in Deutsch, S. and Broomhill, R. (eds) *Recent Developments in U.S. Trade Union Strategies*, Labour Studies, no. 3, December, The University of Aderlain.

Elvander, N. (2002) 'The New Swedish Regime for Collective Bargaining and Conflict Resolution: A Comparative Perspective', *European Journal of Industrial Relations* Vol. 8(2).

European Commission (1997) *Partnership for a New Organisation of Work.* Green Paper COM 97: 128.

Ferner, A. and Hyman, R. (eds) (1998) *Changing Industrial Relations in Europe.* Oxford: Blackwell Publishers.

Freeman, R. B. and Medoff, J. L. (1984) *What Do Unions Do?* New York: Basic Books.

Giddens, A. (1991) *Modernity and Self-Identity: Self and Society in the Late Modern Age.* Cambridge: Polity Press.

Giddens, A. (1998) *The Third Way: The Renewal of Social Democracy.* Cambridge: Polity Press.

Guest, D. E., Peccei, R. and Doupar, W. (1998) *The Partnership Company: Benchmark for the Future.* London: Involvement and Participation Association.

Guest, D. E. and Peccei, R. (2001) 'Partnership at Work: Mutuality and the Balance of Advantage', *British Journal of Industrial Relations* 39(2): 207–36.

Hague, J., Den Hertog, F., Huzzard, T. and Totterdill, P. (2003) *The Convergence of QWL and Competitiveness in Europe.* Report for EU Commission (Innoflex Project).

Hammarström, O., Huzzard, T. and Nilsson, T. (2004) 'Employment Relations in Sweden' in Bamber, G. and Lansbury, R. (eds) *International and Comparative Employment Relations: A Study of Industrialised Market Economies* (3rd edn). Sydney: Allen and Unwin.

Hardt, M. and Negri, A. (2001) *Empire.* Cambridge, MA.: Harvard University Press.

Haynes, P. and Allen, M. (2001) 'Partnership as Union Strategy: A Preliminary Evaluation', *Employee Relations* 23(2): 164–93.

Hirst, P. and Thompson, G. (1996) *Globalization in Question: The International Economy and the Possibilities of Governance.* Cambridge: Polity Press.

Huzzard, T. (2000) *Labouring to Learn: Union Renewal in Swedish Manufacturing.* Umeå: Boréa.

Huzzard, T. (2003) *The Convergence of QWL and Competitiveness: A Swedish Literature Review*, Work Life in Transition 2003: 9, Stockholm: National Institute for Working Life.

Keenoy, T. (1985) *Invitation to Industrial Relations.* Oxford: Blackwells.

Knell, J. (1999) 'Partnership at Work', *Employment Relations Research Series*, No. 7, Department of Trade and Industry, United Kingdom.

Kelly, J. (1998) *Rethinking Industrial Relations: Mobilisation, Collectivism and Long Waves.* London: Routledge.

Kelly, J. (2004) 'Social Partnership Agreements in Britain: Labor Cooperation and Compliance', *Industrial Relations* 43(1): 267–92.

Klein, N. (2000) *No Logo: No Space, No Choice, No Jobs.* London: Flamingo.

Kochan, T. A., Katz, H. C. and McKersie, R. B. (1986) *The Transformation of American Relations.* New York: Basic Books.

Kochan, T. A. and Osterman, P. (1994) *The Mutual Gains Enterprise: Forging a Winning Partnership among Labor, Management and Government.* Boston: Harvard University Press.

Lakoff, G. and Johnson, M. (1980) *Metaphors We Live By.* Chicago: University of Chicago Press.

Locke, M. R. (1996) *The Composite Economy: Local Politics and Industrial Change in Contemporary Italy.* Working paper, MIT, Sloan School of Management.

Lyon, D. (1999) *Postmodernity* (2nd edn). Buckingham: Open University Press.

Mishel, L. and Voss, P. B. (eds) (1992) *Unions and Economic Competitiveness*. Armonk, New York: M.E. Sharp.

Nilsson, T. (1999) 'The Future Role of the Swedish Unions – Increased Local Cooperation for Production Development', *Economic and Industrial Democracy* 20: 461–82.

Parker, M. and Slaughter, J. (1988) *Choosing Sides: Unions and the Team Concept*. Boston: South End Press.

Pfeffer, J. (1998) *The Human Equation*. Boston. MA: Harvard Business School Press.

Phelps Brown, H. (1990) 'The Counter Revolution of Our Time', *Industrial Relations* 29(1): 1–14.

Sandberg, Å., Broms, G., Grip, A., Sundström, L., Steen, J. and Ullmark, P. (1992) *Technological Change and Co-Determination in Sweden*. Philadelphia: Temple University Press.

SIPTU (2000) *Team-Building Programme for Union Teams*. Dublin: SIPTU ADAPT Project.

Stiglitz, J. (2003) *Globalization and its Discontents*. London: Penguin.

Streeck, W. (1987) 'The Uncertainties of Management and The Management of Uncertainty: Employees, Labour Relations and Industrial Relations in 1980s', *Work Employment and Society* 1 (3): 281–308.

Thompson, P. (1993) 'Postmodernism: Fatal Distraction' in Hassard, J. and Parker, M. (eds) *Postmodernism and Organizations*. London: Sage.

Thompson, P. and McHugh, D. (2002) *Work Organizations: A Critical Introduction* (3rd edn). Basingstoke: Palgrave.

Traxler, F. (1996) 'Collective Bargaining and Industrial Change – A Case of Disorganization? A Comparative Analysis of Eighteen OECD Countries', *European Sociological Review* 12: 271–87.

Traxler, F. (1998) 'Austria: Still the Country of Corporatism', in Ferner, A. and Hyman, R. (eds) *Changing Industrial Relations in Europe*, 239–62. Oxford: Blackwell.

Van Klaveren, M. (2002) 'The FNV "Industribution" Project. Trade Union Learning in the Netherlands', *Concepts and Transformation* 7(2): 203–24.

von Prondzynski, F. (1998) 'Ireland: Corporatism Reviewed', in Ferner, A. Hyman, R. (eds) *Changing Industrial Relations in Europe* (2nd edn). Oxford: Blackwell Publishers.

Weick, K. E. (1995) *Sensemaking in Organizations*. Thousand Oaks, CA: Sage.

Willmott, H. (1993) 'Strength is Ignorance, Slavery is Freedom: Managing Culture in Modern Organizations', *Journal of Management Studies* 30(4): 515–52.

Zuboff, S. (1998) *In the Age of the Smart Machine: The Future of Work and Power*. New York: Basic Books.

2
Boxing and Dancing – Trade Union Strategic Choices

Tony Huzzard

Introduction

Although the field of industrial relations is often seen as an overwhelmingly empirical discipline, it is not as bereft of theory as is often made out (Kelly, 1998). This chapter starts by briefly surveying recent contributions to comparative union research and then positions the book in relation to some key theoretical contours of the field. It continues by locating the book within the paradigm of strategic choice and then introduces and elaborates the strategic choice framework of boxing and dancing at the core of the project. It will be recalled from Chapter 1 that a central aim of the book is to inform trade union futures – that is, some of the key choices to be made. Specifically, the strategic choice approach is adopted in our exploration and evaluation of social partnership.

We focus on strategic choice theory, as we are interested in investigating how trade unions have 'a hand in shaping their own destiny' (Ackers and Payne, 1998: 529). This contrasts with the rather more established systems view of industrial relations where unions are largely seen as somewhat passive actors responding to demands of the system (Dunlop, 1958). Our intention is not to deny the role of systemic factors but, rather, to give greater emphasis to the potentials and responsibilities of unions for their own renewal in what is in many respects a widely different contextual backdrop to that which characterised their earlier evolution (Olney, 1996). Although the significance of a strategic choice perspective is becoming widely recognised, it is still relatively under-researched, particularly on truly comparative research on union strategies (Frege and Kelly, 2003: 10). It is our hope that the current volume will help rectify such shortcomings.

Comparative industrial relations

This book is a study of unions in eight countries. As such, it can be considered to contribute to the literature on comparative industrial relations

(Ferner and Hyman, 1992; Bean, 1994; Van Ruysseveldt and Visser, 1996; Traxler *et al.*, 2001; Lecher *et al.*, 2002; Bamber *et al.*, 2004). Although there is a slight overlap between this book and these texts on macro level updates of industrial relations developments, we focus more specifically and uniquely on the issue of strategic choices for unions on co-operation and conflict in the employment relationship. Moreover, we aim to evaluate social partnership as a basis for union renewal. Accordingly, the book is perhaps better seen as a contribution to the rather more specific comparative literature on trade unions (Rigby *et al.*, 1999; Waddington and Hoffman, 2000; Hyman, 2001).

The integration of the similarities and differences between unions into a single, sophisticated theoretical framework is beyond both the scope of the book and the resources of the project on which it is based. But as well as drawing out and synthesising messages for union practitioners, the book does have the ambition of making a contribution to the debate in comparative industrial relations on whether globalisation is prompting greater convergence in industrial relations systems (Smith, 1999; Katz and Darbishire, 2000). Our view is that the European Social Dialogue is indeed an expression of convergence on partnership at the level of discourse, but our cases show considerable divergence of practice. Union action is not just a matter of external triggers 'but is also the outcome of internal discussion, debate and often conflict' (Hyman, 2001: 170). To some degree globalisation poses a uniform set of environmental challenges that suggest pressure for convergence. But this tendency should not be exaggerated: union responses are shaped by their different starting points and country-specific traditions.

Comparative trade union research – recent contributions

Without exception, the comparative literature sees unions as facing increasingly hostile environments conditioned in particular by globalisation and structural change (Olney, 1996). Preferring the term 'responses' to that of 'strategies', Rigby *et al.* (1999) attempt, first, to explore the question of whether European integration has led to convergence in industrial relations systems and second to examine how far union responses have concurred with those identified in the existing literature. Empirically, unions in five countries were chosen each reflecting different industrial relations traditions: Denmark, Italy, Spain, Germany and the UK. The design of Rigby *et al.* is also sector based – a decision which is reflected in how the empirical material is presented in their book.

The authors found that although at the general level some degree of convergence was detectable in that management were seeking to restrict union influence and reduce labour costs, the causes of these trends varied from sector to sector. The key mechanism in manufacturing was the globalisation of markets whereas in banking it was deregulation and in the public sector it was the pressure to reduce government spending. In terms of relations with employers, most responses suggested a move away from oppositional stances towards an increased tendency to collaborative relationships in contexts of decentralisation. Internally, unions were diverting resources into recruitment, organising, communications and training. Increased merger activity was detectable, and more pragmatic political strategies were evident as unions sought to distance themselves from political parties. In discussing the implications for unions, Rigby *et al.* concluded that the scope for unions to develop strategic responses depended on the degree that they had a supportive context – specifically, strong bargaining institutions and a focused union structure. Accordingly, a supportive EU context will continue to be 'an important issue for the unions as they seek to adapt to their new environment' (ibid.: 228).

A similar emphasis on environmental change for unions was also the context for Waddington and Hoffmann's edited volume published by the European Trade Union Institute in 2000. Specifically, the key developments are identified as greater economic internationalisation, the hegemony of neo-liberal economic management practices in preference to Keynesian policies and wide-ranging reform in production regimes including the shift from manufacturing to services. The book includes chapters on union challenges and solutions in sixteen European countries. The final chapter of the volume concludes that European unions require to radically overhaul their policies and structures (Hoffmann, 2000). Interpretations and trajectories of change will vary from country to country, but common challenges can be summarised as: a renewal of collective bargaining policy and workplace representation; recruitment of new employees; adaptation of organisational structures to sectoral change; and the Europeanisation of union work.

Waddington and Hoffmann (2000) see patterns of trade union reform which are discernible through four inter-linked issues. These are, first, the articulation of union activity and organisation between different levels including the European dimension; second, an appeal including representative forms for new groups of workers; third, issues associated with union restructuring through mergers; and fourth the growing importance of union activity at the workplace and the issues associated with how this is supported by central union organisations. However, although reform agendas are underway in the various countries covered by the book, such agendas are invariably contested both within unions and between them. Such diversity of responses reflects different policies, traditions and points of departure in the different nation states suggesting, again, that claims about convergence are decidedly premature.

Hyman (2001) discusses the evolution of different national union movements in relation to a simple model whereby unions can be classified in three ways. First, they can primarily be understood as market bargainers – they are interest organisations with predominantly labour market functions; second they can be understood as mobilisers of class opposition under capitalism – they are key collective actors in a struggle between labour and capital; and third they are partners in social integration – they are vehicles for raising workers' status in society more generally and hence advancing social justice. Each of these ideal types of unionism is associated with a distinct ideological orientation, and the history of trade unionism can be seen as that of a 'triple tension at the heart of union identity and purpose' (ibid.: 3). All unions must face in the three directions, yet inherited traditions vary from country to country. To illustrate this, Hyman suggests that British unionism has evolved between market and class, German unionism between society and market and Italian unionism between class and society.

Hyman concludes that none of the traditional dimensions of union policy retain much credibility within international boundaries. Moreover, practical experiences of socialism have led to the erosion of credible mobilising rhetoric around 'visions of a better future, of *utopias*' (ibid.: 173, italics in original). Although sceptical of the (bipartite) European Social Dialogue in its current format, he nevertheless stresses the importance of internal social dialogue within and between unions as part of the ongoing quest for supranational regulation. But such matters are also intimately linked to the dual challenge of formulating more effective processes of strategic direction and leadership *at the same time* as enhancing the scope for mobilising more vigorous participation at the grassroots. Above all, these challenges require unions to reconstitute themselves 'as bodies which foster interactive internal relationships and serve more as networks than hierarchies' (ibid.: 174; see also Huzzard, 2000a).

Some theoretical contours in industrial relations

Unitarism, pluralism and Marxism

Since Fox (1973), studies of the employment relationship have tended to be seen from three generic perspectives: unitarism, pluralism and Marxism (see e.g. Salaman, 2000: 4). The first of these, unitarism, assumes that organisations are integrated into a single authority and loyalty structure, a common set of values, interests and a single legitimate source of authority, management. Organisations are seen as harmonious, conflict free and tied together by a single organisational culture. This is the domain of 'Human Resource Management' (HRM) where unions are often seen as anachronistic and an unwelcome intrusion: where they are accepted it is usually by force. Management approaches to industrial relations are typically authoritarian or paternalistic.

In contrast to unitarism, pluralism sees the distribution of power and authority at the workplace (and in society) as being relatively dispersed among various groups who have distinct interests. Organisations are competitive in terms of groupings, leadership, authority and values. Inherent conflicts of interest arise, and these have to be managed through a variety of roles, institutions and processes in order to maintain a 'viable collaborative structure' (Fox, 1973: 193). Conflict is both rational and inevitable: this requires to be regulated by institutions through accepted and codified procedures. These may include collective bargaining machineries, provisions for joint consultation, as well as arbitration channels beyond the organisation. In some countries these arrangements are buttressed by legislation such as co-determination in Germany and Sweden, and in other cases the state itself is a central industrial relations actor in tripartite arenas as in the concertation arrangements in Italy. A recent expression of pluralism is that of 'social partnership' which, while recognising the divergent interests of employer and employee representatives, nevertheless stresses the areas where interests may overlap (see later discussion in this chapter). In certain countries such as Sweden and Germany, however, the notion of partnership is less of a novelty.

The third perspective is that of Marxism which shares the pluralist view that interests are divergent and conflictual but adds that these are specific expressions of the nature of the capitalist firm and capitalist society in general. Conflict between employer and employee is seen not just in terms of organisational tensions but also as a symptom of the social and economic divisions between those who own the means of production and those who can only rely on selling their labour power. Joint regulation is seen as a mere temporary accommodation to capitalist work structures. An emphasis is also placed on the inherently unequal nature of the employment relationship and the asymmetries of power between buyers and sellers of labour power (Offe and Wiesenthal, 1980). Trade union organisation goes some way to reducing such asymmetry, but any claims about there being an equal balance of power, are an illusion even where unions are well organised.

It will be of little surprise to the reader that we do not see the unitarist perspective of use given the marginal or non-existent role it affords to unions. We are accordingly closer to the pluralist view although we would not dissent from the Marxist contention that power relations between employers and employees are inherently unequal. The Marxist view sees industrial relations as a process whereby class interests are played out and consciousness is raised as part of a longer-term vision of achieving fundamental social and economic change. The pluralist view has no such vision, the implicit assumption being that union missions are limited to having an ameliorating role under capitalism. But it may be the case that social partnership can have a role to play in either scenario; we thus leave it open for practitioners to decide on matters concerning union missions – it is a matter for them to tackle the basic question of 'what trade unions are for'.

Determinism and voluntarism

A further line of theoretical distinction in the literature is that on the degree of freedom of action enjoyed by unions and employers. This is usually seen in terms of assumptions of determinism or voluntarism, or in the language of sociology between structure and agency (Giddens, 1984). A deterministic view offers actors little discretion – they are tightly constrained by factors such as the actions of others, contextual factors such as technology, market forces, power in society, ideology and regulatory factors. Together, these factors comprise what Dunlop (1958) termed the 'Industrial Relations System'. Naturally, the precise configuration of such systems will vary across countries and even within them. In contrast to deterministic views, other scholars have emphasised the discretion that actors individually and collectively have and how such discretion is exercised. Here individual and collective perceptions of reality are more important sources of behaviour, actions and relationships (Kochan *et al.*, 1984). Actors will be able to make (boundedly) rational judgements about possible courses of action, 'strategic choice', and choose between them – yet such decisions will be mediated by ideology and the power resources at the disposal of the key actors in their organisations (Child, 1972, 1997).

For trade unions, the voluntaristic approach has generated practices of strategic management (Dunlop, 1990; Scheck and Bolander, 1990; Heery and Kelly, 1994) and this in turn has attracted an interest in strategic unionism in research quarters (Stratton-Devine and Reshef, 1996; Boxall and Haynes, 1997; Hannigan, 1998; Huzzard, 2000a). Our focus in this book is firmly within the voluntarist camp – we are interested in how unions might shape their own futures by exploring the strategic choices of regulating the employment relationship through configurations of 'boxing and dancing'. Our approach is to foreground agency over structure: such choices are, naturally, constrained by system factors, yet can lead to changes, however small, that impact on the structures and relationships that comprise the industrial relations system (Giddens, 1984).

The basic choices of co-operation versus conflict in industrial relations are generally associated with what have been termed in the literature as 'accommodative versus combative forces' (Hyman, 1989; Kelly, 1998: 8). But what are the implications of recent changes on the relative significance of such forces and their interrelationship? What are the options for unions and what do these mean for union renewal? It is our argument that such choices and how unions make them are central aspects of union renewal, hence our theoretical focus on the concept of strategic choice. It is to an elaboration of this concept and how we use it that the chapter now turns.

The concept of strategic choice

The concept in the literature

Although such an approach was hardly new to scholars of business policy, the domination of contingency theory and systems theory in the OT (Organisation Theory) and IR (Industrial Relations) literatures respectively meant that the concept of strategic choice came to these fields relatively late. The first appearance of the concept of strategic choice in the organisation theory literature was the seminal article by Child in 1972. In essence, strategic choice theory focuses on ways leaders are 'able in practice to influence organisational forms to suit their own preferences' (Child, 1997: 43). The concept was proposed by Child as a critical response to the overwhelmingly deterministic approaches that had dominated the field up to that time, for example, contingency theory.

A further 12 years elapsed, however, before the concept had reached the industrial relations literature in the work of Kochan and colleagues in the US (e.g. Kochan *et al.*, 1984). Kochan *et al.* did not attempt to supplant systems theory, rather, they sought to add a more dynamic component and propose values and ideology as mediating factors (ibid.: 20). In their formulation, strategy can be defined as follows: (a) strategic decisions occur when parties have discretion over decisions, and (b) strategic decisions are those that *alter* the party's role or relationship with the other actors in the industrial relations system (italics in original).

Accordingly, a strategic approach to unions provides a framework for 'critical choices about the ends and means of [union] organisations' (Boxall and Haynes, 1997: 569). Unions acting strategically are generally considered to engage in activities of forecasting employment changes, production trends, corporate mergers, public policies, conducting research on membership needs and aspirations as well as formulating long term policies 'to anticipate and respond to the changes such processes unleash' (Reshef and Murray, 1988: 90). There is some debate, however, in the strategy literature about whether it is actually possible or even desirable for organisations to make long-term choices given the unpredictability of organisational environments. An alternative view of strategy has thus been suggested as that of a consistent pattern of actions from the past that, through retrospection and learning processes, are deemed to 'work' (Mintzberg, 1994). Hence, strategies may exist even when strategic planning does not.

Although Kochan *et al.*'s initial work focused on strategic choices of employers, the 1990s in particular saw a significant increase in the literature on strategic unionism. Various authors claimed to detect a greater adoption of strategic approaches by practitioners in both the US (e.g. Dunlop, 1990) and the UK (e.g. Heery and Kelly, 1994) including practices of strategic planning and analysis. Such literature, moreover, often sought to develop strategic typologies since those in the mainstream strategic management literature were clearly not applicable to unions. For example, in Germany Streeck (1992: 284) saw unions as having two basic choices: between those of 'independent, powerful representation of member interests' and 'pursuit of general, social and economic interests'. The latter required co-operation, but this needed to be 'forceful intervention in, and regulation of, managerial behaviour with unions potentially and eventually appropriating, through *collective political action* a significant share of the responsibility of productive performance' (italics in original).

A recurrent theme in many of the strategic typologies is that of the choices of conflict or co-operation in relations with employers. For example,

Kelly (1996) saw such choices in terms of moderation versus militancy with, apparently, no middle ground, whereas Jeffries (1996), in a comparative study of union strategic postures in France and the UK, saw a continuum of five choices: conflict, containment/aggression, accommodation, co-operation and collusion. Such typologising has also drawn on the discourse of social partnership. For example, Martinez-Lucio and Weston (1992) suggest union strategies in the UK as being underpinned by three competing logics: new realism/social partnership, extension of collective partnership and oppositionalism whereas Claydon (1998) sees choices as those of militancy, incorporation and partnership.

Strategic choice in the unions – a conceptual framework

Following Kessler and Purcell's analysis of strategic choice on employment relations in public services in the UK (1996), it is useful to conceptualise union strategic choices on a number of different levels. Without exception unions are organisations whose basic mission concerns advancing their members' interests. What we might call 'Level 1' choices on union missions historically are ideologically shaped and form the basic identity of the union organisation. At the next level, 'Level 2' choices are made on the scope of union activities and relationships. This concerns decisions on the range of issues and services to be encompassed within union activities as well as which serviceable job territories to occupy (Willman and Cave, 1994).

Flowing from Level 1 decisions on union identity and mission, choices have to be made on which workers to organise. In terms of advancing members' interests, those of representation in discussions with employers are the most crucial. This requires decisions to be made on which employers to seek recognition and negotiation rights from. In practice, however, unions not only make Level 2 strategic choices in terms of what services they offer to members, they also need to make 'Level 3' decisions in terms of how they engage with employers, how they engage with other unions and how they engage with civil society.

A switch to a more strategic approach to the management of Level 1, 2 and 3 choices has major implications on how unions are governed internally – that is, 'Level 4' choices. These concern how the decisions at the other levels are to be put into practice – here we can talk about organisational level choices on matters such as structures, processes, technology, learning capacities and so on. Heery and Kelly (1994) argue that strategic management in unions is associated with a 'managerial servicing relationship' whereby union members are reactive consumers whose needs should be carefully researched and monitored. This suggests a rather different way for the conduct of union affairs by leaders than that of reactively responding to membership demands channelled through representative structures.

Each of the four levels of strategic choice identified here can feasibly be made at the various levels of trade union organisation: both at the macro

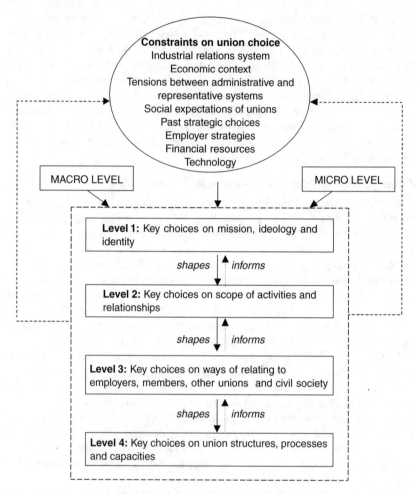

Figure 2.1   A strategic choice model for trade unions.

levels of national, confederational, regional or sectoral unionism or the more micro levels of workplace or branch (local) unionism. No union leaderships, at whatever level, however, will have a free hand to make choices. In reality such choices will be constrained by a number of factors: the industrial relations system, membership voice, employer strategies, the economic context and the social expectations of unions in political markets (Berg and Jonsson, 1991). Unions will also be constrained by their own strategic choices from the past (Rigby, 1999: 20). A tentative model of trade union strategic choice encompassing the various options and constraints outlined here is set out in Figure 2.1.

Figure 2.2 Level 1 strategic trade union choices – class, society and market (Hyman, 2001).

Level 1 strategic choices overwhelmingly concern the basic factors of ideology and identity that shape long-term decision-making within unions. These will perhaps involve well-established and codified traditions in mission statements or rulebooks. Such factors may, however, have a considerable history and be subject to considerable institutional constraint. An illustrative example of Level 1 strategic choice is the framework of Hyman (2001), which usefully illustrates how unions in different countries have followed quite distinct trajectories in terms of ideology and identity. These choices are illustrated in Figure 2.2, which depicts a triangle of three apexes: class, society and market. In practice, Hyman shows that unions in the UK, Germany and Italy tend to incorporate two of these three apexes in forging their identities and ideologies.

This model may not necessarily fit other countries so neatly; for example, the Swedish blue-collar unions appear to be located between class and society whereas their white-collar counterparts fit better between society and market. Nevertheless, the model is useful for mapping out basic ideological positions that shape union strategies at the level of individual unions or even individual union leaders, both nationally and locally. As will become clear in the discussion below, a closer positioning towards a 'class' orientation would feed through to shape Level 3 choices vis à vis employers that we would characterise as 'boxing', whereas a closer positioning towards a 'society' orientation would suggest a closer positioning towards 'dancing'. The model also reflects ideological differences on whether to foreground collective interests (a class orientation) or individual interests (a market orientation) as well as providing a map for the ideological ebb and flow of union electoral preferences.

As to Level 2 choices – those of decisions on what activities to undertake, for whom and which relationships to enter into – these, again, can occur at both macro and micro levels of decision-making in unions. However, it is highly likely that macro decision-making will be informed by dialogue between the centre and regional or local level union organisations as a

	Existing issues/ service mix	New issues/ service mix
Existing members	Mobilisation	Service development
New members	Recruitment/ recognition	Diversification

Figure 2.3   Level 2 strategic choices for trade unions (adapted from Ansoff, 1968).

means to identify strategic opportunities associated with developing new services or targeting new members to recruit. These could be either new groups, where the union already organizes, such as women members, young members, ethnic minorities or groups in non-recognised firms.

Level 2 choices can be usefully illustrated by adapting Ansoff's product/ market expansion grid from the mainstream strategy literature (Ansoff, 1968; see also Heery and Kelly, 1994, and Jeffries, 1996). This model suggests choices between activities of directing existing services to existing members (labelled here as mobilisation), developing new services to existing members (service development), seeking to develop relationships with new members and possibly new employers (recruitment and recognition) and, finally, developing new services to attract new members (diversification). As well as choices with regard to new services, we can also include choices on new or existing issues on which to develop union dialogues. This model is illustrated in Figure 2.3.

In many respects, the importance of Level 2 strategic choice has been over-looked; some unions, however, have paid increasing attention to issues of gender in particular where women members comprise a majority of the union's membership and have traditionally been under-represented. For example, in the 1990s the Swedish Municipal Workers Union (Kommunal), in recognising that 85% of its membership were women, sought a number of novel strategic responses. These included forging new dialogues on the gendered nature of work organisation, low pay and equal opportunities. A key service, the union's training programme, was redesigned to reflect gen-der perspectives. The union's renewal work explicitly included various forms of 'new material and intellectual support, co-ordination, education pro-grammes, mobilisation and programmatic direction' (Higgins, 1996: 185). Accordingly, both 'mobilisation' and 'service development' could be dis-cerned as Level 2 strategies.

This book, however, is specifically interested in Levels 3 and 4 strategic choices (see Table 2.1) – but we limit our focus to the arenas and choices fac-ing unions in how they engage with employers in joint regulation of work

Table 2.1 Level 3 strategic choices for trade unions

Action dimension	Action arena	Strategic choices
Employers (central or workplace levels)	Negotiating machineries Joint consultation Partnership	Zero-sum pressure bargaining (BOXING) Positive-sum integrative bargaining (DANCING)
Members	Representative system Administrative system	Service delivery and voice mechanisms
Other unions	Trade union side meetings International links Inter-union disputes machinery	Joint ventures Mergers Competitive rivalry
Civil society ('political markets')	Activity in political parties Lobbying nationally and internationally Opinion forming Public relations	Advocacy of new legislation or directives Support for single issue campaigns Building community alliances

and the labour market. Clearly such choices will tend to have a focus towards the firm or workplace or members within a particular employer or workplace context. Level 3 choices will also extend to relations with other unions, again in the context of organising at a particular firm or workplace and may also involve interventions in civil society or 'political markets' (Berg and Jonsson, 1991) in the pursuit of a particular activity or campaign.

Level 3 choices, of course, will to a great extent be shaped by Level 2 choices. Unions that seek to pursue an agenda of mobilising their existing members on traditional distributional issues through collective bargaining underpinned by the weapon of industrial action, as exemplified by the fire-fighters in the UK in 2002 and 2003, will naturally opt to box with employers. On the other hand, unions seeking to pursue new issues and offer new services to members may well prefer to dance. A clear example of the latter was the Swedish Working Life Programme from 1990 to 1995 that entailed 24 000 workplace development projects and a new union strategy of developing work and new role as a supporting resource to members at the workplaces involved. Little or no evidence exists that such a strategy was possible through 'boxing' (Gustavsen *et al.*, 1996).

We are also interested, however, in the implications of such choices on the Level 4 choices more concerned with internal union matters. These can be described as comprising 'trade union renewal'. Referring again to the example of the Swedish Municipal Workers Union, it is possible to discern Level 3 choices by Kommunal in relation to co-operating with local authority employers on rationalisation efforts, yet at the same time pursuing a pro-active agenda on redistribution and engaging actively in civil society. This, however, was not considered sufficient: in questioning the 'progress' seen under the Swedish model from a gender perspective, the union set about *critically reflecting on its own gender praxis*. The union's structure of a male-dominated hierarchy acting as a chain of delegation of routine services was seen as being unsuited for collective, proactive political strategies. Programmes to reinvigorate the union at the base were set up together with a more informal meetings culture, which was explicitly sensitive to the needs of women (Higgins, 1996). In this sense, Level 2 strategic choices were feeding onwards, through Level 3 choices, to shape Level 4 choices on internal structures and processes.

In sum, the model of strategic choice elaborated here shows that the range of options for unions is considerable. Our primary concern in this book, however, is on Level 3 choices and it is conceptualised as the basic choice between confrontational approaches to engagement with the employer and co-operative engagement. In the current discourse typified by the European Social Dialogue (see Chapter 3), the former finds its expression in collective bargaining, often backed by the right and readiness to take industrial action, whereas the latter finds its expression in social partnership. As stated in the introductory chapter to the book we use the terms of boxing and dancing as guiding metaphors for the choice of stance adopted by unions vis à vis employers.

Critiques of strategic choice theory

Despite the apparent attractiveness of strategic choice theory as a means of refining systems theory, it is nevertheless fruitful to recognise its limitations. What is often not made explicit is that actors require resources and mechanisms for their choices to be realised. The mere act of choosing does not guarantee the success of the strategy (Martinez-Lucio and Stuart, 2004). The making of choices tells us nothing about outcomes: for this reason trenchant critiques have been made in the strategy literature of too much focusing on content and positioning while downplaying the importance of strategic processes (Mintzberg, 1990).

A further difficulty is that choices are often a great deal more complex in reality than is often suggested in the literature. Multi-dimensional trade-offs often confront decision-makers. Strategic typologies, whilst useful, can vastly oversimplify what is at stake. As we argue in this book, both partnership and collective bargaining, rather than being mutually exclusive, will co-exist in complicated and dynamic configurations – and the politics of partnership may lead to outcomes that are different to those originally envisaged. In reality, moreover, decision-makers will have complex and shifting political agendas and any analysis of strategic choices must take into account the interests, rationales and internal politics of the key actors. Choices may be made on the basis of rational calculation or institutional considerations – or indeed a combination of the two.

The strategic choice literature in industrial relations thus has very little to say about power despite the original highlighting of the concept by Child (1972). As argued by Kelly (1998), it is not only the strategic choices of actors that are important. Also crucial is 'the balance of power which enables some actors to impose their choices on others' (ibid.: 19). This critique can be taken further by arguing that neglecting to make explicit the inherent imbalance of power between employers and organised labour implies that the latter can only prosper or acquire legitimacy by accommodating to the demands of the former. The implication of this, therefore, is that social partnership as a strategic choice inevitably involves subordination of unions to employer interests (Kelly, 1996; Taylor and Ramsay, 1998).

It is also argued that there is also a weakness in the strategic choice literature of dealing with the question of organisational context; it has relatively little to say, for example, on management attitudes – where they come from and why they might differ between companies and countries. A further gap is that of external political factors such as the accumulation of power resources through utilising the state (Kelly, 1998: 19). On the other hand, an alternative view has been advanced by Korpi (1983) who attributes the relative strength of the Swedish labour movement precisely to its strategic choices in relation to both employers and the state (see also Huzzard, 2000a ch. 6). Indeed, it could also be argued that adoption of dual systems of representation in Germany and the Netherlands can be ascribed at least in part to union strategic choices. In similar vein, the rapid decline of union influence in the UK during the 1980s can arguably be attributed to the strategic choices exercised vis à vis the state in the previous decade.

Overall, therefore, although recognising its limitations, we are not persuaded on the arguments for dispensing with the strategic choice approach. The challenges of globalised markets, information technology, flexibility, new production regimes and so on may indeed be general to all the countries covered in this book. And there may indeed be similar responses to such challenges – decentralised bargaining, greater labour market flexibility and a European discourse on social partnership, for example. But behind this apparent convergence lies a number of important differences in point of departure, degree, direction and power of response (Van Ruysseveldt and Visser, 1996). Although unions are rarely in the driving seat, a focus on strategic choice does offer an opportunity to link union responses to change with issues of union renewal – the aim at the heart of our project.

The dynamics of boxing and dancing

Although the advocacy of social partnership in the European Social Dialogue is relatively recent, the employment relationship has always been built around shifting patterns of conflict and co-operation– in this sense the terms boxing and dancing are not representations for new phenomena. For example,

Walton and McKersie (1965) proposed a behavioural theory of labour negotiations whereby two processes of pressure bargaining and integrative bargaining happen face to face across the main table. The first of these concerned itself with distributional issues (and zero sum outcomes) whereas the latter involved issues to do with running the firm (and some potential for positive sum outcomes). This distinction found a later echo in Flanders' (1970: 88) categories of market relations and managerial relations.

As discussed elsewhere in this volume, the 1997 EU Green Paper *Partnership for a New Organisation of Work* (European Commission, 1997) sought to establish changes in work organisation as a new priority for the social partners. The basic argument here is that sustainable work reforms have to be accompanied by broader shifts in HR systems (Marks *et al.*, 1998: 210, but for a contrasting view see Frost, 2000). In practical terms this has meant an increasing union focus on the qualitative agenda of production (and business-related) issues as well as the traditional quantitative agenda of distributional issues (Rigby, 1999). In the view of Hyman (2001: 84), the embrace of production issues has entailed a new direction for unions into civil society. But the implications of production agendas on distribution issues are unclear: does such a strategic shift comprise an opportunity to push for competence based rewards systems and advances up competency ladders (see e.g. Huzzard, 2000a, chapter 7) or does it simply involve a quid pro quo for lowering expectations on wages (Rigby, 1999: 23)?

Throughout this book the metaphor of 'boxing' is used to signify an adversarial approach to conducting industrial relations whereas 'dancing' is used to signify a co-operative approach. At a very basic level, these choices can be summed up as those of collective bargaining and partnership. Yet although collective bargaining is largely an adversarial process, it would be an oversimplification to state that it entails no sites of co-operation. In particular, unions and employers will have a shared interest in policing and protecting the integrity of procedural agreements. Moreover, there are often informal interactions of a congenial and co-operative nature between the sides as a necessary prerequisite of relationship building. Such co-operation has been described in the literature as 'accommodation' (Hyman, 2001: 29).

By the same token, there are issues that we might expect to be dealt with in partnership arenas such as training or health and safety where an ex-ante convergence of interests is apparent. Yet when developing dialogues on such issues, conflict can subsequently arise – for example, on time-off for safety representatives or training activities (Kelly, 1996; Stuart, 2001). It is thus improbable that there will be 100% congruence between 'boxing' and adversarialism or between 'dancing' and co-operation. Accordingly, if the European Social Dialogue is presaging a new era of partnership-based co-operation, this is perhaps best understood in the words of Haynes and Allen (2001: 181) as '... from co-operation in an adversarial context to constrained conflict in a co-operative one'. Nonetheless, as guiding metaphors for conflict and co-operation, the terms boxing and dancing have consistently had analytical purchase during the regular and ongoing dialogue between researchers and international practitioners throughout the project on which this book has been based. The usability of the metaphors can also be illustrated by the fact that we can introduce the associated terms of 'referee' and 'disc jockey' to signify the role of the state as a third actor in industrial relations arenas in certain contexts such as the concertation arrangements in Italy.

In practice the strategic choices of co-operative and conflictual responses by unions are rarely if ever a straightforward matter of either/or. Indeed, in mapping out union responses to HRM in the UK, Bacon and Storey (1996: 48) identified fifteen different configurations ranging along a continuum of hostility versus support for the concept. Collective bargaining and joint consultation, then, involve both adversarial and co-operation elements but have a bias towards the former – hence our label 'boxing'. Likewise, social partnership can have both elements, but of these there is a strong bias towards co-operation – hence our label 'dancing'. Seen as strategic choices for industrial relations, postures, boxing and dancing have quite distinctive characteristics as shown in Table 2.2. These defining characteristics, however, should be seen as ideal types of boxing and dancing; in reality such characteristics are often in a fluid state and the dividing lines between boxing and dancing will often be blurred.

The terms boxing and dancing need, however, to be unpacked further. Not only do we use them to signify the activities associated with adversarial industrial relations and co-operative industrial relations respectively, they also have a spatial dimension suggesting different arenas for each, a cultural dimension suggesting different ways of thinking about each or 'collective minds' (Weick and Roberts, 1993) and an identity dimension suggesting

Table 2.2 Collective bargaining and partnership compared

Collective bargaining ('Boxing') is:	Social partnership ('Dancing') is:
Episodic	A continuous process (but possibly in a project time-frame)
Limited in scope	Potentially open in scope (but may be issue-specific)
Restricted in terms of information access	Informed by high level information flows
Ritualistic and defensive	About joint problem-solving and sharing mutual gains
Sometimes settled in other arenas, e.g. arbitration	Settled internally
Underpinned by positional thinking and negotiation	Underpinned by process thinking and dialogue
About responding to decisions	About shaping decisions
Based on low trust	Based on high trust

Table 2.3 The four dimensions of boxing and dancing

Dimension	Boxing	Dancing
Action dimension mode of engagement between the parties	Discussion/negotiation; then agreement reached through give and take.	Initial identification of shared or overlapping interests and goals; then dialogue.
Spatial dimension arenas of engagement between the parties	Boxing rings: formal negotiation through collective bargaining machinery and joint consultation; co-determination where no consensus.	Dance floors: ongoing dialogue on organisational matters; co-determination on issues where consensus exists; joint development projects.
Cultural dimension mindset governing engagement between the parties	Boxing culture: divergent interests and zero-sum outcomes.	Dancing culture: shared or overlapping interests and positive-sum outcomes; commitment to firm by union and ethical commitment by employers.
Identity dimension roles of the parties	Bearers of class interests – adversaries in struggles over surplus value.	Value-adding partners.

contrasting roles of the parties. The four dimensions of boxing and dancing are illustrated in Table 2.3.

Partnership as strategic choice?

The precise meaning of the term 'social partnership' is somewhat unclear, but has been defined by Cave and Coats (1999) in a publication produced by the Trade Union Congress in the UK as consisting of six principles: commitment to the success of the organisation; recognising legitimate (stakeholder) interests; a commitment to employment security; a focus on the quality of working life; transparency; and adding value to the firm. But although presented in the UK and the US as something new or an idea 'whose time has come' (see e.g. Ackers and Payne, 1998; Guest and Peccei, 2001), it can be argued that it is something that has characterised industrial relations in other countries for some decades. For example, it has been accepted by the Swedish blue-collar union confederation since the 1950s that rationalisation in firms was required to facilitate structural adjustment. Such rationalisation, which implied a co-operative posture towards employers, had to be accepted by the labour movement, albeit alongside active labour market measures undertaken by the state to maintain full employment (Huzzard, 2000a). Perhaps it could also be argued that the spirit of collaboration forged at Saltsjöbaden in 1938 has been cognitively institutionalised (Scott, 1995) to such an extent that semantic debates on the meaning of 'partnership' in Sweden have been rendered somewhat unnecessary.

On a general level, social partnership itself is thus ambiguous as it is by no means clear in the literature or in practice whether it is a workplace phenomenon entailing new channels of worker involvement and participation or whether it is something encompassing the whole repertoire of employment regulation (Claydon, 1998). Moreover, the trajectories and meanings of partnership will depend on a number of factors: the organisational environment, political resources and state support mechanisms (Martinez-Lucio and Stuart, 2004). The logic of partnership as expressed, for example, in the Green Paper and the policy articulated by the Trades Union Congress (TUC) in Britain in the late 1990s (see e.g. Cave and Coats, 1999) is that it provides the potential, at least, for a more effective channel for the workers' voice to be heard, particularly on production and organisational issues. However, the fact that a channel for the elaboration of the workers' views exists is, in itself, no guarantee that it will have much influence on those responsible for planning and implementing change at the workplace.

Many examples can be found of the relative powerlessness of unions in challenging management decisions to downsize (Levie *et al.*, 1984) or outsource (Huzzard, 2000b) even where collective bargaining arrangements were well established and functioning effectively. This is partly because of the limitations in the scope of collective bargaining but equally because of the inability of the bargaining process to gain involvement in the planning stages of any strategic changes. A partnership approach, by contrast, typically tackles such constraints by ensuring its central dialogue process increasingly takes place at an earlier stage – where problems are being identified and solutions formulated. This is a crucial distinction and one that can be illustrated in Figure 2.4.

The vertical axis on the diagram represents the degree of agreement or consensus that exists in the organisation regarding the need for a particular change. The horizontal axis represents the time needed to reach and implement decisions associated with the change. The model assumes that in most organisations support amongst managers for a particular change will be achieved over time by an iterative process of internal discussion. The curved line shows how this internal consensus develops to the point, indicated by the square 'boxing ring', where a conventionally organised company will consult and/or negotiate the implementation of the change with the trade union or workers' representatives.

Depending upon the outcome of those negotiations, the level of support within the organisation for the change can increase, or stay the same, or decline. A circle, the 'dance floor' is located at a much lower level on the consensus curve. This represents the position that a company adopting a partnership approach will typically exhibit. By contrast with conventional consultation and negotiations, which are part of a potentially confrontational

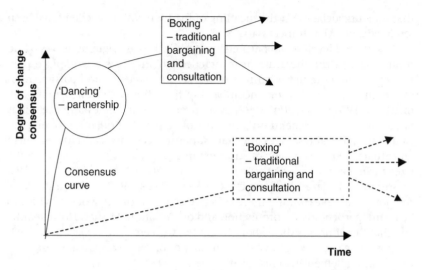

Figure 2.4   Employee involvement in decision-making: boxing or dancing?

'end game' (hence, 'boxing'), a partnership dialogue plays a critical role in reviewing the options and shaping the decisions necessary to make the organisational change. The dialogue takes place well before the management have agreed their final position and is therefore less confrontational and more constructively participative (hence, 'dancing'). The logic of partnership is that earlier involvement will facilitate greater chances of ongoing and even increasing consensus on change than would be the case under collective bargaining.

A partnership approach can be contrasted with a traditional approach to change that relies exclusively on collective bargaining and consultation. This is represented by the broken line and box in the lower part of Figure 2.4. As levels of trust are lower and information disclosure is later, not only does the change process take longer, but also discussions are held at a lower level of consensus for change. *'If only the management had asked us we could have told them that it wouldn't work. ...'* This common criticism, heard frequently in workplaces the world over, neatly illustrates the folly and the cost of not consulting the workforce in advance of making organisational change. A partnership approach, as shown in the model, avoids such outcomes by ensuring that the views of the workforce are introduced at an early enough stage in the process. In addition, partnership offers a number of advantages in terms of both business and social needs when compared with conventional consultation and negotiation. First of all, decisions coming from a dialogue that embraces the experience and the views of the workers' representatives as well as those of management inevitably emerge more extensively pre-tested and reviewed. Second, where this leads to jointly determined strategies to plan and implement the change, the shared 'ownership' that this confers is much more likely to lead to a higher level of acceptability at the workplace – particularly where social interests have been embraced alongside the commercial interests of the business. Third, enhanced accept-ability of the change process is, in turn, likely to lead to more willing adop-tion of the change itself. So much for the theory, then, but is this how partnership plays out in practice?

Critiquing social partnership

Social partnership, however, relies on the willingness of the partners to par-ticipate, a condition that is not at all guaranteed. Not only are there poten-tial objections from employers who may see social partnership as an infringement on management's right to manage, but also the implicitly plu-ralistic framework of social partnership is ideologically unacceptable in certain unions that have more traditional channels of unambiguously independent representation. Some critical accounts have also suggested that social partnership is simply a new label for an old phenomenon – that of accom-modation to employer interests and the manufacturing of consent (Burawoy, 1979; Kelly, 1996). Moreover, sceptics of social partnership have also argued that it inevitably involves accommodation and compromise with employers of such a magnitude that unions, de facto, sacrifice their independence and detach themselves from their members. The ideal of shared interests and mutual gains (Kochan and Osterman, 1994) is a mirage as no attempt at recasting the employment relationship around 'partner-ship' can circumvent the fundamental antagonism at the heart of the labour process (Kelly, 1996). Partnership will inevitably share the incorporationist features of business unionism as the mutual respect of the dance floor gives way to the seduction of the bedroom (Taylor and Ramsay, 1998).

Central features of social partnership are mutual gains (Cohen-Rosenthal and Burton, 1987; Kochan and Osterman, 1994), shared goals (Guest and Peccei, 2001: 212) and high trust (ibid.: 232). Such features can also be asso-ciated with business unionism; however, the endurance of partnership in some firms (see e.g. the cases discussed elsewhere in this volume) suggests that partnership need not imply incorporation. Research in Germany, for example, into member attitudes towards IG Metall's new role of co-operating with employers on production issues saw no evidence of perceived incorpo-ration (Kuhlmann and Schumann, 2001: 207). There is evidence, too, that in some instances employers see trade union *independence* as the prerequisite to added value (see Chapter 5 in this volume). This being so, it appears that both high levels of membership voice/legitimacy (Chaison *et al.*, 1993) and high levels of influence on the employer are simultaneously possible.

The issue of partnership from the point of view of trade union strategic choices and how it is distinguishable from business unionism is illustrated in Figure 2.5. A basic dilemma facing union representatives at the workplace

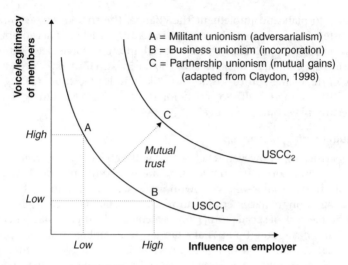

Figure 2.5   Union strategic choices and the role of mutual trust.

is that of serving both employer interests and membership interests (Boxall and Haynes, 1997). These activities entail a basic conflict and can be depicted as a trade-off between proximity to and high influence on employers on the one hand and proximity to and high legitimacy with the members on the other. This trade-off is illustrated in the figure by the union strategic choice curve $USCC_1$. Union leaders have a choice of industrial relations posture on this trade off – between the options of militant unionism and business unionism illustrated in the figure as A and B respectively.

Unions, however, have a further dimension of strategic choice beyond militancy and incorporation – that of social partnership (Claydon, 1998). The crucial point here is that there is a difference between co-operative relations with employers that are resigned and uncritical and co-operative relations that are informed by an independent perspective that accepts potentially divergent interests (Thompson *et al.*, 1994: 58). It seems reasonable, however, that for such relations to endure there is a requirement for mutual trust between the union and the employer (Kochan and Osterman, 1994). Accordingly, a new trade-off of strategic choice is discernible at higher levels of mutual trust – in terms of Figure 2.5. This entails an outward shift in the choice curve from $USCC_1$ to $USCC_2$. The figure shows that, in theory, partnership unionism entails the co-existence of high influence on employers and high levels of member voice and legitimacy.

Concluding comment

This chapter has sought to position this book in relation to the existing industrial relations literature, notably comparative studies, as well as elaborate on the core metaphors of boxing and dancing. In relation to the research questions of the book on social partnership and union renewal, we have sought to draw on and develop the concept of strategic choice as a theoretical tool for evaluating whether and how the choice to dance may or may not be linked to trade union renewal. Does partnership lead to renewal? Or do renewal options require the capacity and choice to dance? Or does renewal really depend on more informed and better-resourced boxing? These issues will be tackled in the chapters on various countries and cases to follow in the book. Before proceeding with our empirical accounts of boxing and dancing, however, some discussion is necessary of the unfolding institutional dimensions of industrial relations at the European level and the debates that have underpinned such developments. It is to these matters that the book will now proceed in the next chapter.

References

Ackers, P. and Payne, J. (1998) 'British Trade Unions and Social Partnership: Rhetoric, Reality and Strategy', *International Journal of Human Resource Management* 9(3): 529–50.

Ansoff, H. I. (1968) *Corporate Strategy*. Harmondsworth: Penguin.

Bacon, N. and Storey, J. (1996) 'Individualism and Collectivism and the Changing Role of Trade Unions', in Ackers, P., Smith, C. and Smith, P. (eds) *The New Workplace and Trade Unionism: Critical Perspectives on Work and Organization*. London: Routledge.

Bamber, J. G., Lansbury R. and Wailes, N. (eds) (2004) *International and Comparative Employment Relations* (4th edn). St Leonards, Australia: Allen & Unwin.

Bean, R. (1994) *Comparative Industrial Relations: An Introduction to Cross-National Perspectives* (2nd edn). London: Routledge.

Berg, P.-O. and Jonsson, C. (1991) *Strategisk ledning på politiska marknader*. Lund: Studentlitteratur.

Boxall, P. and Haynes, P. (1997) 'Strategy and Trade Union Effectiveness in a Neo-Liberal Environment', *British Journal of Industrial Relations* 35(4): 567–91.

Burawoy, M. (1979) *Manufacturing Consent: Changes in the Labor Process Under Monopoly Capitalism*. Chicago: Chicago University Press.

Cave, A. and Coats, D. (1999) 'Partnership: the Challenges and Opportunities', in *Tomorrow's Unions*. London: TUC.

Chaison, G. N., Bigelow, B. and Ottensmeyer, E. (1993) 'Unions and Legitimacy: A Conceptual Refinement', *Research in the Sociology of Organizations* 12: 139–66.

Child, J. (1972) 'Organizational Structure, Environment and Performance: the Role of Strategic Choice', *Sociology* 6(1): 1–22.

Child, J. (1997) 'Strategic Choice in the Analysis of Action, Structure, Organizations and Environment: Retrospect and Prospect', *Organization Studies* 18(1): 43–76.

Claydon, T. (1998) 'Problematising partnership: the prospects for a co-operative bargaining agenda' in Sparrow, P., Marchington, M. (eds) *Human Resource Management: The New Agenda*. London: Financial Times/Pitman.

Cohen-Rosenthal, E. and Burton, C. E. (1987) *Mutual gains: A Guide to Union Management Cooperation*. New York: Praeger.

Dunlop, J. T. (1958) *Industrial Relations Systems*. New York: Holt.

Dunlop, J. T. (1990) *The Management of Labor Unions*. Lexington: Lexington Books.

European Commission (1997) *Partnership for a New Organisation of Work*. Green Paper COM 97: 128.

Ferner, A. and Hyman, R. (1992) *Industrial Relations in the New Europe*. Oxford: Blackwells Business Books.

Flanders, A. (1970) *Management and Unions: The Theory and Reform of Industrial Relations*. London: Faber and Faber.

Fox, A. (1973) 'Industrial Relations: A Social Critique of Pluralist Ideology', in Child, J. (ed.) *Man and Organization*. London: Allen and Unwin.

Frege, C. M. and Kelly, J. (2003) 'Union Revitalization Strategies in Comparative Perspective', *European Journal of Industrial Relations* 9(1): 7–24.

Frost, A. (2000) 'Union Involvement in Workplace Decision Making: Implications for Union Democracy', *Journal of Labor Research* 21(2): 265–86

Giddens, A. (1984) *The Constitution of Society: Outline of the Theory of Structuration*. Cambridge: Polity Press.

Guest, D. E. and Peccei, R. (2001) 'Partnership at Work: Mutuality and the Balance of Advantage', *British Journal of Industrial Relations* 39(2): 207–36.

Gustavsen, B., Wikman, A., Ekman-Philips, M. and Hofmaier, B. (1996) *Concept-Driven Development and the Organization of the Process of Change: An Evaluation of the Swedish Working Life Fund*. Amsterdam: John Benjamin.

Hannigan, T. (1998) *Managing Tomorrow's High-Performance Unions*. Westport CT: Quorum Books.

Haynes, P. and Allen, M. (2001) 'Partnership as Union Strategy: A Preliminary Evaluation', *Employee Relations* 23(2): 164–93.

Heery, E. and Kelly, J. (1994) 'Professional, Participative and Managerial Unionism: An Interpretation of Change in Trade Unions', *Work, Employment and Society* 8(1): 1–22.

Higgins, W. (1996) 'The Swedish Municipal Workers' Union – A Study in the New Political Unionism', *Economic and Industrial Democracy* 17: 167–97.

Hoffmann, R. (2000) 'European Trade Union Structures and the Prospects for Labour Relations in Europe', in Waddington, J., Hoffman, R. (eds) *Trade Unions in Europe: Facing Challenges and Searching for Solutions*. Brussels: European Trade Union Institute (ETUI).

Huzzard, T. (2000a) *Labouring to Learn: Union Renewal in Swedish Manufacturing*. Umeå: Boréa.

Huzzard, T. (2000b). 'From Partnership to Resistance – Unions and Organisational Learning at Ericsson Infocom', *Management Learning* 31(3): 353–73.

Hyman, R. (1989) *The Political Economy of Industrial Relations: Theory and Practice in a Cold Climate*. London: Macmillan.

Hyman, R. (2001) *Understanding European Trade Unionism: Between Market, Class and Society*. London: Sage.

Jeffries, S. (1996) 'Strategic Choice for Unions in France and Britain: Divergent Institutions with Converging Opinions', in Leisink, P., Van Leemput, J. and Vilrokx, J. (eds) *The Challenges to Trade Unions in Europe*. Cheltenham: Edward Elgar.

Katz, H. and Darbishire, O. (2000) *Converging Divergences: Worldwide Changes in Employment Systems*. Ithaca NY: ILR Press.

Kelly, J. (1996) 'Union Militancy and Social Partnership' in Ackers, P., Smith, C. and Smith, P. (eds) *The New Workplace and Trade Unionism: Critical Perspectives on Work and Organization*. London: Routledge.

Kelly, J. (1998) *Rethinking Industrial Relations: Mobilisation, Collectivism and Long Waves*. London: Routledge.

Kessler, I. and Purcell, J. (1996) 'Strategic choice and new forms of employment relations in the public service sector: developing an analytical framework', *International Journal of Human Resource Management* 7(1): 206–29.

Kochan, T. A., McKersie, R. B. and Capelli, P. (1984) 'Strategic Choice and Industrial Relations Theory', *Industrial Relations* 23(1): 16–39.

Kochan T. A. and Osterman, P. (1994) *The Mutual Gains Enterprise: Forging a Winning Partnership among Labor, Management and Government*. Boston: Harvard University Press.

Korpi, W. (1983) *The Democratic Class Struggle*. London: Routledge and Kegan Paul.

Kuhlmann, M. and Schumann, M. (2001) 'What's Left of Workers' Solidarity? Workplace Innovation and Worker Attitudes toward the Firm', *The Transformation of Work* 10: 189-214.

Lecher, W., Nagel, B. and Platzer, H.-W. (eds) (2002) *The Establishment of European Works Councils: from Information Committee to Social Actor*. Aldershot: Ashgate.

Levie, H., Gregory, D. and Lorentzon, N. (eds) (1984) *Fighting Closures*. Nottingham: Spokesman Books.

Marks, A., Findlay, P., Hine, J., McKinlay, A. and Thompson, P. (1998) 'The Politics of Partnership? Innovation in Employment Relations in the Scottish Spirits Industry', *British Journal of Industrial Relations* 36(2): 209–26.

Martinez-Lucio, M. and Weston, S. (1992) 'The Politics and Complexity of Trade Union Responses to New Management Practices', *Human Resource Management Journal* 2(4): 77–91.

Martinez-Lucio, M. and Stuart, M. (2004) 'Swimming Against the Tide: Social Partnership, Mutual Gains and the Revival of "Tired" HRM', *International Journal of Human Resource Management* 15(2): 410–24.

Mintzberg, H. (1990) 'Strategy Formation – Schools of Thought' in Frederickson, J. (ed.) *Perspectives on Strategic Management*. New York: Harper Business Books.

Mintzberg, H. (1994) *The Rise and Fall of Strategic Planning*. Hemel Hempstead: Prentice Hall.

Offe, C. and Wiesenthal, H. (1980) 'Two Logics of Collective Action: Theoretical Notes on Social Class and Organizational Form', *Political Power and Social Theory* 1: 67–115.

Olney, S. L. (1996) *Unions in a Changing World*. Geneva: International Labour Office.

Reshef, Y. and Murray, A. I. (1988) 'Toward a Neoinstitutionalist Approach in Industrial Relations', *British Journal of Industrial Relations* 26(1): 85–97.

Rigby, M. (1999) 'Approaches to the Contemporary Role of Trade Unions', in Rigby, M., Smith, R. and Lawlor, T. (eds) (1999) *European Trade Unions: Change and Response*. London: Routledge.

Rigby, M., Smith, R. and Lawlor, T. (eds) (1999) *European Trade Unions: Change and Response*. London: Routledge.

Salaman, M. (2000) *Industrial Relations Theory and Practice* (4th edn) Harlow: Pearson Education.

Scheck, C. L. and Bohlander, G. W. (1990) 'The Planning Practices of Labor Organizations: A National Study', *Labor Studies Journal* Winter: 69–84.

Scott, W. R. (1995) *Institutions and Organizations*. Thousand Oaks: Sage.

Smith, R. (1999) 'The Convergence/Divergence Debate in Comparative Industrial Relations', in Rigby, M., Smith, R. and Lawlor, T. (eds) (1999) *European Trade Unions: Change and Response*. London: Routledge.

Stratton-Devine, K. and Reshef, Y. (1996) 'Union Planning: A Framework and Research Agenda', *Relations Industrielles* 51(3): 506–22.

Streeck, W. (1992) 'Training and the New Industrial Relations: A Strategic Role for Unions?' in Regini, M. (ed), *The Future of Labour Movements*. London: Sage.

Stuart, M. (2001) 'Contesting Partnership? Evaluating the Demise of a National Training Agreement', *Journal of Vocational Education and Training* 53(1): 5–20.

Taylor, P. and Ramsay, H. (1998) 'Unions, Partnership and HRM: Sleeping with the Enemy?' *International Journal of Employment Studies* 6(2): 115–43.

Thompson, P., Wallace, T. and Sederblad, P. (1994) 'Trade Unions and Organizational Innovation: British and Swedish Experiences', *Employee Relations* 16(2): 53–64.

Traxler, F., Blaschke, S. and Kittel, B. (eds) (2001) *National Labour Relations in Internationalized Markets: a Comparative Study of Institutions, Change and Performance.* Oxford: Oxford University Press.

Van Ruysseveldt, J. and Visser, J. (eds) (1996) *Industrial Relations in Europe: Traditions and Transitions.* London: Sage.

Waddington, J. and Hoffman, R. (eds) (2000) *Trade Unions in Europe: Facing Challenges and Searching for Solutions.* Brussels: European Trade Union Institute (ETUI).

Walton, R. E. and McKersie, R. B. (1965) *A Behavioral Theory of Labor Negotiations.* New York: McGraw-Hill.

Weick, K. and Roberts, K. (1993) 'Collective Mind in Organizations: Heedful Interrelating on Flight Decks', *Administrative Science Quarterly* 38(3): 357–81.

Willman, P. and Cave, A. (1994) 'The Union of the Future: Super-Unions or Joint Ventures?', *British Journal of Industrial Relations* 32(3): 395–412.

3
The Limits of the European Dance Floor: Hard Times for Strategic Choice, Partnership and Union Innovation

Regan Scott

Partnership as process, substance and choice

In this chapter we focus on two closely linked aspects of Europeanisation: these are the European dimension of social partnership, seen through the prism of the European Union (EU)'s 1997 Green Paper on Work Organisation,[1] and second the strategic choices of unions operating at the European level. The Green Paper is seen as a decisive staging-point in EU industrial relations development, and is argued to carry a bigger meaning than was commonly seen at the time. Our special interest was in relating it to the longstanding debate about trade union decline and the strategic choices made about union recovery and innovation. We end the chapter by posing some questions and suggesting some orientations for understanding the likely development and mixtures of conflict and co-operation in ongoing European industrial relations.

First, however, we look at some questions of method and understanding, including what might be called the 'Green Paper conjuncture' and then we present some considerations which derive from our reliance on the concept of strategic choice for unions in their relationship to the wide and complex pathways of the EU's social dimension. We move on then to delineate the Green Paper and present the official co-ordinates of the trade union decline/innovation debate as seen at the level of the European trade union movement.

On the substantive area of the Green Paper, we explore the view that, at least in intention, it signalled an imperative to extend the EU's peak level industrial relations settlement directly down to the productive base of the European economy. It marked a step change in the basic political economy of EU industrial relations: from a dynamic of harmonising and adapting labour market regulation for the single European market to a bid to deliver global competitiveness through a distinctly European model of co-operative industrial relations at the workplace. Since there was no debate beyond the broad terms of existing social partnership – this comes later, as we shall see – we would emphasise that this massive prospect seemed to be envisaged as working through the already existing institutions of representation and bargaining. The initiative can only have been intended as, and was certainly perceived as constructive and supportive of Social Europe, and as counterposed to the growing trend of neo-liberal 'distancing' from traditional social partnership modes. So it has had something going for it.

But there was a new element: it promulgated a new conditionality for social partnership well beyond the scope of labour market harmonisation politics, and aimed at the sharp end of industrial relations, rather than simply developing existing macro-economic themes through the processes started at the Essen and Cologne summits. Within just a few years, as EU governments moved towards a much more overtly neo-liberal consensus, the residue of the Green Paper did however take at least a nominally substantial form. There was an appeal for the social partners to negotiate 'innovation agreements' as a mechanism for delivering the imperative of European modernisation: this formula was apparently introduced into the final text of the Lisbon Summit in year 2000 through union pressure.[2] What followed for the Green Paper, its social partnership assumptions, and its underlying imperatives will be discussed below.

European level perspectives on issues of trade union decline and innovation are then examined partly as a background to the country studies and some of the case studies which deal with new approaches to union organisation, but also to see how the deeper problems of European industrial relations related to these developments.

The discussion of our two focal points makes no pretence to the status of any kind of causal correlation, or indeed any higher 'mega' causality, although the mega level will emerge in both the European Commission's and the unions' literature. Nor have we set out consciously to plough a different path to mainstream academic industrial relations approaches to the Europeanisation of industrial relations.[3] We have nevertheless sensed a conjunctural association between the developmental stage marked by the Green Paper's reach into the traditional arenas of micro bargaining and a trade union politics of uncertainty about strategy, organisational decline and innovatory directions. At the start of the Green Paper period there was a mixed sense of, on the one hand, considerable developmental potential for both unions and for the Social Europe project.[4] On the other hand there was also a sense of foreboding.

It has not been hard to see the parameters of hope and fear: big history was already presenting the European integration project with growing pressures from what we now call globalisation. The author recalls the frequency of inner union discussions in the early 1990s about the unbeatable odds posed by what might be called global social dumping as opposed to the narrower waters of purely European social dumping. The term 'global pessimism' was coined, and while it related sharply to the majority of UK unions' analyses of their prospects and the dramatic downward revision of their aspiration from any future 'New Labour' government, its parameters were plain to see in most European countries.[5] With so many eggs in the basket of European-level political exchange and soft processes of social dialogue, the chosen ideology of EU industrial relations – social partnership – for the first time looked like a narrow and hard path. That this was something more than the long march of unions through the European institutions – it took about 25 years to get European information and consultation rights implemented through European Works Councils (EWCs) – was not debated openly, but the deeper probings about the basic status of industrial relations in Europe started to send a clear message: social partnership would have to transform itself if it was to be capable of impacting on forces deriving more from global competition than straightforward European integration.

Our concern has therefore been to look at social partnership as it has been and is being practised, aiming to detect something more advanced than the traditional patterns of dancing and boxing, and to see if there are clues about how it might or might not become a dynamic process, and even become embedded as the *substantive doctrine* of future European industrial relations. Not the least of our concerns has been how social partnership relates to traditional areas of collective bargaining, for which, incidentally, there had only ever been a slim and blocked treaty base in any case.[6]

The Green Paper as step change?

The special nature of the Green Paper initiative can be best understood by setting it in the context of the many evolving streams of social dialogue and sponsored EU industrial relations programmes. Social dialogue – as the process which takes substantial form in social partnership – evolved from The Coal and Steel Community and Euratom through Val Duchesse and then the two separable paths of industrial or sectoral social dialogue and the macro-economic consultation which came into place with the incomes restraint aspect of the single currency project.[7] These macro processes were given authority by the Maastricht Treaty which in return for wage restraint, as a very visible and powerful form of 'political exchange', created the unique mechanism whereby social partner agreements could substitute for the normal governmental process in formulating and enacting social directives.[8] This has produced some important labour market regulations for atypical workers and parental leave, while older themes from the Social Charter and the new Social Chapter finally delivered the directive on European Works Councils and the more recent and slightly stronger information and consultation directive.[9]

In contrast to these achievements, which while broad in impact have stayed very close to their legal bases in the Social Chapter, the Green Paper revealed the EU for the first time stepping down from its chosen 'peak' or federal level of industrial relations regulation to designate an industrial relations modality – social partnership – for routine workplace relations throughout the European area. The Green Paper said that micro-bargained agendas should come under European influence, and that social partnership should be the mode, rather than traditional conflictual workplace relations and that, implicitly, partnership agendas should certainly be at a much more engaged level than customary works council·co-operation. The fact that there was no direct treaty base for this strategic focus on micro-industrial relations cannot usefully be regarded as a matter of either incompetence or adventurism. We hold to the straightforward view that this decision to push so dramatically beyond the boundaries of the treaties was driven by the new agenda of European modernisation under the shadow of globalisation. It would therefore be a powerful imperative.

Certainly the ensuing period showed that a lot of confident and ongoing industrial relations developments were under severe pressure. Commissioner Flynn's termination of resources for most of the so-called 'parity committee' system of sponsored social dialogue in 1995 served notice on dependent tripartite corporatism, flagging a hard push for unions and employers into free-standing and voluntarist agreements. It was seen at the time as an advance out of the grip of the European nanny state. The achievement of trade union standing as a social partner capable of legislating agreements in place of normal European law-making at Maastricht was seminal at macro level, the fulfilment of the long cherished goal of having hands on the legal enactment process. The Cologne and Essen Summits brought an acceptance of a European-level social compact on national collective bargaining as a support to the Single European Currency programme. This income policy for Europe was widely seen as a watershed for controlling inflationary creep and overcoming the scramble of money, wages trying to keep up with prices. This acceptance in turn spawned a number of national level social pacts. The achievement of an EWC directive was a breakthrough, and a trigger for extensive and largely successful union activity, at least until the cross-border litigation crisis of Renault's arbitrary closure of its Vilvoorde, Brussels factory in February 1997.[10] But overall, the results were not good: not much outcome from sectoral social dialogue, nor many new jointly negotiated directives; not much in the way of new jobs from macro wage restraint and low inflation, or the subsequent National Action Plans for Jobs (NAPs); and real wages starting to decline in many countries too (see above and note 7).

Searching for deeper dancing rhythms?

So it can hardly have come as a surprise that the Green Paper process was followed by a wave of explorations into the deeper working of European industrial relations. The most prominent was the Supiot Report which looked at the degradation of mainstream employment status through extensive labour market diversification, in the sense of the growth of massive atypical work and new individualised working cultures and patterns (Supiot, European Commission 1999).[11] The report took place in the context of an intensive monitoring of the full range and diversity of industrial relations trends by the Commission's agencies and strategic reports such as the Wise Persons' Group (Rodrigues Report, European Commission 2002).[12] Globalisation's impact on European industrial relations – however it might be defined – was explored extensively by a research group based at the European Trade Union Congress Institute (ETUI) (Hoffman, Hoffman, Kirton-Darling and Ramptelshammer, European Foundation 2002). Overt challenges from the competition doctrine to industrial relations created a crisis, arising from the Albany case which was resolved finally by the European Court of Justice. This ruled that competition law did not override embedded industrial relations doctrines.[13] The competition versus social policy issue had been explored and damped down much earlier in the Mollitor Report (Deregulation and Employment, European Commission 1995). And the Gyllenhammar Report on industrial restructuring, coming directly from the Renault crisis, recognised that industrial restructuring had become a routine industrial market process, not simply an occasional corporate crisis mechanism.[14]

Positions were promulgated ranging from the EU being simply a neutral but nevertheless multi-country 'industrial relations space' through to the contemporary doctrine of an imperative for a 'quality industrial relations' – the Rodrigues group formulation – in Europe's engagement with global competitive forces (see above, and note 12). The latest development within the union world is the call for a 'supplementary system of EU industrial relations'. This has emerged from the ETUC's 1999 and 2003 Congresses, and involves seeking to establish a status for cross border agreements and possibly a dispute resolution mechanism at EU level for autonomous agreements between the social partners.[15] On the wider social and welfare front, by the time of the neo-liberal summits at the end of the millennium, official Europe was starting to talk about the comprehensive 'modernisation' of the social model, and a debate about social model governance was started, giving unions and employers another basis for a special role as modernisers in 'civil society'.[16]

Finally, it may be useful to note at this point that the Social Affairs Commission did not seek to prescribe a strategic role to works councils or EWCs in its modernisation-of-work-organisation scenario. Formally, of course, it could not do this in any case since the legal base and objectives of both EWCs and national information and consultation procedures under the 2002 Directive was restricted and studiously neutral to the terrains of collective bargaining. Our project has operated on a parallel view. While we recognise the potential importance of EWCs as an industrial relations mechanism, and understand their prominence in the unions' innovation agendas, the terms of our investigation range wider than any foreseeable development of EWC competences, although they are a major and innovatory social partnership institution, at least in mainstream understanding. The extent of trade union penetration over the ten years or so of EWC development has been impressive, but our sense is that a form of social partnership which goes well beyond works councils would be needed for a fully functioning social partnership to become the modernising vehicle in European labour markets and industrial relations.[17]

A Green Paper for 'New Partners at Work': dancing on the shopfloor?

The Green Paper was launched in April 1997. Its title was carefully but explicitly formulated, if broad in scope and maybe aspiration – 'Partnership for a New Organisation of Work'. It was followed by a Commission Communication in November 1998, 'Modernising the Organisation of Work – a Positive Approach to Change' (EU9901146F). The Commission saw these texts as practical reflections of the much bigger macro-economic process agreed at the Luxembourg Council in November 1997. This established the ongoing Employment Guidelines and the system of agreed and actively monitored NAPs for Employment. The work modernisation initiatives related to the 'adaptability pillar' of the Luxembourg Guidelines.

The text adopted the concept of 'flexible security' as the new social production paradigm, reflecting the complex diffusions of technology into basic production processes.[18] These were seen as now substantially diverse, taking place in changed social circumstances and being driven by strong, open competitive forces which needed managing through a social partnership-based industrial relations system, and workforce participation at enterprise level. The structural imperative was crystal clear: flexible and adaptable work organisation requires workforce participation and change in industrial relations systems.

Three subjects were identified at the level of the enterprise, albeit closely linked and interdependent, but it may be useful to keep their separate identities in mind. These are

1. *work organisation,* which might be interpreted as the organisation of employment relations at workplace levels – a micro industrial relations focus.
2. *the future of work,* an all-embracing formulation with strong unemployment, new jobs aspects – a policy-oriented formula.
3. *new forms of work.* This is sometimes a question of micro organisation – flexibility and associated issues within the enterprise, sometimes having an external labour market focus, whether on the issue of exploitative non-standard employment or on freely chosen new work patterns.

These three foci can be seen as separable elements in the well-established debates about core/periphery workforces, the effect of increasing – and nearly equalising – female participation in the workforce, and the shift from big scale manufacturing to service and knowledge-based industrial employment. The corresponding industrial relations model was positioned strongly in between future (unspecified) innovation and retention of the best bits of the old industrial relations spectrum. So the Green Paper strode through the well-trodden pastures of skill enrichment and high-trust, high-quality industrial relations at enterprise level as part of the European answer to global competitiveness. But equally important, the future 'high road' for Europe could only be completed with worker participation as the principle underlying 'new forms of industrial relations'.

The terrain for the new forms of industrial relations was explicitly comprehensive, descending from global corporations to small and medium-sized enterprises, and equally relevant to public services such as health, education and environmental services.

A familiar litany of plaudits and negatives attended the discussion of the historic role of Tayloristic mass production and its dominance and successful contribution to 20th century wealth creation. But the key insight of the Green Paper is that the narrow segmentation of jobs under this functional and authoritarian system had restricted innovation, impeded skill-upgrading and retarded productivity growth by failing to unlock the human creativity of the workforce. Not surprisingly, quality circles are cited with enthusiasm, the concept of the 'flexible firm' is endorsed and the Toyota production system of continuous improvement is commended.

Three factors which drive change in a wide variety of models of production are located in the fields of human resources, markets and technology. Using mainstream nostrums, the speed of innovation is seen as commanding a skills-and-knowledge revolution on a continuous basis. Second, markets are seen to have changed structurally with an in-built consumer demand for quality production and open markets. Third, the technological revolution (IT – Information Technology) has ushered in a seemingly ceaseless era of relatively cheap and fast change in and around production and supply and resource use.

On the industrial relations front, the analysis is that increased skills in the workforce will lead to more active and mobile labour markets as workers with tradeable skills are able to move to seek better employment terms. This exercise of legitimate mobility rights is seen as eroding traditional industrial relations stability, while on the employers' side there has been a diversification of employment relations through management strategies for downsizing, outsourcing, sub-contracting, networking and joint ventures.

The special burden of this process of change has been to expose the limits of traditional labour law with its assumption of stable employment rights, and single, straightforward identities for employers. Further, these structural changes prompted the European Commission to conclude that the balance of regulatory powers between government on the one hand, and employers and unions through collective bargaining on the other hand, needed fundamental questioning. They introduced a third term to the balance, namely the regulatory role of the individual through personal employment contracts.

But the text contained little sense of developmental direction. Instead, the Commission indicated a whole menu of sites within industrial relationships which were profoundly affected by these changes. These were wage systems, working time, taxation, and social security as the generic areas: only one of many new labour market practices is cited – teleworking. The canvass finished with a flourish of questions for the social partners to address as the concrete outcome of the formal consultation process which the Green Paper had instituted.

Designing the dance in an action framework

The brief interval of seven months between the Green Paper's launch and the ensuing Communication can be taken as a sign that there was little disagreement at the peak level of social partnership, and equally that some concrete agendas had already been in mind when the Green Paper's analytical tour-de-force had been launched. There was little time for any consultation which reached below the peak level of social partner organisations such as Union of Industrial and Employers' Confederations of Europe (UNICE), European Centre of Enterprises with Public Participation and of Enterprises of General Economic Interest (CEEP) and the ETUC and its sectoral affiliates, and no declared impulse to explore what already might have been developing at many levels in routine industrial relations where the very forces both of and for change might already be working some of the passages so elegantly analysed in the Green Paper.

Nevertheless, some confident sounding policy frameworks did emerge. There would be a positive promotion of a new social partnership for a new organisation of work. That was a considerable advance on the Social Charter and Social Chapter's vision of creating a level playing field of basic rights within the existing boundaries of individual countries' industrial relations settlements. And the politics and economics of the situation were clear: Europe needed to speed up its modernisation of work, which in some areas was 'fairly thin on the ground'. In effect, the whole agenda was a new version of traditional, periodic productivity improvement politics.

That the process needed to be anchored at enterprise level, but that the levers and pathways of change lay at European peak level, was recognised. It would be reconciled by two processes: an agreement that the argument about more regulation versus de-regulation should be set aside with a new agreement for more flexibilisation in return for more worker security; and second, by agreement on a mechanism for implementing new modes of work organisation.

The narrative goes further, albeit carefully so. The first example cited was predictably the macro level of the Luxembourg jobs summit with its employment guidelines and NAPs. Existing country social partnership dialogue was supposed to come into play. The next level of approach was seen as the European sectoral level of social dialogue. This held the possibility of changing 'contractual framework(s)': few commentators have been able to interpret the coding here, but something more than encouraging European employers to establish a negotiating mandate was clearly envisaged. The Communication finished by specifying key areas through which social partnership processes – of whatever variety and level and competence – might address the imperatives of change and modernisation. These were:

- training guarantees without age limitation
- new payments systems to enhance productivity
- pursuing annualised working time agreements
- the endorsement and active pursuit of new employment relationships
- developing active strategies for new technology (IT) adaptation
- using worker participation processes to drive work modernisation
- promoting equal opportunities by encouraging women's work, re-entry to work and access to training.

An agenda of some specificity had thus been set, very rapidly, across a wide range and at a level of intervention quite new to the EU social dimension. Its evident weakness was delivery mechanisms. There was a problem of the distance of peak level trade union and employer organisations from the shopfloors and offices and industrial districts of the European economy, and, equally, there was the established reluctance of employer organisations to seek and exercise a negotiating mandate from their own members. So long as the Green Paper imperatives and social partnership stayed at the level of policy *influence* and *ideological* authority, the business of crafting new industrial relations futures might be acceptable. But if fundamental change and positive employer engagement with unions was being envisaged, as far the employers were concerned, delivery of competitiveness by market processes was still preferred.

Not surprisingly, the Green Paper did not progress into the legislative sphere, or even attract any specific funding lines. Arguably, neo-liberalism had started to extend its grip from governments down to the level of the Commission. On a formal level too, the official instruments to pursue an active bargaining level industrial relations strategy were delimited by the terms of the Amsterdam Treaty's Social Chapter.[19]

Set against this background, the substantive message of the Green Paper can be seen as difficult and radical: pushing upstream, against the tides.

Drafting the terms of a step change towards a peaceful, co-operative road for the adaptation of workplace relations to new global challenges would prove to be a different matter to actually dealing with the imperatives. Maybe the Commission had already seen the future: in its Communication in 1998, when it stated 'The Commission did not intend the Green paper process as the basis for a legislative initiative to prescribe a single form of organisation of work'. The aim was to 'launch a debate'.

From union decline to union innovation

The trade union decline debate took on a European dimension in the mid-1990s, having become a practical issue in most but not all countries, perhaps a decade earlier. Prior to this, trade union modernisation agendas had been running to varied timetables in different countries. Issues from the literature both at national, European and international levels can be sum-marised as falling within a social modernisation paradigm, with agendas concerning:

- mergers to achieve critical mass for professional servicing in the increas-ingly complex industrial relations world;
- gender, ethnicity and disability being main-streamed into union struc-tures and programmes, feeding into changed internal governance and bargaining priorities;
- commitment to union organisation in new labour market areas, partly flowing from new gender sensibilities;
- individual member rights mainly through reformed democratic decision-making, both in ballots on agreements and authorising action;
- union policy-making transparency, development of media profiles and organisational branding;
- development of commercial and professional services for members as a client group.

In the main, however, the substances of collective bargaining and workplace relationships were not seen as part of the early debates about union mod-ernisation.

The European level debate in official trade union circles commenced with sympathetic researchers' probings through the ETUC's Research Institute (ETUI), with the start of its journal Transfer in 1995. This work culminated in a massive report published in 2000, Trade Unions in Europe: Facing Challenges and Searching for Solutions (Waddington and Hoffman, 2000). This report was prefigured by an ETUC Conference in 1998 on the theme of 'new workforces, old unions', based on a presentation of union challenges (Waddington *et al.*, 1997). The review in the ETUI's Transfer journal identified two essentially atrophied and structurally crucial relationships between

1. unions as organisations and union members, and
2. unions and workplaces.

Action areas were identified as

- relating recruitment to labour market change
- revising trade union structures, socially and in terms of mergers
- articulation and cohesion in union-to-member relations
- recognition of employer needs in terms of bargaining levels and issues
- trusting that decentralised flexibility could be protected under national social pacts
- engaging with participation and employee involvement working methods (from the HRM movement)
- responding to Europeanisation.

It is worth noting that five out of the seven action areas can be seen to be cautiously embracing – albeit cautiously – bargaining and workplace imperatives, matters over which the European level of trade union organisations had no established competence. By 1998, the ETUC conference analysis had acquired a broader rhetoric: conference proceedings openly discussed unions becoming 'attuned to the new socio-economic order' and suggested two strategic changes. First, that unions should demand and support direct worker participation cultures, rather than relying on indirect union representivity and second that unions should endorse as a new duality decentralized industrial relations and simultaneous Europeanisation. Policy cohesion would be secured through 'pattern bargaining' and 'organisational decentralisation'.

The full ETUI Report was published in 2000 – a 700-page compendium and the first fully discussed and articulated 'autobiography' of official European trade unionism, albeit resting squarely on 16 country chapters. There is a valuable presentation of de-unionisation experience and literature which records the mainstream view that in the 1980s direct participation of workers in new working methods and consultation systems did not lead to union exclusion or loss of influence, whether in single or dual system countries. However, in the 1990s union exclusion in the single channel countries did make real inroads, and that in dual system countries, most notably Germany, and also the Netherlands, opening clauses and agreement-making by works councils had started to erode central union authority.

The Report's conclusions generally favoured European and co-ordinated (united) solutions, and targeted collective bargaining co-ordination, whilst accepting that national collective bargaining traditions – if not their scope and effect – seemed not to have changed in any visible ways despite the admitted challenges and agendas of change. The essential analysis does not differ greatly from mainstream academic research findings (Rigby *et al.*, 1999).

Meanwhile, whatever paper-based imperatives of union modernisation might have been formulated, European inter-governmental structural reform programmes, mainly concerning the reduction of welfare costs and labour market protection, have brought a renewal of confrontation to the wider industrial relations scene. These levels and sites of conflict continue to hold their own authority. The recent World Bank report, Unions and Collective Bargaining: Economic Effects in a Global Environment (World Bank, 2002), aside from a valuable literature review, is an authoritative reminder that trade union functioning in the collective bargaining field seems to persist relatively independently of other agendas, and to be of continuing and detailed concern to employers and governments. Further, on the globalisation front, the Dublin Foundations' 2002 Report – Europeanisation of Industrial Relations in a Global Perspective (Dublin Foundation, 2002) and its accompanying massive literature review by Hoffman, Hoffman, Kirton-Darling and Rampetlshammer offers a careful and cautious assessment of the overall pattern of recent structural change in European industrial relations. They assert that a re-alignment of industrial relations has taken place through company-centred bargaining, but that there has not been an erosion of the system and its basic structures. This reflects Hyman's opposition of Europeanisation or erosion (Hyman, 2001b), but draws a more optimistic conclusion.

One of the larger research programmes on trade union 'revitalisation' (EJIR, March 2003) covers five countries and employs the 'strategic choice' paradigm, drawing on the concept of 'framing' or 'cognitive processes' for understanding unions' responses to changing environments (structural conditions). The research asks three questions: what types of action are unions taking to address challenges, what explains cross-country difference, and, more judgementally, how effective are these actions for revitalisation? The project recognises a sense of a crisis in unions which exists relatively independently of the actual degree of union decline. It studies organising (membership), organisational change in unions (as institutions) and thirdly coalition building (a kind of political exchange). Partnerships with employers at any and all levels count here alongside more traditional political action seeking friendly legal enactment. The results to date are not surprising, but we find some comfort for our own project in the following evaluation of the paucity of research on union strategic choice and truly comparative research on union strategies. We quote from the introductory article by Frege and Kelly (2003: 1):

> It is surprising that although Kochan, Katz and McKersie (1986) introduced the concept of 'strategic choice' to industrial relations literature in

the mid-1980s, there is hardly any research on the different strategic choices made by unions. Moreover, although multi-country studies of industrial relations are increasingly popular, there has been little truly comparative research on union strategies in different countries.

The prospects and problems of European partnership

The strategic weight of the Green Paper initiative raised many questions. Was it realistic, or even likely, that workplace modernisation could be pursued by social partnership rather than traditional bargaining? Could a powerful enough dynamic be launched through the existing institutions and understandings of the EU's peak level industrial relations settlement? If unions did and could respond, what did employers think, and what could the EU actually do about its initiative? What would it mean for trade union thinking, and did it imply a strategic choice about a new balance or set of interrelations between conflict and co-operation? The sheer weight of these questions meant that the project in the form of an immediate action programme was quickly sidelined. A lot more work needed to be done, even if the will to pursue the path would remain in place.

As we have seen above, what actually happened was that deeper issues came to the surface in the form of reports and inquiries driven either by the logic of policy development or, more likely, by sheer events, like the Renault crisis. In effect, the imperative remained to drive a period of deeper analysis and political movement. Four aspects of the ensuing period merit closer attention. These might be termed the Supiot agenda, the Gyllenhammar agenda, the politics of social policy agenda and finally the underlying trade union agenda which saw an emergence of conflictual activism caused by co-ordinated neo-liberal agendas against the old welfare settlement in Europe. We look briefly at these four areas, and return to reflect on some possible lessons of the European experience.

Supiot: new and strong dance rhythms needed?

The controversial report into the 'Transformation of labour and future of labour law in Europe' was commissioned in July 1996, reporting in June 1999. Under the chairmanship of Professor Alain Supiot, it made uncomfortable reading, not least in its recommendations – sympathetically intended for workers' rights and union futures – for

> active support from public (in particular Community) authorities for recasting collective bargaining; broadening the scope of bargaining and extending the parties covered and tasks involved should be encouraged as the sole response to demands for flexibility that is consistent with traditional labour law. Such support may (might -author) consist of rules for mandatory bargaining and procedural rules on representation.

The report described the widespread devolution to company bargaining as 'risky', and commends the dual system for its essential complimentarity of conflictual and co-operative functions in industrial relations systems. It also found collective bargaining where it existed 'astonishingly dynamic'. Some of the report's radicalism derived from its very wide-ranging terms of reference. Two related studies, The Regulation of Working Conditions in the Member States of the European Union, Vol. 2 in 1998, and Vol. 1 in 1999, penetrate to fundamental industrial relations structures, and especially the legal status of trade union/employer agreements and the constitutional standing of collective bargaining processes for producing these agreements. For Year 2000, a new and very focused series of annual Industrial Relations in Europe Reports was launched by Social Affairs Commissioner Diamontopoulou. These gave a status to the problems and challenges of industrial relations which had been given in the 1990s to unemployment and labour market change through the annual EU Employment Reports. Then another Expert Group was set up to report on the future of industrial relations as a formal system at all EU levels. The ensuing Rodrigues Group Report (2001) came after the turn to open markets signalled by the Lisbon Summit and while not innovative, can only be viewed as essentially supportive of the EU continuing to have a comprehensive and fully constitutional system of industrial relations. It did however flag the notion of European innovation agreements in industry. Also a High Level Task Force on Skills and Mobility was set up in 2001 to examine pan-European labour markets and new economy dynamics. An important five-year research project emerged on Benchmarking and Europeanisation of Industrial Relations, based at Warwick University, UK. The project included an examination of emerging boundaries in sectoral and enterprise level collective bargaining.

Gyllenhammar: is restructuring dancing or boxing?

Prior to the Supiot Report, the Gyllenhammar Report had been commissioned to respond to the crisis of information and consultation relationships when Renault closed its Brussels Vilvoorde factory without notice to its French union dominated EWC. The wise person's group under former Volvo Chief Executive Officer (CEO) Pehr Gyllenhammar took on board a broader concept of information and consultation through its recognition, at the prompting of the European Metalworkers Federation, the parent body of the Renault unions, of industrial restructuring as a routine management process, not simply a crisis instrument. While the overt outcome of the report was the setting up of an Industrial Restructuring Observatory based at Europe's Dublin Foundation, at the behest of the European Metalworkers Federation (EMF), the message was clear: normal commercial management practices in response to rapidly changing market conditions would mean virtually permanent change in employment terms and opportunities at levels not reached by much of the established collective bargaining machinery of the European countries. By implication, it viewed the running sore of employee and union rights to substantively challenge and change corporate restructuring decisions as a matter for EU law to prescribe, with the goal of facilitating change, not impeding it (as employers would see the matter). Union approaches to hard consultation rights could have come either by an extended and resourced period of consultation or by exploring legal rights to a resort to boxing supported by a legal period of suspension for the intended action. The problem of finding a formula was handed over to the dual processes of reviewing the EWC directive and at long last formulating a basic information and consultation directive. The latter was achieved in 2002. For our broad purposes, this new and major pathway in industrial relations challenges invites questions about whether a restructuring rights settlement can be achieved simply within a works council context, without the support of a broader framework of social partnership. And if the wider framework is needed, what character might it take? Would soft and uncodified and legally unsupported partnership cultures be able to take the strain? Some of our case studies look at these questions.

The five-year social programme: the dance master tries out new steps

In 2000, it was decided that instead of two-year Social Programmes, there would be a grander if legislation-light, five-year programme. The social partners under the Maastricht negotiating facility were invited to look at industrial relations issues at the system level. This was not a remit to consolidate industrial relations, but to agree the principles upon which the social model could be modernised, and second, to look for a mechanism by which existing legislative and contractual rules might be reviewed.

The five-year social programme took the form of a working agenda, rather than a strictly budgeted social and legislative *programme*. It was comprehensive and traditional in the sense of having a strong position for equalities and social inclusion, and continued to pursue full employment issues. At the same time, it included for the first time after the Green Paper, the 'new work environment', and fundamental rights. The atypical workforce issues were the only headline commitments, these being presented in part as 'family friendly' since their legal base was to be equal treatment. On the industrial relations structure agenda, the concept of 'quality industrial relations' was launched, signalling an interest in leading-edge models, best practice and benchmarking rather than harmonisation through legislation. There is a specific invitation to the social partners to think of negotiations and collective bargaining, 'where appropriate', on issues related to work organisation and new forms of work, based on the premise of 'the shared responsibility between business and employees regarding the employability and adaptability of the workforce, in particular with regard to occupational mobility'. The promotion of 'quality industrial relations' sounded rather grand and a hostage to fortune, but landed at a more familiar if obstinate airstrip: the runway of sectoral social dialogue. It was closely focused around improving existing EU level social partner dialogues, exploring links between national and European level sectoral structures, and aside from the initiation of reflection groups and social forums, proposed setting up a system of 'national labour inspectors' to monitor the implementation at member state level of European social directives.

Overarching the new Social Programme was the ominous presence of the new political mode of 'open coordination', due to take root in the heart of EU practices in the ongoing process of creating a new treaty settlement for Europe. This could mean that the will to design and implement social directives would wither, leaving the dance floor without a powerful magnet to bring the partners together. Political exchange was being flagged as no longer necessarily leading to legal enactment. Overall, it seemed that the Green Paper's major imperatives were being displaced back to the decentralising dynamic of market industrial relations. It seemed that even if key aspects of industrial relations were deemed to be a big European problem, they were certainly not going to be dealt with by a robust social dialogue leading to bargained social partnership agreements.

... and boxing returns on social wage issues

At the same time, traditional conflictual industrial relations had started to take on a new life, directed largely at member states and, by extension, at official Europe's social reputation because of the Cardiff and Lisbon Summit commitments to neo-liberal political economy. The most prominent issue has been pension reform. Workfare retrenchments on the welfare state settlement also provoked conflict with a European level aspect. The failure of National Action Plans for jobs to produce results also contributed. The fact that there was no direct European treaty competence in social security and welfare matters meant that the social wage consequences of the European Growth and Stability Pact – the macro-management system of monetary union – could not be dealt with in formal social dialogue: so at a testing time, the cohesion designed to be drawn from broad social partnership ideology and process was simply not available. The message from the peak political level to the practical levels of European industrial relations cannot have been positive.

The Green Paper that ended with a whimper seemed nevertheless to send loud reverberations around European industrial relations. What might be termed the Supiot problems remain, and will most likely grow less tractable as time passes. The Gyllenhammar problems remain at the heart of global corporate practise, quite apart from the post-Enron crisis in corporate governance which seems, in turn, to be threatening the basic fabric of the pre-existing movement for corporate social responsibility.[20] European new governance seems to be evolving away from legal regulation in the social field and some unions, in some countries, have found broad social issues on which to base a renewal of traditional boxing skills. It looks therefore as though the Green Paper period has ended with a hard conjuncture, with only one certainty: that is, that the imperatives of the Green Paper and its analytical progeny have not gone away.

The politics of partnership and new unionism

If Europe were to succeed with its social dimension intact and credible, and able to compete globally, it seemed that it needed to become an even more active maker of its industrial relations heritage. If there was an important new dimension to add to or re-make co-operative industrial relations, how might it relate to unions' politics? Social partnership and social dialogue might work for narrowly defined European purposes as a supplement to national systems and traditions, but would not there be political problems for unions in the process of moving beyond *supplementing* industrial relations to *substituting* them from the European level?

Social partnership had never been a policy or value free area, of course, within trade union tradition and doctrine, and the search for trade union recuperation in the form of strategic innovation and variants of new union-ism is not in itself new or unidirectional. Our own period contains a wide range, from the wholesale embracing of social partnership, as with the UK TUC (the 'New Unionism' turn of the mid-1990s) to multi-level and specif-ically engineered experiences in Sweden around the mantra of 'good work' (Huzzard, 2000) and the carefully defined workplace co-operation in Germany focused on 'new production concepts' (Kern and Schumann, 1984). Union history is littered with variants of 'new unionism', and an ironic twist especially in the UK case.[21] It seems in principle, therefore, that choices for innovation, renewal and modernisation can vary considerably over the boxing/dancing continuum, and in ideological substance. This is what we find in the dynamics of our country and case studies.

But on the matter of European level influence, if the Green Paper impera-tives were to be embraced and social partnership became a multi-level and legally sustained modality within a framework of classical employer/trade union agreement, surely these largely domestic agendas of innovation would themselves change. There would be new equations of boxing and dancing, and, in principle, new dominances and subordinations between the many levels. If such an outcome were to be called social partnership, and how else could it conceivably be branded, would it not be seen as a new and somewhat different animal to traditional union corporacy and collusion, to dancing at the cost of boxing? Might there not be a genuinely new animal in the industrial relations zoo?

A final disclaimer is needed about European industrial relations politics: we do not in any sense share the view that there is an essential dynamic vested in the European federal project to create a rational and fully mature industrial relations system for the European social space. Certainly there are strong developmental forces vested in the treaties and the institutional arrangements, not the least of which is the irreversibility mechanism of market and social harmonisation underpinned by the European Court of Justice rulings. This has been reinforced to date by the perceived need to keep trade unions on board for Social Europe. But the politics of being on board has posed a deep dilemma in recent times as neo-liberal politics has fed into the social market system of the European Union. This has been the political direction since the Green Paper period, when arguably the European politics of globalisation first took hold. The trade union political equation – the mix of boxing and dancing – therefore now looks somewhat different to what might be termed the European rescue of the national industrial relations systems, and especially the weaker ones.[22] So maybe a heavier trade union politics – a re-activation of the best of classical boxing – will be needed to deliver a power balance capable of a sustained European social partnership. This may be the shape of the European innovation.

Notes

1. The Green Paper 'Partnership for a New Organisation of Work' (European Commission EU9707134F) was published in April 1997. It was followed by a Commission Communication in November 1998, 'Modernising the Organisation of Work – a Positive Approach to Change' (EU9901146F). In June 2000, the Commission started the process of consulting the social partners about aspects of the 'modernisation of the European social model'.
2. Lisbon Summit Conclusions, 23/24.3, 2000, para. 29. 'Innovation agreements' is a broad policy concept which may not fit the particular institutional structures of industrial relations in individual member states, of course. But the idea had the possibility of carrying more specificity than most of the existing 'social pacts' littered across the member states. They would obviously take the form of framework agreements, and had at least the merit of agreed agendas and procedures, and could be related to specific collective agreement modernisations in various countries. These can be monitored through English language periodicals: see European Industrial Relations Review and Incomes Data Services Employment Europe. A literature started to emerge about the idea after it was incorporated in the Social Programme for 2000–05 (see e.g. European Foundation for the Improvement of Living and Working Conditions, 2002: 3–26).
3. Academic discourses are being played out around a range of themes resting on aspects of the integration question and its relationship to ongoing structural trends (see e.g. Marginson and Sisson, 2002 on the convergence/divergence debate). The development/atrophy dimension is explored by Hyman (2001b). A pessimistic view of political exchange balances (pessimistic for unions and joint regulation) in broad overview is set out by Martin and Ross (1999). Sectoral assessments for four key industries, with a measured optimism about European agendas, can be accessed through Rigby *et al.*, (1999). A sober sense of the globalisation period comes from the extensive comparative work of Bamber and Lansbury (1998).

Hyman (2001a) is noticeably prescriptive, embracing a civil society networking concept as the political pre-requisite of union recovery, with an outward turning and vocal defence of labour market status, especially for the most vulnerable. Closer attention to the legal and institutional politics of European industrial relations, drawing on the ample literature of European labour law, would enrich much of the formal industrial relations literature. The same might be said for industrial and sectoral economics. After all, unions coping with European problems have to embrace all three areas in their routine work.

4. Union optimism had several sources: EWCs had largely come under union influence from the very outset, rather than being a bulwark to NER (Non-union Employee Relations) as many unions feared. Shorter working time policies were spreading, and being seen as being able to make inroads into unemployment, and some union coordination had started about strategies for total working time regulation, notably through the European Metalworkers Union Federation which formulated the 1750 hour benchmark. Unions had started to organise themselves more actively as lobbyists of the European Parliament, as it gained more influence, rather than relying on their special if rather narrow access to the Brussels Commission. And, of course, it looked as though de-regulated labour markets might come under some form of control as the atypical family of directives started to be negotiated under the Maastricht facility. Industrial policy looked possible, even if it had to be 'new' industrial policy not based on subsidies and special protections. The ETUC brought the sectoral unions into its governing structures, counterbalancing the traditionally more corporate and ideologically traditional union centres.

5. Global pessimism, a formula to which the author lays claim when he discovered that the adaptive quiescence of most UK unions to emergent New Labourism was reflected quite widely across European unions, even if it was cloaked sometimes in robust positions. He was appointed National European Coordinator by his union in 1992. Typical of European pessimism was a decoded version of boxing in German union politics to the effect that the real strategy was to make Germany a 'good investment space'. It seemed therefore as if an element of beggar-my-neighbour strategy coexisted with seeking level playing fields.

6. The road block in the existing Social Chapter consists both in the single country veto for measures and actions by the European authorities to be subject to a single country veto about 'representation and collective defence of the interests of workers and employers including co-determination' (Article 137, Clause 3, Point 3, Consolidated Treaties 1997) and the whole of Article 137 being subject to any such action not applying 'to pay, the right of association, the right to strike or impose lockouts' (Clause 6). The strong treaty base for information and consultation of employees and their representatives, in what became subsequently the Social Chapter, enabled the political will to see EWCs come into successful existence through the famous EU Budget Line group, B3 4000. Innovation agreements, hard social partnership agreements and other practical mechanisms of co-operation and dancing near to productive relations would need similar financial support if they were to take off. The grave treaty weakness is compounded by the doctrine of subsidiarity and the fact that most social policy measures come through directives, rather than regulations, and are open to wide national interpretation. The combined effect of subsidiarity and loosely formulated directives is that there is still no common legal base to European collective bargaining institutions and structures. To quote the Social Chapter, EU social law must take into account 'the diverse

forms of national practices, in particular in the field of contractual relations'. Legal debate is starting to focus on the status of collective agreements: a useful discussion can be found in Deinert (2003). On the other hand, the new fundamental human, social and economic rights coming through the year 2000 Nice Treaty (and already having effect through the European Court of Justice prior to gaining explicit treaty status) could change the picture radically. For the first time there will be a right to collective bargaining and industrial action:

> *Article 28   Right of collective bargaining and action*: Workers and employers, or their respective representatives, have, in accordance with Community law and national laws and practices, the right to negotiate and conclude collective agreements at their appropriate levels and, in cases of conflicts of interest, to take collective action to defend their interests, including strike action.

A second layer of interpretation of the new fundamental right is however of considerable importance to the health of collective bargaining: this concerns the question of whether this new provision will bring the right to enjoy collective agreements collectively and fully across a bargaining unit whether in a company or a whole sector. This process of legal extension characterises most mainland European countries. Countries outside this doctrine of erga omnes (Latin for 'therefore everyone') might find the new right limiting not simply the ability of employers to default on agreements, but also their right to seek to vary them, and in effect undermine them, by agreements with individual workers. If this construction proves correct, it would re-dynamise, if not revolutionise industrial relations in the UK and Ireland, and maybe a lot of Eastern Europe, bringing them into line with mainstream Europe. The fact that some countries with doctrines of extension are also seeing the erosion of collective bargaining cover through employer withdrawal and/or workers not joining – or being easily able to join – unions means this new right may help these countries too.

7. One point needs to be made here on top of the well-understood goals and processes of macro-economic dialogue. It is simply that many European countries have had incomes restraint policies in place with the effective support of trade union centres, and some for many years. Belgium has taken this stance to the extreme of having a permanent statutory ceiling on money wage increases. But the common perception has been that national and decentralised union bargaining doctrine has been much freer and effectively seeking redistribution of national wealth. However the common doctrine of inflation plus a share of productivity, espoused vigorously by IG Metall in Germany and many other unions in non-incomes policy countries is itself a moderate wage doctrine. It has resulted in a declining share of national wealth going to wages across Europe, and real wage statis in some cases. It seems therefore that even free collective bargaining unions have in reality made a strategic choice for European wage moderation. The European Metalworkers Federation Collective Bargaining Committee has systematically tracked these processes.

8. The so-called Maastricht facility represented a revolution in social partnership, quite different to traditional corporacy and even classical tripartism, which while rare now in national industrial relations remains the governance system of the ILO (International Labour Organisation). Even at the ILO, tripartism is a bit of mis-nomer since governments have two votes, and unions and employers one each! The Maastricht facility has become Article 139, Clause 1 (Consolidated Treaties 1997): 'Should management and labour so desire, the dialogue between them at Community level may lead to contractual relations, including agreements ... .' The

constitutional power stipulated in Clause 3 restates that agreements in areas subject to a veto remain subject to that veto when they are ratified by the Commission and the Council (of Ministers) i.e. governments, and subject to qualified majority voting where this pertains in the Social Chapter.

9. In comparison to the EWC Directive's processes of consultation, the new Information and Consultation Directive 2002 while still weak does provide for information 'at such a time, in such a fashion and with such content as are appropriate to enable adequate study and prepar(ation) for consultation'. Consultation is also subject to 'appropriate' timing, method and content.

10. Renault announced the closure of its Brussels specialist car factory and termination of 3500 jobs on 27th Feb 1997, without any notice to unions, and most amazingly, not even through its French dominated European Works Council. It created a political crisis for EWCs, and European law. Solidarity action took place notably from Spain and some from France, and a work-in at Vervoorde made militant political headlines. The issue of cross-border employment law was evaded, in the end, by a symbolic fine on the French national CEO of Renault in a Belgian court under pre-existing Belgian consultation law. The case was taken by a white-collar union member. Europe's chosen instrument for information and consultation was dramatically exposed, social partnership widely seen as useless at the point of need. The EWC Directive is currently (2004) under review.

11. The so-called Supiot Report (see Supiot, 1999), named after its chairperson, a French legal anthropologist, took analysis of labour market degradation and changed employment cultures far further than may have been anticipated by the European Commission. A classical text in deep structural trend analysis, moving from social policy goals through employment law to historic sociologies – there is a thematic about feudal vassalage, a kind of workforce branding – it led to other research reports and a Supiot debate. For his subsequent reflections, see also Supiot (2000). The Supiot Report should be read in conjunction with the 2 volumes of European Commission reports 'The Regulation of Working Conditions in the Member States of the European Union', Vol. 1, 1999, and Vol. 2, published earlier in 1998.

12. The Rodriguez Report on Industrial Relations and Change in Europe, a 'wise persons' report, was a formal celebration of social partnership and regulated industrial relations systems as necessary and effective lubricants of change. It legitimised the doctrine of 'quality industrial relations', led to a benchmarking methodology, but was studiously neutral about the extension of the European dimension of existing industrial relations.

13. The Albany case caused a major legal crisis about EU industrial relations, just like the Vervoorde Renault incident. A European Court of Justice (ECJ) ruling in September 1999 came out in favour of the binding nature of sectoral collective agreements, in this case and two others in respect of supplementary pension schemes in the Netherlands textile industry. An inward investing company, Albany, wanted to opt out of established and collectively bargained sectoral arrangements, arguing that they should be subject to EU industrial competition rules. Had Albany been lost, the house of cards would have been exposed perhaps mortally. The house of cards is European sectoral, regional and cross industry (inter-professional) agreements. The legal background was brought together in a very important report on competition law and collective bargaining, sponsored by the EU Commission. See COLCOM: a study of competition rules and their impact on collective labour agreements, June 2000, Employment and Social

Affairs Directorate, in the Industrial Relations and Industrial Change series. Much earlier, the Mollitor Group Report – Deregulation and Employment: Policy Perspective Group (1995) on the relationship between EU competition doctrine and industrial relations established the idea of social benchmarking as a technical means for comparisons of social regimes and employment. This independent/employer and union group decisively rejected overt de-regulation and lowering of social standards to raise employment levels, putting the burden of change on to the platforms of social partnership. This report was undertaken by consultants McKinsey, in association with the OECD.

14. Anger at the Vilvoorde closure was very effectively channelled through the European Metalworkers Federation, riding on the real solidarity of the Vilvoorde work-in, under which the workers' occupation sold completed cars to Renault to finance their work-in. Some real European level solidarity action in Spain and to a lesser extent, in France contributed. This was in parallel with the unions' (Belgian and EMF (European Metalworkers Federation)/FEM) search for legal redress. The author, representing UK autoworkers through the TGWU (Transport and General Workers' Union), co-wrote the EMF/FEM's evidence to the inquiry set up by the European Commission, which was under the chairpersonship of former Volvo CEO Pehr Gyllenhammar who had led the experiments in group working at one of Volvo's factories in Sweden. The EMF/FEM evidence was called 'Cold facts'. Aside from winning a modest Industrial Change Observatory, as an EU-funded project, it established that restructuring had become a routine, rather than a crisis, mechanism of transnational management under intensifying competitive conditions. The crisis and strong European level union intervention benchmarked the issue of effective industrial consultation rights, leading to a modest improvement in the rights specified in the national level Information and Consultation Directive 2002, and to intense debate in the mandatory review of the EWC Directive's rights and powers. The failure of new legal redress caused not simply the crisis about EWCs as hard industrial relations institutions, but also a crisis in French industrial relations law about the respective sites of authority in France's industrial dispute and consultation mechanisms. The contemporary agendas of corporate governance and corporate social responsibility after the Enron, WorldCom and Parmalat crises has opened another pathway for organised worker influence, as have global framework agreements.

15. ETUC Congresses 1999 and 2003. The Danish LO (Landorganisationen) has taken a particular interest in these matters because of its autonomist traditions, submitting an open paper to the ETUC (end 2003).

16. This literature needs to be set in the broader context of global social policy and politics. Unions have a presence in frameworks agreements with about 25 global companies, the minimum standards prospectus drawn from the ILO, their special role in the ILO, and voices through the OECD's Trade Union Advisory Committee (TUAC) and the ICFTU (International Congress of Free Trade Unions). Presently the EU-union position is stronger than this, of course. But if (negative) globalisation intensifies further, the most important issue from global social policy could be the further enfranchisement of NGOs in social policy governance. If the EU were to adopt a dominant mode of 'open policy co-ordination' and benchmarking for any further action in social policy, rather than positive regulatory harmonisation and the improvement of social standards by legislation, NGOs as substantial social policy players could threaten trade unions' exclusive locus as

social partners. The problem comes not in matters which are clearly the concerns of 'management and labour', this being the treaty formula, but when broader social policy is negotiated by these two partners. A dispute about consultation over the parental leave directive, involving the European Small Business Association, was resolved by the European Court of Justice on the basis that organisations wishing to intervene in the labour/management field need to have mandates industrial relations from their members. But it is not far-fetched to see that NGOs through social responsibility agreements with companies might be able to claim agreement making capacity, if not in industrial relations as such. But the closing down of the present grey areas between industrial relations and social policy does not augur well for unions' broader hegemony and political voices.

17. The question of EWCs and their potentials in both dancing and boxing is very important, but so far, little explored in the extensive research literature on them. The view that the political parameters of EWC development were present from the earliest stages of EWC agreements goes against the 'evolutionary trends' approach common in the literature. Scott's (1999) paper to the Bremen University Arbeitkammer conference, December 1999 sets out early negotiating experiences from first hand experience of organising the UK's first EWC union conference. The paper discusses mature union policy towards EWCs, especially in respect of sectoral grouping for industrial policy influence. See Conference Proceedings, Kooperation Journal, Bremen University (German).

18. The doctrine of 'flexible security' is now mainstream, but originates in the UK with union responses to 'New Management Techniques', 'Employee Involvement' and 'Quality Circles', which were the advance guard of the subsequent strategic HRM invasion across the Atlantic. Flexible security needs to be understood as a bargaining doctrine, not an accommodation to neo-liberalism and de-regulation. The author's first written note using the term dates from a 1992 seminar at Ruskin College, Oxford. The doctrine is now undergoing differentiation into 'flexploitation' associated with the labour process school of research, while the EU Commission has a research programme running under its 5th framework research programme supporting work on 'Innoflex', that is, innovatory work and firm performance.

19. See the background in Note 6 above. And further, in belt and braces style, it is limited by the subsequent and notorious Clause 6. This needs to be understood fully: it states, 'the provisions of this Article (137) shall not apply to pay, the right of association, the right to strike or the right to impose lock-outs'. This has normally been deemed to rule out any European competence in traditional collective bargaining areas.

20. The emerging field of corporate governance reform and the pre-existing movements around corporate social responsibility are being linked to traditional trade union interests through global social agreements, though the agreements being pursued by NGOs mainly concern human rights and ecological issues. Corporate governance is being linked through the use of employee funds (pension and savings funds, mainly in the US, but possible in the UK where occupational pension funds are invested in corporate equity) in association with shareholder revolts against excess corporate power vested in chief executives and boards of directors.

21. This is not however the place for a history of 'new unionism'.

22. See Milward (1992). This reflects accurately UK industrial relations politics, and the author suspects, substantial dependencies in other countries too.

References

Bamber, G. J. and Lansbury, R. D. (ed.) (1998) *International and Comparative Employment Relations (3rd edn)* St Leonards, Australia: Allen & Unwin.

Deinert, O. (2003) 'Models of Implementing European Collective Agreements and their Impact on Collective Autonomy', *Industrial Law Journal* December 2003: 317–25.

European Foundation for the Improvement of Living and Working Conditions (2002) 'Industrial Relations Developments in Europe 2002', 3–26.

Frege, C. M. and Kelly, J. (2003) 'Union Revitalization Strategies in Comparative Perspective', *European Journal of Industrial Relations* 9(1): 7–24.

Hoffman, Hoffman, Kirton-Darling and Ramptelshammer, European Foundation 2002.

Huzzard, T. (2000) Laboring to Learn: Union Renewal in Swedish Manufacturing. Umea: Boréa Boeförlag.

Hyman, R. (2001a) *Understanding European Trade Unionism*. London: Sage.

Hyman, R. (2001b) 'The Europeanisation – or Erosion – of Industrial Relations?' *Industrial Relations Journal* 32(4): 280–94.

Kem, H. Schumann, M. (1984) The End of the Division of Labour? Rationalisation in Industrial Production. Munich: Verlag C. H. Beck.

Marginson, P. and Sisson, K. (2002) 'European Integration and Industrial Relations: A Case of Convergence and Divergence?' *Journal of Common Market Studies* 40(4).

Martin, A. and Ross, G. (eds) (1999) *The Brave New World of European Labor*. New York: Berghahn Books.

Milward, A. S. (1992) *The European Rescue of the Nation State*. London: Routledge.

Mollitor Report (Deregulation and Employment, European Commission 1995).

Rigby, M., Smith, R. and Lawlor, T. (eds) (1999) *European Trade Unions: Change and Response*. London: Routledge.

Rodrigues Report, European Commission 2002. *The Future of Industrial Relations*.

Scott, R. (1999). *Personal papers*.

Supiot, A. (1999) *Beyond Employment: Changes in Work and the Future of Labour Law in Europe*. Brussels: European Commission.

Supiot, A. (2000) 'The Dogmatic Foundations of the Market', *Industrial Law Journal* December.

4

Dancing in the Dark: UK Unions and Strategic Choice

Denis Gregory

Introduction: union dance partners seek opportunities

Recent years have seen a vast shadow cast over the traditional UK industrial relations system. While it may be banal to say that 'system' is in crisis, it may be useful from the start to ask whether anything which might be called a 'system' is any longer in sustainable operation in the UK. The extent and nature of change may have been so great that the century-and-a-half long heritage of voluntarism and single channel representation of employers and workers needs to be approached in quite a different way. This chapter argues that the old system has become so atrophied that it is more useful to talk now, in an exploration of strategic choice, innovation and partnership, about the new trends and patterns that are emerging rather than seeking to fit old categories into the UK's hollowed-out model of voluntarism.

The UK case studies attached to the volume offer company level, private sector data that illustrates developments which we have seen emerging from both brown and greenfield industrial relations sites: the question is what sort of trend might they represent? How should they be understood? How does an emergent model relate to conflict and co-operation, to boxing and dancing? The chapter proceeds with a brief historical overview and discussion of the evidence on the partnership experience to date. It then sets out a framework of understanding. There is an attempt to see what might be different about the emergent model, with a preliminary attempt at a theoretical formulation. The chapter concludes with a brief reflection on the severity of change which has impacted on the old UK 'system'.

Strategies and developments in the UK

In the UK for most of the last century trade unions and employers took a strategic choice to rely on a system of voluntary collective agreements to reconcile and mitigate their respective interests. Thus, the pay and conditions of work for many workers were predominantly determined by forms of collective bargaining that were binding in honour but not in law. In this respect the experience of the UK and Ireland, which also favoured the voluntary approach, was markedly different from their European neighbours. The influence of the law in UK industrial relations was, until the 1970s, mostly limited to specifying the framework for individual employment contracts and providing health and safety regulation at the workplace (Lewis and Simpson, 1981).

The apparent wisdom of this strategic choice was measured in the post-1945 growth of trade union membership and in the burgeoning power and influence that union leaders enjoyed in the 1960s and 70s. By the late 1970s, for example, individual membership of trade unions in the UK reached a record 13 million (about 55% of the workforce) and three in every four workers had their pay and conditions determined by voluntary collective agreements (Cully *et al.*, 1999). Moreover, powerful trade union leaders regularly used their industrial power base to exercise major influence over governmental policy irrespective of the political party in power (Taylor, 1991). Frequently this was decisive as when the Trades Union Congress (the central union body in the UK) persuaded the then labour Government to drop its controversial 1969 industrial relations reform *In Place of Strife*. Shortly afterwards, they effectively sidelined the Conservative Government's 1971 Industrial Relations Act (Marsh, 1992). Both events were symptomatic of the unions (and for that matter many employers') determination to keep the law out of industrial relations. The fact that a dispute with the National Union of Mineworkers brought down the same Conservative Government in 1974 showed the ultimate political power the unions wielded. This dispute in particular, though, gave rise to the anti-union strategies to be adopted by successive Conservative governments led by Margaret Thatcher between 1979 and 1990.

Declining union power and influence: after the ball was over ...

The second half of the 1970s is widely regarded as constituting the high point in trade union power and influence in the UK. A labour government between 1974 and 1979 repealed the restrictive legislation of the previous conservative government. In its place came legislation which boosted union power at the workplace (for example the Trade Union and Labour Relations Act 1974, Employment Protection Act 1975 and the Health and Safety at Work Act 1974) and raised the profile of unions at national level through the growth of tripartite bodies such as the Health and Safety Commission and the Manpower Services Commission. These latter bodies, in effect, added new 'dancing' opportunities for the UK social partners. Along with the detailed tripartite economic dialogue at national and sectoral level which flowed from the National Economic Development Office established in the late 1960s, it is fair to say that the second half of the 1970s witnessed more dancing than has ever happened either before or since.

However, persistent low growth in productivity combined with rising public debt, spiralling inflation and the onset of oil-price-induced deflationary policies in Europe precipitated an economic crisis for the labour government beginning in 1976 when IMF pressure forced cutbacks in public expenditure. The strategic response of unions and employers was to enter into a 'Social Contract' with the government. This tripartite deal saw unions agreeing to moderate wage demands whilst employers accepted price controls and the government agreed to preserve public expenditure levels. Despite early successes in achieving pay restraint and some reduction in inflation, the deal soon unravelled as pressures built up from low-paid public sector workers seeking improvements in real pay whilst higher-paid workers sought to maintain or improve their pay differentials. Thus, the social contract fell apart in a succession of public-sector-led pay disputes in the so-called 'winter of discontent' of 1978/79. Such grim experience, often grossly misreported by a UK media determined to blame the unions, led to the defeat of the Labour government and the election in 1979 of the most radical post-war Conservative government headed by Margaret Thatcher.

Between 1980 and 1993 successive Conservative Governments followed a strategy aimed at destroying trade union power. Margaret Thatcher had been a junior minister in the Heath Government brought down by the miners in 1974. She learned from this and from the mistakes of the 1971 Industrial Relations Act. Her legislative strategy was very different and (in her terms) very much more successful than that of her predecessors. Instead of one all encompassing Act she introduced a series of precisely focused pieces of legislation aimed at reducing the power of trade unions (Brown, 1991). The Government's strategy here has been described by one respected commentator as a 'massive and detailed intrusion by the state into the functioning of trade unions as voluntary organisations' (Taylor, 1994). The end result was to leave Britain with probably the most restrictive trade union legislation within the EU (Dickens and Hall, 1995).

At the same time the Thatcher Government abandoned Keynesian national economic management for monetarism and free market economics in the early 1980s. This prompted a restructuring of the UK economy that decimated trade union strongholds in sectors such as mining, engineering and steel production (Levie, 1984). Widescale privatisation further undermined trade union influence throughout the 1980s and early 1990s as privatised enterprises shed tens of thousands of jobs and in many cases adopted tougher strategies for dealing with trade unions.

A predictable outcome of these changes was a sharp rise in unemployment which rose from just over 1 million in 1979 to more than 3 million by the mid-1980s. This 'reserve army' of the unemployed did not fall below the 2 million mark until late in the 1990s, and introduced a culture of fear into many work places. The consequent reduction in workforce militancy and the weakening of the unions' ability to mount credible threats to counter rising managerial power exposed the frailty of a voluntaristic system of industrial relations. In addition, the spectacular industrial defeats suffered by the traditional 'vanguard' of the trade union movement – the Miners in 1984/5, the Print Unions in 1986 and the Mersey Dockers in the early 1990s – served only to reinforce this conclusion.

The political and economic pressures which bore down on trade unions throughout the 1980s and early 1990s also had a lasting impact on trade union membership levels. From a high point of 13.2 million members in 1979 membership virtually halved to around 7 million by 2000. Against this backdrop it is hardly surprising that the coverage of collective bargaining, traditionally the bedrock of union power and influence in the UK, has declined to the point where only around a third of all employees have their pay and conditions determined by collective agreements.

The EU's influence: a new dance hall beckons ...

Whilst the UK trade union movement was suffering the most concerted political attacks it had faced since the 1920s, political forces elsewhere in Europe were, from the mid-1980s, developing a wholly different view of the future shape of progressive industrial relations. The so-called 'social dimension' of the drive towards greater integration of the EU, particularly when codified into the Social Charter, provided UK trade unions with some potential relief from the relentless legislative battering they had received from successive UK governments and the potential restoration of some of the rights they had lost in the process. In 1988, at the TUC Conference Jacques Delors, the then President of the Commission set out the Commission's vision of 'Social Europe' so persuasively that much of the scepticism which trade unionists felt about the European Union (EU) thereafter withered away.

Although it took nearly ten more years for a UK Government to sign up to the Social Charter, the TUC's shift in 1988 was influential in helping to introduce and legitimate the concept of unions as 'social partners' and to infiltrate the language of partnership and social dialogue into mainstream industrial relations. The ground was, in effect, laid for a new, European dance floor. Initially, trade unions and employers were constrained from joining the European dance floor as both the Thatcher and Major administrations refused to sign up to the Social Charter. Interestingly, it was a trickle of powerful UK companies who broke ranks with the government in the early 1990s and enabled their workforces to form or join European Works Councils.

Constrained choices and the emergence of new dances in the UK

Throughout the 1980s and well into the 1990s, UK trade unions were very much on the defensive. Their strategic choices were heavily constrained by falling membership, restrictive legislation and the rise of Human Resource Management strategies which either attacked directly or nibbled away at the institutions and processes of collective bargaining. There were some positive developments during this time, for example, Rover's 'New Deal' and Welsh Water's Partnership showed dialogue-based approaches with extensive union involvement to be more effective at handling complex organisational change than had hitherto been the case with conventional methods of consultation and collective bargaining. These were the exception rather than the rule, however. By the time New Labour was elected in 1997, trade union membership had fallen to very low levels in the private sector, was barely touching young workers and was making very little impression in the growing service sector. The new heartlands of the trade union movement were to be found in the public service sector. Even here though, privatisation was undermining trade union strength.

Unlike previous Labour governments, the Blair administration had made no significant promises to the trade union movement prior to winning the general election in 1997. Indeed, in the run up to that election they had steadfastly refused to commit to the repeal of all the anti-union legislation that the Thatcher and Major governments had put in place. Instead, the unions were offered 'fairness not favours' and were promised the government would sign up to the Social Charter and introduce a national minimum wage and a new Employment Relations Act. Insofar as 'restoring trade union influence at national level' it soon became clear that the Blair administration's pursuit of 'social justice' left no room for a return to tripartite forums. Instead, as part of their search for a 'third way' (Giddens, 1998), the government embraced and elaborated the notion of 'partnership' at the workplace. Tony Blair, for example, writing in the 1998 White Paper 'Fairness at Work' that preceded the Employment Relations Act said: '... modern and successful companies draw their success from the existence and development of partnership at work.' The government backed this enthusiasm with a £5 million fund to help support the development and spread of partnership at the workplace.

From a trade union perspective, the first few years of New Labour, whilst a welcome relief in important respects were, nevertheless, something of a disappointment. The Chancellor's adherence to the previous Conservative Government's spending plans was aimed explicitly at appeasing the city of London financial community. For public sector trade unions it meant the continuation of downward pressure on pay and conditions. The level of the national minimum wage (£3.20 per hour) was pitched to head off complaints by the Confederation of British Industry (CBI) and the Institute of Directors (IOD). The widely articulated demands of the unions for at least £5 per hour were simply ignored. The Employment Relations Act 1999 did, at least, introduce some important rights for trade union recognition that have subsequently helped unions to arrest the long-term decline in membership. It did nothing, however, to redress the asymmetry of information access that had bedevilled trade unions and impaired collective bargaining ever since the Donovan Report first highlighted the problem in 1968.

In addition to these general elements, unions in the private sector have received little or no support from the government when restructuring and job losses have been announced. Equally, unions in the public sector have been confronted with the government's continued support for privatisation and their relentless drive to decentralise the sector's industrial relations procedures and collective bargaining structures. Moreover, the government has shown itself more than willing to face down the unions in public sector disputes. Both postal workers and fire fighters have, in recent years, found the government to be unflinching in their opposition.

Whilst the development of collective bargaining within an industrial relations framework built on voluntarism rather than legal rights had served trade unions well for most of the 20th Century, the impact of employers and government strategies in the 1980s had brutally revealed the weaknesses of such a system. Their changed circumstances forced unions to look more carefully at their strategic options and modus operandi. Predominant here has been the debate over the balance unions should strike between 'servicing' and 'organising' their membership. Latterly, the TUC, with the formation of its Organising Academy, has shifted the emphasis towards recruitment and organisation. Individual unions, too, have to varying degrees adopted the organising model. In the meantime, a more pragmatic approach to collective organisation at the workplace has been emerging. Again, the TUC's leaders have provided strong support for the establishment and development of partnership approaches at workplace level. John Monks, then General Secretary of the TUC stated unequivocally in 1999 that partnership was ' … central to the TUC's approach to industrial relations.'

The launch of the TUC's Partnership Institute in 2001 was further testimony to their commitment and fundamental belief in partnership as a 'better way' to structure workplace industrial relations. The TUC have been careful to distinguish partnership from concession bargaining and have stressed that it is neither a substitute for collective bargaining nor a design for compliant trade unionism. A summary of boxing and dancing in the UK is set out in Table 4.1.

Defining the dance

"It is important that Partnership does not become another management fad, consigned to the industrial relations dustbin after a less than illustrious history … Partnership has to be more than warm words. It is a concept in need of a tighter definition." ('Partners for Progress' TUC 1999)

"We at British Aerospace are particularly proud of the way our partnership with trade unions has developed. We live in an increasingly competitive

Table 4.1 Boxing and dancing in the UK: a classification

Level	Boxing	Dancing	Prospects
Global/ International	Few boxing rings e.g. European Works Councili's treatment of plant closures.	EWCs learning to dance on information disclosure and consultation.	Most unions seeking opportunities for greater influence internationally. Prospects of
National	Government and employer resistance to EU Directive on Consultation. Little national level bargaining arrangements apart from the public sector.	Discourse on 'Fairness at Work'. Employment Relations Act has granted tightly regulated recognition rights. Some government support for partnership through the Partnership Fund. TUC Partnership Institute. Some partnership initiatives in the public sector (e.g. the Health Service), otherwise at company level.	Government change of heart on EU Consultation Directive? Prospects for partnership otherwise strained by restructuring moves. Union elections may be Indicative of return to the boxing ring.
Sectoral/ Regional/	Centralised public sector collective bargaining (CB) diminishing private sector CB	Civil Service Cabinet Office Partnership Agreement. Decentralisation of government agencies.	Increased dancing prospects?
Local/ Workplace	Traditional company level CB. Boxing dominant but CB coverage in decline.	Some progression towards partnership agreements at company level.	Mixed picture: Increased dancing at some workplaces, but elsewhere partnership fragile.

world and I am convinced that this partnership creates competitive advantage." (Sir Richard Evans Chairman British Aerospace plc. 1999)

"Partnership at work may be an idea whose time has come. But to many it is a vague idea, perhaps linked to some laudable principles but difficult to put into practice." (David Guest and Riccardo Peccei, 1998).

These quotes in many ways reflect the range of contemporary attitudes to the notion of 'partnership' in the UK. The TUC, although supportive are nevertheless anxious that partnership should have some continuity. Employers see partnership as a prop to their business imperatives whilst the academics sound notes of caution. Knell, for example, has pointed out, in the UK, at least, partnership '... is not a term that carries with it any precise theoretical or practical connotation' (Knell, 1999).

John Monks the (then) General Secretary of the TUC has described partnership as 'unions and employers working together to solve shared problems, to boost productivity, improve organisational performance and improve the quality of working life' (TUC, 1999). The TUC suggested that partnership could be effective in three overlapping areas. First of all, developing the workplace by the greater involvement of employees in the creation of 'high performance workplaces' with an emphasis on shared decision-making and the promotion of high-trust relationships between employees and management. In the second place, it could assist the enterprise's learning capacity and enhance both the vocational training and educational development of employees. Finally, at the macro-economic level, partnership could increase the input from unions to the national debate on improving the UK's competitiveness and can serve as a vehicle for the dissemination of 'best practices' at the workplace. The TUC's six partnership principles are listed in Exhibit 4.1. In effect these set out what might be described as the defining characteristics of partnership at enterprise and workplace level.

Implicit in this attempt to define 'partnership', are the notions of joint problem-solving and achieving a balance of employer and employee interests. This latter point has been further elaborated by defining the key employer and employee interests a partnership approach should address and integrate.

In Exhibit 4.2 we list four business needs that can reasonably be said to be critical success factors for an enterprise. Similarly, we list four social needs that characterise good employment practices from an employee's point of view. The challenge for a partnership approach lies in the need to produce

---

Exhibit 4.1   The TUC's Partnership Principles:

- Commitment to the success of the enterprise: effective partnerships are ones where unions and employers have a shared understanding of the organisation's business strategy and a joint commitment to its success.
- Recognising legitimate interests: genuine partnerships recognise that unions and employers will have differences in interests and views. There should be arrangements to resolve those differences in an atmosphere of trust.
- Commitment to employment security: many employers embrace partnership as a way of increasing flexibility in the workplace. Good partnerships complement flexibility with action to increase employment security in the workplace.
- Focus on the quality of working life: partnership should broaden the scope of employment and organisational issues tackled by unions and employers. It should lead to improvements in terms and conditions and more opportunities for employees to participate in decisions about their work.
- Transparency: with successful partnerships, managers share information with unions about the business at an early stage and conduct meaningful consultations with unions and staff.
- Win-win: the hallmark of an effective partnership is whether it delivers concrete improvements to business performance, terms and conditions and employee involvement. Partnership is about mutual gains for unions and employers. (TUC, 1999)

Exhibit 4.2 Partnership fundamentals: a basic framework for integrating and balancing employer and employee interests

Employer (business) needs:

- Maximising value adding activity, reducing non-value adding activity;
- Flexible utilisation of human and capital resources;
- Faster and more effective decision-making;
- Economic and social productivity growth.

Employee (social) needs:

- Employment security;
- Progressive and reliable remuneration;
- Vocational and intellectual development;
- Effective representation and participation.

---

outcomes that provide gains to satisfy both business and social needs. Whether a partnership exists or not can be measured both by the processes that are used to generate the gains and in the balance of the gains achieved. In other words, a partnership that in practice is simply a vehicle for management to impose on a workforce pre-planned decisions that confer only business benefits, cannot be said to be a genuine partnership.

Partnership in practice

In certain academic quarters, partnership in the UK was pronounced a dead letter before it had left the starting blocks (e.g. Kelly, 1996). Others sounded a more sanguine note (Ackers and Payne, 1998). Such accounts, however, tell us little about the prospects and pitfalls of partnership in practice. Empirical studies, however, have tended to present a somewhat mixed picture (Oxenbridge and Brown, 2002). The quantitative work of Guest and Peccei (2001) sought to assess partnership in terms of its impact on key stakeholders, namely, unions, employees and management. In terms of stakeholder outcomes, their analysis reveals that mutual gains were achievable, but with the balance of advantage skewed towards management. Notably, they also argue that three distinct perspectives or approaches to partnership are discernible, namely unitarist approaches that subsume partnership under Human Resource Management (HRM), pluralist approaches that recognises distinct stakeholder interests and hybrid approaches that combine the first two. But, as do many others, Guest and Peccei see the possibility that partnership can simply be 'a way of re-focusing old debates' (ibid: 211).

More recently, Kelly (2004) has sought to investigate the outcomes of partnership agreements using matched comparisons. His conclusion is that where markets are contracting and employment is declining, jobs are shed more quickly in partnership firms than non-partnership firms. On the other hand, jobs have been created more rapidly in partnership firms than non-partnership firms in expanding product markets. There is no evidence that partnership has affected union density or wage settlements, and he is sceptical about whether partnership can lead to union revitalisation in the UK context. The alternative possibility, namely that certain renewal choices might require co-operation, is apparently not considered.

A particular tension of partnership has been the perceived threat that the dance may compromise union independence. The dilemma is put succinctly by Marks *et al.*, (1998: 220) who, reporting from case study research of the Scottish spirits industry, argued that:

> ... [the] paradox of the mutual gains workplace is that it extends the scope of union influence inside corporate decision-making processes as it renders the authority of the shop-floor union delegate more precarious.

In other words, local stewards are finding it increasingly difficult to deal with immediate workplace issues – and the workload for the local level trade union activist has notably increased.

Haynes and Allen (2001), for example, drawing on case study data from the insurance and food retailing sectors argue that partnership is not only compatible with, but dependent on, stronger workplace organisation. A similar view is put forward by Findlay *et al.* (2002) who argue from quantitative data on employee attitudes that the risks of incorporation need not be qualitatively different from those arising from traditional bargaining relationships. Accordingly:

> ... unions should explore partnerships arrangements providing that distinctive interests are acknowledged, potential benefits exist in terms of involvement in governance at all levels, and an independent union agenda is retained and maintained (ibid: 19).

Munro's research on partnership in a case study of the UK National Health Service, echoes such views. Although revealing concerns about partnership dilemmas in terms of conflicts of attitudes, she in fact suggests that this problem is not necessarily a problem of partnership per se but rather is likely to occur in the absence of adequate workplace union organisation or capacities (Munro, 2002). If such a view is generalisable, it suggests that partnership arrangements can be drawn up such that they require an expansion of union bases and capacities, at various levels, rather than union marginalisation. Whether this is achievable in practice, of course, is highly dependent on attitudes and understandings on the management side.

In the stories of both endurance and breakdown in the literature to date, recurrent themes in much of the work appear to be the roles of the prevailing economic environment, the regulatory infrastructure and the ideological stances of the key actors as influences on the evolution and outcomes of partnership (Martinez Lucio and Stuart, 2004). These can be either facilitating or hindering factors. In the UK, there are grounds for believing that partnerships can be very fragile not least because of the absence of a supportive regulatory infrastructure and in many cases deep-seated attitudinal and ideological opposition towards co-operation. This is not just the case on the trade union side (Whitston *et al.*, 1999) – it can be even more significant in the case of management (Stuart and Martinez Lucio, 2002).

The fragility of partnerships in the face of external pressures is well-illustrated by the Vertex case set out in Appendix A7 and summarised in Exhibit 4.3. In this case the vulnerability of call centre employment to outsourcing has put the partnership under some strain.

Tensions, too, can seriously question the existence of partnerships from within. The UK is generally considered to have an adversarial industrial relations culture with low levels of trust between unions and management. The case of Anglian Water as set out below in Exhibit 4.4 shows the difficulties of trust building even in a sector such as utilities that historically has not been particularly dispute-prone or characterised by union militancy. A more general expression of the fragility of the dance and a sense of failure to deliver for union members has been that of a succession of victories in union elections by candidates openly critical of partnership in 2002 and 2003.

Exhibit 4.3   Partnership under strain at Vertex

In the late 1990s, Vertex, a UK private sector call centre operation, granted formal recognition to UNISON. The union had also been involved in assisting the company in framing and making bids for contracts for work outsourced from the public sector. This latter activity saw the conclusion of an agreement covering Local Authority Business, and the parties began to establish a partnership approach. In order to avoid a rapid return to the adversarialism of the past, though, collective bargaining at the Vertex Bolton call centre was embedded within a partnership framework. This was designed to promote social dialogue and joint problem-solving as an alternative to the more adversarial approaches.

Two notable challenges have tested the partnership in recent years. The first has been the management desire to produce a harmonised pay and conditions structure to cover all the various workplaces that Vertex had acquired. Secondly, Vertex acquired call centre capacity in India where labour costs are a fraction of those in the UK. The idea of 'formation dancing' with a harmonised pay structure has been partially achieved, although the difficulties experienced in trying to finalise pay negotiations in 2003 demonstrated that at that time this was one dance too far as unions balloted their members and some contemplated industrial action. At the time of writing, the dialogue continues on how best to deal with the 'global' dance represented by India.

Exhibit 4.4   Partnership at Anglian Water – tensions from within

A paper written by the trade union side chair of the Anglian Water Company Council in 1996 acknowledged that: 'it is no longer sufficient simply to react to whatever the employers propose'. On the contrary, he argued: 'The Trade Union Side need to seize the initiative and set the agenda.' Accordingly, the unions took to the dance floor in a dialogue-based 'partnership' approach to manage change at the company. But the unions' evaluation of the first year of the Council showed the consultation process (the dance) was in danger of becoming a means for the company to force through a range of difficult restructuring policies. The unions found themselves dancing almost exclusively to the company's tune. Despite changes in the structure and functions of the Company Council and the amicable settling of pay negotiations, the partnership was, by common consent, stretched to the limits between 1997 and 2003 due to residues of low trust and the increasingly complex strategies of the Anglian Board.

Some participants, on both sides, were uncomfortable with the dialogue approach. Sharing information and reaching consensus-based decisions was a time consuming exercise, which challenged management prerogative and potentially compromised trade union independence. Peer group pressure amongst senior management and training in joint-problem-solving were launched as a strategic response to these problems. Both elements worked to an extent. However, the trust that was built up through them was fragile. Yet the unions preserved collective bargaining, maintained pay levels and achieved an impressive extension of the regulations on the transfer of undertakings. The partnership also led to better inter-union relationships. In a difficult period both sides made the strategic choice to continue the dance.

Most notably, perhaps, was the defeat of Ken Jackson in his attempt at re-election as General Secretary of Amicus, the engineering and electrical union that had strongly and explicitly advocated social partnership.

Voluntarism by default: a bargained partnership model?

In our view the case studies and other evidence sense a distinct model emerging. It may not be robust, or especially new, and to some extent it is negatively characterised. The model might be termed *bargained partnership* in a framework of *voluntarism by default*. Its putative strength may be its bargained nature, whilst its obvious weakness would be that it has no supporting framework, either from a second channel of employee representation along European lines (see below) or from stronger framework bargaining structures (sectoral minimum standards agreements). From a union viewpoint, it might be termed *dancing in the free market*, a formula which expresses a strategic choice by some unions and some union memberships first, to go beyond traditional boxing (which may in many respects be very difficult because of repressive labour law) and secondly, to express a mature recognition that mutual gains stances in employer/employee relations may be a balanced reflection of real (negative) labour market forces but also of real (positive) market opportunities.

The *voluntarism by default* formula relates directly to the fact that there is no government support for partnership or collective bargaining of any kind – other than a small partnership fund and a more recent union modernisation fund. In effect, partnership enjoys or suffers the same fate as any form of collectively organised industrial relations. It is not favoured, nor, as it is claimed in the famous New Labour mantra, is it going to develop so as to allow the unions to gain economic or political power such that they are ever again 'feared'. The UK partnership model has emerged in a cold climate where traditional collective bargaining, is severely undermined even where it survives.

Innovatory by comparison?

It has become clear that the emergent model needs to be viewed as something more than a continuum of traditional industrial relations partnership: the latter has a long UK history. This has primarily been a matter of peak level exchange ideology (tripartite industrial policy, tripartite dispute resolution) with little practical transformation to micro levels, except in the sense of wage restraint. When partnership was a bargained product at macro level, it produced dramatic proposals for industrial democracy (the Bullock Report 1978) and fair wage extension (the 1976 fair wages Schedule) and strongly meant union recognition rights. But these have gone, unlikely to return in the foreseeable future.

Is the model anything more than UK style company bargaining? Our company level social partnership cases contain classical aspects, and in some respects, they build on the long experience of productivity bargaining developed in the 1970s under the joint pressures of wage restraint policies imposed by government and sometimes agreed by unions, and a decentralisation into multi-level bargaining positively chosen by progressive unions concerned about the low wage straitjacket of traditional sectoral bargaining.

The bargained partnership model is separable from, but not incompatible with, the immense pressure to go over to a dual system (works councils and sectoral bargaining by unions) on mainland European lines, something already embraced by UK unions in their successes with EWCs, but being currently frustrated in the minimalism of the government and employers' approach to the Information and Consultation of Employees Directive.

Bargained partnership within voluntarism by default is also separable from the recent restoration of boxing and contestation in public sector areas (railways, fire service, post offices, civil service) subject to forced 'modernisation' by government. Whilst unions are willing in these sectors to be part of the solution, not part of the problem, the terms of governmental modernisation block off partnership options. Modernisation means lowering labour costs and standards to the level demanded by unregulated market forces. Since the modernisation process is not natural to what was the public sector, and since the redefinition of the sector has been a political matter, partnership terms would themselves need to be politically bartered and agreed. That is a different context to natural private sector market exposure and adjustment, whether in manufacturing or key services like banking and finance.

What of life after the rejection of concession bargaining by new union leaderships in some of the big mainstream general unions? Whilst there was often a partnership element – frosty and fragile, in many cases, one suspects – in concession bargaining, it is fair to assume that partnership would be seen, in the return to boxing, as a topping-out of a new balance of bargaining power, rather than as a new model which integrates boxing and dancing through a partnership process. In the sense that concession bargaining paid for wage advances through labour productivity, the new model might offer some attractions.

The European questions are twofold. First, can such a model be sustained by a positive embrace by government and employers of a dual system of representation along the lines of the European mainland's works councils and sectoral bargaining processes? Prospects here are bleak, regardless of the balance of opportunities and problems presented by such a transformation. UK government minimalism holds sway, at the behest of employers, on any import from the European social model. Second, in terms of legitimation for social partnership from the European social model, and Europe's own theoretically more consensual model of modernisation (see Chapter 3) the constitutionalism of the TUC would certainly tend to support such a model as an alternative to a return to more robust ways. But the TUC has little established authority, or competence, in matters of bargaining strategies. It is a spectator, not a boxer or indeed, where it might matter most, a dancer either.

The model is also separable but maybe not incompatible with a renewal of classical voluntarist trades unionism demanding a restoration of full legal freedoms and support for collective bargaining. This 'real politik' emerges from the concession bargaining sectors, and has a natural preference for strong single channel representation based on shop-floor activism. The trend contains within it, currently, two streams comprising some unions seeking a break with an exclusive political exchange relationship with a hostile New Labour government, and a group of restorationist union leaders committed to securing a classical single channel settlement with full legal empowerment through the policy mechanisms of the Labour Party. For the latter group, bargained partnership will be seen as a high-trust option based on a much fairer balance of power between unions and employers, but an option to be pursued by a mix of boxing and dancing, not a move to a dancing dominance.

Two general points remain to be made. First, notwithstanding the many qualifications set out above, the new model seems to have slipped through many traditional hurdles, rather than to have slipped at them. There is a traceable grain of optimism about the formula, as it takes its place alongside many other pathways to union recovery. Second, gainsaying the common assumption that diversification processes are open-ended and relatively freely developing, it needs to be understood that in the UK, as no doubt elsewhere, the politics of trade union models is highly contested. It may be however that since bargained partnership is in a framework of voluntarism by default, the same framework may afflict rival models too.

Conclusion: blizzard conditions for boxing and cold dance floors

Any path of union revitalisation will not be easy. The change in overall labour market conditions, in the basic regulatory and supportive structures of industrial relations and indeed core doctrines of UK political economy has been severe. The UK economy is much less of a mixed economy than conventionally assumed. Government doctrine is to modernise the whole economy by allowing market forces as much freedom as possible in the private sector, and in the old public sector by introducing market forces as a 'modernisation' dynamic.

The UK workforce toils long hours, is flexible, poorly supported by low investment, and contains about one-third of ordinary manual and white collar workers on atypical employment contracts, that is, part time work, fixed term contracts, agency supply work, forced self-employment and, indeed, illegal working without even basic contracts or social insurance. The nominally low but practically substantial level of unemployment – there is extensive 'churning' in and out of low grade, marginal jobs – is enforced by dozens of workfare schemes through which rights to very low levels of social security support are increasingly conditional on return to work under terms which are regulated by the sole mechanism of a national minimum wage which is set at a very low level.

Collective bargaining cover is low in the private sector, very low in new service sectors though there are exceptions in banking and finance and call centres. An overall skill shortage and low literacy and numeracy levels in the unskilled workforce has enabled many workers to bargain their own terms and conditions of work, and employment contract law allows collective bargaining cover to co-exist with personal contracts, although a major victory has been achieved recently for union members through the Wilson and Palmer judgement of the European Court of Justice outlawing discrimination against individual union members by their exclusion from terms offered to non-union employees. In the short term, these can be better in some respects.

Union freedom is very limited: union recognition is possible with ballot victories above 40% of workforce, but the bargaining unit has no extension.

Ballots on industrial action legalise action only on the direct terms and conditions of employees of the enterprise: secondary action is unlawful. Action in the pubic sector against, for example, privatisation, is unlawful and has resulted in unions being forced to disbar militant members. In this setting, almost any strategic choice model, any union innovation model and any positive versions of social partnership are going to have be tough to grow: the virtues of historic voluntarism now look like a weak default.

Yet the concept and practice of partnership remains a highly contentious issue in trade union circles. On the one hand, some critics who see partnership as a 'sell out' with unions at best compromising their independence and at worst ending up as management stooges. For them collective bargaining remains the only way for the workers' voice to be articulated and given effect. On the other hand, some see partnership with its access to information, early involvement in decision-making and much wider frames of reference as the 'better way'. The need to transpose the EU directive on participation and consultation into UK law by March 2005 might just tip the balance in favour of the partnership approach.

References

Ackers, P. and Payne, J. (1998) 'British Trade Unions and Social Partnership: Rhetoric, Reality and Strategy', *International Journal of Human Resource Management* 9(3): 529–50.

Brown, W. (1991) 'The Changed Political Role of Unions under a Hostile Government' in Pimlott, B. and Cook, C. (eds) *Trade Unions in British Politics*. London: Longman.

Cully, M., Woodland, S., O'Reilly, A. and Dix, G. (1999) *Britain at Work*. London: Routledge.

Dickens, L. and Hall, M. (1995) 'The State: Labour Law and Industrial Relations' in Edwards, P. (ed.) *Industrial Relations: Theory and Practice in Britain*. Oxford: Blackwell.

Findlay, T., McKinlay, A., Marks, A. and Thompson, P. (2002) 'Mutual Gains or Mutual Strain? Exploring Employee Attitudes to Partnership', Paper presented at the 20th International Labour Process Conference, University of Strathclyde, Glasgow, 2–4 April.

Giddens, A. (1998) The Third Way: The Renewal of Social Democracy. Cambridge: Polity.

Guest, D. and Peccei, R. (1998) *The Partnership Company*. London: Involvement and Participation Association.

Guest, D. and Peccei, R. (2001) 'Partnership at Work: Mutuality and the Balance of Advantage', *British Journal of Industrial Relations* 39(2): 207–36.

Haynes, P. and Allen, M. (2001) 'Partnership as Union Strategy: A Preliminary Evaluation', *Employee Relations* 23(2): 164–93.

Kelly, J. (1996) 'Union Militancy and Social Partnership' in Ackers, P., Smith, C. and Smith, P. (eds) *The New Workplace and Trade Unionism: Critical Perspectives on Work and Organization*. London: Routledge.

Kelly, J. (2004) 'Social Partnership Agreements in Britain: Labor Co-operation and Compliance', *Industrial Relations* 43(1): 267–92.

Knell, J. (1999) *Partnership at Work*. Employment Relations Research Series no. 7. London: Department of Trade and Industry, HMSO.

Levie, H., Lorenzen, N. and Gregory, D. (1984) *Fighting Closures*. Nottingham: Spokesman.

Lewis, R. and Simpson, B. (1981) *Striking a Balance*. Oxford: Martin Robertson.

Marks, A., Findlay, P., Hine, J., McKinlay, A. and Thompson, P. (1998) 'The Politics of Partnership? Innovation in Employment Relations in the Scottish Spirits Industry', *British Journal of Industrial Relations* 36(2): 209–26.

Marsh, D. (1992) *The New Politics of British Trade Unions*. London: Macmillan.

Martinez-Lucio, M. and Stuart, M. (2004) 'Swimming Against the Tide: Social Partnership, Mutual Gains and the Revival of "Tired" HRM', *International Journal of Human Resource Management* 15(2): 410–24.

Munro, A. (2002) '"Working Together – Involving Staff": Partnership Working in the NHS', *Employee Relations* 24(3): 277–89.

Oxenbridge, S. and Brown, W. (2002) 'The Two Faces of Partnership? An Assessment of Partnership and Co-operative Employer/Trade Union Relationships', *Employee Relations* 24(3): 262–76.

Stuart, M. and Martinez-Lucio, M. (2002) 'Social Partnership and the Mutual Gains Organization: Remaking Involvement and Trust at the British Workplace', *Economic and Industrial Democracy* 23(2): 177–200.

Taylor, R. (1991) 'The Trade Union "Problem" in the Age of Consensus' in Pimlott, B. and Cook, C. (eds) *Trade Unions in British Politics*. London: Longman.

Taylor, R. (1994) *The Future of Trade Unions*. London: Andre Deutsch.

TUC (1999) Partners for Progress. TVC Report.

Whitston, C., Roe, A. and Jeffreys, S. (1999) 'Job Regulation and the Managerial Challenge to Trade Unions: Evidence from Two Union Membership Surveys', *Industrial Relations Journal* 30(5): 482–98.

5
Dancing Queen? Partnership, Co-determination and Strategic Unionism in Sweden

Tony Huzzard and Tommy Nilsson

Introduction: continuity and change

In Scandinavia, something akin to a spirit of co-operation has enabled forms of partnership to prevail for many decades. Such a spirit was a feature of the Saltsjöbaden Agreement of 1938 between the labour market parties that laid the foundations of the renowned 'Swedish Model'. Some four decades later, co-operative industrial relations found further expression in the passing of laws on co-determination. Organised labour has thus enjoyed relatively fertile territory for the defence of union recognition by employers, collective bargaining, high membership densities and relatively high levels of influence (Kjellberg, 1992; Huzzard, 2000a). Indeed, when drafting the 1997 Green Paper, its main author, a former Finance Minister from Sweden, drew considerably on Swedish experiences of partnership from programmes of job redesign (Gustavsen *et al.*, 1996) in his analysis of the challenges facing Europe on work organisation.

It would be a mistake, however, to conclude that industrial relations are marked by a historically stable state based on well-established models of social partnership. Changed conditions at the workplace in Sweden in the 1990s were marked by what one researcher has termed a managerial 'ideology of rationalisation' (Bäckström, 1999). In some sectors this has called into question the basis for high trust and mutual interest on which partnership has been based. Indeed, there is case study evidence suggesting that some arrangements are built on precarious foundations (Huzzard, 2000b). Moreover, union agendas have been changing since the 1980s and the employers have actively sought to decentralise industrial relations by withdrawing from corporatist arrangements and national level collective bargaining (Thörnqvist, 1999). An increased human resource focus on learning and knowledge has also altered the backdrop against which industrial relations processes are played out.

We accordingly argue in this chapter that Swedish unions have been actively engaged on dance floors for some considerable time and that partnership is therefore nothing new. On the other hand, there are changes both in the forms that partnership is taking and in its relationship with collective bargaining. One commentator has gone so far as to claim that new arrangements at the central level have ended a phase of relative conflict and instability in Swedish industrial relations that prevailed from the late 1960s until 1997 (Elvander, 2002). Partnership is overwhelmingly the preferred basis on which unions are pursuing their agendas on work organisation at the local level and this often takes place in development projects outside the formal procedures arising from co-determination. Both blue- and white-collar unions are also dancing with the employers at the central (sectoral) level in the form of a series of process agreements signed in the 1990s which sought to introduce more consensus into wage negotiations. Here both boxing and dancing are intimately linked as part of a dynamic process that also includes wider issues that might affect sector performance such as training, research and development and energy policy.

We proceed with a brief historical account of Swedish industrial relations since the Saltsjöbaden Agreement and continue by describing contemporary boxing and dancing activities at both central and workplace levels with reference to case study data.[1] The chapter then discusses the implications of the current trend in boxing and dancing dualism for trade union renewal. We conclude that the process agreements at the central level can be construed as a paradigm shift in industrial relations, albeit one which has evolved separately from the European Social Dialogue. On the other hand, dance floors at the workplace, in particular on development issues on the blue-collar side, are hardly new. They date back to the mid-1980s at least, but now face considerable challenges from the rationalisation and restructuring which increasingly appear to characterise both public and private sectors (Huzzard, 2003).

Contextual overview

Saltsjöbaden and after

It could be argued that a spirit of consensus between unions and management was established by the Saltsjöbaden agreement of 1938. Following a long period of conflict and turmoil, both sides accepted the non-desirability of direct government intervention in collective bargaining, and second, the LO (Landsorganisationen) accepted Clause 23 of the SAF (Swedish Employers Confederation)'s[2] statutes that management had 'a right to manage'. This 'historic compromise' thus came to be characterised by centralisation, co-ordination and self-regulation. It was agreed that governments would bring about economic growth so as to guarantee full employment, and that organised labour would not challenge the capitalist nature of production.

Traditionally, therefore, the representatives of capital and labour in Sweden have shared a consensus that they themselves are best able to regulate their mutual activities without recourse to legislation. However, although the joint regulation of the labour market was to a great extent characterised by traditional collective bargaining (boxing) in the decades after Saltsjöbaden, the spirit of consensus also generated a series of joint initiatives in the development of work organisation. Moreover, as early as 1951 the LO warmly embraced the logic of new technologies and rationalisation and accepted the argument of the employers that flexibility was required to facilitate structural adjustment (Meidner, 1986). Such rationalisation had to be accepted by the labour movement, albeit alongside active labour market measures undertaken by the state to maintain full employment (Huzzard, 2000a). The spirit of partnership was also evident in the support of the unions for legislation on co-determination (Swedish Co-determination Act, MBL) in 1977 and its subsequent implementation at the workplace. MBL, however, was initially opposed by the employers who saw it as one of a series of union-led legislative measures that undermined the consensus established at Saltsjöbaden. Arguably, such a spirit had lapsed by the end of the 1960s (Elvander, 2002).

The 1980s

In the 1980s, centralised bargaining came under increasing pressure and eventually broke down. A change of leadership in SAF and bitter experiences of conflict in the 1980 wage negotiations confirmed a collapse in the hitherto robust consensus. Moreover, an ideological shift to neo-liberalism in the SAF leadership was also detected. The demands of international competitiveness required restructuring, higher productivity and payments systems whereby rewards were determined by prevailing market conditions. In the sphere of work organisation, the decade also saw employer-led innovations drawing on ideas infused from Japan and the United States in areas such as total quality management, continuous improvement and organisational culture. Further evidence of SAF's unilateralism was evident in the early 1990s through its attempt to promote work reorganisation through the 'co-worker' concept at the company level whereby the traditional dividing line between blue- and white-collar work would be abolished (Mahon, 1994). This, however, was met with considerable resistance from the unions, at least at the company level.

By the mid-1980s, pressure for innovation was also evident in union quarters. In 1983–84 the Metalworkers Union National Executive set up a programme committee 'on the value and terms of industrial work'. The work of this committee was sub-divided into a number of separate working groups each dealing with different topics: wage and distribution policy; employment and social security; research, the working environment and work organisation; training information and organisation and information; and international issues. The findings of these groups were combined into the report on 'Good Work' to the 1985 Congress that sought to develop a union vision on production issues beyond the traditional focus on distribution issues (Metall, 1985). This policy set out a new union role in the design and development of workplaces in a progressive direction on a basis of mutual gains for both union and employer (Kochan and Osterman, 1994). Such an approach was subsequently endorsed at the confederational level by LO's adoption of 'Developmental Work' in 1991 (Metall, 1985, 1989; LO, 1991).

At the centre of the changes perceived in union circles were new conditions affecting firm competitiveness, both domestically and internationally. The 1980s were seen as being marked by a wide-ranging reorganisation in Swedish industry. Large-scale production was being replaced by flexibility and customer adaptation; and former corporate strategies of maximum utilisation of production capacities were being replaced by a more customer-focused approach based on segmentation and niche marketing. Organisational forms were becoming more decentralised and results-based rather than centralised and function-based.

The new strategy elaborated was therefore to 'develop work' by promoting group-based work organisation, integral job training and the encouragement of job enrichment and new payments systems. The challenge, nevertheless, was to devise a means by which these were to be achieved whilst remaining true to the spirit of the 'solidaristic wages' policy, which remained sacrosanct. Nevertheless, the newly emerging strategy marked a clear departure in that a new emphasis was being placed on production issues in the context of the transition to what some writers came to describe as post-Fordism (Mahon, 1991; Nilsson, 1999). Union goals were evolving to include work of a progressively developing nature in healthy, risk-free workplaces as well as the traditional notions of distributive justice (Huzzard, 2000a).

Subsequently, the LO Congress of 1996 discussed the role of the unions in the development of new production systems. The general view expressed was that the unions needed to develop activities associated with the theoretical ideas and design of new methods for working on the interconnected issues of productivity, efficiency and quality at the workplace. Accordingly, the Congress gave LO the task of setting up development projects in areas such as linking changes in work organisation to new payments systems and regional development networks (Nilsson, 2002).

The current Swedish industrial relations scene – a brief summary

Around 80% of Sweden's 4.2 million labour force are members of unions, and collective agreements comprehensively regulate the labour market. There are three main union confederations; LO (the Swedish Trade Union Confederation) and TCO (the Swedish Confederation of Professional Employees) dominate the blue- and white-collar sectors respectively. A third confederation, SACO (The Swedish Confederation of Professional

Associations), consists of professional unions organising employees who generally possess an academic degree. The various unions affiliated to these bodies organise on a sectoral basis, or on a profession basis in the case of SACO. The links between LO and the Social Democratic Party (SAP) are traditionally very strong.

Although Swedish unions are centralised, this does not mean that they are weak or inactive at the local level. Wherever there are ten or more members at a workplace, it is usual that a local branch (or 'club') of the union is formed. Nevertheless, the employers have pursued a strategic objective of decentralising industrial relations processes over the last 20 years or so. Despite this, the unions have successfully defended bargaining at the sector level, for the time being at least. Traditionally, industrial relations have been left to the employers and unions without government involvement. However, during the 1970s a new framework for industrial relations regulation emerged as new laws were introduced in areas such as the work environment, employment protection and co-determination (Hammarström *et al.*, 2004).

Our early interviews with employer representatives and union leaders in both white- and blue-collar unions suggest that arenas exist for both boxing and dancing at different levels, yet the relative roles of boxing and dancing are undergoing a process of change as is the form and content of each. Arenas of union–employer interaction are discernible on four levels: the global/international level, the national level, the sectoral/regional level and the local/workplace level. A preliminary classification of current boxing and dancing activities in Sweden as well as future prospects is sketched out in Table 5.1.

Table 5.1   Boxing and dancing in Sweden: a classification

Level	Boxing	Dancing	Prospects
Global/ International	Few boxing rings e.g. European Works Councils treatment of plant closures.	Main business of EWCs on information disclosure and consultation.	Most unions seeking opportunities for greater influence internationally.
National	Bargaining role of union confederations now curtailed in private sector as a result of moves to sectoral bargaining. Central negotiations in the state sector.	Historical legacy of corporatism. Some dancing in . public sector process agreements. Some developmental initiatives e.g. SIF's Competence Development Project (1989–93).	Increased pressure for decentralisation to the sector level. Employer withdrawal from dancing in corporatist arenas. Less state funding for development projects.

Table 5.1   (Continued)

Level	Boxing	Dancing	Prospects
Sectoral/regional	Later stages of process agreements e.g. Industry Agreement.	Early stages of process agreements e.g. Industry Agreement. Some development initiatives in regional networks. Competence development initiatives in sector agreements.	Increased dancing through process agreements, particularly on the white-collar side.
Local/workplace	Co-determination in relation to restructuring and rationalisation (though some dancing element). Traditional salary negotiations. Later stages of local process agreements.	Early stages of local process agreements e.g. Astra Zeneca, but less evident on the blue-collar side. Co-determination where ex-ante alignment of interests e.g. health and safety. Job and workplace development projects. Application of sectoral agreements on competence development. Union representation on consultative bodies including company boards.	Both boxing and dancing, but some evidence of union preference for the latter.

Boxing and dancing at the central level[3]

Process agreements – the theory

During the 1990s the Swedish bipartite arena was characterised by greater co-operation both at national and local levels. At the central level an increased number of 'co-operation agreements' (or 'process agreements') were concluded within both the private and the public sectors. On 18 March 1997 a new 'Agreement on Industrial Development and Wage Formation' (Industry Agreement) was signed in Stockholm arising from the belief on both sides that wage formation in Sweden had evolved without any regard to growth in the Swedish economy (Hammarström *et al.*, 2004). Signatories included the SAF led by the Engineering Employers Federation, the ALMEGA Industrial and Chemical Employers Federation, six unions belonging to LO including Metall as well as the industrial unions affiliated to TCO and SACO. The agreement has been described as 'an entirely new model for collective bargaining and conflict resolution' (Elvander, 2001: 15). In effect, the agreement covers the entire competitive sector in the Swedish economy comprising, in all, 19 bargaining arenas and aims to facilitate joint dialogue and consensus on Sweden's economic and to some extent political conditions for industrial enterprise and has put distributional discussions into such a context. This was supplemented by a subsidiary procedural agreement for collective bargaining and conflict resolution in the industrial sector aimed at constructive negotiations that sought to avoid conflict.

A key feature of the Industry Agreement is joint dialogue on general conditions that precedes negotiations on the distributional aspects. Such dialogue seeks consensus in a number of areas including competence development, research and development and energy policy, an activity described by SIF (Swedish Association for Professional and Technical Workers in Industry) leaders nationally as 'creating salary space'. However, the current context of Swedish industrial relations is that of decentralisation. In practice, companies have some degree of negotiating autonomy. This means that separate negotiations at the company level occur. The final agreement reached at the central level acts as a safety net if negotiations at the company level fail. This arrangement, known as a 'stupstock agreement', offers an extra inducement for the parties locally to find common ground. The idea behind the process, and the relationship between levels, is illustrated in Figure 5.1. The first step of the process agreement is intended to be consensual and, in aiming to achieve common ground, can reasonably be described as 'dancing'. The next step bears a closer resemblance to traditional

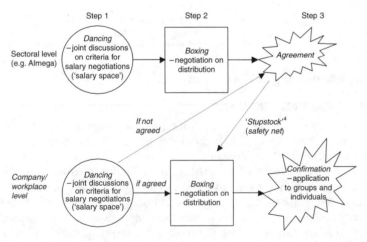

Figure 5.1 Dancing between levels – an ideal typification of process agreements.

positional bargaining and is better termed as 'boxing'. However, there may well be some discrepancy between aspiration (as depicted here) and reality as, in practice, consensus on creating 'salary space' is not always easy to achieve. In particular, disagreement remains on the blue-collar side on the extent to which payment systems should reward workers individually or collectively.

Process agreements – the practice

Although much interest has focused on the Industry Agreement (Elvander, 2001; 2002), other examples of recent agreements at the central level also have process characteristics where consensus and dialogue are preferred to conflictual bargaining and negotiation. One such example is that signed at Föreningssparbanken, one of the major Swedish banks, which is called Handslaget, 'The Handshake'. It was signed at national level, but all individual offices have their own agreement. The aim of the agreement is to increase the productivity and competitiveness of the company, which in turn improves job security for the staff. Examples of national agreements in the public sector are: 'Utveckling 92' (Development 92) from 1992 in the local government sector; 'Samverkan för Utveckling' (Co-operation for Development) in the state sector (1997) and 'En Satsning till 2000' (Towards 2000) covering local authority teachers (1996 – see below). In these agreements the unions and the employers together take responsibility for business development (productivity and service quality) and work development.

The working of the process agreements in practice is well illustrated by the co-operation agreements signed in the teaching profession (see Exhibit 5.1). These agreements, signed between the employers and the two teaching unions The Swedish Union of Teachers (LF – a TCO union) and The National Union of Teachers in Sweden (LR – a SACO union) in 1996 and 2000 involved an acceptance by the unions of individual supplements to the centrally agreed deal in return for greater engagement in the development of their schools with a view to boosting quality at all levels in the profession. The actual negotiation of the 1996 agreement was unique in that the negotiation process was conducted in terms of dialogue rather than exchanges of written positional statements. The agreement recognised the key role of the education sector in determining Swedish competitiveness and both sides explicitly accepted the link between salary policy and quality in schools. Crucially, the central agreement, motivated by such factors, laid down the criteria on which local individual supplements were to be designed.

Both parties at the central level shared responsibility for the intentions of the agreement to be realised. In this sense the role of the parties centrally in the new agreements can be understood as that of advisory rather than norm setting. The agreement also obliged local actors to reach supplementary development agreements at the workplace with local sub-goals linked to the national curriculum. The parties centrally also established joint support

---

Exhibit 5.1   Boxing and dancing in the Swedish teaching profession

The early 1990s in the Swedish public sector saw increasing pressure for decentralisation of salary setting from the state to local authorities as well as determination on the employers' side to push for individualised components. In response, at the end of 1996 the Swedish Teachers Union, LF (215 000 members) and the Swedish Association of Teaching Professionals, LR (75 000 members) signed a national agreement, the School Development Agreement. This entailed an acceptance of greater teacher involvement in and responsibility for developing schools through local development agreements.

Union leaders expressed the view that the traditional approach of high salary demands backed by strike threats simply hadn't delivered and new solutions were called for. Moreover, Sweden's competitive standing depended on better educational standards and higher levels of quality in schools as part of the country's vision of becoming a 'knowledge society'. In consequence, they felt able to explicitly endorse in the new agreement the view that '... salary increases should first of all be awarded to employees who make special contributions to the development and renewal of schools.' Such thinking was widely seen as heralding a systemic shift in the negotiating culture of the profession. A similar development agreement was signed in 2000.

In return for serious engagement on development issues, union members enjoyed significant real salary increases. The 1996 agreement resulted in guaranteed increases 10% above the national average as well as individual supplements. Many teachers saw salaries increase by 27–28% over five years. As to the developmental aspects, a survey of 5000 teachers in 1999 revealed that three quarters of these had been involved in school development dialogues on many or some occasions.

---

teams whose task has been to promote local processes of work organisation development, salary policy and new decisions on teachers' working hours. This is very much a dancing activity – but the possibility of disagreements on distributional aspects was not discarded and the support teams thus also had the role of providing mechanisms for resolving such disagreements in boxing rings locally. The subsequent agreement signed in 2000 had similar provisions for local development and also stressed the need for linkages to be made to the increasing problem in the Swedish public sector of work intensity (see appendix for full case study).

Process agreements – the outcome

Although the process agreements have been heralded as a new epoch of co-operative industrial relations (Elvander, 2002), there are still elements of boxing involved. This was made quite clear by the President of the Metalworkers Union when discussing the Industry Agreement in an interview. In his view:

> Sometimes it's a dance, sometimes it's boxing. We also have a referee when we box in the form of the [agreement's] rules. We have also talked

about how big the ring should be, how many rounds there should be and what one should hit and shouldn't hit.

Although both boxing and dancing existed previously, their nature had changed:

> ... if you take the old dance floor – we both boxed and danced. But one danced sometimes after one had boxed, in order that boxing matches weren't too long ... now it's about 90% dancing and 10% boxing. With three-year deals there are very short boxing matches ... But it's bloody important that we don't stop boxing ... we wouldn't get any legitimacy for the Industry Agreement if it wasn't quite clear that we can also take industrial action.

As to the concrete benefits of the Industry Agreement, he took the view that it was remarkable that two rounds of negotiations had resulted in agreements that have held. Moreover, genuine gains had been registered both for union members in terms of real salary increases and for industry in terms of stability. A further positive aspect was that the agreement gave the unions the possibility of long-term voice – responsible trade unions committed to Swedish competitiveness enjoyed high levels of legitimacy in the eyes of employers and thereby influence on the dance floor. On salaries, the agreement gave scope for even better deals locally than that agreed centrally.

Leaders of the teaching unions also saw the outcomes of the co-operation agreements in a positive light. The fact that the agreements had stuck was clearly an achievement; moreover, the salary increases in real terms were the best the unions had ever secured. One respondent stated that parity with private sector white-collar employees had been achieved on salary development for the first time in decades. The 1996 agreement resulted in guaranteed increases 10% above the national average. When individual supplements were included many teachers saw salaries increase by 27–28% over five years. As to the developmental aspects, a survey of 5000 teachers in 1999 revealed that three quarters of these had been involved in school development dialogues on many or some occasions. A leader from the local LF club in Östersund was also of the view that the new agreements have changed the union role:

> We are going from a negotiating to a monitoring role. Our task is becoming that of educating the members – discussing with them what they can do.

The assessment of more independent observers of the new agreements has also been positive. Elvander (2002), for example, points out that the two rounds of the Industry Agreement were concluded without giving notice of industrial action and the outcome of salary negotiations corresponded at least as favourably as with salary developments elsewhere. Even though the Industry Agreement covers only 20% of the Swedish Labour market, its attractiveness can be measured by the fact that its ideas were copied throughout the public sector and in some smaller areas in the private sector.

The independent economic council advising the parties to the Industry Agreement undertook an in-depth evaluation of the first two periods of the agreement in September 2003. This revealed that the real purchasing power of employees covered by the agreement rose by 3.5% per year from 1998–2000, and by 3.8% from 2001–03. This compares with a figure of zero during the 1980s when the unions boxed to secure money wage increases in line with inflation. The experience on competitiveness was that although labour costs per hour had increased at a greater rate than those of Sweden's competitors, productivity had increased by over 4% annually. This, combined with a weaker exchange rate, had meant that competitive parity had been maintained. In the public sector, there is less evidence available on macroeconomic outcomes of the various co-operation agreements. What is clear, however, is that the agreement has led to considerable activity at the local level on workplace development projects. In September 2003 the website of the state authority overseeing the public sector agreements reported some 90 projects supported by 70mSEK.

Boxing and dancing at the workplace

Blue-collar unions: workplace development projects

At the same time as unions and the employers organisations have been concluding agreements at national level, various types of formal and informal co-operation arrangements between local unions and management have evolved. A recent study of how local union representatives can increase their competencies at change processes through exchanges of experience in networks showed that at 75% of the workplaces covered (n = 147), change occurred through some form of co-operation between management and the local union (Nilsson, 2002). In the remaining cases, management alone implemented change. In the cases where co-operation was reported, 20% occurred according to the Swedish co-determination laws (MBL) that afford unions some degree of limited influence. A further 25% occurred through some form of 'informal' partnership, but with the union having little influence. As many as 64% of the cases reported change occurring through some form of informal partnership between the partners where the union had major influence on the process of change. Such influence typically involved arrangements whereby 'the parties, through dialogue, arrive at possible solutions together that are seen by both sides to be advantageous' (ibid.).

Even if the findings of the study referred to here are not generalisable as it involved learning in a particular network, and the term 'informal' partnership is not clearly defined, it nevertheless suggests that change is afoot in industrial relations locally. This appears to consist of a move away from collective bargaining and an agreement mindset towards greater 'informal' co-operation between the parties. The trend is coinciding with increased union engagement on operational issues and assuming greater responsibility for the development of the organisations in which their members are employed (Nilsson, 1999). Such issues include work organisation, organisational change, competence development, new payments systems and so on.

According to Levinson (1997) a new type of co-determination is developing. The 'integrated form' is increasing while the 'negotiation form' is decreasing. The 'integrated form' means that the trade union organisations are integrated into the decision-making bodies of the enterprise, thus diminishing the need for negotiations. At the Volvo Torslanda factory, for example, this informal type of co-operation is highly developed (see Nilsson, 1997). But local co-operation is not new in Sweden. As early as the 1950s and onwards the local parties were engaged in discussions on work and time studies related to the piece–rate system. Often local unions had developed high degrees of competence on the MTM-system (method, time, measurement), and at times management used union experts as quasi-consultants. But local co-operation since then has intensified – perhaps with the exception of the 1970s – and the previously reactive unions have become increasingly proactive; but, as the evidence suggests, many joint development projects are occurring as 'integrated' rather than 'negotiated' co-determination (Levinson, 1997). Exhibit 5.2 depicts a union view of how a local development process can ideally work.

There are reasons to believe, however, that the prospects for making gains on the dance floor on development issues are receding, especially in the private sector. The doctrine of leanness appears to be becoming increasingly pervasive: here the priority is standardisation and elimination of waste rather than experimentation and development. In a report published in 2003, Metall assessed that around 50% of their members were working under lean production (Metall, 2003). Moreover, in longitudinal survey research in the private sector, it has also been noted that employees see the significance of work organisation as an issue for co-determination as being on the decline (Levinson, 2004).

White-collar unions: dancing on distribution issues

The involvement of white-collar unions in workplace development projects is less common, but there are cases where SIF clubs have been involved, particularly where job redesign involves production engineers (Huzzard, 2000a). 'Development' on the white-collar side tends to be at the individual level with a particular focus on competence and career development; some local SIF clubs were involved in joint projects with employers in this area in the early 1990s (ibid.). More recently, SIF have sought to develop partnership

Exhibit 5.2   Dancing in development projects – a model (source: LO teaching materials)

Activity stage

- preparatory work

Process of partnership

Union (anchorage   Management
with members)   (anchorage with
                     company board)

1 *Interest arousal*
  - Analysis of current situation
  - Environmental analysis

◄──────── Discussions ────────►

2 *Investigation phase*
  - Start: appoint a steering committee
  - Where are we?
  - Where are we going?
    o Form working groups
    o Analyse resource needs
    o Discuss consequences
  - Agreement on 'what' and 'whither'

◄──────── Dialogue ────────►

Goals   Goals

Means   Means

Partnership agreement

3 *Implementation*
  - Concrete action plans
  - Sub-goals, setting of deadlines and allocating responsibilities
  - Measurable key targets

Co-operation

4 *Follow-up*
  - Reflection!

What have we done and how do we go forward?

arenas at the workplace level, parallel to those associated with the central level process agreements, on the basic distributional issues of pay and conditions.

One such example of dancing locally on distributional issues is the evolution of the partnership arrangements at Astra Zeneca, a large pharmaceutical multinational that has its R and D headquarters in Södertälje (see appendix for full case study). When interviewed, the SIF club leaders at the plant stated that the current partnership activity could be traced back to the early 1980s when the club leadership consciously sought close relations with the company and a high level of influence on decisions in the then Astra. A key aim of the agreement signed at that time was for as much common ground as possible to be reached between the union and employers as a precursor to distributional bargaining. Such a view was taken up by SIF nationally in the 1990s with the process approach to bargaining as exemplified by the union's endorsement of the Industry Agreement. Historically, therefore, the SIF club at Astra Zeneca had been engaging in dancing activities across a range of issues prior to the moves in that direction nationally. In reality, those interviewed stated that they did not in practice need to fall back on the provisions of the agreement to make the partnership work. The newly elected chair of the SIF club, moreover, stated that whilst he was aware of the agreement's existence, he'd 'never seen it – and never needed to see it either'.

The process-based approach to bargaining at Astra Zeneca was illustrated by the club leaders by reference to the issue of salaries. Initially, dancing activities entail discussions on establishing joint salary criteria based on a common view of affordability in the context of the developmental trajectory of the business. This results in a written agreement on the aims and direction of the salary round without specifying figures. Thereafter salaries are set on an individual basis. A provision exists for negotiation between union and management where there is disagreement on the individual salary awarded, but this is rare in practice. It can thus be seen from this case that although partnership arenas are being exploited by union representatives, they are not totally replacing collective bargaining. *In other words, boxing and dancing are not mutually exclusive choices but are linked dynamically in a single process that is perceived to be of benefit to both sides.* The process is illustrated in Exhibit 5.3.

Exhibit 5.3 The white-collar salary setting process – Astra Zeneca AB (source: adapted from company documents)

Step	Activity	Actors
0	Planning and development dialogue	Line manager and individual employee
1	Dialogue on issues of major importance in the salary round. Produces written document.	HR managers and local union leaders (Dancing)
2	Individual salary setting: performance-based pay at company, functional and individual levels	Line manager
3	Salary dialogue	Line manager and individual white-collar employee
4	Formal negotiation (only if disagreement at step 3)	HR managers and local union leaders (Boxing but rare in practice)
5	Confirmation and implementation	HR manager

It was argued by club interviewees that early influence helps head off decision makers in the company from taking entrenched positions from which they can't easily escape and is thus a useful means of conflict avoidance. Moreover, the mandate of union representatives legitimises the voice of union leaders in partnership discussions. The club leaders also stated that they could supply, on the dance floor, unique knowledge to the company particularly in relation to the individual characteristics and needs that helped inform subsequent salary discussions. This helped boost the status of the club as a legitimate actor. In the view of the HR Manager interviewed, knowledge from the line managers tended to be distorted by considerations of self-interest: the union was thus seen as a more reliable source. *In such a view, the added-value provided by the union under partnership is conditional on it retaining its independence rather than being incorporated within a unitarist view of the firm.* SIF club leaders also saw dancing as an opportunity for the company and the club to act together as allies against other stakeholders. The example of the merger of 1999 between Astra and Zeneca was cited as an example of this in that both the union and the Astra management supported the move whereas many shareholders were opposed.

Implications for union renewal

What, then, are the implications of the changing face of Swedish industrial relations for strategic trade unionism? Following Boxall and Haynes (1997) and others we argue it is appropriate to tackle this question by mapping out the strategic choices for unions in context. *It is quite clear that there has been an extension in union agendas from distribution issues to operational, production and development issues* (Nilsson, 1999; Huzzard, 2000a). So far as development issues are concerned, however, it is important to draw a dividing line between blue- and white-collar employees. The notion of 'job development' when seen as an operating issue means different things for the two groups of employees. For blue-collar staff development means taking on a broader range of duties both vertically and horizontally in the context of team-working. For white-collar employees, on the other hand, development until recently has tended to involve individual career development which need not have any relationship with the development of work organisation (Nilsson, 1996; Brulin and Nilsson, 1997). Nevertheless, two approaches to strategic choice are discernible along what Boxall and Haynes (1997: 572) call the dimension of worker relations: distributional unionism and developmental unionism. As to the dimension of employer relations, two broad modes of engagement are discernible, boxing and dancing, notwithstanding the need for these to be nuanced further as argued in this chapter.

One choice is to stick with traditional collective bargaining, boxing, on distributional issues. Indeed, so long as union members continue to see matters relating to pay and conditions as being of central importance (Nelander and Lindgren, 1998), work on these issues will remain a core union activity.

Yet there is considerable evidence that unions are increasingly seeking more co-operative arenas in which to resolve distributional matters, notably the process agreements (including the Industry Agreement) and the search for consensus on what constitutes the desirable 'salary space'.

On the other hand, the unions' pursuit of a development agenda can be traced back to the push for co-determination in the late 1970s as part of a drive for greater industrial democracy. The initial thought behind the idea was to enact legislation that allowed unions much greater scope on operational and development issues particularly at the local level. But the forms of joint consultation that became the model mode of engagement nevertheless presupposed some divergence of interests and a boxing mentality. In the view of our respondents from various unions, the experience of co-determination, however, has been rather disappointing from a union perspective. In practice the arrangements are usually used in situations of redundancies, restructuring and downsizing and have not delivered in terms of the proactive union agendas on workplace or career development. Accordingly, unions have sought to experiment in joint projects with the employers on workplace development and in regional development networks. White-collar unions have also sought to develop services associated with career development. Such projects, often outside the bargaining procedures laid down by MBL, have been designed on the basis of consensus and joint problem-solving.

We can thus construct a typology of trade union strategic choices as in Figure 5.2. We make no claims about the generalisability of this typology beyond Sweden. The four choices are not mutually exclusive, indeed, there

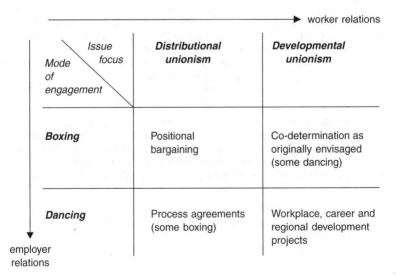

Figure 5.2 A typology of strategic choice for trade unions in Sweden.

is evidence that unions are engaged in all four to greater and lesser degrees. Moreover, the distinctions between boxing and dancing are not clear-cut as, for example, both boxing and dancing are evident in the process agreements and in co-determination. It is also becoming difficult to separate distributional and developmental issues which are in many respects becoming interdependent. However, there does appear to be a trend whereby unions are seeking to move towards terrains of co-operation in order to dance with their employer counterparts. A transition from positional thinking to process thinking in the unions was explicitly evident in our interviews with union leaders. In practice at the workplace such a change involves seeking an earlier union influence on company decision-making as well as union leaders listening to members first and then acting proactively on what is heard, rather than reacting to messages from their respective representative systems (Child *et al.*, 1973).

Finally, there are signs that the developmental agenda not only requires partnership arenas, but also poses considerable demands on union competencies. The Astra Zeneca case study here suggests that local union leaders can no longer restrict their competencies to knowledge of laws and agreements. There needs to be training in the clubs on business administration, psychology and communication skills. This is also a key finding of a recent

---

Exhibit 5.4 The RUD Project – union learning in development networks

In 1997 an agreement was reached between LO and the National Institute for Working Life, NIWL, to start a development programme to support local union activists in handling change processes at the workplace. The idea of the programme was to start cross-union networks in which unionists could develop their change competences. The logic was that the experiences unionists get at the workplace from work organisational changes should be reflected on with other unionists in the network meetings. The results of this reflection would be taken back to the workplace for action and new experiences, and these partly new experiences would be reflected in the cross-union networks, and so on. The programme ran from the beginning of 1998 until the end of 2001.

Each network was led by a 'co-ordinator', who was also a local union activist, and she or he was selected by the steering committee. In this development programme the co-ordinators were chosen because of their specific qualifications: a high level of work organisation competence and knowledge of change processes at workplaces. The members of the networks ('networkers') met normally four times a year.

The overwhelming majority of the 200 or so 'networkers' had learned considerably from the network. They improved their capacity to understand work organisation processes as well as change processes and how to act in these processes. They also increased their self-confidence, both in relation to management and to union members at the workplace.

study of the RUD (The Union Role in Workplace Development) project, an LO initiative aimed at developing union learning in regional networks. This also suggested that local development projects require a special set of skills associated with the execution of change. These include: early identification of problems and detection of new opportunities; having a total view of the organisation; building contacts; information search; anticipation of the barriers to change; planning and implementation of change; bearing tacit knowledge, for example, being a 'champion' of change; active participation and the leading of change; and sensitivity to the uniqueness of the change context (Nilsson, 2002). This study clearly points to a potential role for unions as change agents at the workplace, but naturally, on union terms. A summary of the project is set out in Exhibit 5.4 above and a complete case study is included in the appendix.

Conclusions: boxing and dancing interdependency

The framing of trade union strategic choices in terms of either/or – social partnership or a more adversarial, distanced approach to labour process regulation – is to oversimplify the issues at stake. This chapter has shown how Swedish white-collar unions in particular have sought to pursue distributional goals in partnership arenas. The evidence also suggests that blue-collar unions at the workplace have often adopted a partnership approach on production issues, yet have acted more adversarially on distributional issues. They have built legitimacy in the sphere of the former to make gains in the latter. Strategic choices for unions might thus be conceived as finding an appropriate balance between (a) supplying union knowledge as a valuable input into learning and development in companies, and (b) generating union knowledge as a power resource for gaining extra leverage over employers in distributional bargaining. *The choices of boxing and dancing are thus not mutually exclusive; on the contrary they are dynamically self-reinforcing.*

Social partnership can be on equal terms where either side can initiate dialogue or led by the employers; it can be formal or informal as well as structured or unstructured. Relations between the parties locally can either take the form of negotiations or co-operation or both; and the former has traditionally been the means for resolving distribution issues whereas the latter has been sought to resolve operational issues. More recently, however, such a distinction has become blurred as unions have sought to adopt more co-operative forms in the distributional arena. Moreover, co-operation and consensus has not always been possible on operational issues particularly in connection with downsizing and restructuring. From the 1970s until a few years ago the latter issues have been dealt with under the co-determination arrangements. But a number of new forms of local social partnership have developed alongside the traditional MBL procedures – it would be incorrect, therefore, to equate social partnership with co-determination.

Choices on the precise configuration of boxing and dancing depend on the issue at stake as well as how the parties perceive each other – as adversaries or co-players in the dance – and how they see the relationship between employees and employers more generally. Where the latter relationship is seen as being fundamentally adversarial and that the parties have no common ground, then the only real option is negotiation, agreements and any associated forms of conflict. If, however, the relationship is seen in such a way that employees and employers do share at least some common interests, for example, the survival and long-term development of the firm and the belief that win–win outcomes are possible, then there is scope for co-operation and the emergence of mutual trust. Social partnership, at least when it is on equal terms, is hereby characterised by openness, and the principle that the arguments of the parties are central and that such arguments are founded on the competencies of the actors on the issues in question.

At the central level it has been argued that the Industry Agreement and similar process agreements in other sectors can in many respects be seen as the restoration of a stable framework for co-operative industrial relations following an interregnum of conflict between the end of the 1960s and the mid-1990s. Indeed, Elvander (2002: 201) has drawn parallels between such a framework and that of the Saltsjöbaden Agreement by describing both as forms of 'institutionalised partnership'. At the central level it could thus be argued that there is a paradigm shift in industrial relations, albeit one which has evolved separately from the European Social Dialogue.

On the other hand, the partnership arenas at the local level, in particularly on development issues on the blue-collar side, are hardly new. They date back to the mid-1980s at least, yet are under threat from the frequent waves of rationalisation and restructuring which now appear to have become the norm rather than the exception (Bäckström, 1999; Huzzard, 2000b). Nevertheless, it appears that as we enter the new millennium, trade union strategic choices are reflecting a greater element of dancing at both central and local levels. Centrally, union leaders see partnership as a better basis for delivering *real* salary increases, whereas locally blue-collar union agendas remain focused on work organisation issues. There is little basis for suggesting that the latter can be successfully pursued in boxing rings.

The Astra Zeneca case and evidence elsewhere from Sweden suggests therefore that partnership need not imply incorporation or collaborationist sell-out (see also Huzzard, 2000a, ch. 10). On the other hand, partnership has been deeply embedded in the country's unique institutions and high-trust culture and the translation of Swedish ideas on partnership to other national contexts is decidedly problematic. We can certainly speculate on whether the industrial relations trajectory in Sweden over the last six or so decades has been because of partnership or despite it. Yet the fact remains that where partnership has had the longest history of the countries covered in this book, it has coincided with the strongest trade union movement.

Notes

1. Case study data was obtained through interviews with HR managers, and union leaders at central and local levels as well as company and union documents.
2. The Swedish Employers Confederation. Renamed 'Swedish Enterprise' (SN) in 2001.
3. The term 'central' here means the sectoral level in the private sector and the national (state) level in the public sector.
4. 'Stupstock' is the Swedish term for the stocks used in former times to publicly contain and display alleged miscreants. The idea is that local employers who do not conform to the central agreements would have such behaviour put on public display.

References

Boxall, P. and Haynes, P. (1997) 'Strategy and Trade Union Effectiveness in a Neo-Liberal Environment', *British Journal of Industrial Relations* 35 (4): 567–91.

Brulin, G. and Nilsson, T. (1997) *Läran om arbetets ekonomi*. Stockholm: Rabén Prisma.

Bäckström, H. (1999) *Den krattade managen: svensk arbetsorganisatorisk utveckling under tre decennier*. Department of Business Studies, Uppsala University, Doctoral Thesis No 79.

Child, J., Loveridge, R. and Warner, M. (1973) 'Towards an Organizational Study of Trade Unions', *Sociology* 7 (1): 71–91.

Elvander, N. (2001) '*The Industrial Agreement: An Analysis of its Ideas and Performance*'. Stockholm: Almega.

Elvander, N. (2002) 'Industriavtalet och Saltsjöbadsavtalet – en Jämförelse', *Arbetsmarknad och Arbetsliv* 8 (3): 191–204.

Gustavsen, B., Wikman, A., Ekman-Philips, M. and Hofmeier, B. (1996) *Concept-driven Development and the Organization of the Process of Change: an Evaluation of the Swedish Working Life Fund*. Amsterdam: John Benjamin.

Hammarström, O., Huzzard, T. and Nilsson, T. (2004) 'Employment Relations in Sweden' in Bamber, G. and Lansbury, R. (eds) *International and Comparative Employment Relations: A Study of Industrialised Market Economies (3rd edn)*. Sydney: Allen and Unwin.

Huzzard, T. (2000a) *Labouring to Learn: Union Renewal in Swedish Manufacturing*. Umeå: Boréa.

Huzzard, T. (2000b) 'From Partnership to Resistance – Unions and Organisational Learning at Ericsson Infocom', *Management Learning* 31 (3): 353–73.

Huzzard, T. (2003) *The Convergence of QWL and Competitiveness: A Swedish Literature Review*. National Institute for Working Life, Stockholm: Work Life in Transition 2003:9.

Kjellberg, A. (1992) 'Sweden: Can the Model Survive?', in Ferner, A. and Hyman, R. (eds) *Industrial Relations in the New Europe*. Oxford: Blackwell Business Books.

Kochan T. A. and Osterman, P. (1994) *The Mutual Gains Enterprise: Forging a Winning Partnership among Labor, Management and Government*. Boston: Harvard University Press.

Levinson, K. (1997) 'Medbestämmande i Förändring', *Arbetsmarknad och Arbetsliv* 3 (2).

Levinson, K. (2004) Lokal partssamverkan – en undersökning av svenskt medbestämmande. National Institute of Working Life, Stockholm: Arbetsliv i omvandling 2004 (5).

LO (1991) *Det utvecklande arbetet*. LO: Stockholm.

Mahon, R. (1991) 'From Solidaristic Wages to Solidaristic Work: A Post-Fordist Historic Compromise for Sweden?', *Economic and Industrial Democracy* 12: 295–325.

Mahon, R. (1994) 'Wage-Earners and/or Co-Workers? Contested Identities', *Economic and Industrial Democracy* 15: 355–83.

Meidner, R. (1986) 'Swedish Union Strategies Towards Structural Change', *Economic and Industrial Democracy* 7: 85–97.

Metall (1985) *Det goda arbetet*. Stockholm: Metall.

Metall (1989) *Solidarisk arbetspolitik för det goda arbetet*. Stockholm: Metall.

Metall (2003) 'Metallarbetarna och lean produktion', Stockholm: Metall.

Nelander, S. and Lindgren, V. (1998) *Röster om facket och jobbet: rapport nr 1 – synen på fackligt medlemskap och fackets uppgifter*. Stockholm: LO.

Nilsson, T. (1996) 'Lean Production and White-Collar Work: the Case of Sweden', *Economic and Industrial Democracy* 17: 447–72.

Nilsson, T. (1997) 'Fackets nya Roll. Från Förhandling till Partssamverkan i Lokalt Utvecklingsarbete', *Arbetsmarknad & Arbetsliv* 3 (3).

Nilsson, T. (1999) 'The Future Role of the Swedish Unions – Increased Local Co-operation for Production Development', *Economic and Industrial Democracy* 20: 461–82.

Nilsson, T. (2002) *Att Starta Fackliga Kunskapsnätverk för Förändring*, Working Paper, Stockholm: National Institute for Working Life.

Reich, R. B. (1991) *The Work of Nations – Capitalism in the 21st Century*. New York: A. A. Knopf.

SIF (1997) *Handlingsprogram för kongressperioden 1997–2000*. Stockholm: SIF.

Thörnqvist, C. (1999) 'The Decentralization of Industrial Relations: The Swedish Case in Comparative Perspective', *European Journal of Industrial Relations* 5 (1): 71–87.

6
Tiptoe through the Tulips: The Uneasy Development of Strategic Unionism in Polder Country

Maarten van Klaveren and Wim Sprenger

Introduction: the 'polder model'

Since 1945, Dutch labour relations have been characterised by intricate combinations of boxing and dancing at all levels. In the context of a religiously divided society and an open economy, the consensual 'polder model' rose to the surface – reconciling colliding interests and defence mechanisms against external constraints simultaneously. This model, defined broadly, has deep roots in Dutch history. The relatively democratic and consensual government of polders and towns in the Middle Ages, prolonged in the socio-political structures of the Republic (1579–1795), can be regarded as the undercurrent on which the Dutch system of labour relations was shaped in the last quarter of the nineteenth century: a system characterised by peak-level bargaining between trade unions and employers' organisations (Van Zanden, 2000). In a more limited sense, the polder model was prepared during the Second World War in illegal meetings of union leaders and employers (Van Bottenburg, 1995). As a result, in 1945 the bi-partite Foundation of Labour (STAR) was founded, where union confederations and employers' federations still meet to discuss socio-economic and wage developments and to propose recommendations to their affiliates. The creation of STAR was explicitly meant to draw the class struggle to a close (De Rooy, 2001).

In 1950, the government gained more power in the socio-economic dance floor. The tri-partite Social-Economic Council (SER) was created, with trade unions, employers and independent members appointed by the government advising about broader issues. STAR and SER developed as well-equipped dance floors. In the next two decades, Dutch labour relations were characterised by the dominant role of government and by centralised bargaining. The underlying corporatist arrangements were based on far-reaching trust placed in statutory provisions. The three 'recognised' union confederations formed stable elements in these relations. In 1944–45, a fourth confederation with communist influences stirred. This group, the Communist Trade Union Confederation (EVC), was excluded from the STAR. The other three supported an industrialisation strategy based on low wages, by a system of annually adjusted statutory wage guidelines. Forced by tight labour markets, this system broke down and in 1963–65 wages 'exploded' by 42%. By 1970, the Netherlands was a high wage economy, although still relying on labour intensive industries. In that year, union leaderships were overwhelmed by shop-floor militancy and embarrassed by massive strikes in the port of Rotterdam. Under pressure from the cultural and intellectual revolts of 1964–69, the Dutch union movement had to let go of its paternalistic features. It integrated leftist intellectual inputs and, somewhat later, inputs from the feminist movement rather smoothly (Visser, 1995; Visser and Hemerijck, 1997).

The Wage Act of 1970 handed wage setting back to unions and employers, although the government retained the power to order temporary wage freezes. With unemployment growing after the first oil crisis (1973–74), several of such measures were taken, undermining the basis of trust between unions and employers on the one hand and government on the other. In the same period, the traditional cleavage between the general or Social Democratic, Catholic and Protestant currents in the union movement disappeared, as the general peak organisation NVV merged with the Catholic NKV into FNV (initially in 1976 and finally in 1981). The Protestant CNV confederation attracted a number of independent Catholic unions, and MHP (Trade Union Confederation for White Collar Groups), a confederation of white-collar unions, was also formed (Visser, 2000).

The 1970–82 period can be seen as a relative conflictive intermezzo in Dutch labour relations. In 1982, against the background of rapidly growing unemployment, the representatives of the union confederations and the employers' federations in STAR agreed upon wage moderation in exchange for reductions in working hours. This Wassenaar Agreement, the 'Mother of all Accords', and subsequent STAR recommendations not only minimised government intervention in wage setting (formalised in the 1987 Law on Wage Formation). It also stimulated decentralisation towards sector/regional levels and partnering at those levels. Partnering received a further impetus in 1993, when the union confederations and employers' federations signed the 'New Course' accord. Again, in a recession, both parties stressed the need to improve competitiveness as well as employment. The 1993 agreement paved the way to broaden collective bargaining to fields like employability, career structuring, working time schedules (legal monitoring), provisions for disadvantaged groups, child care, and reinsurance of entitlements reduced in government welfare reforms – issues that the governing coalitions mainly left to the social partners or, like the reinsurance issue, provoked them to settle (Van der Meer *et al.*, 2002). In doing so, the unions entered fields where many works councils had already developed competence, engaging these councils in an uneasy co-management relationship (Visser, 1995).

An overview of the Dutch context

One has to keep in mind a number of contextual factors. The Netherlands industrialised later and less intensively than its neighbouring countries. Large-scale industries developed in the 1910s and 1920s, decades in which the six industrial Dutch-based multinationals (Philips, Unilever, Shell, Akzo Nobel, Hoogovens, DSM) came to maturity. Between 1945 and 1950, they accepted company collective agreements, tailored to their needs in an open economy (one of the most open in Europe, with imports and exports making up 85% of Gross Domestic Product) (Van Zanden, 2000). Dutch civil society was much less 'open'. It developed along political–religious cleavages. Protestants, Catholics, socialists and liberals, all had their own 'pillars' with political parties, mass media, unions and so on. This 'pillarised' system formed the basis for neo-corporatism. From the late 1950s on, it gradually disintegrated, but the pillars are still rather strong in politics (De Rooy, 2001). The Dutch union movement mainly developed along the guidelines of Henri Polak, leader of the Diamond Workers' Union and in 1906 co-founder of the Dutch Confederation of Trade Unions (NVV): industrial unionism, strong internal discipline, based on the work of full-time paid officials and having adequate strike funds grounded on high membership fees. The Catholic and Protestant movements, founded somewhat later, based themselves on the same principles. The first national collective agreements were agreed upon in the early years of the twentieth century. The law of 1927 gave contractual status to such agreements (Visser, 2000).

By 1947, employment in commercial services had already surpassed that in manufacturing industry. The Netherlands went through its industrial stage quickly, developing into a service economy. In 2001, just over 1 million employees worked in manufacturing industry, less than 15% of all 7 million wage earners – except for Luxemburg, the lowest share in the European Union (EU). The employment rate for women (working women as a percentage of the population aged 15–64), until 1980 one of Europe's lowest because of women withdrawing from the labour market after marrying, rose quickly to attain 66% in 2002, well above the EU average – although Dutch employers maintained segregation by gender rather strictly (EC, 2003; Van Klaveren and Tijdens, 2003). The Wassenaar Agreement has been important here because it stimulated all forms of working time reduction. The Netherlands developed into the first part-time economy in the world, with a share of part-timers in the female work force of 73% in 2002 (and 21% in the male work force). Under pressure from a coalition of unions and women's organisations, part-time work escaped from marginalisation. A large majority of Dutch part-timers is covered by collective contracts, enjoying legal protection and working conditions equal to full-timers (Visser, 2002; EC, 2003). In a second round of shortening working time following the 1993 STAR recommendations, a standard 36 hours working week was agreed upon for a majority of employees (Tijdens, 2002).

In the light of the militancy of the 'factory cores' in the 1930s and directly after the Second World War, employers' federations and mainstream unionism tried to codify co-determination. A dual labour relations system developed. Under the 1950 Works Councils Act, employees were entitled to representation in joint councils, chaired by the employer. A 1971 law provided for separate meetings of employee representatives. In 1979, the law was revised again, providing for mandatory councils elected by and from the employees, independent from employers and endowed with powers of information, consultation and, on matters of personnel policy regulations, co-determination. Like their German colleagues, the Dutch unions have succeeded in getting members elected to works councils. Although candidature and voting are open to all employees, in elections from 1979–93 the FNV unions gained on average 40% of the votes, twice their membership share. By 1990, the works councils had become the centres of employee representation in firms (Visser, 1995). A majority of the councils want to function rather independently from the unions, but do not have ambitions to take over collective bargaining powers (Van het Kaar and Looise, 1999). Indeed, when in 2002 the chairman of the main employers' federation suggested that employers should start collective bargaining with 'their' works councils, only a minority of works councillors favoured this idea (NRC-Handelsblad, 2002).

At the beginning of the 1980s, union power was tested by a rapid process of de-industrialization and steeply rising unemployment (officially 11% in 1983). In December 1979, union membership reached a peak of over 1.7 million, a density of 40%. In the next seven years, the unions suffered from a net loss of 260 000 members, bringing density down to 32% at the end of 1986. On the one hand, union strongholds in manufacturing such as textiles and shipbuilding, with densities of 40%–50%, were reduced drastically. On the other hand, the unions hardly succeeded in lifting up their very low density in commercial services, already the largest sector in 1980 and even expanding in the recession. In 2000, FNV unions organised only 8% of all employees in commercial services. Between 1985 and 1995, FNV and affiliated unions reduced staff levels by one-third. Their ranks of unpaid activists were even more heavily depleted. The remaining pool of activists is ageing. From 1986 on, the numbers of union members grew again, but this growth was surpassed by the more rapid growth of employment. Union density gradually fell to 25% in 2002. The density rate of the FNV unions fell from 25% in 1979 to 16% in 2002 (Visser, 2000; Hooiveld *et al.*, 2002a).

Between 1988 and 2000, the Dutch economy grew rapidly, especially after 1994. Job creation and real GDP growth rates were way above EU averages, until in 2001 a recession started with just 1% GDP growth (OECD, 2001; EC, 2002). Before that hard landing, 'the Dutch disease' had been transformed into 'the Dutch jobs machine'. Clinton, Blair and Schröder sung the praise of Wim Kok, in 1994–2002 leader of the two 'purple' government coalitions (and former FNV chairman), for guiding them on their Third Way. In the decade following 1988, the revitalised consultation machinery, still based on the dance floors created in 1945–50, functioned rather effectively. The contribution of rejuvenated labour relations to the Dutch economic miracle is spelled out by Visser and Hemerijck (1997). Macro-economic stability and growing micro-economic dynamism created near-full employment (2002: 4% official unemployment). Yet, between 1985 and 1995, and in all probability also afterwards, they resulted in growing income inequality, with a falling share of income distribution for the bottom 20% (Förster and Pellizzari, 2000; De Beer, 2002). The macro-economic successes blinded the 'Purple II' coalition, in power since 1998, from the obstinacy of major societal problems, especially concerning:

• health care
• the education system
• the social security system
• public transport
• the large cities, with growing relative poverty among groups of immigrants.

As far as costs were involved, these problems were a price that had to be paid for the EMU and Stability Pact orthodoxy of the Dutch administration (Hemerijck and Visser, 2002). The lack of new policies was the price of self-satisfaction and low propensity to change during prosperity – familiar phenomena for students of organisational learning, maybe aggravated in a corporatist setting as in the Netherlands (cf. Van der Meer *et al.*, 2003).

In December 2001, world-famous American economist Michael Porter warned the Dutch policy makers that their model of essentially keeping wages down and costs low was ending (Porter, 2002). Various commentators interpreted Porter's lecture as writing off the polder model. In our view this is wrong. Porter lectured about economic policies, arguing that pursuing wage moderation for too long was seriously hampering innovation and productivity. It cannot be denied that labour productivity growth in the Netherlands has been quite low: between 1985 and 2000 the lowest of all EU countries (De Beer, 2002). Thus, the Dutch economy is in urgent need of speeding up productivity growth and innovation (cf. *The Economist*, 2002). It remains to be seen whether the unions are ready to use this need as a strategic crowbar. The CNV union confederation (350 000 members in 2002) has advocated an innovation agenda aiming at productivity increase. However, 'big brother' FNV (1 230 000 members) has seemingly hesitated in combining such an agenda, associated mainly with 'dancing', with the usual bargaining input, associated with 'boxing'. The FNV obviously judges company union representation to be too weak to mobilise for productivity rises in a socially acceptable way (cf. Leenders, 2002).

Yet, there have been many efforts in the Netherlands towards innovative union activities and partnerships. We will now go into these initiatives, first those at sectoral/regional levels and then those at company and workplace levels. A classification of current boxing and dancing activities in the Netherlands as well as their prospects can be found in Table 6.1.

New union initiatives

Sectoral and regional levels

In the 1980s, few sectoral and/or regional union initiatives could be called innovative. Yet, there were two exceptions, both touching upon work organisation. One was the introduction of employment plans at company level, set up by union activists fighting closures, inspired by the Lucas Aerospace Corporate Plan and other UK proposals for alternative products. In some

Table 6.1   Boxing and dancing in the Netherlands: a classification

Level	Boxing	Dancing	Prospects
National	Confederations occasionally boxing during conflicts with government.	Common dance floor with employers dominant (SER, STAR), particularly following accords of 1982 and 1993, last 5 years less outspoken.	Pressure for decentralisation of preparation of collective bargaining, differentiation of issues will be continued.
Sectoral/Regional	Dominant in traditional, declining sectors, coordination by confederations and Mandatory Expansion of contracts limiting boxing conflicts.	In new con figurations and regionally, accompanied by some boxing.	Increased dancing in large stabilised sectors and in projects aiming at specific groups of employees.
Company/ Workplace	Weakness of unions at this level restricts boxing potential. In collective bargaining new roles for works councils could enhance some boxing. In work organisation fewer process arrangements with works councils, fewer union projects, means more boxing.	Continuing in prolonged work organisation projects, rather new in preparation of collective bargaining in major companies.	If recession continues, more boxing; for unions new forms of dancing bringing together collective and individual empowering of members.

towns these initiatives were broadened to encompass regional union projects. The second exception was the renewal programme of the Transport Union FNV in the port of Rotterdam. This started after the wildcat strikes of 1979 in order to regain the confidence of (potential) membership. With the help of a company modernisation programme set up by the Rotterdam Port Authority (GHR), the three parties involved, including the local employers' federation, became aware that they needed a joint platform. In the early 1990s, the Transport Union tried to transfer experience from strongholds like the Rotterdam port, with 70%–80% union density, to 'white spots' or 'deserts'. Most of the new networks, corridors and clusters that developed throughout the Netherlands turned out to be such 'union deserts', with densities of less than 10%.

Other FNV unions followed. They started activities aiming at attracting members and at creating social infrastructures: recognition of unions, dance floors to deal with employers, works councils and vocational training facilities. In the course of these activities, empowerment of a differentiated membership by offering differentiated services came into prominence. Headquarters and regional officers of the FNV confederation often played co-ordinating roles. They did not have to start from scratch. Derived from the dance floors at national level, in all regions and most sectors elaborate networks of union representation were already in existence and laid down a standard. Government often supported their expansion to the 'union deserts', for example, by subsidising vocational training facilities and recognising training certificates. In the 1990s, a number of union projects developed into partnerships. Most partnerships led to union-controlled labour supply and training arrangements, and some improvements in working conditions (mainly in health and safety, and less short-cycled jobs). Yet, as often in the consultation economy, the unions came across the 'claim problem': how to convince sceptics that union inputs are indispensable for achieving partnership results? (Van Klaveren, 2001).

The knowledge transfer from union projects to partnership practices also occurred in the reverse direction. The FNV confederation and a number of affiliated unions used experience from partnerships for union projects. From 1990 till 2002, in the FNV at least 13 projects at sub-sector and regional levels or aiming at specific groups were implemented. These covered (in chronological order, considering the year of start-up):

- retail trade
- wholesale trade
- audiovisual media
- banking
- Schiphol airport
- industribution
- Rotterdam mainport

- cleaning
- information and communications technology (ICT)
- call centres
- self-employed workers
- home workers and teleworkers
- workers with occupational disabilities

These initiatives showed a growing individual servicing content, and the latter three included a high level of individual arrangements. Recently, new union services have been developed aiming at individual employees not defined in numbers beforehand. An example is the FNV career service.

The overall picture of the results of these projects varies. If FNV union density is the yardstick, the projects in wholesale, retail, banking, industribution and cleaning were rather successful, with densities doubling or more between 1985 and 2000. Yet, densities in ICT and call centres are still in the 5% range (Hooiveld *et al.*, 2002a). Some projects showed considerable learning effects, especially as regards the possible combinations of boxing and dancing. During these projects, a number of bipartite and tripartite arrangements were agreed upon, concerning labour supply (vocational) training

---

Exhibit 6.1   The FNV Industribution Project – dancing and boxing in a 'union desert'

In the early 1990s, industribution activities boomed in the Netherlands. 'Industribution' is a contraction of 'industry' and 'distribution'. Such activities have been developing where industrial, logistic and servicing activities meet, for example in assembly of printers, pre-assembly of car parts, and in reconditioning of shoes and clothing. In 1996, the FNV confederation and four affiliated unions (in manufacturing, food, transport, services) started a joint project, as this boom, in the words of the project leader, 'went on without collective agreements, with low wages, bad working conditions, and with a depressingly low union density' – all features of a 'union desert'. Research commissioned by the unions demonstrated that the prevailing employers' policies, hiring workers from temp agencies at random, caused problems of loyalty, reliability, costs and performance. Regional authorities and local employers' organisations accepted joint labour pools as an alternative. FNV officers found legal forms and subsidies for these pools, and took the initiative to create vocational training facilities. After the merger of the four unions into FNV Bondgenoten (February 1998), the new union tried to use project experience in collective bargaining practice. This meant a strategic change from mere dancing to combinations of dancing and boxing. In July 1999, collective agreements covered 60% instead of 33% of the spearhead companies, the number of union activists had doubled and that of members tripled.

Source: FNV Bondgensten Internal Consultancy Report.

and, career development (cf. Van Klaveren *et al.*, 1997). Based on a detailed evaluation of three sub-sector/regional projects (Van Klaveren, 2001), we can add some outcomes and recommendations.

- Failure factors in projects pointed to weak project management, including a lack of goals, planning, feedbacks and of easily accessible documentation: unions still lack any 'collective memory'.
- During most projects the distance grew between a first echelon of paid officials, eager to develop competencies such as creativity, the ability to improvise, early awareness of changes needed and a second, more bureaucracy-oriented echelon.
- Trade unionists should try to bring their project experiences, especially of mobilising and building-up organisational power at shop floor level, into collective bargaining practice.

Company and workplace levels

The Dutch union movement still feels many disadvantages of being developed 'outside the factory gates'. From the early days of unionism, distributive strategies dominated and craftsmanship-based strategies remained on the margins. It was not until 1964 that the Metal Union NVV started building a system of company union groups. In the first 20 years of this 'company work', its activities concerning work organisation were often subordinated to considerations of national union (wage) policies (Buitelaar and Vreeman, 1985). The company union groups only matured in a few large companies, such as the Hoogovens steel works (now Corus); everywhere else they remained impotent. This has to do with the statutory position of the works councils, the depletion of the ranks of union activists, and the dominance of sub-sector collective bargaining. Most union bargaining delegations maintain rather weak bonds with works councillors and union groups. Moreover, potential shop floor conflicts tend to be 'depoliticised' as they are mostly transferred to human resource management (HRM) staff, if necessary negotiating with paid union officials (Hooiveld *et al.*, 2002a).

In the 1980s, the Netherlands witnessed a public debate concerning the quality of work. Studies pointed to the increasing gap between job levels and skill levels of the labour force. This 'qualitative gap' was widely seen as a major argument for the introduction of new forms of work organisation. The Dutch variant of the Modern Socio-Technical Approach (MST), based on the seminal work of De Sitter, had the potential to become an important vehicle here. MST was developed in interaction with the (re)design of work and organisation in Dutch manufacturing firms. De Sitter blamed the unions for not entering this new dance floor. He was partly correct. For example, the chairman of the Industrial Union FNV characterised efforts towards a better quality of work as 'sticking plasters on a wooden leg'. He and other union leaders warned about compromising and dissuaded his members from involvement in organisational change. Of course, individual union leaderships had to consider the rather sad state of their company representation, but they did not even try to shift the frontiers of control. In the 1980s, the company union groups mainly influenced health and safety conditions. In their own perception, these groups had to execute the boxing aspects of their work quite carefully, as they had no legal status and lacked any legal protection. A supportive context developed for the works councils, but not for the union groups. In 1985, a bill settling their status was withdrawn from parliament and 'put on ice' – where it has stayed until now. De Sitter and his MST adherents underestimated this weak point of the Dutch unions (Van Klaveren and Bouwman, 1993).

The case of Dutch Railways, described briefly in Exhibit 6.2, is interesting as the parties involved did *not* go tiptoe through the tulips. On the contrary, they met great difficulties in returning to the dance floor and seemed to deny the achievements of Dutch consultation machinery. The case is an illustration of the limitations of the Dutch labour relations in situations where employees feel threatened by developments like privatisation, distrust tends to dominate and communication patterns are poorly developed.

From 1985 on, the FNV confederation and its unions left their defensive boxing positions. A main trigger to dance was the development of demands for the social use of new technology. Six FNV unions managed to use government funds for sector technology training programmes combined with company pilots. These programmes and pilots stimulated union work at the company level. In 25–30 cases, joint efforts of paid officials, union activists and works councillors grew into long-term workers' projects: efforts to

---

Exhibit 6.2   Dutch Railways: from dancing to boxing – and back

Between 1990 and 2002 a process of privatisation of the Dutch railway system took place. Dutch Railways (NS) developed into an autonomous company, still running most of the lines. Influenced by this process as well as by new, more antagonistic management strategies the relations between management and employees (unions and works council), formerly dominated by dancing, gradually developed into distrust. In the second half of the 1990s, a series of conflicts escalated around the so-called 'trip-around-the-church', a management plan to restructure shifts and logistic personnel planning. Many NS employees saw this plan as another attack on their autonomy, at the same time preparing parts of the railway network for outsourcing. In 2001 the works council and an employees' consultant succeeded in developing an alternative planning system, which was accepted by the employees and by newly appointed and more partnership-oriented managers. Since then, new combinations of boxing and dancing seem to be developing, although mutual trust still is very fragile. How to realise effective new combinations of boxing and dancing strategies in a period of rapid change – that's the key question here.

influence the design of technology and organisation. In 1990 the FNV confederation commissioned evaluation research. The ten projects selected proved to have been successful in at least one out of three fields: better quality of work, better union and/or works council positions in company decision-making, and better relationships with the rank and file. Two projects showed successes in all three fields, four in two fields (Van Klaveren, 1991). These successes are remarkable, not least because the intentions of the union confederations to negotiate technological change did not materialise well: only a few technology agreements were as substantive and mandatory as the unions wanted.

Some of the technology projects are very interesting from a labour relations perspective, notably those in the Rotterdam port. In a context until then characterised by elaborate boxing practices and the country's highest strike incidence, officers of the Transport Union FNV and the works councils of the four main stevedoring companies created dance floors. The Transport Union leadership transferred responsibilities from paid officers to works councils, judging the latter to be better qualified and equipped with legal rights. Indeed, the rights of works councils to be trained, to form special committees, to meet during working hours and to hire experts proved to be decisive in getting projects off the ground. In their further development, learning to express 'social design claims' and finding sustainable coalitions became crucial (Van Klaveren, 1991; Van Klaveren and Bouwman, 1993).

Nevertheless, the legal rights attributed to the Dutch works councils did not lead to their broad and lasting involvement in the design of work organisation and technology. Many councils got stuck in procedural approaches (Levie and Sandberg, 1991). Based on two FNV surveys we had to conclude that the councils' perceived influence on technological change was even smaller in 1992 than four years earlier, in 1988 (Tijdens and Van Klaveren, 1997). A large majority of works councils kept on relying on management initiatives on work organisation. For example, in 1995–96, activities of 41 councils in this field received press coverage. Thirty-two of them were confronted with major reorganisations. Only ten councils mentioned their own initiatives, mostly in the form of projects. Moreover, this minority of ten faced major difficulties in acquiring lasting influence. An inventory of their main problems showed that

- change processes were often frustrated by middle management
- relationships with the rank and file worsened as relations with management developed and entered into strategic areas
- border conflicts with union officers occurred more frequently as projects developed.

Some works council projects grew into bipartite management – works council projects. In those cases, partnerships of top management, works councils and employees' consultants were useful in breaking through the conservative resistance of middle management. These development projects often had a high dancing content. Yet, these partnerships at company level remained few in numbers. It is symptomatic that rather fragile coalitions, like those at Unitcentre (Rotterdam stevedoring, 1989–91) and Interpay (bank clearing, 1996–97), received nationwide attention (Van Klaveren *et al.*, 1997). Obviously a corporatist setting at national level, and some top-level dancing experiences do not guarantee successful partnerships at company level – they hardly even stimulate such partnering. Maybe this has to do with the lack of stimuli for the unions to care about their company organisation implied in the Dutch collective bargaining system: see our final paragraph. In general partnership projects at sectoral and regional levels proved to be more successful and durable. The latter had the advantage of being developed in or close to existing networks, and were also more directly stimulated by the national accords agreed upon since 1982.

Trade union innovation and collective bargaining

As we have already suggested, most union projects have developed rather independently from collective bargaining practice. As collective bargaining remains the core business of the Dutch union movement, we have to explore the relationship between this business and the new union activities evolving since 1985. Although union density declined dramatically in the Netherlands, bargaining coverage remained unabatedly high. In 1980, 82% of all private sector employees were covered by collective agreements. Although not completely comparable, official figures state that in 2001 84% of all Dutch wage earners were covered by such agreements (Rojer, 2002). This coverage was 90% or more in manufacturing industry, building, retail, transport and communication, and health care. However, the coverage was 49% in commercial services (including ICT) and 60% in other services (Minister van SZW, 2002). The latter two sectors contain most sub-sectors in which FNV started up projects.

The gap between 25% union density and 84% bargaining coverage is large, and in the EU only exceeded by France. Although union leadership points to the latent support for the union movement that about 80% of the Dutch wage earners express in surveys, it cannot be denied that the 1937 Law on Mandatory Extension (ME), still in force, has been the main instrument here. This law states that if a collective agreement covers a substantial share of an industry's employees, the Minister of Social Affairs can extend the agreement to the entire industry. This is even automatic if the share is 60% or more. The ME practice gave rise to two kinds of debates.

First, mainstream politicians have often criticised ME, which is supposed to raise the general wage level, as being rigid and frustrating the decentralisation of collective bargaining. This too has been the position of leaders of the liberal party (which in the Netherlands is right-wing), and the populist politician Pim Fortuyn shortly before he was assassinated in May 2002. Thorough analyses, however, demonstrate that ME has had no or very small upward wage effects (Freeman *et al.*, 1996; Rojer, 2002). Freeman *et al.* (1996: 33) explain that ME:

> helps to keep together the federation of unions. A similar argument applies to employer federations. Employers gain from the system by the fact that unions do not care too much about having a strong organisation within the firm, so that distributional conflicts are resolved outside the firm. The essential characteristic of the system is the balancing out that the organisations of workers and employers have to perform.

It is hard to imagine ME operating without a national dance floor: the system puts considerable pressure on unions and employers to control and co-ordinate negotiations centrally, even including joint decisions about bargaining priorities.

Second, there is the latent debate about the representativeness of the peak organisations. Certainly, ME provides employers with an incentive to join their associations, as around 80% of Dutch employers do nowadays. Moreover, it is understandable that the Dutch employers' associations are more cautious than their political allies in criticising ME. In times of low unemployment the unions may feel provoked to leave the dance floor and start boxing for higher wages. Until now this has hardly happened. Even in the 1998–2001 period, with tight labour markets, the initial wage rises were lower than the ceilings in wage claims set by the FNV confederation. Internal wage coordination in the FNV confederation has proved to be effective, even more so than in the early 1990s (Rojer, 2002). On the other hand, a major problem on the union side is that ME takes away incentives for employees to join them (Visser, 2000). Although majorities among Dutch employees have always been 'free riders', the decline of union membership has brought the union movement closer to the danger zone. Maybe a 20% union density marks this critical zone.

The Dutch collective bargaining building is remarkably stable. In the last three decades, the number of company agreements has expanded by 85% (450 in 1975, 836 in 2002), but their coverage has grown only slightly, from 15 to 20% of all wage earners under collective agreements. The number of sub-sector collective agreements grew slowly, from 180 in 1975 to 231 in 2003. The splitting up into company agreements has been limited to small sub-sector agreements, with one major exception, the creation of company agreements in the banking sector. Until now, empowerment at lower levels has been orchestrated and controlled from the national level (Tros, 2001; Hooiveld *et al.*, 2002b; Ministerie van SZW, 2003). Indeed, as comparative studies indicated earlier (Ferner and Hyman, 1998), the Netherlands is one of the few EU member states not characterised by decentralisation of the bargaining system.

The content of collective bargaining has broadened and differentiated, hand in hand with the enlargement of dancing opportunities, especially at sub-sector level and in large companies. While in the 1980s national co-ordination concerned content with quantitative targets (percentage of wage moderation in exchange for a certain number of 'extra' jobs), since the early 1990s co-ordination has concentrated on processes and, in a multiple choice model, various other issues (Van der Meer *et al.*, 1999; Van der Meer *et al.*, 2003). We do not agree with the latter authors' suggestion that nearly all innovations in Dutch labour relations were realised under pressure from the government using either the carrot or the stick. STAR is continuing to try to influence the negotiation agenda by recommending issues for collective bargaining, such as training and employability (1996, 1998) reconciling work and family life (1997), and possibilities for individual choices within wage limits (à la carte agreements, 1999). Within three years, these issues were taken up in over 50% of the negotiation proposals from single unions and in about 20% of the collective agreements. Moreover, the confederations advise their affiliated unions annually to try to include specific themes, not agreed upon in STAR, in collective agreements. An example is 'less work pressure', advised by the FNV in 1999. Thus, quite often both the unions themselves and the unions in conjunction with the employers have felt the need to take up new initiatives. This definitely held for fields where the government played a quite passive role for years, the most notorious example being childcare.

The new centre-right government coalition appearing in 2003 has announced huge cuts in social insurance for the 2003–07 period, at the same time ignoring SER and STAR as the national dance floors. It is already clear that the union movement feels compelled to concentrate on boxing, mainly using sub-sector bargaining. Matters are complicated by plans of the new administration to forbid unions to 'repair' social insurance and other state cutbacks by collective agreements. Contract liberty is at stake here, and the related passing on of costs has already mobilised the employers' federations against the administration too. This situation will put the brakes on further decentralisation in collective bargaining.

In any event, decentralisation *within* collective agreements has also been limited until now. Between 2001 and 2003, the share of agreements with decentralised, layered structures remained at 2% (Tijdens and Van Klaveren, 2003). The most innovative developments seem to have taken place in collective bargaining *processes*. In some large companies, elements of mutual trust and dancing have been strengthened in early stages of bargaining preparation. These elements prepared the ground for innovative arrangements (cf. the Akzo Nobel case: Miltenburg and Veerman, 2000; and the Unilever case: Suijkens and Miltenburg, 2000). Another innovation is the ploughing back

Exhibit 6.3 The FNV Career Service Project

In 1998, the FNV confederation and its largest affiliate, FNV Bondgenoten (485 000 members), started experimental training in career development for women and low-skilled members – and non-members. A broad debate about employability was already going on in the Netherlands. The pilot was a success. A survey identified a large potential market. Many respondents did not immediately consider the union to be a serious career consultant, but after being informed what such union services might be they were in favour of this union offer. Nowadays, a regular union career service is up and running, for which purpose FNV Bondgenoten and the second largest FNV union, Abvakabo FNV (civil servants, 325 000 members), co-operate in 'FNV Loopbaanadvies' (FNV Career Consultancy). This service offers individual consultation; workshops on special themes; individual assessment, and training schemes. Forty paid union officials are responsible for the regional organisation, and 130 union members are acting as consultants or trainers. They have been trained on the union's behalf and receive annual re-training. Ninety of them are relatively high-skilled 'new' union activists.

Source: FNV Bondgenoten Internal Consultancy Report.

of experiences from career development consultancy into union policies on employability (see Exhibit 6.3 and case study in this volume).

However, such innovations are exceptional. It is widely recognised that projects on individual servicing and at sub-sector and regional levels show considerable learning effects, especially in testing new combinations of boxing and dancing. Yet, such experiences are hardly ploughed back into collective bargaining. In bargaining practice, policy development can still be traced, but developing and using instruments for empowering individual members or small groups of members is scarce. This may be connected with the fading away of union leadership training. Union training institutes concentrate on the market of works council training, which is secured by statutory levies on companies' wage sums. Analyses and instruments are lacking for developing union training expertise. The experiences of officials and activists involved in collective bargaining, cherishing their boxing attitudes, are hardly confronted by those of their colleagues involved in projects and individual servicing, who are busy developing dancing practices (Van Klaveren, 2001).

Yet, it is hard to accept this rather sad state of affairs in view of the risk that the Dutch union movement will end up with a minimum level of representativeness and credibility. It is worth exploring further the suggestion that the Dutch unions should concentrate on those collective arrangements and individual services (information about work, incomes, careers) that are meant to empower members and that can be linked closely with each other.

Effective combinations of these activities may create unique positions for the trade unions versus competitors like insurance companies, lawyers and HRM departments (cf. Hooiveld *et al.*, 2002b).

Summary and lessons for the unions

In summarising this chapter, we can also draw some lessons:

- Dutch labour relations have strong consensual tendencies, characterised as they are by bargaining between trade unions and employers' organisations with a high dancing content.
- Since 1982, a number of national accords have stimulated partnerships at sector and regional levels and have broadened the bargaining agenda to include employability, career structuring, working time schedules, child care and the like.
- Union density fell heavily during in the early 1980s and is still declining; the gap with the unabatedly high bargaining coverage is mainly explained by the ME of sub-sector agreements and the related pressure on the union and employer federations to co-ordinate negotiations and achieve results.
- The Dutch unions had difficulties entering the company level dance floors and making use of socio-technical and other movements for organisational change as they still encountered the disadvantages of their development 'outside the factory gates'; moreover, contrary to the works councils, the company union groups did not gain any legal status.
- Since the mid-1980s, demands for the social use of new technologies and a better quality of work formed the basis for a new strategic unionism, although clever use of works council rights often turned out to be a decisive factor.
- Since the early 1990s, the FNV confederation in particular undertook a number of sub-sector and regional projects, aiming at attracting and empowering members as well as creating a social infrastructure.
- Until now the many lessons from the new technology/quality of work projects, from the regional/sub-sector projects and from the individual servicing/empowerment projects have hardly been used in collective bargaining, the strategic core of Dutch unionism: within the unions a lot is still to be learned and reorganised to better achieve this.

References

Buitelaar, W. and Vreeman, R. (1985) *Vakbondswerk en kwaliteit van de arbeid. Voorbeelden van werknemersonderzoek in de Nederlandse industrie*. Nijmegen: SUN.

De Beer, P. (2002) 'De inhaalslag van Nederland. Sociaal-economische prestaties in Europees perspectief', *Tijdschrift voor Arbeidsvraagstukken* 18: 381–99.

De Rooy, P. (2001) *Republiek van rivaliteiten. Nederland sinds 1813*. Amsterdam: Mets en Schilt.

EC (2002) Eurostat.

European Commission (EC, 2003) *Employment in Europe 2003. Recent Trends and Prospects*. Luxembourg: Official Publication Office EC.

Ferner, A, and Hyman, R. (eds) (1998) *Changing Industrial Relations in Europe*. Oxford: Blackwell.

Förster, M. F. and Pellizzari, M. (2000) *Trends and Driving Factors in Income Distribution and Poverty in the OECD Area*. Paris: OECD.

Freeman, R., Hartog, J. and Teulings, C. (1996) *Pulling the Plug. An Analysis of the Role of Mandatory Extension in the Dutch System of Labour Relations*. The Hague: OSA.

Hemerijck, A. and Visser, J. (2002) 'Het "Nederlandse mirakel" revisited', *Tijdschrift voor Arbeidsvraagstukken*, 18: 291–305.

Hooiveld, J., Sprenger, W. and Van Rij, C. (2002a) 'Twintig jaar na FNV 2000 (1)', *Zeggenschap*, 13 (3): 34–40.

Hooiveld, J., Sprenger, W. and Van Rij, C. (2002b) 'Twintig jaar na FNV 2000 (2). Vakbondswerk anno 2010', *Zeggenschap* 13 (4): 32–6.

Leenders, P. (2002) 'Economendebat: de loonmatiging voorbij?', in Noordermeer, P. (ed.) *CAO-Jaarboek 2002/2003. Onderhandelen bij krimpende wind*. Amsterdam: FNV.

Levie, H. and Sandberg, Å. (1991) 'Trade Unions and Workplace Technical Change in Europe', *Economic and Industrial Development*, 12: 231–58.

Miltenburg, J. and Veerman, A.-C. (2000) 'Een experiment met gevolgen bij Akzo Nobel', in Van der Meer, M. and Smit, E. (eds) *Innovatie of imitatie? CAO-vernieuwing op ondernemingsniveau*. The Hague: Elsevier.

Minister van Sociale Zaken en Werkgelegenheid (SZW, 2002) *Brief aan de Voorzitter van de Eerste Kamer der Staten-Generaal*, 222a, nr. 9c, July 8.

Ministerie van Sociale Zaken en Werkgelegenheid (SZW, 2003) *Voorjaarsrapportage CAO-afspraken 2003*. The Hague: SZW.

NRC-Handelsblad (2002) 'Vakbonden nog onmisbaar' August 6.

Organisation for Economic Co-operation and Development (OECD, 2001) *OECD Employment Outlook. Employment*. Paris: OECD.

Porter, M. E. (2002) *Innovation Lecture 2001*. The Hague: Ministry of Economic Affairs.

Rojer, M. F. P. (2002) *De betekenis van de CAO en het algemeen verbindend verklaren van CAO's*. The Hague: Ministerie van Sociale Zaken en Werkgelegenheid (Ministry of Social Affairs and Employment).

Suijkens, M. and Miltenburg, J. (2002) 'De ontwikkeling van een decentrale CAO bij Unilever', in Van der Meer, M. and Smit, E. (eds) Innovatie of imitatie? CAO-vernieuwing op ondernemingsniveau. The Hague: Elsevier.

The Economist (2002) 'Modelmakers. A Survey of the Netherlands' May 4.

Tijdens, K. and Van Klaveren, M. (1997) 'Statutory Regulation and Workers' Competence. The Influence of Dutch Works Councils on the Introduction of New Technology', *Economic and Industrial Democracy* 18: 457–88.

Tijdens, K. G. (2002) 'Arbeidsduurverkorting en het Akkoord van Wassenaar', *Tijdschrift voor Arbeidsvraagstukken* 18: 309–18.

Tijdens, K. and Van Klaveren, M. (2003) *Een onderzoek naar CAO-afspraken op basis van de FNV CAO-databank en de AWVN-database*. Amsterdam: AIAS.

Tros, F. (2001) 'Arbeidsverhoudingen:deventralisatie,deconcentratie en empowerment', *Tijdschrift voor Arbeidsvraagstukken* 17: 304–18.

Van Bottenburg, M. (1995) *Aan den Arbeid! In de wandelgangen van de Stichting van de arbeid 1945–1995*. Amsterdam: Bert Bakker.

Van der Meer, M., Benedictus, H. and Visser, J. (1999) 'De cao: van inhoudelijke naar procedurele coördinatie', *Zeggenschap* 10 (4): 34–7.

Van der Meer, M., Van Liempt, A., Tijdens, K., Van Velzen, M. and Visser, J. (2002) *The Trade-Off between Competitiveness and Employment in Collective Bargaining: The National Consultation Process and Four Cases of Company Bargaining in the Netherlands*. Geneva: ILO.

Van der Meer, M., Visser, J., Wilthagen, T. and Van der Heijden, P. F. (2003) *Weg van het overleg? Twintig jaar na Wassenaar: naar nieuwe verhoudingen in het Nederlandse model*. Amsterdam: Amsterdam University Press.

Van het Kaar, R. H. and Looise, J.C. (1999) *De volwassen OR. Groei en grenzen van de Nederlandse ondernemingsraad*. Alphen aan den Rijn: Samsom.

Van Klaveren, M. (1991) *Scoren op speerpunten. Vakbondservaring met technologische vernieuwing*. Amsterdam: FNV.

Van Klaveren, M. (2001) *De FNV en de regionale overlegeconomie. Rapport voor de FNV*. Eindhoven: STZ.

Van Klaveren, M. and Bouwman, T. (1993) *New Technology, Employment and Working Conditions at the Port of Rotterdam*, presentation International Transport Workers Federation (ITF) World Technology Conference. Hamburg: May 3.

Van Klaveren, M. and Tijdens, K. (2003) 'Substitution or Segregation? The Impact of Changes in Employment, Production and Product on Gender Composition in Dutch Manufacturing 1899–1999', *Economic and Industrial Democracy* 24: 595–629.

Van Klaveren, M., Van de Camp, A. and Veersma, U. (1997) *The Dutch Comment on the Green Paper of the European Commission: Partnership for a New Organisation of Work*. Eindhoven/Tilburg: STZ / Tilburg University.

Van Zanden, J. L. (2000) 'Post War European Economic Development as an Out of Equilibrium Growth Path. The Case of the Netherlands', *De Economist* 148: 539–55.

Visser, J. (1995) 'The Netherlands: From Paternalism to Representation', in Rogers, J. and Streeck, W. (eds) *Works Councils: Consultations, Representations, and Cooperation in Industrial Relations*. Chicago: University of Chicago Press.

Visser, J. (2000) 'The Netherlands', in Ebbinghaus, B. and Visser, J. (eds) *The Societies of Europe. Trade Unions in Western Europe since 1945*. New York/London etc.: Grove/MacMillan.

Visser, J. (2002) 'The First Part-Time Economy in the World: a Model to be Followed?', *Journal of Social European Policy* 12 (1): 23–42.

Visser, J. and Hemerijck, A. (1997) *'A Dutch Miracle'. Job Growth, Welfare Reform and Corporatism in the Netherlands*. Amsterdam: Amsterdam University Press.

7
Where now for the German Tango Partners?

Martin Kuhlmann

Introduction

German unions in general and even the present system of industrial relations and its institutional regulations are under heavy pressure. For decades, the dual system of industrial relations has been self-sustaining with, on the one hand, strong sector based unions focused on traditional bargaining and industrial corporatism and, on the other hand, independent company or establishment based works councils representing the whole workforce, regulating management actions and co-operating on a wide range of work-related and social issues. This system has been universally regarded as more or less stable. Most elements of the institutional infrastructure were legally based. The system was rooted in a long tradition of joint regulation and its outcomes were highly valued respectively by employers (for competitiveness and industrial peace) and by employees (for improvements in wages, working time and social security). Even today, the level of institutional stability is still high, although unions are currently confronted with a number of significant changes.

Long lasting unemployment has gradually eroded the bargaining power of unions and has triggered a growing willingness to deregulate at least some elements of labour market protection, even by the current Social Democratic government. Employers who have made extensive use of the instrument of concession bargaining on the micro-level since the 1990s are now putting extra pressure on their bargaining partner on all kinds of issues, including the basic relations at sectoral and national level which cover wages and working times. This is coming through pressure for more opening clauses in collective agreements.

These current discussions about ongoing changes in industrial relations need to be understood in the context of other union problems discussed since the 1980s. There have been difficulties in recruiting young members and women, white-collar and professional workers; in coping with the industrial and economic changes in the wake of globalisation and the integration of East Europe; difficulties because of the break up of traditional stakeholder structures of governance in Germany along the lines of a shareholder economy and, last not least, difficulties because of the still problematic industrial structure in Eastern Germany, where unions are weak, and where in 2003 IG Metall, still the strongest union, for the first time in decades lost a major strike (on bringing working times down to the level in West Germany). This failure in particular has fuelled strong anti-union voices.

Although more and more actors on the political scene are advocating far-reaching legal initiatives to restrict union power, professional observers still stress the stability and flexibility of the present system. But, for the first time in the life of this system, even some academic researchers are no longer ruling out the possibility of a major erosion or transformation of at least some elements of the dual system (Bispinck, 2003; Schroeder and Weinert, 2003; Streeck and Rehder, 2003). They reason that the complex mix of old and new problems might be too great to sustain union power in a changing, increasingly dual economy characterised by long-lasting high unemployment. They argue that slow economic growth and increasing competitive pressures on the high-wage German labour market are adding further to the weakening of collective bargaining power. Even with the formal structures remaining in place, major changes of power relations between employers, unions and works councils could lead to the system working in quite a different manner.

Rather than aiming to give an overview of the situation in German industrial relations and the problems German unions are facing in sustaining union influence, this chapter focuses on the interrelationship of conflict and co-operation in the German system, using the metaphor of boxing and dancing.[1] The chapter sets out the background for understanding a case study of how IG Metall tried to sustain and extend union influence on the structures and organisation of work. This is included in the appendix to this book. From a comparative perspective the German experience of combined boxing and dancing is important, because this is how German unions worked when they tried to sustain and extend union influence on how work is structured over a period of years. We therefore look at how boxing and dancing were organised institutionally, assess what German unions achieved by combining both strategies, and look at some of the lessons they learned in sustaining and developing this specific combination of boxing and dancing.

The main argument will be that boxing and dancing is not only a question of strategic choice in the sense of policy or type of action but that the strategic choice for a combined approach has to be rooted in specific institutions. From this perspective, the German system of giving legal rights to both unions and works councils had important consequences for the specific interaction between works councils and unions. Although this structure is under heavy pressure nowadays, the dual structure of the German system of industrial relations has, to date, been working to make sure that both boxing and dancing continue to take place. Further, while there may be significant changes in the institutional framework in the future, as it looks now, the dual system will remain in place.

Contextual overview – boxing and dancing in the German system of industrial relations

Researchers in Germany stress that German industrial relations are characterised both by conflict – for example, the strike actions around working times during the 1980s and against reductions in sick leave compensation in 1996 – and by a long tradition of co-operation. Key examples here have concerned the management of the vocational training system and the productivity processes which resulted from major union policies. A good example of the interrelatedness of boxing and dancing is that German unions go for a strike if necessary, but at the same time are willing to permit overtime afterwards to produce output that has been lost because of the strike. A widely known German source book on industrial relations (Müller-Jentsch, 1999) is called 'Konfliktpartnerschaft' (partnering conflict). Other authors use similar constructions such as 'antagonistic co-operation'or 'co-operative conflict resolution' (Weltz, 1977).

Institutional background

The institutional backbone of the industrial relations system in Germany is its dual structure of unions at the sectoral level and works councils on the plant, establishment and company levels. This structure has its roots in the Weimar Republic of the 1920s, but the legal framework and the complex web of institutions and policies came into place after the Second World War and have been continuously refined and elaborated by the law on co-determination (1976) and several amendments of the law on collective agreement ('Tarifvertragsgesetz') and by the works constitution act ('Betriebsverfassungsgesetz'). This law defines the role of the works council and has also been amended several times (especially 1972 and 2001) to keep it in touch with changes in industrial and company structures. These changes have strengthened the legal position of the works councils and provided more resources for their work. It is noteworthy that since the 1970s there has been a continuous dynamic of professionalisation of the role and work of work councils (Kotthoff, 1994; Schmidt and Trinczek, 1999; Wassermann, 2002).

After more than a decade of mergers the union structure has reached a somewhat consolidated structure with three big unions left (IG Metall, IG BCE and ver.di) and a number of smaller unions focused on specific sectors such as the IG BAU (construction work, agriculture, environment), NGG (food, catering), GEW (education, science), Transnet (railways), GdP (police). In the private and the industrial sector IG Metall is still the biggest union with 2.65 million members in 2002, followed by IG BCE (Mining, Chemical, Energy) with about 850 000 members (2002). These unions mark, at the same time, the two poles in the political discussion inside the DGB-Confederation. IG Metall is more conflict-oriented and has, for example, a long history of collective agreements reached by strikes as ultima ratio. In IG BCE there is virtually no strike experience, collective bargaining is much more centralised and is based on a social partnership approach of industrial relations. In the service sector (including both public and private services, white- and blue-collar employees as well as areas like printing and the media), ver.di is nowadays the biggest union with 2.75 million members (2002). It was founded quite recently as a merger between four unions from the DGB-confederation (ÖTV, public services, transportation; DPG, postal employees; HBV, retail, banking, insurance; IG Medien, printing, media), and the white-collar organisation DAG (white collar employees from different sectors). Politically, ver.di leans more towards IG Metall and at least some sections of the new union also have many experiences of strike action. The Big Three organise over 80% of DGB-union members. The DBB (Deutscher Beamten Bund) – outside the DGB – has 1.2 million members and is the head organisation of 39 professional organisations especially for public servants ('Beamte') and the Christian 'anti-DGB'-federation CGB (Christlicher Gewerkschaftsbund). The latter has about 300 000 members in more than 15 unions whose legal status as unions is heavily disputed and CGB-organisations were only recently able to sign a collective bargaining agreement in some cases in Eastern Germany.

The most important role of the unions in the German industrial relations system is their constitutionally backed right to strike and to sign legally binding collective agreements either with employer federations or, to a much lower extent, single employers ('Tarifautonomie'). Traditionally, collective bargaining takes place at the regional and sectoral levels ('Flächentarifvertrag')[2] and it includes wages, working times and holidays, pay systems, systems of workload regulation and different types of additional compensation such as overtime, shift work, work on Saturdays and Sundays, or strenuous work. In areas where legislation exists such as on working time and sick leave compensation, the logic of collective bargaining is to achieve standards higher than the minimums set by the law. However, the goals of collective bargaining became much broader during the 1970s as a reaction to work intensification and rationalisation, a process which accelerated during the 1980s and 1990s, with the unions putting more and more emphasis on so-called 'qualitative' collective agreements about employment, work and competence development ('qualitative Tarifpolitik') as a supplement to traditional wage and working times policy ('quantitative Tarifpolitik').

The works council as a second level looks different from a union, at least formally (Müller-Jentsch, 1995; 2002; Schmidt and Trinczek, 1999). The most important difference between unions and works councils is that the latter are not allowed to organise industrial action. Legally, their role is defined as trust-based co-operation with management in the best interests of the firm and its employees. Members of works councils are elected for four years by all employees (not only by those who are union members), so there is both a legal structure and a political necessity for them to work in the best interests of the employees as a whole. The historical starting point of the idea of a plant-based system of worker representation in the second half of the nineteenth century, that is, the concept of the constitutional firm ('konstitutionelle Fabrik', Frese, 1909) is still a good guide to the relationship between works councils and management.

The existence of works councils depends very much on number of employees. In very small firms (up to 50 employees) firms with works council are under 10% (year 2002), but the percentage rises very quickly from 51–100 employees (45%) over 101–199 employees (72%) and 200–500 employees (85%) to 95% in firms with more than 500 employees (Kohaut and Schnabel, 2001; Ellguth, 2003: 194). The last amendment of the Works Constitution Act made it easier for employees in small firms to elect a works council by simplifying its legal procedure. As with the German industrial relations system as a whole, the works councils are an example of institutionalised class compromise. Müller-Jentsch described it as 'a bastard born of two conflicting historical social movements: the worker councils of the pre - 1914 German Empire which were voluntarily created by employers, and the revolutionary councils of 1918/19' (Müller-Jentsch, 2002: 51). Here, boxing and dancing can be found in a nutshell.

The main focus of the works council is on concrete working conditions, a wide range of employee-related questions and the different areas of co-determination (on social and economic issues). The works council also has the right to control whether collective bargaining or legally fixed standards are met. Works councils have a very strong legal position in Germany. This arises not only from their far-reaching information and consultation rights, but also from the strong co-determination rights in important areas like the application of working time and pay systems. The personal position of a member of the works council is protected and strong. Elected by all employees for a period of four years, it is almost impossible for a works councillor to be forced to resign and, in any case, they have far-reaching employment security. Depending on the number of employees, there are full-time jobs for at least some members of the works council, while the works council as a body has extensive rights to its own technical infrastructure, including the right to hire consultants.

Throughout history there have always been attempts (usually unsuccessful) to use works councils as counter-organisations to union influence, but although works councils are legally independent from unions, there is normally a strong connection between them and unions. Even in the matter of political and ideological orientations, there is no evidence that there are any fundamental differences between the attitudes of works councils and the unions. In industrial relations research, it is commonly understood that unions and works councils are complementary to each other and mutually dependent (Thelen, 1991; Müller-Jentsch, 1995; Keller, 1999; Schmidt and Trinczek; 1999). Most members of works councils are, in fact, also union members. Normally works councils are dominated by union members from the DGB confederation, and this becomes more so in larger companies with more than a few hundred employees.[3]

At the same time, works council members are normally the most active and most influential people amongst union members. The heads of large works councils play a decisive role in local, regional and national union committees, and normal full-time careers as union officials very often start with works council membership. The daily work of unions and works councils strengthens this relation of mutual dependence even further. This works two ways. On the one hand, works councils attract and recruit union members since unions in the German system have no institutionalised position inside companies. This is facilitated because ordinary workers/rank and file members see no distinction between the works council and the union. On the other hand, works councils are heavily dependent on the information services, consulting skills and training infrastructures that are provided by unions.

Shop stewards ('gewerkschaftliche Vertrauensleute'), which means elected union representatives, often exist only in large firms. Through the shop steward system, unions have direct access to the workplace, but even the shop stewards rely heavily on the works council. In practice, the shop steward system is often run by the works council. It exists only when there is a strong, union-oriented works council. Mostly, the shops stewards are the information and communication substructure of the works council, and the works council recruits its candidates from experienced and popular shop stewards. Where shop stewards are in place, this position is the first step of a union career, member of the works council the second step, while becoming a union official or head of a big works council may be the third step.

A high level of integration and coordinated policy-making is very evident between unions and works councils in large companies. This is especially true for the large joint-stock companies ('AGs') where union officials and members of the works council occupy seats on the employee side in the supervisory boards ('Aufsichtsrat'). Here, they work closely together in controlling and influencing management decisions.

Boxing and dancing in Germany

Because of the dual structure of German industrial relations, there are strong actors representing employees both at the sectoral level (unions) and the local level (works council) with a clear division of labour between them. But, to make the picture more complete, it is important to note that there are at least three levels of regulation (see Table 7.1). Although wages, compensation and working times are at the centre of collective bargaining with a high level of constitutionally guaranteed autonomy for the employers and the unions ('Tarifautonomie'), there is some legal regulation of work-related issues in several areas (for example, working time, occupational health, statutory notice). Often, collective bargaining at the sectoral level builds upon these minimum standards. The collective agreements of the IG Metall in all West German regions include, for example, 35 hours working time instead of 48 hours by law, 30 days holiday instead of 20, a three-month period of notice instead of four weeks and a long list of supplementary compensations and benefits.

At the sectoral and mostly regional level, the employers and the unions are free to reach legally enforceable agreements on all kinds of issues from wages and wage systems to working time, training and other working conditions. The works council at the plant or company level too has the right to sign agreements. This is frequently done and has become one of the major tasks of works councils in large companies, where the same pattern of additional or supplementary agreements is found.

The capacity to make plant agreements ('Betriebsvereinbarungen') is controlled by a legal principle that these agreements signed by works councils are not allowed to violate the collective agreements signed by unions. From the point of view of the employees, those regulations apply which favour them best. The law states that agreements signed by a works council that fall below collective bargaining standards are illegal. This is one of many regulations that are under heavy attack nowadays from the employers and the Christian Democrat and Liberal parties. So-called opening clauses do exist already for a range of cases – like for instance a company near bankruptcy. In order to prevent a change in legislation giving more authority to the local level of single employers and works councils, the unions and the employers' federation have stated that they will start consultation to reach an agreement which makes local agreements easier to reach.

In practice, forms of co-operation and conflict exist on every level (see Table 7.1). The levels are integrated with each other, through the close links between works councils and unions, through practices of co-ordination at the sectoral and national level – both on the employer and on the union side – and because the government normally does not interfere with collective bargaining. Government's role is to formulate procedures and give legal rights to the actors. Even more important for the integration of the different levels are corporatist arrangements in areas like vocational training, labour market administration, social security and the tradition of co-operation in all kinds of associations ranging from occupational health to industrial engineering (Herrigel, 1996).

Table 7.1   Boxing and dancing in Germany: a classification

Level	Boxing	Dancing	Prospects
Global/ International	Few boxing rings, for example, European Works Councils, contested treatment of plant closures.Few rare/ cautious initiatives in transnational co-ordination of wage bargaining.	Main business of EWCs and GWCs on information disclosure and consultation. Weak forms of co-determination by works councils with global initiatives depending on strength of position in their home base. Initiatives like Global Compact or Social Charter at the company level. Some areas (e.g. construction work) with legislation on wages according to national/ sectoral wages ('Entsendegesetz').	Most unions seeking opportunities for greater influence internationally.
National	National agreements/ bargaining in some sectors (public white collar), some professions, on some issues. Unions have a strong position in several bi/tripartite institutions and other bodies (social insurance, labour market administration, vocational training systems).	Historical legacy of corporatism. Rare (mostly failing) examples of formalised tripartite co-operation ('Bündnis für Arbeit') due to strong emphasis on the autonomy of the social partners ('Tarifautonomie'). Unions and employers have a seat in several bi/ tripartite institutions and other bodies (social insurance, labour market, vocational training systems, research funding).	The national level is still important depending on the issue and the government. National Co-ordination between unions is still important on basic issues, but eroding on policy issues and collective bargaining.
Sectoral/ Regional	The normal level of collective bargaining. Ongoing erosion of sectoral bargaining ('Flächentarifvertrag') because of opening clauses and sub- standard agreements (co-ordinated and wild decentralisation).	Several bipartite institutions and nowadays agencies (pensions, training). Long tradition of co-operation and joint initiatives in several areas (training, labour market policy, industrial policy).	More boxing *and* more dancing depending on the issue. The future of the sectoral bargaining ('Flächentarifvertrag') is under discussion; different forms of decentralisation are becoming more and more important.

Table 7.1 (Continued)

Level	Boxing	Dancing	Prospects
Local/ Workplace	Collective agreements (boxing) at the company/plant level are becoming more and more important (wage systems, working times, employment pacts, re-organization).	Union representation on company boards ('Aufsichtsräte'). Strong tradition of co-coperation on various issues because of works councils. Active involvement in developmental issues (critical co-management) is becoming more and more important.	Boxing *and* dancing. Boxing (instead of controlling) as a new agenda for works councils because of decentralisation.

A short history of boxing and dancing

Historically, it makes sense to differentiate three approximate phases of boxing and dancing, building on Schroeder's work on periods in the German industrial relations system after the Second World War. The first period, ranging deep into the 1960s, was characterised as a 'founding period' that then led into a first phase of a 'golden age' ranging from the mid-1950s to the mid-1960s (Schroeder, 2000: 391). In these years, during which Germany was run by a conservative government, the whole system of industrial relations and the main institutional elements were built-up: the dual structure of unions and works councils,[4] the works constitution act which institutionalises the works council as the dominant actor and gives it a comparatively strong role, the legislation on collective bargaining, and co-determination rights, initially at least in the steel industry. The dominant actors in industrial relations were at the national level, where the unions criticised the government heavily because of its policy of economic restoration and restricting union influence. Throughout this period, there were several major strikes and lockouts on issues of wages, working time, holidays and different types of compensation, but at the same time the process of integration of the unions at the national level began, which then developed into corporatist structures.

Schroeder sets out the second phase of the golden age[5] as lasting from 1967 until 1977 which started in the heyday of corporatism and formed the basic institutions, policies and practices which still hold today. In this period the social democratic government extended the consultation and co-determination rights of unions and works councils and the process of giving unions (and employer federations) a major role in all kinds of public authorities. From the union perspective, the 1970s not only strengthened their legal position, but they were also able to reach further improvements in collective agreements extending into new issues like rest times, and the effects of rationalisation and technological change.

The period from the late 1970s until today can be characterised as a period of transition. The first phase of transition started with comparatively strong unions although unemployment figures went up quickly and union membership started to decline. When IG Metall went out on a major strike in 1984 for a further reduction of working times as an instrument against unemployment, this was done from a position of strength and in a climate of pure boxing. Although IG Metall succeeded in getting working time reduced further (other sectors gradually followed), the concrete results and procedural agreements opened, as an unintended effect, a new path in the development of German industrial relations (Promberger *et al.*, 1993; Herrmann *et al.*, 1999; Lehndorff, 2001; Promberger, 2002).

Accordingly, in the 1980s, a process of differentiation started, with decentralisation and flexibilisation in the field of bargaining and industrial relations. These trends accelerated during the 1990s, partly because not all sectors – and later, regions – were able to follow the forerunners, and partly because the implementation of the reduction in working times fostered a broad range of different solutions. Also important for the process of differentiation and decentralisation was the political change towards a conservative government that gradually started policies of deregulation. Although a new era was commencing, most commentators stressed the remarkable stability of the German system of industrial relations until the 1990s and its positive outcomes compared to other countries. Not least because of Germany's competitiveness, the late 1980s and early 1990s saw major attempts of presenting the country as a case of good practice in industrial development and industrial relations (Dertouzos, 1990; Thelen, 1991; Turner, 1991; Streeck, 1992).

A second phase in the period of transition started around 1993, shortly after reunification, when the boom was over and Germany fell into the deepest recession since the 1930s. Unemployment rose even further and remained more or less stagnant at a high level. Since then, the decline in union membership and in membership in employer groups accelerated and a wave of concession bargaining started at the company level (Bahnmüller and Bispinck, 1995; Schroeder, 1995). This then spread into collective bargaining at the regional and sectoral levels. On the political scene, policies of deregulation and the privatisation of public services became gradually more widespread and the legal regulation of employee rights such as protection against dismissal, working times restrictions and sick leave compensation were cut back. In an international comparative perspective it is important to note that although these changes went in the same direction as in the UK under Thatcher, they had a very different impact. The conservative party (Christian Democrats) during the Kohl-era was much more in line with Rhenish capitalism (Albert, 1993). Throughout the 1980s the debate about deregulation did not impact on the high level of compromise and co-operation between unions and employers.

Although Gerhardt Schroeder's Social Democratic government (since 1998) in the beginning dropped some conservative legislation and amended the works constitution act to strengthen the legal position of works councils (2001), in the face of opposition from the employers, the main deregulatory developments proceeded. Since the mid-1990s, most employer federations took a more and more critical position towards union influence. In the leading sector of the metal industry, the employer federations came under pressure especially from their members in small and medium firms who had become increasingly dissatisfied with the results of collective agreements and the whole system of sectoral/regional bargaining. Since the mid-1990s, several attempts to form corporatist tripartite pacts for employment failed because unions and employers could not reach agreements that went beyond the scope of a moderate wage policy.

Today, after several years of negative wage drift and a gradual cutting back of other achievements, a highly conflictual debate between unions, employers and the state is focusing on local employment pacts, opening clauses and a possible breakdown of sectoral/regional bargaining. The Christian Democrats have already stated that they are prepared to implement major legislative changes to restrict union influence. Overall, the present period in the development of industrial relations is loaded with debates and political conflicts, which partly could result in major changes of the present system of industrial relations and which have already led to processes of significant erosion in the scope of collective agreements. However, at the same time as IG Metall is in deep conflict with employers on the future of collective bargaining, both sides have nevertheless reached a number of major new agreements on issues like pay systems, further training and pensions (Huber and Hofmann, 2001). These agreements have even led to the formation of new jointly managed bodies. So in the end, even in a phase of strong conflict between labour and management, the German system still has a capacity for compromise.

Boxing and dancing today

Sometimes German industrial relations are perceived as if the division of labour between unions and works councils is aligned with different styles of employee representation. This view assumes that unions take on the boxing part dealing with collective bargaining on distributional issues, while works councils operate in a more co-operative way. This type of division of labour does exist in at least some firms. But there are other examples too. Empirical research on types of interaction between employers or management and works councils has shown that a broad range of patterns exists from complete integration or subordination over different types of co-operation, to permanent conflict (Kotthoff and Reindl, 1990; Kotthoff, 1994; Bosch *et al.*, 1999; Artus *et al.*, 2001). Of course, in the long run works councils generally have to preserve a co-operative relationship with management to gain real influence, but the picture of completely different orientations is misleading.

Most unions in the German industrial relations system, because of their role in collective bargaining and their still strong legal position, are prepared to go into conflict with the employers. Boxing is therefore a normal way of defending their members' interests. The picture of a division of labour along the line of boxing and dancing holds fairly well in the arena of collective bargaining on wages and working time ('quantitative Tarifpolitik'), although German unions from time to time have been quite co-operative by accepting moderate wage policies. So even in collective bargaining, where mutual gains are less common than, for example, in the field of vocational training, German unions are not exclusively boxers. We already mentioned that even the most conflict-experienced IG Metall has always been and still is involved in a number of dancing activities on different levels such as training, industrial policy and local initiatives especially on employment issues.

The large IG BCE (the mining, chemical and energy union) has been able to reach roughly the same results as IG Metall in collective agreements with a much more co-operative, social partnership approach (Kädtler and Hertle, 1997). Until the 1970s this union too had a more conflict-oriented approach. However, the positive results of collective agreements have to be seen against the background of much more favourable economic conditions in this industry and the much lower importance of labour costs. For the present debate about the future of collective bargaining, the situation in the chemical industry is important, because the much more centralised employer federation in this sector (compared to engineering) is on the side of those who defend the existing system against complete decentralisation and deregulation. All in all, German unions have a tradition of both boxing and dancing. Some are more frequent dancers, others have a stronghold in bargaining.

The picture of a complete division of labour between unions and works councils is also distorted, because, nowadays, works councils are much more engaged with conflicts around distributional issues than before. The wave of concession bargaining which started in the 1990s has forced more and more works councils into a situation where they have to combine conflict and co-operation, boxing and dancing, even more than they did during the golden age of the 1960s and 1970s. It has always been normal for German works councils to trade-off their legal rights to approve overtime and a positive attitude towards changes in working time regulations or wage systems for influence on operational or work-related issues, where the legal position of the works council has always been much weaker.

In the daily operation of works councils, boxing and dancing has always been interconnected: but nowadays both conflict *and* co-operation have become more important. This is caused both by the overall competitive pressure on German wages and labour standards, areas which are much more conflict-loaded, and by much more proactive and professional roles being played out by works councils. This in turn has followed from the legislation on co-determination that came into place during the 1970s and from the positive experiences with co-operation especially during the 1980s. Overall, works councils today are much more integrated into management decisions. Moreover, the normal working relationship between management and works councils includes both conflict and co-operation. Normally, a works council would not go into complete opposition against management because the members know that their position is much stronger if they have access to information and management's internal decision-making processes. Often the works council gains particular strength by taking into account that management is not homogenous (Hyman, 1993) and by forming coalitions with managers. The conventional wisdom among German managers is that it is almost impossible to make organisational changes *against* the works councils, but that you can manage almost everything if you do it *together with* the works council.

The example in our case study (see Appendix A13) of policies on work organisation aims to show, in more detail, how this flexible system works and the range of outcomes that can be reached through it. The field of work organisation is a good example of the fact that a two-way relationship really exists. During the 1970s, the issue of work organisation renewal was discussed and developed at the sectoral level, inside the unions. However, local initiatives and works councils' policies were fuelled only gradually. Today, the initiative often rests with the works councils (together with management) and influences union policies. There are other issues, where unions have taken up locally developed initiatives, too.

In general, unions have been able to gain from the various forms of dancing activities at the local level and from the combination of boxing and dancing. This gave them an active role in shaping work-related issues even at times when there were no major improvements at the sectoral and regional levels. Since membership, both in terms of numbers and loyalty, is a major issue for union renewal nowadays, the co-operation between works councils and unions and the institutionally backed possibility to mix and, sometimes, integrate defensive and proactive policies has strengthened the unions' role and reputation. One, still open, issue for unions is whether and how this dual approach and type of co-operation can be built up in new fields of employment and against the background of much higher levels of economic differentiation. Of growing importance and in the long run what may be decisive for the future of German unions will be whether the rapidly growing transnational expansion of big firms and labour markets and globalisation in general will erode the present institutions, forms and policies of employee representation or whether new collective actors and institutions like European Works Councils (EWCs) emerge which could be integrated with present policies (Hoffmann *et al.*, 1995, 1998).

Conclusion

Summing up the experiences from the German case, it is important to note that it would be misleading to pin boxing and dancing against each other. Historically there have been phases when either boxing or dancing was more in the forefront. However, the mixture of boxing and dancing varies between issues. The main lesson is that boxing and dancing can be blended and that unions favour strategic choices that integrate developmental and distributional issues. Boxing *and* dancing has a long tradition in Germany and is rooted in specific institutional structures of antagonistic co-operation. The German system is not some kind of middle point, halfway between co-operation and conflict. Instead, it is organised to stimulate both boxing *and* dancing. The institutions and the traditions of policy-making are able to facilitate both co-operation *and* conflict. The mode depends on the field or level of action, on whether mutual gains are a realistic perspective or not, and on the historical circumstances. The dual system based on highly unionised works councils is flexible in the sense that it is able to manage co-operation and conflict at the same time. It weaves a complex web of parallel but connected actors and scenes where both boxing and dancing takes place. Different levels and actors can be integrated in a mutually reinforcing way. Because of their legally strong position, German unions and works councils are relatively well placed to engage in dancing activities from a mutual gains perspective without blurring differences between management and employee representatives. The still strong position of German unions is very much under attack nowadays and there are serious problems with membership levels and the reach of collective agreements. Moreover, there is for the first time a conservative agenda against the present industrial relations system. Nevertheless, the basic structure of the German system, with its dual character and combination of conflict and co-operation, is likely to continue.

Notes

1. An overview of the present state of industrial relations in Germany can be found in Müller-Jentsch and Weitbrecht (2003) and Schroeder and Weßels (2003). A good discussion about the future of industrial relations in Germany is also in Wagner and Schild (2003) and two special issues of leading industrial relations journals: Industrielle Beziehungen 2/2003 and WSI-Mitteilungen 7/2003.
2. This holds true for the mainstream of collective bargaining, but in some sectors there are collective agreements on the national and company level as well (see Table 7.1).
3. There are no official statistics on the number and composition of works councils, but even a recent study of the employer-oriented IW which reports lower union membership of works council members than other studies, counts over 80% DGB-union membership in industry and around 60% overall. Overall 70% of the heads of the works councils come from a DGB-union.

4. The conservative government institutionalised works councils as a counterbalance to union influence. The unions were in the beginning strictly against works councils because of their independent status and tendency towards peaceful solutions. In the first period of industrial relations the unions were still sceptical about works councils. The active role of works councils in the unions, the close co-operation and mutual dependency between works councils and unions of today evolved only gradually especially during the 1970s and 1980s.

5. Golden Age here means two things. On the one hand this period was characterised by an increase in membership on both the union and the employer sides and by the ability of both sides to reach sectoral agreements at the national or regional level. On the other hand during these years those institutions were formed which are important even today. Of course this term also refers to the French concept of regulation (Marglin and Schor 1990; Boyer and Saillard 2002).

References

Albert, M. (1993) *Capitalism against Capitalism*. London: Whurr.

Artus, I., Liebold, R., Lohr, K. and Schmidt, E. (2001) *Betriebliches Interessenhandeln, Band 2. Zur politischen Kultur der Austauschbeziehungen zwischen Management und Betriebsrat in der ostdeutschen Industrie*. Opladen: Leske & Budrich.

Bahnmüller, R. and Bispinck, R. (1995) 'Vom Vorzeige- zum Auslaufmodell? Das deutsche Tarifsystem zwischen kollektiver Regulierung, betrieblicher Flexibilisierung und individuellen Interessen', in Bispinck, R. (ed.) *Tarifpolitik der Zukunft. Was wird aus dem Flächentarifvertrag?* Hamburg: VSA.

Bispinck, R. (2003) 'Das deutsche Tarifsystem in Zeiten der Krise – Streit um Flächentarif, Differenzierung und Mindeststandards', *WSI-Mitteilungen* 56(7): 395–404.

Bosch, A., Ellguth, P., Schmidt, R. and Trinczek, R. (1999) *Betriebliches Interessenhandeln, Band 1. Zur politischen Kultur der Austauschbeziehungen zwischen Management und Betriebsrat in der westdeutschen Industrie*. Opladen: Leske & Budrich.

Boyer, R. and Saillard, Y. (eds) (2002) *Regulation Theory. The State of the Art*. London: Routledge.

Dertouzos, M. and Solow, L. R. (1990) *Made in America. Regaining the Productive Edge*. New York: Harper Perennial.

Ellguth, P. (2003) 'Quantitative Reichweite der betrieblichen Mitbestimmung', *WSI-Mitteilungen* 56(3): 194–9.

Frese, H. (1909) *Die konstitutionelle Fabrik*. Jena: Fischer.

Herrigel, G. (1996) *Industrial Constructions. The Sources of German Industrial Power*. Cambridge: Cambridge University Press.

Herrmann, C., Promberger, M., Singer, S. and Trinczek, R. (1999) *Forcierte Arbeitszeitflexibilisierung*. Berlin: Ed. Sigma.

Hoffmann, R., Jacobi, O., Keller, B. and Weiss, M. (eds) (1995) *German Industrial Relations under the Impact of Structural Change, Unification and European Integration*. Düsseldorf: Hans-Böckler-Stiftung.

Hoffmann, R., Jacobi, O., Keller, B. and Weiss, M. (eds) (1998) *The German Model of Industrial Relations between Adaption and Erosion*. Düsseldorf: Hans-Böckler-Stiftung.

Huber, B. and Hofmann, J. (2001) 'Der Tarifvertrag zur Qualifizierung in der Metall- und Elektroindustrie Baden-Württembergs', *WSI-Mitteilungen* 54(7): 464–6.

Hyman, R. (1993) 'Strategie oder Struktur? Die widersprüchliche Handlungskonstellation des Managements der Arbeit', in Müller-Jentsch, W. (ed.) *Konfliktpartnerschaft*. München: Hampp.

Kädtler, J. and Hertle, H-H. (1997) *Sozialpartnerschaft und Industriepolitik. Strukturwandel im Organisations bereich der IG Chemie-Papier-Keramik.* Opladen: Westdeutscher Verlag.

Keller, B. (1999) *Einführung in die Arbeitspolitik.* München: Oldenbourg.

Kohaut, S. and Schnabel, C. (2001) *Tarifverträge – nein danke!? Einflussfaktoren der Tarifbindung west- und ostdeutscher Betriebe.* Erlangen-Nürnberg: Friedrich-Alexander-Universität.

Kotthoff, H. (1994) *Betriebsräte und Bürgerstatus. Wandel und Kontinuität betrieblicher Mitbestimmung.* München: Hampp.

Kotthoff, H. and Reindl, J. (1990) *Die soziale Welt kleiner Betriebe. Wirtschaften, Arbeiten und Leben im mittelständischen Industriebetrieb.* Göttingen: Otto Schwartz.

Lehndorff, S. (2001) *Weniger ist mehr. Arbeitszeitverkürzung als Gesellschaftspolitik.* Hamburg: VSA.

Marglin, S. and Schor, J. (eds) (1990) *The Golden Age of Capitalism. Reinterpreting the Postwar Experience.* Oxford: Clarendon Press.

Müller-Jentsch, W. (1995) 'Germany: From Collective Voice to Co-management', in Rogers, J. and Streeck, W. (eds) *Works Councils.* Chicago: University of Chicago Press.

Müller-Jentsch, W. (ed.) (1999) *Konfliktpartnerschaft. Akteure und Institutionen der industriellen Beziehungen.* München: Hampp.

Müller-Jentsch, W. (2002) 'Works Councils – a German story', *Die Mitbestimmung* 48(8): 50–5.

Müller-Jentsch, W. and Weitbrecht, H. (eds) (2003) *The Changing Contours of German Industrial Relations.* München: Hampp.

Promberger, M. (2002) *Das VW-Modell und seine Nachfolger. Pioniere einer neuartigen Beschäftigungspolitik.* München: Hampp.

Promberger, M., Schmidt, R. and Trinczek, R. (1993) *Was wird aus der Arbeitszeit?. 'Modernisierung' der betrieblichen Arbeitszeiten in der Metallindustrie zwischen Verkürzung, Pluralisierung und Differenzierung.* München: Hampp.

Schmidt, R. and Trinczek, R. (1999) 'Der Betriebsrat als Akteur der industriellen Beziehungen', in Müller-Jentsch, W. (ed.) *Konfliktpartnerschaft.* München: Hampp.

Schroeder, W. (1995) 'Arbeitgeberverbände in der Klemme. Motivations- und Verpflichtungskrisen', in Bispinck, R. (ed.) *Tarifpolitik der Zukunft. Was wird aus dem Flächentarifvertrag?* Hamburg: VSA.

Schroeder, W. (2000) *Das Modell Deutschland auf dem Prüfstand.* Wiesbaden: Westdeutscher Verlag.

Schroeder, W. and Weinert, R. (2003) 'Zwischen Verbetrieblichung und Europäisierung. Oder 'Can the German Model Survive'?' *Industrielle Beziehungen* 10(1): 97–117.

Schroeder, W. and Weßels, B. (eds) (2003) *Die Gewerkschaften in Politik und Gesellschaft der Bundesrepublik Deutschland. Ein Handbuch.* Wiesbaden: Westdeutscher Verlag.

Streeck, W. (1992) *Social Institutions and Economic Performance. Studies of Industrial Relations in Advanced Capitalist Economies.* London: Sage.

Streeck, W. and Rehder, B. (2003) 'Der Flächentarifvertrag: Krise, Stabilität und Wandel', *Industrielle Beziehungen* 10(3): 341–62.

Thelen, K. (1991) *Union of Parts. Labor Politics in Postwar Germany.* Ithaca: Cornell University Press.

Turner, L. (1991) *Democracy at Work. Changing World Markets and the Future of Trade Unions.* Ithaca: Cornell University Press.

Wagner, H. and Schild, A. (eds) (2003) *Der Flächentarif unter Druck.* Hamburg: VSA.

Wassermann, W. (2002) *Die Betriebsräte. Akteure für Demokratie in der Arbeitswelt.* Münster: Westfälisches Dampfboot.

Weltz, F. (1977) 'Kooperative Konfliktverarbeitung. Ein Stil industrieller Beziehungen in deutschen Unternehmen', *Gewerkschaftliche Monatshefte* 28(5,8): 291–301, 485–94.

8

The Last Waltz: Are Italian Trade Unions Leaving the Dance Floor?

Mirella Baglioni[1]

Introduction

This chapter looks at the development of industrial relations and collective bargaining practice over the last 15 years in order to make an assessment of the current options open to Italian trade unions. During this period Italian trade unions have collaborated with actors in the political system and this approach has yielded positive results for their political and contractual legitimisation. This has happened in spite of falling membership and relevant changes in the labour market. Here, as everywhere else in Europe, a large number of traditionally unionised jobs have disappeared especially in manufacturing industry, and new 'atypical' jobs have partly compensated this decline in employment. On the other hand, at the sector and company levels, unions have exercised strategic choices to both box and dance. The picture, however, is a fragmented one and overall patterns are difficult to discern.

In contrast to some of the other countries covered in this book, industrial relations in Italy has historically been featured by a central role for the state. In particular, the need to control inflation and to reform the welfare system has led to a process of close interaction between public (i.e. state) and collective labour market actors in what is generally understood as 'concertation'. Concertation on the one hand has limited the scope for collective bargaining, making it subject to macroeconomic constraints. On the other hand, it has increased trade union legitimisation, both in the political economic arena and from the point of view of actual and potential membership. In recent articles, Baccaro *et al.* (2003a,b) in fact show that Italian trade unions have been able to compensate for their lower degree of bargaining autonomy with better worker consultation procedures. Draft collective agreements are in fact regularly submitted for worker approval before final signatures are entered.

A well-established dance floor in Italian industrial relations now features the processes of peak level trilateral concertation, where unions, employers' associations and government agree on a number of shared public goods and objectives. But collective bargaining follows its own rituals and procedures that have been consolidated over time, and these tend to feature industrial action rather than dancing steps. The interaction between overall macro-economic agreements and collective bargaining is dynamic, uncertain and variable. Therefore choices on the balance between boxing and dancing must be understood as occurring where collective bargaining takes place, that is, at the sector level where strategic choices have to combine contingent and structural factors. The analysis will have to neglect the various dances taking place at the local level (i.e. province, region and district level). These dances, extensively analysed by Locke (1995), Trigilia and Burroni (2000) and, in their socio-political implications, by Putman (1992), would lead us to consider too many actors and to go into the description of different and particularistic contexts. At the *macro level*, on the other hand, the dynamics of the dance that takes place in concertation is embedded into the relationship between collective actors and the political system.

During the 1990s, trade union confederations played an important role in helping the European convergence process and they also displayed a positive attitude towards mediating between macroeconomic interests and collective autonomy. It is widely thought that the role of collective actors compensated for the increasing delegitimation of the political parties. Some critics (e.g. Salvati, 2003) go so far as to say that collective actors even replaced political parties. Indeed, when the political situation changed and a strong right-wing government, destined to remain in power, was elected in 2001, trade unions began to face serious problems. The neo-liberal programme of the Berlusconi government in fact has implied a progressive reduction in the role played by collective actors in policy-making.

Currently, there are two main types of problem in internal trade union dynamics:

- *Increasing inter-union competition*: the Italian trade unions, in spite of different origins and different political affiliations, have showed themselves over time to be able to act unitarily. But the recent situation, with a stable right wing majority in government, appears to be breaking down this solidarity.
- The internal *cohesion* of trade union organisations seems to be sacrificed in favour of overall unity of action. The different problems peculiar to each sector persist and limits decided at the macroeconomic level are accepted only to varying degrees. This becomes transparent through an analysis of two sectors such as chemicals and metalworking that exhibit two different orientations towards sector and company partnerships.

Case studies of these two sectors are included in the appendices to this volume and are drawn upon in this chapter, including the implications of sector-dependent factors for boxing and dancing at the company level.

Boxing and dancing as a response to the political arena

Before discussing the recent history of industrial relations dynamics in Italy, it is perhaps instructive to describe briefly the main union actors. Italy has three main union confederations, the *Confederazione Generale Italiana del Lavoro* (CGIL – The General Confederation of Italian Workers), the *Confederazione Italiana Sindacati Lavoratori* (CISL – The Italian Confederation of Workers' Unions), and the *Unione Italiana del Lavoro* (UIL – The Union of Italian Workers). Each of these has a separate structure for retired members (see later in chapter). Immediately after the Second World War, Italian unions were combined into a single confederation, CGIL. In 1948, however, a substantial Catholic element left CGIL to form CISL (Hyman, 2001). Two years later, various Republicans and Social Democrats also left CGIL to form the UIL (Pellegrini, 1998).

Today, after the political collapse, it is difficult to explain the persistence of three separated confederations. The famous theory of political patronage (La Palombara, 1964) on societal interests, among which, workers' interests played a major role should have lost its significance, but many inertial factors still shape the organisations for workers, the behaviour of the politicians and the styles of the political representation. So it can be said that the largest of the three, the CGIL, organises workers who sympathise for the left-oriented components of the centre–left coalition, while CISL and UIL members' preferences are probably distributed between the two poles of political representation.

For many years Italian trade unions were seen as militant organisations expressing class interests rather than associative interests. Excluded from production units, they developed an adversarial style of collective bargaining at the sector level. Only in the 1970s did trade unions enjoy the basic rights of worker representation at plant level. At that time company and plant bargaining was often perceived as an opportunity to test the employers' resistance and anticipate the contents of national negotiations at the most vulnerable production units.

A change of perspective that meant moving from the strategy of boxing towards some dancing started at the end of the 1970s, when the Italian government entered the procedure of trilateral consultation with the aim of experimenting a new alliance with organised interests (Cella and Treu, 1998). This kind of alliance – better known as neo-corporatism – was already in place in other parts of continental Europe. At that time, CGIL took the very important strategic choice – at the EUR Congress – of leaving the boxing ring and proceeding towards negotiating with the government on the basis of political exchange (Crouch, 1993). Nevertheless the exchanges negotiated from 1977 to 1984 could not succeed in establishing a new framework for industrial relations for the following reasons:

- frequent changes of government;
- union pluralism that led to many diverse and conflicting tactical responses by trade unions;
- prevailing boxing attitudes within the sector associations.

The mindset to dance did not reach the shop floor negotiators until the mid-1980s. The decentralisation of production was a leading factor behind the strategic decisions taken by the negotiation partners. Unions were caught up in the need to contribute to changes in the company or otherwise be excluded from them and lose influence, representative capacity and capacity for worker protection. As noted by Baccaro *et al.* (2003a), actors at the local level were actively engaged in discussions on coming up with innovative solutions on industrial restructuring by the early 1990s. In many respects, however, the main arena of change in terms of boxing and dancing in Italian industrial relations in the more recent period has been at the sector level. For this reason case studies of contrasting stories of sector level developments have been selected for inclusion in this book. The analysis of boxing and dancing in the section to follow, however, discusses developments at all three levels.

Boxing and dancing at multiple levels

In order to discuss various aspects of the choices made by Italian trade unions, our analysis develops the following three levels:

(A) The *peak level* of associations (confederation level), where the dance takes on connotations of tripartite agreements combining public aims (control of inflation, employment protection, social policy and improvements in economic factors) with collective interests (maintenance of salary purchasing power, contractual autonomy).

(B) The *sector level*, where the readiness to dance or to box appears to be correlated to long-term structural variables rather than political variables located at level A.

(C) The *company level*, where the actors feel mainly, although not exclusively, the weight of tradition of struggle or involvement expressed at level B.

The different and sometimes contradictory choices made by Italian trade unions will be explained here by taking into account their organisational characteristics as well as the structures of collective negotiations. Such an analysis, however, is by no means straightforward. Briefly, the main problems of interpretation are as follows:

(A) Segmentation of organisational systems and implied differentiation:
   • the persistence of three peak confederations (inter-organisational differences);
   • the internal differentiation of trade unions (intra-organisational differentiation).
(B) Structural factors:
   • overall employment and cycles;
   • sector cycle and technology.
(C) Traditional union culture:
   • differentiation between manufacturing and civil servants;
   • differentiation within the different sub-sectors.

Unfortunately, the high level of influence on the parties exerted by the political actors has often diverted the attention of analysis away from trade union organisational features and resources, which is a matter that deserves further investigation and will be examined below.

The peak level

First of all it is worth noting that in spite of the differences in the founding principles of the three main trade union confederations, they have not undertaken significantly different courses of collective action over the course of time. For most of their existence, the CGIL, the CISL and the UIL have signed the same agreements and thus made similar strategic decisions. The unity of collective action was mainly determined by strategic choices taken by political parties: the lack of legal status of trade unions, the absence of legally binding collective contracts and the constitutional principle of the individual right to strike were originally conceived of as instruments for helping union development and growth (Cella and Treu, 1998). In fact this lack of regulation led the three not to compete amongst themselves and to emphasise their status as encompassing organisations able to represent the interests of all workers and thus work towards the common or public good.

By virtue of this wide profile of collective action, the three unions were invited to take part in governmental socio-economic regulation. This happened in different phases and with different implications in content and extension of their participation. From ritual consultation they became involved in regular information and consultation on numerous issues and partnership in concertation (Regalia and Regini, 1998). This happened at a time when the government was able to carry out a programme of convergence in line with the Maastricht parameters. Such a process was largely possible due to union commitment to an incomes policy. In fact in that period of political disorder caused by the legitimacy crisis of the political parties, the unions represented the only existing channel for consensus building. Unlike the political parties, however, the unions did not descend into crisis. They rather came to fill the political vacuum and devoted much energy to central and local concertation.

Starting from the early 1990s, collective bargaining, especially wage dynamics, became subject to incomes policies to which peak unions and business had adhered (Protocol 1993). But the consequences on sector or company level bargaining were not automatic. At sector or company levels the sides had to conform to constraints laid down by the superiors from their respective hierarchies, but long-term structural variables affecting different negotiating traditions shaped the behaviour of the actors and could thus help or hinder the decisions on whether to engage in dancing or boxing.

Contrary to the experience of political exchange that took place in the 1970s, the process of trilateral decision-making that developed during the 1990s provided the institutional framework for further developing experiences of social partnership. The key features, including strategic choices, of the era of political exchange between 1977 and 1984 are contrasted with the key features and strategic choices associated with the concertation of the 1990s in Exhibits 8.1 and 8.2. It can be seen from these exhibits that the

---

Exhibit 8.1 Tripartite negotiations in Italy (I)

POLITICAL EXCHANGE 1977–84

Contents: slowing down of real wage dynamics through revision of indexation mechanism (scala mobile) and reform of indirect wage structure.

Political balance

1977: Italian communist party external support to the government.
1979–84: coalition government with the exclusion of the PCI.

Trade Unions

CGIL

1977 strategic choice: submit wage dynamics to macro-compatibilities.
1984: defence of indexation mechanism 'scala mobile'.

CISL

Internal resistance against reduction of sectoral autonomy.
Approval of the revision mechanism.

UIL

Strategic choice: take part in consultation mechanism.
Internal resistance against reduction of sectoral autonomy.
1984: approval of the revision mechanism.

Exhibit 8.2   Tripartite negotiations in Italy (II)

CONCERTATION 1993–1996–1998

1993 Protocol

Framework: meeting the Maastricht requirements.

Government: coalition government led by non-politicians (Amato and Ciampi).

Substantial content: incomes policy and subsequent wage dynamics.

Procedural content: two annual trilateral sessions on incomes policy.

Collective bargaining system: the agreement formally regulates the structure and levels of collective bargaining for the first time. Collective bargaining outputs linked to the inflation rate.

No overlapping between issues settled in national and company agreements.

Sector collective agreements: to be negotiated every four years. Wage adjustments to inflation rate every two years

Company collective agreements: to follow the national agreements. No wage increases if not linked to performance indices.

Strategic choice (shared among the three unions): to revise the collective bargaining structure and conform to incomes policy.

The Pact for Work 1996

Framework: White Paper (Delors) and the EU reforms to labour market and employment.

Government: centre–left coalition (Ulivo).

Pact content:
Reform of labour market agencies.
Privatisation of manpower intermediation.
Application of equal opportunity policy.

Consequences: increased union participation in central and peripheral committees on (a) vocational training (b) equal opportunity policies (c) concertation on whole labour policies.

Strategic choice (shared among the three trade unions): to reform the labour market and to co-manage labour policies.

The Pact for Economic Development 1998

Framework: European social dialogue on growth and competitiveness.

Government: centre–left coalition (Ulivo).

Procedural content: extension of actors in concertation (32 peak level associations sign the pact.

Substantial content: economic development and bureaucracy modernisation.

> *Main consequences*: participation of collective actors in policies of economic development of marginal areas through territorial pacts, where economic interests, trade unions, local political actors combine together in order to accompany projects to be supported by European funding.
>
> *Strategic choice*: to engage in territorial pacts for economic development, to help regulate the black economy.

main substantive content of both the political exchange era from 1977–84 and the early period of concertation associated with the 1993 Protocol concerned pay-related issues – salary setting mechanisms and procedures as well as salary structures. More recently, discussions have extended to include manpower policy and regional developmental issues. As to strategic choice, it is clear that the union choices to dance, which became more evident from the mid-1990s, have necessarily required inter-union collaboration at the confederal level.

As a consequence of concertation, the tasks performed by the peak associations have greatly increased and mainly developed towards participation in public policy. Following the definition criteria of the International Questionnaire on the Basic Dimensions of National Labour Relations Systems conceived and subsequently elaborated by Traxler *et al.* (2001),[2] Italian trade unions can be said to perform the following tasks:

- influence national governments or parliamentary bodies with regard to labour market issues;
- represent members' labour market interests on national corporatist (i.e. bipartite or tripartite) institutions;
- conduct general consultations with employers' confederations;
- co-ordinate collective bargaining of affiliates;
- participate in the formulation of public industrial policy programmes;
- participate in the formulation of public regional development programmes;
- participate in the formulation of occupational programmes (including apprenticeship) and active labour market policy;
- implement occupational training programmes (including apprenticeship) and active labour market policy, or participate in implementation;
- participate in the formulation of policy on social security.

Following the Pact of 1998 (see Exhibit 8.2), unions also began to take part in the implementation of public industrial policy programmes at national and regional levels (Baglioni, 2002). More generally it can be said that the spirit of the Protocol has affected sector negotiations (Regini, 1997).

The sector level

National Sector unions associated to three confederations are the signatories of collective agreements that regulate the conditions of work and pay for the different sectors. Although dating back to the 1950s, the timing, and procedures associated with such agreements were explicitly acknowledged in the 1993 Protocol. Such agreements generally cover topics such as job classification and descriptions, working hours, overtime, rewards systems, leave entitlements, discipline, information disclosure and union rights. It appears that exchanges between the parties at this level, notably collective bargaining, have also enabled unions to exert some influence on employer investment strategies, subcontracting and technological change as well as the content and administration of vocational training (Pellegrini, 1998). Sector level exchanges of a largely dancing character have also materialised in joint commissions and observatories.

At the sector level, the unions themselves are in disagreement, however, on the strategy of dancing. In the metalworking sector, social partnership is an integral part of policy for FIM-CISL and UILM-UIL. These unions see no contradiction between 'boxing' and 'dancing'. In fact, one should supplement the other, as the same people are involved in joint commissions as in bargaining. The FIM proposed re-launching the culture of participation in the policy statement of its most recent national congress in 2001. The following statement is illustrative of the FIM position:

> The relaunch of bargaining is essential in order to reaffirm in the workplace and local areas the culture of sharing and participation of workers in company life and to promote bilateralism in the management of union relationships. (Congress document, FIM-CISL, 29 May–1 June 2001)

So for FIM, relaunching boxing means promoting dancing too. The sentence clearly expresses the approach of this federation. Conflict and participation are not alternatives but integral parts of one and the same strategy.

In the same sector, FIOM-CGIL, however, appears to have opted for redistributional unionism where bargaining power is derived from conflictual pressure. In the FIOM congress of the same year, 2001, the policy document expressed fears for the survival of national sector contracts, repeatedly criticised by the employers' association Federmeccanica. Decentralising negotiating shifts it from the central collective to the company level and FIOM has restated its own strategy of safeguarding workers at the sector level and its faith in traditional means of pressure. It does not explicitly refute partnership, which would not be reasonable, as it too has taken part in the establishment of observatories and commissions. But it expresses the fear that by dancing, employers could incorporate unions so as to support their own aims. A remark by a national sector official reveals the FIOM point of view:

> We are not saying 'no' to concertation but it must be subordinate to bargaining because this is the only way the union can remain independent. And anyway, the employers do not appear to want concertation to continue.

There have always existed different perceptions of the relative importance of dancing and boxing among unions, but in recent years the differences have become more pronounced and visible in the different negotiating rounds. For example, in 2001, when the national contract was due for its partial intermediate review, in other words wages were to be brought in line with inflation, FIOM–CGIL judged the increase insufficient and refused to sign the agreement. In 2002 in preparation for contract renewal, FIOM, FIM and UILM all put forward different platforms and different negotiating strategies. This led to different outcomes; FIM and UILM signed the contract renewal and FIOM refused. This divergence became even clearer subsequently. In the early summer of 2003 FIOM-CGIL opted to pursue company agreements with the aim of delegitimising the national agreement signed by the other two unions. In order to do this, FIOM has put forward negotiating platforms in many companies and has already won some wage increases higher than those allowed by the national agreement.

In the chemical sector the dynamics of 'dancing' and 'boxing' are somewhat different. As shown in the case study in the appendix of this volume, the strategic choice of concertation or dancing has been a traditional feature of the sector. Increasingly, this has become institutionalised in the form of the bipartite observatory for the sector that was recognised by law in 1997. Social partnership, however, does not in fact prevail in equal measure across the sector. It is less evident at national contract renewal and in larger companies, but more frequent in small- and medium-sized enterprises.

Another important factor in the chemical sector is that the continuous processes of rationalisation, company closures, concentrations and redundancies have created an atmosphere unfavourable to collaboration and can sometimes be a source of bitter conflict in defence of workers' interests. There are major differences between what happens nationally and in some of the large companies and what happens in more decentralised levels and in small companies. Trade union leaders are aware of this and are now trying to decentralise the concertation model and apply to the whole sector the experience of joint commissions, which have only operated nationally up to now. And the national agreement itself explicitly invites the sides to reach company level agreements.

Case studies on the two sectors are included in the Appendix (A1 and A2) and summarised in Exhibit 8.3.

Exhibit 8.3 Institutional partnership at the sector level

(a) *The chemical sector*
- National joint observatory and bilateral commissions were set up at the beginning of the 1990s.
- The scope of the National Commission is to collect and analyse data on the sector including employment.
- The scope of bilateral commissions: to analyse specific problems and to develop a joint approach.
- The problem solving process undertaken by trade union officials and employers' association officials benefits from a widespread consultation process with shop stewards and middle management.
- The institutional partnership is progressively transforming labour relations by inducing an attitude in favour of social partnership

(b) *The metal industry*
- Joint bodies at the national level only exist on paper.
- Bilateral commissions at the territorial level have been working on specific matters.
- The system of partnership is not widespread.
- Conflictual attitudes prevail – some distance from being social partnership.
- Collective bargaining retains the central role in shaping labour relations.

The company level

Collective bargaining has been significant at the company level since the late 1960s and early 1970s when shop stewards were increasingly recognised and union representatives became protected in law (Pellegrini, 1998). Although moves to extend company level collective bargaining were heavily circumscribed between 1975 and the early 1980s, the enterprise level nevertheless became a focal arena for restructuring processes thereafter upon which local level concertation began to develop. The enterprise level was further strengthened by the 1993 Protocol that laid down matters of both substance (performance payments) and procedure for local level bargaining as well as rights for new unitary trade union representative bodies (RSUs). At the same time, a number of ad hoc joint committees were formed for handling issues on a more co-operative basis.

There are several examples in the chemical sector of the relationship between national concertation and company and local union organisation. At the end of the 1990s, there were serious environmental problems concerning toxic waste at the big oil refinery at Marghera near Venice. The National Observatory set up a joint commission to look into solutions. The RSU of the Marghera plant took part and with the help of outside experts the commission drew up a series of joint proposals. This 'Area Project' was discussed with the Environment Ministry, with the local authority of Marghera and the province of Venice and environmental associations, and was finally approved.

Another example was evident in Varese, in northern Italy, where there is a high concentration of small companies. The area was identified as suitable for investment in research and development. Here, too, the national commission worked with union and business representatives of the companies. This commission, with its wide membership, made a proposal to Varese local and provincial authorities regarding the development of infrastructures, company services and vocational training. Life-long learning is another example of local level concertation. There is a permanent national joint commission which discusses it with company or industrial estate representatives interested in setting up training programmes.

These examples show that relationships in the chemical sector between national commissions and decentralised union structures in the different provinces and companies are very elastic and work according to different criteria of efficiency. The entire organisation by both unions and management in this sector is governed by the principle of meeting targets and rapid problem solving.

In the metalworking sector the example of Fiat shows what the obstacles are to dancing. Over the years Fiat was management-led and decisions were unilateral. Only in 1996 did the negotiating parties sign an agreement on a new model of industrial relations. The aim was to pave the way from hierarchical organisation to worker involvement and participation. It was based on the establishment of bipartite commissions or working parties at company and plant level. These commissions were to deal with company services, safety and accident prevention, new technological and organisational patterns and product quality. The unions seemed to be positively oriented towards this, as the boxing ring had become increasingly conflictual and dangerous. But after a promising start, some of the commissions met with difficulty in that some of their members brought to the partnership the attitudes and approaches they were most familiar with, in other words, fighting out differences in the boxing ring. The commissions were unable to fulfil their task of opening up new spaces on the dance floor. They were successful only on 'soft' items such as company services and canteens and safety and the environment.

The procedural rules of the commissions were also subject to disagreement. Decisions could only be taken unanimously, and work was halted if either side disagreed. So conflict reappeared. And commission members had no time to change their approach, because subsequent management crises led to far-reaching rationalisation and significant cuts in the workforce in all car plants. Accordingly, the actors returned to the boxing ring.

In other large- and medium-sized companies in the metalworking sector, however, dancing activities went ahead. The personnel management at Aer-Macchi, an aeronautics manufacturer in northern Italy, which was rationalised extensively in the 1990s, attempted to impose unilaterally a new classification of personnel. There was united opposition from employees, and management was forced to review its approach. A joint union – management commission was formed to draw up a new system, and this took account of the union proposals for wider income bands. Because the new agreement resolved common problems in an innovatory way, it became a point of reference for the whole sector. Its lessons and experience was taught on national RSU training courses and conferences, and the way it had been reached as well as its content was used as an example nationally. Finally, the national secretariat of FIM put it forward as a demand in the renewal of the national contract in 2002 with a view to it being extended to all companies.

In the case of two firms reported on in our case study of the metalworking sector – Aer-Macchi and ZF (see Appendix) – it is also clear that these made recourse to dancing only when the failure of negotiations to take account of workers' needs after rationalisation made it the only viable course of action. Both sides in these firms appear to have learnt that dancing is the best way of facing continuous and rapid changes in the market, in technologies and work organisation.

More generally, new dancing activities were discernible at the company level from the Pact for Work of 1996 (see Exhibit 8.2). This sought to encourage local partnerships aimed at promoting economic regeneration through 'area contracts' in crisis areas and through 'territorial pacts' largely in the south. These efforts were often supported by EU funding and characterised by local development initiatives rather than top-down solutions. Baccaro *et al.* (2003b) report that by 2000 some 61 agreements had been signed; in many cases these drew in external actors as a means of building social capital (Putnam, 1992). On the other hand, it must not be thought that dancing is common in the Italian metalworking sector. Concertation is moving forward only very slowly. In most cases negotiation is carried out by boxing, or boxing alternating with dancing. As a regional secretary from Lombardy remarks:

> Companies want to be friends with unions and invite them to supper only when they have to give bad news to their employees. When things are going well they are no longer interested.

Dancing and dancers

It can be seen from the discussions above that the experience of national social partnership influenced the joint management of collective agreements by means of observatories, joint committees and bilateral bodies. That there was indeed more collaboration in negotiating arenas in the 1990s is demonstrated by the overall decline in levels of industrial conflict (see Figure 8.1). On the other hand, looking at the reality of industrial relations rather than

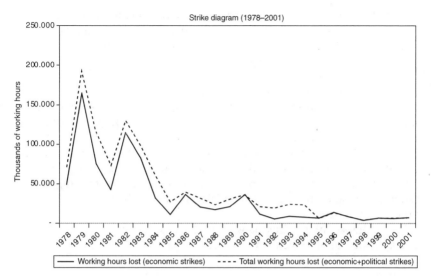

Figure 8.1   Strikes in Italy 1978–2001.
Source: Istat.

the agreements on paper, different situations have been emerging depending mainly on three factors: levels of negotiations, sectoral tradition and issues negotiated.

How is the dance at the peak level linked to the day-to-day options of sectors, observatories, joint commissions and collective bargaining? In order to answer this question attention must be paid to union *organisation cohesion*. Many studies have been made of Italian trade unionism, often with a particular focus on the relative importance of the three main confederations CGIL, CISL and UIL (Codara, 1998). There have been fewer studies of the intra-organisational features (Della Rocca, 1998) which confirms the point made above that the perceived pre-eminence of politically important indicators are more significant than membership composition factors. Attention in such studies has tended to be focused on the relative weight of the three components. This, however, has not varied significantly over time; changes in membership, a rise or fall in numbers in one of the three confederations has had no consequences on the other two, which also suggests that inter-union competition has been weak.

The most significant events of the last 30 years in terms of trade union organisation have been the following:

• An increase in unionism in the 1970s due to new generations entering the labour market, particularly the public sector.
• A decline in membership in the 1980s following industrial reorganisation.

- Variations in the relative importance of internal membership. Pensioners' unions have grown continuously. The public sector has maintained its strength but unions in the private sector, particularly manufacturing, have continued to lose members.

Accordingly, unionisation in industry has declined with the crisis of the Fordist production model. The public sector has remained unionised, but the importance of pensioners' unions has grown steadily since the 1980s. It has been shown that these members are ex-workers who maintain unbroken links with the union, but there are also new members who have been joining in order to receive administrative assistance on receiving their pension. In Olson's terms, the unions provide workers in retirement with semi-authoritative goods and this explains the increasing numbers of pensioners in union membership.

Italian trade unions thus base their strategic choices on the following multiple membership factors within their organisations:

- The importance of retired workers (see Table 8.1)
- The importance of the state sector
- The importance of employment categories exposed to product market fluctuations

Membership composition confirms the persistent importance of different negotiating arenas: general agreements or pacts for the protection of social rights, national sector agreements for the public sector and collective bargaining for market-exposed sectors. However, both pension unions and the public sector unions are affected by negotiations with the government, and thus the political system is still a central influence on trade union action.

Currently the situation is extremely fragmentary, and the absence of empirical research makes it very difficult to interpret the reality of partnership and union responses in Italy. Uncertainty in our location of union action increases with the heterogeneity of organisational domain. Peak associations have only a political influence on member associations; the organisations are loosely linked so confederation decisions are not automatically transmitted to all affiliates. Moreover, negotiating practices, and more generally the behaviour of the actors, are naturally influenced by structural factors and their previous experiences of negotiating and industrial conflict. There is thus no clear-cut division between boxing and dancing at the different levels.

Boxing and dancing in collective bargaining

As stated previously, even though collective bargaining has traditionally been a boxing activity, there is evidence to suggest an increasing dancing element in certain arenas. How can the moves towards dancing in collective

Table 8.1   Trade union membership in Italy

(a) Retired members

Unions	1990	1997
CGIL	2 353 891	2 875 459
CISL	1 274 489	1 909 832
UIL	268 076	418 437
Total membership	3 896 456	5 203 728

(b) CGIL, CISL, UIL employed members and associations

Year	Membership	Number of confederal affiliates**
CGIL		
1997	2 288 141	15
1998	2 303 653	16
1999	2 327 954	16
2000	2 385 468	16
CISL		
1997	1 882 623	23
1998	1 895 713	23
1999	1 934 854	24
2000	1 941 931	23
UIL		
1997	1 119 768	23
1998	1 123 988	20
1999	1 260 000	16
2000	1 130 833	16

Note: **excluding retired and unemployed members.
Source: CGIL, CISL, UIL.

bargaining be explained? In order to answer we concentrate our attention on sector dynamics. The analysis of negotiating practice and the experience of participation in joint bodies in two sectors, chemicals and metalworking, helps us to better understand the often contradictory mix of dancing and boxing. Structural features such as sector trends, average wage and employment levels appear to be decisive in union decisions to opt for one or the other strategic choices. These focus on the role played by joint institutions of partnership such as observatories and bilateral commissions in enlarging the dance floor and reducing the boxing rings.

Looking at the different sectors covered in our case studies, chemicals and metalworking, social partnership has been more widely and efficiently applied where a stronger tradition of co-operation between the sides had already developed. This means that dancing has constituted a development or structural improvement to an existing model of co-operative relationships. As well as in the chemical sector, this was also the case in retailing and in agriculture. But in these latter sectors where there was a strong tradition of conflict, the new model has met with greater resistance. This was the case in the metalworking, transport and public sectors.

The experience of partnership has found more fertile terrain where the joint bodies (observatory or joint committees) discussed less controversial issues like vocational training, the environment, health and safety, labour market regulation, equal opportunities and services. But dancing has been more difficult on those issues that were traditionally more controversial such as salary increases and working hours. The overall mix of boxing and dancing is tentatively summarised in Table 8.2.

As stated, there is a shortage of empirical research on partnership in Italy. But what appears to be clear is that a participation approach was tried throughout the 1990s, an approach that could reasonably be equated with social partnership. The foundations of this, however, were somewhat shaky. One reason for this, as mentioned above, has been that neither trade unions nor employers' associations have as yet made a clear decision to discard the old contractual model in preference for the new concertation arrangements. There appears to be widespread cognitive indecision on both sides; moreover, new factors have been adding further uncertainties to this picture. Nevertheless, the unions' unanimous support for concertation has gradually proved to be more apparent than real, and during the late 1990s, trade unions increasingly disagreed about the extent of their support for the political actors on the dance floor.

Background ideological factors became more important when the government coalition changed from centre–left to centre–right. In 2002 the new government relaunched tripartite consultation on work flexibility and proposed a new definition of some basic workers' rights. The choices advocated by CGIL and CISL unions in response to this can be summarised as follows:

Trade unions	Wage policy	Basic rights
CGIL	Increases in minimum wages	As defined in the Fordist era
CISL	Plant negotiations on productivity	New definitions (post Fordist)

The incompatibility of these two strategic choices has caused CGIL to oppose the government proposal and revert to boxing. It subsequently called two general strikes. CISL and UIL, who were unwilling to lose the roles they had gained for themselves during the period of concertation, have maintained a dancing approach, and negotiated and signed a new tripartite

Table 8.2 Boxing and dancing in Italy: a classification

Level	Boxing	Dancing	Prospects
National	Mix of B and D. Different orientations with respect to the centre–right governments: CGIL is against its neo-liberal approach to labour matters, while CISL and UIL seek co-operation and political legitimisation.	Important trends towards dancing have developed during the last decade. These experiences took place within a system of concertation where collective actors and public actors defined their common objectives.	The prospects for dancing have become uncertain. The present government has replaced the model of concertation with a pro forma consultation that is being evaluated differently by the unions.
Sector	The practice of boxing for wages and working hours is evident on occasions of collective bargaining renewal. Historical trends and the negative conjuncture of manufacturing favour the practice of boxing in engineering, the public sector and transportation.	The practice of social partnership has helped new experiments in dancing at the sector level. These concern healthy and safety, the work environment, equal opportunities and vocational training.	Increased and stabilised dancing in chemicals, telecommunication and construction. Trends to replace dancing with boxing in the metal industry.
Company	Occasional boxing on wages and working time. These conflicts appear to be linked to local variables (union leaderships), and to structural variables of the local economy.	Widespread practices of dancing as far as shiftworking, flexibility, outsourcing are concerned. The ability to dance is not equally distributed across the different areas.	Dancing prevails over boxing.

agreement (Patto per l'Italia). Subsequent events have forced CGIL to continue boxing, the most important of these being their exclusion from the preliminary meeting with the government on economic planning and the Fiat crisis that has caused a high number of layoffs. Last but not least, the recent engineering collective agreement was signed by FIM-CISL, and UILM-UIL, but not by FIOM-CGIL.

To sum up, recent events have shown not only that unions from the different confederations have exercised divergent strategic choices, but also that such choices are subject to considerable constraint or limitations in terms of 'policy space'. Such constraints on union choice can be summarised as in Table 8.2

Constraints on union choice

- *Industrial relations system* as defined by the 1993 protocol (political commitment).
- *Economic context*: *wages* at rate of agreed inflation. EU *Labour market* liberalisation policy.
- *Business organisation* (Technology): *small- and medium-sized* plants.
- *Social expectations*: defence of the welfare state and more generally of social rights.
- *Employer strategies*: trends towards plant level bargaining and individualisation of work contracts.
- *Membership voice:* organisational weight of pensioners and public servants (political negotiations).

Strategic choices for unions: what do we learn from the Italian story?

Strategic options for Italian trade unions at the beginning of the third millennium are largely conditioned by the Berlusconi government. From its first days in office, the right-wing government initiatives were met with two distinct union responses. CISL and UIL, motivated by the need to keep open all opportunities to take part in political and economic consultation with the government, were willing to dance. But CGIL intended to box in order to defend the union's traditional distributional role. The differences between the three unions for many years had lain dormant, but the recent divergence has clearly opened them up. CISL has proclaimed its associative identity several times in contrast to the class identity still claimed by CGIL. The former has shown itself to be adverse to boxing in an atmosphere which would cost its members dear. A close look at the membership figures, however, shows that the three unions have a similar internal membership composition. There is no reason why CISL's concern not to go against the interests of its pensioner or state employee members' interests should not be shared by the other unions, especially given that all three have to engage in dialogue with the government.

But in negotiations in sectors exposed to market forces, the decisions made by the three have been even more diverse. In the metalworking sector, the split between FIOM-CGIL and the other two unions has been especially marked. FIOM-CGIL not only refused to sign the national collective agreement of 2002–03, but, where the situation was favourable, it also initiated company level negotiations with the clear aim of delegitimising the agreement signed by the other two unions. Accordingly, the dance that started in Italian industrial relations in the mid-1980s appears to be increasingly uncertain. Where once joint committees and bilateral negotiations had opened up numerous fronts for consultation on issues that were once strictly confined to managerial prerogative, divergences between peak associations are now spreading downwards and interrupting the dance.

Union strategic choices have evolved along the model of encompassing representation that helped to develop institutional partnerships at the different levels of concertation, to advocate welfare rights and social citizenship and also to favour a move towards partnership on work organisation. Looking back over the last decade, union choices have been based upon their encompassing role and a recognition of and respect for the constraints imposed by the 1993 Protocol. On the other hand, the neo-liberal orientation of the Berlusconi government has severely curtailed the space on the dance floor. Unions, increasingly deprived of the opportunity to dance, appear now to be locked into different boxing rings and will soon be forced to renew their strategic choices that will influence the already established choices in the different arenas.

In sum, there is evidence of unions adopting a positive approach to dancing at the peak level as well as having a propensity towards developing social partnership in negotiation processes at company level. On the other hand, union divisions have allowed the government to divide and rule and this has been a factor preventing the continuation of social partnership experiences. Finally, it appears that the unions still retain an overdependency on the balance of forces in the political arena.

Notes

1. This chapter provides an overall view of Italian industrial relations and elaborates on sector analysis conducted by Aldo Marchetti and summarised in the following appendices. The translation from Italian to English was undertaken by Lois Clegg.
2. The project on Internationalization, Labour Relations and Competitiveness funded by the Austrian Fonds zur Forderung der wisseschaftlichen Forshung, was based on a very extensive questionnaire of 50 pages completed by different authors (Mirella Baglioni for Italy) through different phases. The overall picture covers the years from 1970 to 2000. The analysis is now formalised in Traxler *et al.* (2001).

References

Baccaro, L., Carrieri, M. and Damiano. C. (2003a) 'The Resurgence of the Italian Confederal Unions: Will it Last?' *European Journal of Industrial Relations* 2003(1): 43–59.

Baccaro, L. Hamann, K. and Turner, L. (2003b) 'The Politics of Labour Movement Revitalization: The Need for a Revitalized Perspective', *European Journal of Industrial Relations* 2003(1): 119–33.

Baglioni, M. (2002) 'Collective Actors and Public Policies: The Case of Territorial Pacts', in Széll G. and Cella, G. P. (eds) *The Injustice at Work*. Campus: Verlag.

Cella, G. P. and Treu, T. (1998) 'La contrattazione collettiva', in Cella G.P. and Treu, T. (eds) *Le nuove relazioni industriali*. Bologna: Mulino.

Codara, L. (1998) 'la Sindacalizzazione', in CESOS (ed.) *Le Relazioni Industriali in Italia. Rapporto 1997–1998*. Roma.

Crouch, C. (1993) *Industrial Relations and European State Traditions*. Oxford: Clarendon Press.

Della Rocca, G. (1998) 'Il sindacato', in Cella, G. P. and Treu, T. (eds) *Le nuove Relazioni Industriali*. Bologna: Mulino.

Hyman, R. (2001) *Understanding European Trade Unionism: Between Market, Class and Society*. London: Sage.

La Palombara, J. (1964) *Interest Groups in Italian Politics*. Princeton: Princeton University Press.

Locke, R. (1995) *Remaking the Italian Economy*. Ithaca: Cornell University Press.

Olson, M. (1965) *The Logic of Collective Action*. Cambridge, MA: Harvard University Press.

Pellegrini, C. (1998) 'Employment Relations in Italy', in Bamber, G. and Lansbury, R. (eds) *International and Comparative Employment Relations: A Study of Industrialised Market Economies (2nd edn)*. Sydney: Allen and Unwin.

Putnam, R. D. (1992) *Making Democracy Work: Civic Traditions in Modern Italy*. Princeton: Princeton University Press.

Regalia, I. and Regini, M. (1998) *Italy: the Dual Character of Industrial Relations*, in Ferner, A. and Hyman, R. (eds) *Changing Industrial Relations in Europe*. Oxford: Blackwell.

Regini, M. (1997) 'Still Engaging in Corporatism? Recent Italian Experience in Comparative Perspective', *European Journal of Industrial Relations* 1997(3): 259–78.

Salvati, M. (2003) 'Il sindacato: quanto conta la rappresentanza effettiva?' *Stato & Mercato* 2003(1): 109–16.

Traxler, F., Blaschke, S. and Kittel, B. (2001) *National Labour Relations in Internationalized Markets*. Oxford: Oxford University Press.

Trigilia, C. and Burroni, L. (2000) 'Italy: Economic Development through Local Economy, in Crouch, C. (ed.) *Local Production Systems in Europe*. Oxford: Oxford University Press.

9
Ireland: Shall We Dance?

Kevin P. O'Kelly[1]

Introduction

Because of the close ties between the British and Irish trade union movements, going back to the nineteenth century when for a time they were united under one Trade Union Congress, the Irish system of industrial relations has evolved from the British voluntarist model. Indeed, for many years after Ireland gained independence, both systems of industrial relations and the scope of legal power given to trade unions was governed by the same set of UK statutes, in particular the Trade Union Acts of 1871 and 1913 and the Trade Dispute Act, 1906.

The legacy of the industrial and political upheavals in the first decades of the century are still reflected in the trade union structures today. The present Irish Congress of Trade Unions (ICTU) represents unions in both parts of Ireland, therefore, Congress functions under two different legal frameworks and two different political and economic entities. Ireland is also unusual, in that foreign (UK) registered unions are members of ICTU and operate within the political jurisdictions of the Republic and of Northern Ireland. Many of these unions, and, indeed, unions registered in the Republic, have members both north and south and take an active part in the development of policies which impact on both parts of the island. It is also important to note that Northern Ireland has developed its own structures and particular system of industrial relations, reflecting its position of straddling the British and Irish systems (Cradden, 1993).

The approach of Irish business to industrial relations has also been dominated by the substantial trade links with Great Britain since long before Irish independence, links which are still strong today. With these close business and, indeed, cultural ties and with so many subsidiaries of UK companies based in Ireland, the traditional Anglo/Saxon adversarial model of employee/management relations, with its emphasis on collective bargaining, has been dominant in solving workplace problems, in the introduction of change and as a system of information disclosure. This approach has been re-enforced in recent decades by an increasing number of US companies, in particular non-union electronic enterprises, setting up plants in Ireland. So 'boxing' rather than 'dancing' characterises the evolution of the Irish industrial relations system.

The State has, for its part, supported the continuance of this system by encouraging the voluntarist model and adopting a minimalist approach to interference through legal or other controls. Negotiations, without interference from Government, between voluntary employee and employer organisations have been encouraged. For this voluntary approach to work, it presupposes that trade unions are accepted and recognised as legitimate representatives of their membership and that both sides recognise their respective social and commercial responsibilities and that once an agreement is reached, it will be honoured by the two parties. The State also provides the dispute resolution machinery for much of this sector and for the private sector and these institutions strive to maintain industrial peace within the parameters agreed at national level.[2]

Labour market organisations

Irish Congress of Trade Unions (ICTU)

The ICTU is the central trade union authority with 66 unions affiliated, representing a membership of 767 000 (Report of the Executive Council, 2001–03). Of these, 552 000 members are part of the workforce in the Republic and the rest are employed in Northern Ireland. Some 350 000 of the total membership are women (45.5%). Of the 57 affiliated unions, 26 are British based and 2 are exclusively Northern Ireland unions. Of these, 12 operate only in Northern Ireland while the remaining 14 have members both north and south of the border – 71 600 (9.3%) members in the Republic are members of these unions. Four of the unions based in the Republic have members in Northern Ireland.

The movement is dominated by a number of large unions. Services, Industrial, Professional and Technical Union (SIPTU), the biggest affiliated union, accounts for some 29% of the ICTU membership. In the Republic, SIPTU, with almost 200 000 members has 36% of unionised workers. Together with SIPTU, the next eight biggest unions represent over 80% of trade union members in the Republic. The ICTU estimates that 45% of trade unionists are employed in the private sector and 52% are employed in the public sector.

Against the trend in other European countries, trade union membership in Ireland has increased in recent years, after a serious decline during the 1980s. As the Irish economy experiences unprecedented growth, there is significant creation of employment and, as a result, total union membership increased by 24 200 between 1995 and 1997 and again the figures show a further increase of 10.6% in the Republic and of 7.7% in Northern Ireland between 1997 and 2003. However, this hides a steady decline in unionisation in the Republic, from an estimated 60% in the early 1980s to an estimated 46% in 2002, as a percentage of the workforce (see Turner and Morley, 1995; D'Art and Turner, 2003).

The function of ICTU is to co-ordinate the national policies and work of the affiliated unions. It regulates aspects of inter-union relations, including the transfer of members and inter-union disputes. It represents the membership on government advisory bodies, State boards and in negotiations with government and employers in national bargaining. It nominates members to the Labour Relations Commission and Labour Court. Congress also works closely with the European Trade Union Confederation (ETUC) on European Union issues, the International Trade Secretariats and other international agencies.

Irish Business and Employers Confederation (IBEC)

IBEC is the major organisation representing employers within the labour market. The membership of IBEC includes 3700 companies in both the public and private sectors employing over 300 000 workers. It also comprises 53 sectoral associations and transnational trade organisations, including the Small Firms Association. Its role is to develop and co-ordinate economic, commercial and social policies for employers and to influence national decision-making, so that national policies are enterprise and employment friendly. It represents Irish business and industry in discussions on matters of trade, economics, finance, taxation, planning and development, with government, the European Union (through UNICE) and other international organisations.

It also co-ordinates the views of business on all topics relating to industrial relations, labour and social affairs. IBEC represents employers in discussions with government and participates in the work of a wide range of advisory groups both nationally and internationally. It nominates the employer members of the Labour Relations Commission and Labour Court and participates in centralised bargaining on national agreements with ICTU and the Government (IPA, 1998–2003).

The system of industrial relations

Voluntarism

As already stated, the Irish system of industrial relations is based on the concept of voluntarism, that is, the right to choose to join a trade union or an employer organisation, to bargain collectively or individually and to agree or not to agree on the issues in dispute and that the disputes between the parties should be resolved without the intervention of outside forces. A fundamental principle of this voluntarism is the absence of legally imposed structures.

Rights, obligations and the regulation of behaviour by both parties should be arrived at without State intervention and collective bargaining, not legislation, should be the primary source of regulation in the employment contract. In general these principles are supported both by the trade unions and employers (although on occasions there are calls from one side or the other, or from other quarters, for legal intervention on specific issues).

However, since Ireland joined the European Economic Community (EEC) in 1973, the State has become much more involved in the employee/management relationship by enacting a series of protective and control laws, thereby removing many aspects of this relationship from determination by collective bargaining. These laws, in general, set out certain minimum standards or a floor of statutory rights which may be improved upon by collective bargaining but cannot be taken away or diminished (Redmond, 1980). This trend towards the establishment of workplace rights, together with the emergence of centralised agreements since 1987, has reduced the 'pure' voluntarist approach and has given the State a much greater influence in the employment relationship.

Legislation is only acceptable by the social partners as a facilitator by providing the framework within which the industrial relations system can function and in providing structures for the settling of disputes. In its capacity as legislator, therefore, the State has, on the whole, taken a supportive role in the development of the industrial relations system. However, as the biggest employer in the labour market it has a major influence on the outcome of collective bargaining as regards labour costs and conditions of employment and has been a strong advocate of centralised agreements as a way to provide economic, social and employment stability within an open European and global market place.

Collective bargaining

Since 1946, wage increases have been regulated through a series of National Wage Rounds during which all workers received a cost-of-living increase for a given period, usually every two years. This system of regular bargaining at first was unplanned but eventually became institutionalised within the industrial relations system. This system was characterised by annual rounds of semi-structured boxing.

On a number of occasions, agreement on a Wage Round was negotiated centrally by the ICTU and the employers' organisations. However, these experiments never lasted longer than a single Wage Round, until 1970 when, under the threat of legislation to control incomes and prices, the employers' organisations and trade unions negotiated the first National Wage Agreement.

Seven such agreements were to follow. They set out the maximum levels of pay increases allowed and they also set strict controls on the scope for enterprise-level bargaining. They allowed such local negotiations in cases of productivity payments and flexibility arrangements and they also contained special minimum increases for lower paid workers. This process introduced more structure into the negotiations and, consequently placed boxing within a set of agreed parameters.

Initially, the Government participated in the negotiations on the National Wage Agreements as an employer but as the decade drew to an end it became apparent that taxation and budgetary policies were having a major impact on incomes and living standards. Between 1979 and 1981, therefore, two tripartite National Understandings were agreed. They covered, not just pay levels in the public and private sectors, but also a wide range of national economic and social policies, such as taxation, social welfare and health, education and training, labour law, housing and a commitment from the three parties to work together to achieve significant increases in employment. The first elements of dancing began to appear into the system.

In 1981, ten years of centralised agreements came to an end and there was a return to boxing. There were two reasons for this change of direction. A new right-of-centre government came to power which was not committed to negotiations with the trade unions and employers on such issues. Second, many private sector employers believed that they could achieve greater control over labour costs and in this way control their overall production costs at a time of global economic recession resulting from the second OPEC oil crisis.

However, the original objectives of de-centralised agreements were not realised – the economy continued in recession, the national debt escalated, unemployment increased, wage agreements in the private sector were higher than had been hoped and were higher than the norms laid down by the government and employers' organisation. Emigration also re-emerged as a major national problem.

National Agreements

With the next change of government, in 1987, all parties were committed to build on the earlier experience of dancing and a return to centralised bargaining, so a new National Agreement was concluded between the trade unions, employers, farming organisations and Government – the Programme for National Recovery (PNR) – covering a period of three years. Under this agreement very modest wage increases (below the rate of inflation) were allowed and these were to be negotiated through local bargaining so as to take into consideration the particular circumstances of individual firms. There was a return to the principle of special increases for low-paid workers. The Programme also included a range of measures on employment creation (by the private sector), taxation reform, labour legislation, education and training and a commitment by the parties to providing an economic climate which would assist growth and employment.

The PNR and the following, much more detailed, agreement – Programme for Social and Economic Progress (PESP) – were very successful in achieving the agreed objectives. Pay bargaining at enterprise level remained within the terms of the agreements. The rates of pay increases were just below or in line with inflation. The three-year period of the agreements provided a stable business environment which resulted in strong manufacturing and export performances, an average annual economic growth of 4%, increased competitiveness and increased employment. The PNR also included allowances for agreement through local bargaining of a reduction in working hours, the first reduction for over ten years.

Both of these national agreements had introduced a period of stability into Irish industrial relations and industrial disputes over pay became almost non-existent during this six-year period. Indeed, workdays lost due to industrial disputes continued to fall during the 1990s until in 2001 disputes had fallen to the lowest number since records began. The Irish system had made a quick and successful shift from boxing to dancing during this period.

These two National Programmes can be taken together as a period of economic recovery and to have provided the foundation for the unprecedented economic growth and job creation in the Irish economy in the latter half of the 1990s. The subsequent National Programmes fall into two distinct phases:

- Economic and social progress (1993–99):
  Programme for Competitiveness and Work (PCW) (1994);
  Partnership 2000 (1997);
- Social cohesion and an inclusive society (2000–2005):
  Programme for Prosperity and Fairness (PPF) (2000);
  Sustaining progress (2003).

In the negotiations on Partnership 2000 representatives from over twenty civil society organisations and non-govermental organisations (NGOs) were invited to participate. Consequently, the focus of the National Programmes has shifted from issues affecting the economy, the labour market and employment, to the improvement of living standards, social inclusion, equality and other social problems (housing, migration, disabilities etc).

While each National Agreement is negotiated between the parties without any commitment to continue the process, one point of interest is that there is now general political support for the process. All the major political parties represented in the Oireachtas (parliament) have been in government during the present series of centralised agreements and all are in support of continuing these centralised agreements. Sections of the trade union movement are more sceptical about continuing centralised negotiations as there is a view that workers, while restricting demands for pay increases, have not benefited in other ways from the process, such as their demands for greater levels of involvement and partnership at workplace level and for a legal right to union recognition.

Collective bargaining, therefore, is carried out primarily at national level, but there is also bargaining at the enterprise level in relation to the implementation of the National Programmes. Enterprise level negotiations covering such issues as employment contracts, wage/salary structures, conditions of employment, organisation of work, introduction of new technology and automation, disciplinary procedures, working time/holidays, training and others, are the subject of collective negotiation. Sectoral level bargaining is almost non-existent. A summary of boxing and dancing in Ireland together with future prospects is set out in Table 9.1.

Table 9.1 Boxing and dancing in Ireland: a classification

Level	Boxing	Dancing	Prospects
Global/ International	Few examples of boxing. Many large US-based companies in the information and electronic technology and biotechnology sectors are non-union, with a management emphasis on Human Resources Management (HRM).	Five Irish-owned companies have set up European Works Councils (EWCs), while there are Irish representatives on numerous other EWCs.	Irish trade unions will continue to play a full role in the European trade union movement and in the sectoral trade union organisations.
National	As collective bargaining is now conducted at the national level there has been a significant reduction in boxing. However, trends in the Public Services (education, health transport, etc.) show an upward shift in workplace conflict.	A series of three-year National Programmes on economic and social issues since 1987. Originally quadripartite – government, union, employer and farming organisations now multipartite, by including NGOs and community organisations. Under these programmes a National Centre for Partnership and Performance (NCPP), to promote 'dancing' at national and enterprise levels, has been set up.	While the present National Programme runs until end-2005, it is becoming more difficult to continue dancing and to reach consensus. There is no guarantee that the present arrangement will continue. However the NCPP will continue to work to promote partnership at national and enterprise levels.

Table 9.1 (Continued)

Level	Boxing	Dancing	Prospects
Sectoral/ Regional	There is no sectoral level bargaining in the Irish system.	Not applicable.	Little prospect of sectoral bargaining as it is not part of the Irish IR (Industrial Relations) tradition.
Local/ Workplace	in the private sector, issues around work organisation, flexibility, re-structuring, the introduction of new technologies and automation, and competitiveness are important subjects for collective bargaining, but seldom lead to open conflict.	Growing commitment to the introduction of different forms of employee involvement, dealing with a wide range of topics of common concern to management and the work force. A system of employee board-level representatives (worker directors) is in place in State-owned companies and agencies.	With transposition of the EU Directive on Information and Consultation there will be continued expansion of the partnership, dancing approach. However, a collapse of the National Programmes would result in a return to local level bargaining and an increase in boxing.

Employee participation[3]

Employee board-level representatives (Worker Directors)

With the failure of the social partners to agree on how to move from boxing to dancing in Irish workplaces, during the 1970s, the Government took the view that if anything was to happen regarding workers' participation then it would have to provide a stimulus. Consequently, in 1977 legislation was enacted giving employees in seven State-owned commercial companies the right to elect a third of the directors to the boards of these organisations (Worker Participation (State Enterprises) Act, 1977). This legislation was amended in 1988, extending the worker director system further and introducing a system of sub-board-level information and consultation committees within State-owned enterprises and agencies.

Trade unions or staff associations, recognised for the purpose of collective bargaining, with members in the company or agency, have the sole right to nominate the candidates for election and all employees, including certain part-time workers, are entitled to vote in the election of these board-level representatives. Once elected, and appointed by the relevant Minister, worker directors have the same rights and duties as all other directors. Following the introduction of the two Acts and the extension of the concept to other State-owned enterprises and agencies, there are now some 54 employee representatives who are members of over 20 boards, mainly in the public sector but also a few in the private sector.

However, this form of employee participation is under threat as of the seven original companies covered by the 1977 Act, three have been privatised. In one, B&I Shipping Co., the system of worker directors was terminated by the new owners. In the other two, NET (fertiliser manufacturing) and CSE (sugar production), the former boards are retained, which include the worker directors, but all commercial, operational and policy decisions are taken by a second board, representative of the private shareholders, and from which the employee representatives are excluded, thus having no influence on decision-making.

In another case (1996) the state sold the state telephone company, Telecom Éireann, to a joint Swedish/Dutch consortium, which, in turn sold it on to a Irish-American group. As part of the legislation to facilitate the privatisation of the company, the worker directors were removed from the board. In a parallel development the company and Government also sold 14.9% of the company to an ESOP Trust owned by the coalition of unions, in exchange for changes in work practices and cost reductions. This employee share-ownership in the company (now Eircom) has been increased to 29.9% under agreement with the new owners.

Social partner commitment

Recognising the success of consensus at national level, the ICTU and the FIE (now IBEC) published a Joint Declaration on the most acceptable approach for the private sector in 1991, setting out an agreed framework for employee involvement. This document relies heavily on the voluntarist nature of Irish industrial relations and it outlines in broad terms, the type of initiatives and suggested models which would be acceptable.

Building on the Joint Declaration, the third National Programme (the PCW), contained a section on developing partnership at work. It recognised the emphasis placed by the Joint Declaration on employee involvement and the role it could play in achieving higher levels of productivity and competitiveness at enterprises level. The commitment was further expanded in the Partnership 2000 agreement (see page 168). In the PPF there was an additional agreement on the introduction of partnership structures into the public services, in particular in the health services, local authorities and third-level Institutes of Technology.

It was also agreed to set up the National Centre for Partnership on a statuary footing, within the new National Economic and Social Development Office (to be called the National Centre for Partnership and Performance – NCPP). The role of this centre is to promote dancing at national and enterprise levels, identify cases of good practice, promote research and studies into the workplace of the future and to facilitate the social partners in reaching agreement on issues which will increase co-operation and consensus. Research carried out on behalf of the NCPP suggests that social partners and many firms, workforces and trade unions have already acquired significant experience with the operation of various forms of partnership (NCPP, 2002). One example of 'good practice' on the dance floor suggested by the NCPP is that of Jury's Hotel Group, summarised as Exhibit 9.1 (full case in the Appendix).

Other forms of employee participation

With the resistance of employers' organisations to agree to employee participation arrangements and the reluctance of the Government to introduce legislation without social partner agreement, the introduction of EU legislation for the establishment of European Works Councils brought a new concept to the Irish labour market by introducing, for the first time, statutory information and consultation rights into Private Sector employment. Five Irish multi-national enterprises have set up EWCs and an estimated 300 transnational enterprises with subsidiaries based in Ireland are covered by the Directive. Many of these have already established EWCs with members representing Irish workers at European-level meetings (Gallagher and Geraghty, 1997; Kerckhofs, 2002).

Exhibit 9.1   The partnership approach at Jury's Doyle Hotel Group

The Jury's Doyle Hotel Group is Ireland's leading hotel group. It employs approximately 4000 people in some 32 hotels in Ireland, the UK and US. Sixteen of these hotels with a workforce of 2600, are in Ireland. Following participation of its 'flagship' hotel, in Dublin, in an EU-funded ADAPT project in 1998, designed to examine issues around workplace partnership, a steering committee was set up, which included the general manager and other senior management representatives and key union personnel. The initial focus of the steering committee was on team dynamics and building trust (industrial relations issues were excluded from the work of the steering committee). Training on decision-making, communications and financial information was provided to facilitate the process. As the process progressed a number of achievements were recorded, for example:

- job-sharing in Reservations Section;
- housekeeping staff were consulted on the re-design of rooms;
- reception staff were involved in the re-design of the reception area;
- productivity deals and Save-as-you-Earn (SAYE) schemes were agreed.

The introduction of dancing in the Jury's Doyle Group has provided it with a competitive advantage in its response to the extremely difficult period in the sector over the past few years, post-September 11, 2001. It has enabled the Group to respond with greater flexibility to the developing crisis and provided a mechanism to ensure staff were aware of and understood the survival strategies and actions undertaken by management.

(*Working Together for Change and a Modern Workplace* NCPP, Dublin (2002) – case study 4).

The transposition of the EU Framework Directive on Information and Consultation (COM/98/612) will extend this process further and employee involvement will have been achieved through the EU route, something the unions have advocated for decades, but until now, without success, because of the insistence of employers' organisations on the voluntary introduction of employee involvement arrangements at the enterprise level.

Responding to the trend emanating from the European Union (EU), the ICTU published a guide to assist union representatives in the establishment of workplace partnerships and for working within a dancing environment (ICTU, 1997). In this document Congress sets out its objectives for:

- The widest possible diffusion of the partnership concept.
- Greater union involvement within companies in managing change and better facilities to represent members.
- A meaningful improvement in working conditions and rewards for workers.

The guide recommends that affiliate unions adopt the development of workplace partnership as a key objective and that they should set a goal of establishing a partnership process in a majority of workplaces in which unions are represented.

The Jury's Hotel's case illustrates well how a partnership can encompass the broad area of employee participation. There is also evidence, however, that the substance of other partnerships have extended to include the traditional distributional issues that we would normally associate with the boxing ring. For example, a recent deal at AIB Banks has involved agreement on a 35-hour week (see Exhibit 9.2).

Attitudes to trade unions

After 16 years of national partnership, the trade union movement is debating its future attitude to centralised agreements. This debate is fuelled by a number of developments, such as the perceived disenchantment of low-paid workers with their wage increases; the slow progress in establishing workplace partnership; the danger of the role of unions being marginalised at enterprise level; and the increased difficulties unions are facing in recruiting new members, which is linked to the union recognition debate.[4]

In an effort to determine its future policies on these and other issues, Congress sponsored a national survey on attitudes to unions (ICTU, 1998). The survey found that the vast majority of the public have a positive attitude towards trade unions and to national social partnership. It highlighted a number of opportunities for unions in Ireland, but also a number of problems. Of those surveyed who were employed, 59% of non-unionised workers said that they would join a union if they had the opportunity. For

Exhibit 9.2   AIB partnership deal includes 35-hour week

In April 2003, 6000 staff of AIB Banks voted to accept a 3-year industrial relations agreement that includes a 35-hour working week, as part of an ongoing partnership approach to change between the bank and the Irish Bank Officials' Association (IBOA).

The new deal is the most concrete development in the partnership process involving AIB and the IBOA, which started almost five years ago as part of a wider effort to develop workplace partnership in AIB. The agreement was concluded with the assistance of an independent consultant, Phil Flynn, a former President of the Irish Congress of Trade Unions. Mr Flynn described the AIB/IBOA model as one of the 'best of its kind in operation in these islands'.

Apart from the introduction of a 35-hour working week, which is relatively rare in Ireland, significant aspects of the deal include:

- long service-increments that are to benefit several hundred longer serving staff;
- a commitment on no-closures of rural branches for the duration of the agreement;
- no voluntary redundancies for three years;
- discussions on 'gainsharing', under specific headings such as 'profit share', 'share options' and 'bonus payments'.

For AIB, the key to the proposed deal is that it firmly commits IBOA to engage positively and proactively in meeting the market-driven demands of the business. The agreement states there should be 'no strait jacket' put on the bank's change and 'transformation' agenda. Meanwhile, 'best practice' should apply in regard to consultation, adherence to agreements and 'consensus-based bargaining'. Key roles in negotiating the deal on the management and union sides were played by the bank's head of employee relations and the general secretary of the IBOA.

The agreement is seen as a major landmark in the context of Irish industrial relations and as a milestone in the slow development of enterprise-level partnership, which is being strongly promoted by the NCPP. The Executive Chair of the NCPP also chairs the AIB/IBOA partnership steering committee.

AIB is one of the big two banks operating in Ireland, the other being Bank of Ireland. Between them, they have dominated the Irish banking scene for decades.

(www.eiro.eurofound.eu.int/2003/05/inbrief/ie0305201n.html)

the 18–24 year-olds this figure increased to 65%. This goes against the perceived view that young people do not have a positive attitude to unions. The preference for union membership was also high among lower paid workers – 66% of skilled manual, semi-skilled and unskilled workers said they would join a union if they had the opportunity.

Ninety-four per cent of those surveyed viewed the role of ICTU in national social partnership very positively. However, almost a quarter (24%) of union members had the view that unions could represent them better than through participation in national agreements. However 65% of members wanted more involvement in workplace decisions concerning their jobs (56 per cent for non-union respondents).

In the context of the centralised partnership model and the challenge of remaining relevant to their memberships, trade unions in Ireland are having to change. In the face of growing European and global competition there is as much pressure on workers' representatives to find new ways of working, as there is on management. There are indications that both sides are stepping back from confrontation to find different ways of addressing workplace problems and resolving disputes. Even though the conflict resolution machinery, such as the Labour Relations Commission and Labour Court, is still available, there is not the same tendency to use these facilities as in previous times. Although very often using dancing as a way of working together may not be formalised or accompanied by the introduction of structures, there is a tendency for it to be 'institutionalised in an informal way'.

However, this trend towards dancing is also dependent on the business sector. The more open the sector is, the greater the possibility there is of the actors dancing. While in other sectors where employment is not as sensitive to business trends, such as the public services, existing employment relations structures are more formal and work practices are more entrenched, consequently, change is more difficult to bring about and the difference between boxing and dancing is more finely balanced.

Conclusion

The ICTU survey shows that trade unions in Ireland are in a healthy position but, with other movements in Europe, they are faced with major challenges in remaining relevant within a quickly changing working environment. The resolution of key targets, such as on trade union recognition and workplace employee involvement, will determine the future direction of the relationship between the unions, employers and government and the future of the series of national level agreements, which have served the Irish economy so well in recent years.

Since the beginning of these National Programmes and, in particular, since the fourth agreement (Partnership 2000) in 1997 there has been an increase in the level of interest and implementation of enterprise level consensus problem solving and the establishment of partnership fora. The process has been assisted by institutional and structural support through the NCPP and through close co-operation between ICTU and IBEC on a range of joint programmes and promotions. It is also been driven by the pending transposition of the EU Framework Directive on Information and Consultation, so the management of many enterprises are moving in anticipation of this new legislation.

There are also some dark clouds – for example, the well-established and successful system of worker directors (board-level representatives) has been, to some extent, sidelined and put under pressure. In the light of the experiences of worker directors, past and present, the future for board-level employee participation in the policy formation and decision-making process is not very encouraging. There is an underlying suspicion and opposition to any form of employee representation on boards of companies and the political climate is not as supportive as previously, seeing other forms of employee involvement, such as direct participation, as more relevant.

While dancing has become the dominant form of employment relations in Ireland during the past 16 years, a reasonable degree of trust has been built between the social partners at national and, to a lesser extent, at local levels. However, as each National Programme is always seen as a 'stand alone' agreement, with no commitment by the parties to the negotiation of a successor, the prospect of a return to boxing and workplace conflict is always lurking close to the surface.

To sum up, the Irish system has seen an evolution from a highly conflictual approach to a greater degree of mutual understanding and emphasis on consensus problem solving in dealing with challenges at the enterprise, company and national levels – a significant shift from boxing to dancing across a wide range of issues. The trade unions and employer organisations have always had an influence on the formation of national policies and this has grown even stronger in recent years through the National Programmes. Nevertheless, in the Irish context, dancing is a fragile art and the possibility of reverting to boxing is never too far away.

Notes

1. I would like to acknowledge the contributions to this chapter of Jack Nash, Regional Secretary, SIPTU, Martin Naughton, Head of Education and Training, SIPTU, and Andy Burke, SIPTU representatives in Jury's Hotel, Ballsbridge.
2. Some examples of legal intervention in the industrial relations process are legislation in 1966 to prohibit disputes in the national electricity board (ESB). A number of workers in dispute were imprisoned for continuing to picket in defiance of a Court injunction. This resulted in a nation-wide power blackout and eventually, as part of the settlement, the Government gave an undertaking to repeal the legislation. On two occasions during the mid-1970s legislation was enacted to prevent the associate banks from paying their staff, members of the IBOA, increases in excess of the terms of the National Pay Agreements, which were voluntary agreements and, in themselves, did not have any legal status. The banks and the IBOA were not parties to the negotiations on the National Agreements. While this legislative involvement in a collective bargaining agreement produced the desired results on both occasions, these Acts were eventually declared to be un-constitutional by the Supreme (Constitutional) Court, thus preventing the use of this option by future governments.

3. For developments in employee participation see the Department of Labour 'Report of the Advisory Committee on Worker Participation' (1986) – Chapter 2. This Advisory Committee was set up arising out of discussions on the Government Paper *Worker Participation – A Discussion Paper* (1980). As a result of the recommendations of the Advisory Committee two booklets were issued by the Department, 'Guidelines for Employee Participation' (1986) and 'Case Studies in Employee Participation' (1989) to promote the concept of workers' participation in Irish enterprises.

4. The issue of trade union recognition has come to the fore in the debate on the future of industrial relations in Ireland as a result of a number of high profile industrial disputes related to this problem – for example, Pat the Baker, Nolan Transport and Ryanair. In most cases, which are heard by the Labour Court as recognition disputes, the Court recommends recognition of union representation but in a number of cases, as in these three, the companies have refused to implement the Court findings, thus further antagonising the unions.

References

Cradden, T. (1993) 'The Tories and Employment Law in Northern Ireland: Seeing Unions in a Different Light?' *Industrial Relations Journal* 24(1) 59–71.

D'Art, D. and Turner, T. (2003) 'Union Recognition in Ireland: One Step Forward and Two Steps Back', *Industrial Relations Journal* 34(3): 226–40.

Department of Labour (1980) *Worker Participation – A Discussion Paper*. Dublin.

Department of Labour (1986) *Report of the Advisory Committee on Worker Participation*. Dublin.

Federation of Irish Employers (FIE) / Irish Congress of Trade Unions (ICTU) (1991) Joint Declaration on Employee Involvement in the Private Sector.

Gallagher, N. and Geraghty, D. (1997) *European Works Councils – Information and Consultation Rights*. Irish Productivity Centre.

Government Stationary Office (GSO) (1994) *Programme for Competitiveness and Work*.

Irish Business and Employers' Confederation (1993) *Teams in Action – A Report on Team Working in Leading Irish Companies*. Dublin.

Irish Congress of Trade Unions (1997) *Partnership in the Workplace – Guidelines for Unions*. Dublin.

Irish Congress of Trade Unions (1998) *What People Think of Unions*. Dublin.

Institute of Public Administration (IPA) (1998–2003) *Administration Yearbook*. Dublin.

Kerckhofs, P. (2002) *European Works Councils: Facts and Figures*. Brussels: European Trade Union Institute.

Kerr, A. and Whyte, G. (1985) *Irish Trade Union Law*. London: Professional Books Ltd.

Kirwan, C. (1991) Presidential Address to ICTU Annual Delegate Conference.

Labour Relations Commission (1996) *Improving Industrial Relations – A Strategic Policy*. Dublin.

National Centre for Partnership and Performance (2002) *Working Together for Change and a Modern Workplace*. Dublin.

Redmond, M. (1980) 'The Law and Workers' Rights' in *Trade Unions and Change in Irish Society* Nevin, D. (ed.). Cork: Mercier Press/RTE.

SIPTU (1993) *Total Quality – Implications for Competitiveness and Positive Trade Unionism: The SIPTU Position*. Dublin.

Turner, T. and Morley, M. (eds) (1995) *Industrial Relations and the New Order*. Dublin: Oak Tree Press and Graduate School of Business, Dublin: University College.

Further reading

European Foundation for the Improvement of Living and Working Conditions (Dublin), *EIROnline* (www.eiro.eurofound.ie), various items on social partnership in Ireland, for example:
  Union Recognition Report Supports Continuation of Voluntarist Approach (Jan., 1998);
  The Problem of Trade Union Recognition: Endangering Social Consensus in Ireland? (Mar., 1998);
  Social Partners Launch Major Training Initiative (July, 1999);
  Survey Finds Strong Support for Pay Moderation and Social Partnership (28 Jan., 2000);
  New National Centre for Partnership and Performance Established (April, 2001);
  Social Partners Debate Priorities as Economy Slows Down (Nov., 2001);
  Employers Set Out Blueprint for Social Partnership (Oct., 2002).
FIE (1991a) (now IBEC) Press Statement to coincide with the publication of the Joint Declaration (June).
FIE (1991b) (now IBEC) Guidelines on Employee Involvement. Dublin.
Government Stationary Office (GSO) (1977) Worker Participation (State Enterprises) Act.
Government Stationary Office (GSO) (1988) Worker Participation (State Enterprises) Act.
Government Stationary Office (GSO) (1987) *Programme for National Recovery*.
Government Stationary Office (GSO) (1991) *Programme for Economic and Social Progress*.
Government Stationary Office (GSO) (1997) *Partnership 2000*.
Government Stationary Office (GSO) (2000) *Programme for Prosperity and Fairness*.
Government Stationary Office (GSO) (2003) *Sustaining Progress*.
Irish Congress of Trade Unions (1993) *New Forms of Work Organisation – Options for Unions*. Dublin.
Irish Congress of Trade Unions (1995) *Managing Change*. Dublin.
Irish Congress of Trade Unions (1997) Report to Conference. Dublin.
Irish Congress of Trade Unions (2003) *People in Unions are Better Off – Report of the Executive Council, 2001–2003*. Dublin.
National Economic and Social Forum, Dublin (1997) *A Framework for Partnership: Enriching Strategic Consensus through Participation* (Forum Report No. 16).
O'Brien, J. F. (1990) *The Role of Employer Organisations in Ireland* in 'Industrial Relations in Ireland'. Dublin: University College.
O'Dowd, J. (1998) *Employee Partnership in Ireland – A Guide for Managers*. Dublin: Oak Tree Press.
O'Kelly, K. P. (1995) *A Joint Approach to Direct Participation – Ireland*. European Foundation Working Paper (WP/95/01/EN).
O'Kelly, K. P. (1996) *The Role of Worker Directors in the European Union* (ed.) Irish Worker Directors' Group – Proceedings of a transnational seminar (September).
O'Kelly, K. P. (2000) 'Ireland: Shifting from Voluntarism to National Agreements' in *Trade Unions in Europe – Facing Challenges and Searching for Solutions*, Waddington, J. and Hoffmann, R. (eds). Brussels: European Trade Union Institute.
O'Kelly, K. P. and Doyle, P. (1997) 'Workers' Participation in Ireland and the Guinness Brewery Council' in Markey, R. and Monat, J. (eds) *Innovative and Employee Participation through Works Councils*. Aldershot: Avebury.
Wedderburn, K. W. (1971) *The Worker and the Law*. London: Penguin.

10

Romania: Learning to Dance

Aurora Trif and Karl Koch

Introduction: radical change in 1989

This chapter explores the strategic choices of trade unions in Romania, during a period of radical change from a centrally planned economy to a market economy model. In Romania, partnership (dancing) as well as collective bargaining (boxing) between independent unions and (private) employers are new phenomena, which emerged after the collapse of the communist regime in 1989. In the unitary communist system, with its centrally planned economy, trade unions were the largest mass membership organisation, but their main functions were to support the accomplishment of the economic plan decided by the communist apparatus as well as to distribute social benefits (Thirkell and Vickerstaff, 2002: 58). At the company level, there were no clear boundaries between unions and the management. However, in contrast with business unionism in Western countries, the trade union leadership was integrated, and totally subordinated to the Communist Party (Nelson, 1986: 108). Hence, Romanian trade unions did not even seek to have strategic choices before 1989.

The fall of the communist regime in Eastern Europe in 1989 conferred unions the freedom to dance and box with the employers. Despite a general climate that favoured the market mechanism and resulted in a massive decline of union membership as well as a decrease in the living standards for most employees, evidence suggests that unions generally have chosen a partnership (dancing) approach to industrial relations, except when their survival was at stake. As a result, various incipient forms of partnership between trade unions and employers have emerged in the precarious transition context, but the social partners are still learning to dance.

The chapter focuses on trade union strategic choices in relation to employers. It begins by presenting an overview of the current state of industrial relations in Romania from a union perspective. Subsequently, boxing and the main types of dancing operating at the national (transsectoral), sectoral and workplace levels are examined.[1] In the concluding part, perspectives and implications for the unions in Eastern Europe are explored. The case of the Romanian trade unions illustrates an example of opportunities and constraints faced by unions in Eastern Europe in the context of transformation from the centrally planned economy to a market economy model.

Contextual overview

Before and during the communist regime

In Romania, there is a weak tradition of partnership as well as voluntary collective bargaining between trade unions and employers. Since the 1920s, legislation has played an important role in industrial relations (Burloiu, 1997; Moarcas, 1999). The Law No.41/1921 provided legal recognition of unions as well as the right to conclude collective agreements (Moarcas, 1999), but the trade union movement was not well developed, having only 519 000 members in 1945 (Nelson 1986: 108). Laws passed before 1945, outlawed trade unions for a year in 1920 (following a general strike) and between 1938 and 1944 (when the Royal dictatorship was established – see Burloiu, 1997: 369). Additionally, laws on collective labour disputes required conciliation and/or arbitration by the state representatives, if no agreement was achieved. As a result, a number of collective agreements were concluded between trade unions and employers before 1945, but most of them were either settled through arbitration procedures or after an industrial conflict took place (Moarcas, 1999). Therefore, dancing was not a feature of industrial relations before the communist regime.

It could be argued that a sense of co-operation between unions and the management had developed at company level during the communist period. Beginning with 1945, a single trade union was established in each company covering almost the entire labour force. Company unions were united under an umbrella federation in each industrial sector, which formed a single confederation in 1966. As the union leadership was part of the party apparatus, trade unions did not seek to have any strategic choices in Romania during the period of communist rule, performing so-called political 'transmission belt' functions (Nelson 1986: 108). Their role was strongly influenced by the ideological belief that there were no divergent interests between employees, management and the state (Hethy, 1991: 125). Furthermore, as the central plan mechanism allocated resources (e.g. raw materials, wages and human resources), trade unions had a common interest with the management to get as many resources as possible at company level to fulfil the plan (Kornai, 1992). Additionally, since 1978 trade unions were part of the management board (Kollonay-Lehoczky, 1997). Hence, co-operation between trade unions and management had developed, but it resulted generally in business unionism rather than partnership (as defined by Huzzard in Chapter 2).

The 1990s

With the collapse of the communist regime in 1989, unions acquired the freedom to dance and box with the employers. The communist unions were abolished or transformed and new, often rival, organisations to the former ones were set up immediately after 1989 (Draus, 2001: 11). However, their choices have been influenced by inherited legacies. For instance, in large public companies, trade unions have generally chosen to maintain co-operative relations with the management team, especially to get subsidies for their company or other favours from the government.[2] However, some fierce boxing matches (strikes) with the government in the public sector, particularly related to the closure of loss-making companies, have occurred (e.g. in the mining sector – see Martin, 1999). Therefore, dancing and boxing have been taking place simultaneously in Romania, but unions are still learning how to dance alongside boxing to achieve benefits for their members.

The transition process represented an opportunity for unions to participate in the establishment of the new labour legislation as well as in the economic and political strategies. Across Central and Eastern European countries (CEECs), tripartite forums for national consultation among the government, trade unions and employers' associations were established, as a source of mutual legitimisation of the parties involved (Draus, 2001; Thirkell and Vickerstaff, 2002). Apart from consultation with regard to the establishment of labour institutions, trade unions participated in public policy formulation regarding income, wage, employment and social policies (Hethy, 2001: 14). Nevertheless, in contrast with Western Europe, tripartism in Eastern Europe has developed in a context of economic recession and it did not result in a positive outcome for labour (Ost, 2000). Furthermore, Thirkell and Vickerstaff (2002) convincingly argue that trade unions were actually involved in the decision-making process only when governments needed union support to share the responsibility for the economic burden. As the economic situation is precarious in Romania, tripartite forums are still important in 2003, but their significance is likely to diminish when the transformation process is over. In Romania, union partnership choices (tripartism) resulted in labour legislation fairly favourable to labour, which may be considered an important achievement of trade unions. However, as in other CEECs, it did not result in substantive advantages in terms of wages and working life quality, as unemployment increased while the living standards of most employees had declined (Martin and Cristesco-Martin, 2002: 524–5).

The current state of Romanian industrial relations from a union perspective

Trade union density declined from around 90% in 1991, to 77% in 1995 and 58% in 2000 out of the near eight million labour force (Centrul de Resurse Pentru Sindicate, 2000). Another source indicates that trade union density in 2002 was between 40% and 46% (Clarke *et al.*, 2003: 144). It is not clear how reliable these union membership data are, but there was certainly a huge decline in trade union membership during the 1990s. The reasons for the decline are partly due to specific circumstances of the transition period, such as the emergence of small- and medium-sized enterprises with virtually no trade union representation, the restructuring of all sectors that had over-employment, and the closure of many large enterprises (Martin, 1999; Clarke *et al.*, 2003). Additionally, there has been a decrease in the manufacturing sector and an expansion of employment sectors where unions are not well represented, such as services and agriculture. Hence, the transition period resulted in a huge decline in trade union membership during the 1990s, but union density is still higher in Romania than other countries where economic reforms are more advanced, such as Poland (15%) and Hungary (20%) (Stanojevic and Gradev, 2003: 38).

There are three main layers in the union hierarchies, namely national (confederations), sectoral (federations) and the company, which is the basic unit. At the peak level, the five largest union confederations[3] are the following:

- *The National Free Trade Union Confederation of Romania – Fratia* is the largest confederation covering 33.7% from a total of around two million trade union members.[4] It was created in 1993 through a merger of the reformed official union and a new union (Fratia), both confederations initially established in 1990. It includes 48 federations from various industrial sectors and services (e.g. petroleum and telecom).
- *The National Trade Union Block* was created in 1991 and it represents 20.6% of all trade union members. It includes 39 union federations representing mainly the machine-building industry, the chemical and oil industry, arts and culture and transportation.
- *The National Democratic Trade Union Confederation of Romania* was created in 1994 as a result of a split from the CNSRL-Fratia and it comprises 16.5% of total union membership. It includes 22 federations being mainly represented in the education, health and food sectors.
- *The National Trade Union Confederation Cartel Alfa* was created in 1990 and it represents 16.4 % of trade union members. It comprises 27 federations being represented in various sectors of industry (e.g. steel and mining), services and agriculture.
- *Meridian* was created in 1994 and it covers 8.9% of all trade union members. It includes 22 federations being represented mainly in mining, oil, chemicals and light industry.

The two largest confederations support the Social Democrat Party (the party in power since 2000), while the third supports the Christian-Democrats (Rusu, 2002). As Rusu (2002: 26) argues, it appears that the ideological fragmentation of the Romanian confederations is based on the pragmatic interests of the confederation leaderships rather than an expression of the ideology of union members.

The main goal of all confederations is to defend and promote the professional, economic and social aims of their members (Moarcas, 1999: 233). Since 1989, their main influence has been in the creation of the new labour legislation (interviewees). Additionally, confederations' have been involved in establishing the minimum terms and conditions of employment via tripartite bodies and collective bargaining at the national level. They also assure legal assistance to their members and support federations in collective bargaining if they so require. However, since the minimum labour standards are very low and the legal framework is often not implemented, the benefits for employees at the company level are not always visible. Therefore, the strategic choice of the unions to focus on national level issues has resulted in legislation fairly favourable to labour, but it has not resulted (yet) in a positive outcome for many of their members.

Trade union federations are generally not well consolidated. Federations are constituted from company trade unions from the same industry. As only two company unions are legally required to form a federation, they are fragmented and competing (Mihes and Casale, 1999; Rusu, 2002). Additionally, the financial resources available to the union federations are very limited. For instance, in the construction sector less than 20% of membership dues goes to the federations and confederations, while 80% remains with the company unions (which collect the membership fees see – Clarke *et al.*, 2003). Federations generally deal with industry specific labour legislation, collective bargaining and professional training (Rusu, 2002: 31). In 1998, only 12 industrial sectors were covered by collective agreements comprising 42.6% of the total labour force.[5] Furthermore, the collective agreements concluded at the sectoral level establish only the minimum set of terms and conditions in the respective sector, which are often similar to those concluded at transsectoral level (Mihes and Casale, 1999). Therefore, in contrast with most of Western Europe, the company level is the main arena where terms and conditions of employment are established in most Eastern European countries (see Lado and Vaughan-Whitehead, 2003).

The basic units of trade union hierarchies are company unions.[6] These unions are constituted from at least 15 employees working in the same firm. One or more unions may operate in the same company, but only those covering more than 30% of the labour force have the legal right to negotiate collective agreements. Apart from concluding and monitoring the implementation of the collective agreements, company unions deal with individual issues for their members, depending on their own statutes and resources (Moarcas, 1999). Their financial resources come primarily from their membership fees, which are generally around 1% of the wage. The decentralised structure of unions alongside companies' survival issues in the precarious transition context favoured a decentralised industrial relations system, which resulted in great variation across sectors and companies.

Nevertheless, in contrast with many countries in Western Europe, legislation in Romania heavily regulates the relations between trade unions and employers. This legislation requires management to initiate CB annually within any company with more than 20 employees (Law 143 of 1997). Additionally, the law allows only a single collective agreement to be negotiated at national, sectoral and company levels, which should cover all employees from the bargaining unit. The legislation also stipulates the requirements which should be fulfilled by the parties to be allowed to

Table 10.1 Boxing and dancing in Romania: a classification

Level	Boxing	Dancing	Prospects
Global/ international	Virtually no boxing rings.	Virtually no dance floors.	Participation via EWC (European works Councils) in the few large MNCs (Multinational companies) operating in Romania.
National	First stage of collective bargaining (CB) (Transsectoral agreement): Bargaining role of (the five representative) union confederations, but results in a minimal framework for lower levels of negotiation.	Historical legacy of authoritarian corporatism. Incipient dancing in the tripartite Economic and Social Council (e.g. co- determination on labour legislation, consultation on social policy and EU enlargement).	Less scope for dancing after labour legislation would become more stable. Increased pressure for decentralisation to the company and sector levels.
Sectoral (no regional boxing rings or dance floors)	Second stage of CB (Industry Agreement): Bargaining role of union federations, but still a minimal framework for the company agreement.	Incipient dancing in the sectoral tripartite commissions (e.g. information and consultation on sectoral issues, such as bad weather funds in the construction industry). Early stages of collective agreements (e.g. Industry Agreement).	Potentially increased dancing with the consolidation of the sectoral tripartite bodies established.
Local/ workplace	Third stage of CB (Company Agreement): The final stage of CB in which the actual terms and conditions of employment are established, including wages. Co-determination in relation to restructuring (though some dancing element).	Company agreements (e.g. Petromidia). Co-determination where shared interests (e.g. privatisation, subsidies from the state in the public sector, training and health and safety). Union representation on consultative bodies including company boards.	Both boxing and dancing. Evidence of union preference for dancing, but also indicating as well a tradition of unions being co-opted by the management ('sleeping together').

negotiate the single collective agreement at a particular level (e.g. membership level). Additionally, it indicates the minimal scope of a collective agreement and the fact that provisions included in collective agreements at lower levels have to be similar or more favourable for employees than those agreed at higher levels. Therefore, statutory legislation still plays a major role in the relations between trade unions and employers.

Evidence suggests that boxing and dancing between trade unions and employers and their representatives are taking place at three main levels. A preliminary synopsis of current as well as prospects of dancing and boxing at various levels is presented in Table 10.1. Unlike in the EU (European Union) member states, in Romania unions have virtually no relations with employers at international level. This is likely to change, when Romania joins the EU. Trade union strategic choices after 1989 and prospects of dancing and boxing at the national, sectoral and company levels are examined in detail in the next section.

Boxing and dancing at the national (transsectoral) level

The state-led dance at the national level

Since the beginning of the transition period, tripartism has been the strategic choice of the social partners throughout CEECs due to pragmatic reasons (Hethy, 2001; Thirkell and Vickerstaff, 2002). First, tripartism was a source of mutual legitimisation for the parties involved, which have been facing deficits of support (Hethy, 2001: 10). Second, tripartism was a means of securing legitimacy for political and economic transformation, and to maintain social peace in a context of economic recession (Martin, 1999: 379; Hethy, 2001: 10). Third, there was a long tradition in CEECs of governments dealing with trade unions at national level as well as relying on unions to implement their policies (Vidinova, 1997: 86). Finally, international organisations, such as the International Labour Organisation (ILO) and the EU, also recommended tripartism (Hethy, 2001: 11). For unions, the short-term choice to share the burden of the transformation was outweighed by the privilege to be a reform maker and to ensure restructuring without major losses in employees' rights in the long term (Vidinova, 1997). Nevertheless, across Eastern Europe, tripartism was primarily an action initiated by the state seeking the support of trade unions (which have been the largest mass organisation) for its reform.

Tripartite forums have been designed to deal with dancing as well as boxing activities. According to Hethy (2001: 14), the main functions of the tripartite bodies in the region have been as follows:

(a) consultation with regard to the establishment of new labour institutions and the legislative framework;
(b) national level wage negotiation;

(c) participation in public policy formulation with regard to income, wage, employment and social policies;
(d) settlement of national industrial conflicts.

Of these, only (a) has primarily dealt with shared interests, as all three partners have been committed (at least initially) to establishing a legal framework that facilitates the development of social dialogue and voluntary collective bargaining (Lado, 2002), while (b), (c) and (d) are predominantly adversarial issues. Hence, the creation of tripartite bodies has been based on long-term commitment between the parties, but it was accepted that arenas should be set up for dancing as well as boxing activities.

In Romania, the first tripartite institution was created in 1993, part of a Phare assistance programme (Mihes and Casale, 1999: 277). The Tripartite Secretariat for Social Dialog was established to provide support in setting up labour institutions and a legal framework that would facilitate the dialogue between unions, employers' associations and the government. This institution was dissolved in 1997, when the direct funding from Phare ceased. Nevertheless, a new Economic and Social Council was created in 1997 by the government (Law no. 141/1997). This Council had an advisory role in developing economic and social policy. It endorsed draft legislation primarily regarding wages, employees' rights and duties, unemployment, social insurance and pensions. Additionally, it mediated collective conflicts if the parties involved required its assistance. Despite fairly extensive legal rights, its General Secretary (interviewed in May 2001) revealed that its effectiveness in representing employees' interests has generally been reduced. He indicated that employers' associations were still very weak and dominated by the state representatives. As a result, the state could often pursue its initial proposals, assuming a double role, as government and as employer in the tripartite forum. Hence, the national arena is dominated by the state, which frequently dictates the 'dancing steps' for the unions and the undeveloped employers' organisations.

The commitment to dancing (partnership) has been reinforced in recent years. A tripartite National Agency for Employment and Professional Training was set up in 1999. Its main scope is to deliver training services for job seekers, job mediation and to manage the unemployment fund (Mihes and Casale, 1999: 281). Additionally, the first social pact (*Acord Social*) was signed in 2001 between trade unions, employers' associations and the newly elected government. Trade unions agreed to refrain from industrial action for one year in exchange for government commitment to take measures to increase the living standards of the population and to create new jobs (Martin and Cristesco-Martin, 2002: 529). As the government was unable to fulfil these promises, the second largest union confederation, the Cartel Alfa, withdrew from it after six months. The social pact also included provisions to establish a tripartite forum for every industrial sector, which would meet whenever a party requires debating issues specific to that particular sector (interviewee – a state official).[7] The social pact was renewed in 2002, but only three out of the five largest union confederations signed it (Rusu, 2002: 29). Hence, incipient dancing activities have been taking place in the national arena, but the social partners are just learning to dance.

Romanian trade unions have also used the national arena for boxing activities. As indicated in Table 10.1, the first step of the collective bargaining process takes place at the national level.[8] Despite the fact that it establishes only a minimal framework for lower levels of collective bargaining, it has sometimes led to industrial action. At the beginning of the 1990s, strikes were quite frequent and related primarily to wages and job security (Kideckel, 2002: 103). Apart from 'bread and butter' issues, Romanian trade unions, particularly mining organisations,[9] have been involved in political strikes. Although strikes generally started with demands for wage increases, the miners strike and march on Bucharest in September 1991 for example, led directly to the fall of the first democratically elected government (Martin and Cristesco-Martin, 1999: 399).[10] Additionally, under union pressure, the government favoured particular industries. For instance, the Government Ordinance 22/1997 entitled miners that worked for more than 15 years to receive a severance payment worth 20 monthly wages, while workers in the other sectors are entitled to less than 12 months wages (Kideckel 2002,: 107). Furthermore, wage increases achieved by unions were regularly followed by a higher increase in inflation (Pert and Vasile, 1995; Rusu, 2002). Therefore, 'boxing matches' resulted in some accomplishments, but these were generally short-lived solutions.

Union achievements did not result in a positive outcome for labour where it counts most. Overall, unions failed to preserve or expand either labour's purchasing power or employees' jobs (Kideckel, 2002: 97). Additionally, the disrespect of employers and the government of the labour laws as well as the expansion of the black market labour made the success of the unions very limited at operational level (Interviewees – trade union officials and employers' association officials; see also Clarke *et al.*, 2003). Romanian unions have been among the most militant in Eastern Europe (Martin, 1999; Kideckel, 2002), but they have become more committed to partnership than to adversarial relations as the developments at the sectoral and the company levels indicate.

Fragile dancing and boxing arenas at the sectoral level

Formal arenas for dancing and boxing have been established at the sectoral level, but there is a weak development of the relationship between the social partners. The legislation provides for the establishment of Consultative Commissions of Social Dialogue at ministries and at the prefects' offices. These are tripartite consultative bodies consisting of representatives of the ministry concerned (or local authorities), trade union federations and the employers' association from a particular industry (or area). In these forums, social partners are consulted on draft laws concerning the specific industry as well as enterprise restructuring measures, and they can bring up any claims and proposals to be considered (Mihes and Casale, 1999: 281). Additionally, other incipient forms of tripartite bodies have emerged, such as the Social House of Builders in the construction industry. Its main functions are to manage the bad weather funds and to deal with training issues in the construction industry. Therefore, a dance floor at the sectoral level has been established in Romania, which formally is more solid than in other CEECs (see Clarke *et al.*, 2003).

However, evidence indicates a low level of effectiveness of the tripartite forums in practice, primarily due to a very weak commitment by the employers. For instance, in the case of the chemical industry, where a sectoral employers' association named the Fepachim has been operating since the 1990s, an official revealed that it is very difficult to get a common position among their members. A further illustration of the little importance given by the members of the employers' association, is the fact that the staff of the Fepachim consisted of four officials of whom only one (the vice president) was working full time for the organisation. Additionally, their headquarters consists of a room in the same state-owned enterprise with that of the largest union federation. The Fepachim illustrates a fairly typical case of the degree of (under)development of employers' associations in Romania. The slow development of the private sector has made the Romanian employers' association among the weakest in Eastern Europe. However, their lack of experience combined with the heterogeneity of the new employers as well as their strength at the company level has resulted in a weak development of employers' associations throughout Eastern Europe (Draus, 2001). Hence, it has been very difficult for unions even to learn any 'dance steps' at the sectoral level, with a dancing partner from the employer side not able and/or willing to decide which type of dance they want to perform.

As regards boxing activities, the sectoral level represents the second stage of collective bargaining (see Table 10.1). In contrast with Western Europe, the sectoral collective bargaining sets only a minimal framework for that particular sector. It deals with a wide range of issues, from wages, to training and health and safety standards. The provisions of the sectoral agreements cannot be set below those established by the national collective agreement and the Labour Code. As in other CEECs, the main reasons for collective disputes at the sectoral level have been pay levels, delays in the payment of wages in the public sector and the restructuring of basic industries, such as mining, railways and steel (trade union officials interviewed; see also Martin and Cristesco-Martin, 1999: 396).

Although Romanian unions have generally been able to mobilise their members in the public sector, the number of strikes has declined. Trade union officials interviewed were of the view that during the 1990s they learned that dialogue with employers' representatives generally resulted in a better outcome for their members than strikes. Furthermore, the prolonged economic recession, the reduction of the public sector due to privatisation alongside increasing unemployment and a huge decline in trade union membership resulted in unfavourable conditions for unions. Hence, the social partners have learned from their experiences during the 1990s that dancing brings generally more benefits than boxing. However, dancing and boxing arenas at the sectoral level are still fragile in Romania, similar to other CEECs (see Kohl and Platzer, 2003; Lado and Vaughan-Whitehead, 2003). The unions' Level 4 strategic choices (see Huzzard, Chapter 2) of decentralised internal structures did not support the development of sectoral and regional institutions in Eastern Europe as will be shown in the next section.

Limited strategic choices for unions at the company level

As in other Eastern European countries, the strategic choice of trade unions in Romania has been to preserve their company based membership and the institutional monopoly that existed before 1989. Trade unions as well as employers were against the introduction of a dual channel of representation (see Kohl and Platzer, 2003). However, the EU regulations on minimum information and consultation rights made necessary the introduction of works councils' structures like in the candidate countries. The solutions adopted by different countries varied. In Romania, similar to the Czech Republic, a single channel of representation remained in place, but since March 2003 employees in companies with at least 20 employees, which have no union representation, have the right to elect representatives for up to two years (Labour Code, 2003). The elected representatives have similar legal rights of information, consultation and collective bargaining with trade unions. Therefore, in countries such as Romania, trade unions as well as employees' representatives in non-unionised workplaces have formal rights to deal with boxing and dancing activities at the company level.

The reform process created opportunities for the trade unions, as well as a large number of constraints. The main opportunities for unions at the company level indicated by our interviewees are as follows:

- The restructuring and privatisation processes have given unions the chance to participate in the decision-making process (e.g. Petromidia case study).
- The massive reduction of personnel represented an incentive for employees to join unions in order to protect them from unfair dismissals and to get a reasonable severance package if they were made redundant.
- In the context of low living standard, employees from very large companies revealed that they joined unions to get some financial help (e.g. loans

with a low interest rate, reimbursement of expenses in the case of medical problems etc).

However, there have been a large number of constraints that affected company unions according to the respondents, such as:

- The rationalisation process, which resulted in a massive reduction of personnel among whom many were trade union members.[11]
- The fact that many companies were making losses, which resulted in a prolonged economic recession[12] and no benefits to share between employer and employees.
- The emergence of new small- and medium-sized companies, where employers generally did not accept unions.
- Additionally, the strategic choice of the unions to operate within the companies often resulted in the co-optation of unions by the management.

These opportunities and constraints affected unions to different degrees throughout Eastern Europe (see Lado and Vaughan-Whitehead, 2003; Stanojevic and Gradev, 2003). Since in Romania the marketisation process is less advanced than in countries such as Poland and Hungary, trade union density is still higher than the average in Eastern Europe (see Stanojevic and Gradev, 2003: 38). However, the restructuring and privatisation of the loss-making companies that are still subsidised by the state are likely to lead to further decline in trade union membership in the near future.

Research findings suggest that after 2000, when the privatisation and restructuring process have been almost completed in many CEECs, most unions had very limited choices at the company level. Stanojevic and Gradev (2003: 45) classified workers' representation at the company level in Eastern Europe into three categories:

(a) The first type refers to small and medium enterprises where there is usually *no union representation*. Although this is also common in Western Europe, in countries such as Romania, unions cannot be established in the small companies. This is because the legislation requires at least 15 members to create a company union and gives the legal right to CB only in companies which employ more than 20 employees. Hence, unions have generally no strategic choices of dancing and/or boxing in the growing number of small and medium sized companies.

(b) The second type consists of companies where trade union representation exists, but they are *under different degrees of management control*. In these companies, CB usually takes place, but trade unions have very limited influence in the organisational decision-making process. Trade union officials from national confederations and federations indicated that between 50% and 66% of company trade unions fall in this category in

Romania. In most companies, employees interviewed confirmed that they have doubts about the degree of independence of unions from the management.

The company union officials revealed that it is very difficult to develop a professional union team at company level, because the management offers management positions to the best unionists with very attractive conditions. If they refuse the job or continue to support employees' interests, the management finds a reason to dismiss them. Interviewees also indicated that it is very difficult to get a job after you have been a union official in a company. Offering management positions to union leaders seems to be a fairly common management strategy to curb union influence at company level in Eastern Europe (see Croucher, 1998: 29; Pollert, 1999), but in Romania this tactic appears to be used more 'efficiently' by the management due to low living standards. Hence, in the precarious transition context, trade union leaders often dance too close to their partners to protect their private interests. Despite the fact that this usually happens just to ensure the basic needs for their family, the co-optation of company unions by the management (or employer) represents a major impediment for the development of a genuine partnership approach at the company level.

(c) The third type covers companies where *autonomous trade unions* operate, such as in the Petromidia case study. Trade unions only have the choice between boxing and/or dancing with the employer in these companies. Union officials revealed that in the first years of transition, Romanian unions were inclined towards an adversarial approach, having sometimes exaggerated claims that could not be fulfilled by employers (usually the state). Furthermore, even when the state-employer surrendered to wage increase claims following industrial action, inflation quickly reduced purchasing power. Gradually, trade unions have learned that a constructive long-term approach would be more efficient to protect their members' interests (see also Clarke *et al.*, 2003: 143). As a result, since the second half of the 1990s, elements of CB together with partnership have developed in these companies.

Research reveals that the prevalence of boxing and dancing activities varies across companies as well as within a particular company in time. Our interviewees and other evidence indicated that after 2000, boxing activities prevailed at the company level only when employees' jobs were at stake or when employees did not receive their agreed wages or other benefits (see Martin and Cristesco-Martin, 2002). As illustrated by the Petromidia case study, dancing between company trade unions and the management was generally the approach when the survival of the company was at risk. Additionally, in the public sector, unions and the management still have a shared interest in getting as many resources from the state as possible (e.g. subsidies, exemption from paying certain taxes etc). However, findings indicate that genuine partnership is possible only in companies where the employer has financial resources and the willingness to adopt a dancing approach. Although dancing between unions and employers appears to be rarely found in Romania, certain MNCs (e.g. Xerox) and Petromidia have successfully adopted a partnership approach (interviewees). Summing up, findings suggest that dancing and boxing have developed together, but in many companies trade unions have very limited choices. Nevertheless, the experiences of genuine partnership indicate that even in the precarious transition context of Romania, dancing is likely to result in benefits for both parties.

Implications for trade unions

Unions around the world have had to adapt to a fairly hostile environment since the 1980s, in which the free play of market forces rather than social values have been promoted (see other chapters in this book). Whilst unions in developed countries had to adjust and redefine their scope and strategies, in Eastern Europe independent unions had to be established in this context. Despite an initially high trade union density, the weighted average in 2002 in the eight Eastern European countries that joined the EU in 2004, was 21.1%, as compared to the 30.4% weighted EU average (Stanojevic and Gradev, 2003: 38). As indicated previously, trade union density in Romania is around 40%, but unions are not necessarily independent from the management, which is a precondition for unions to have strategic choices. Hence, instead of considering unions' renewal, this section focuses on the implications of unions' strategic choices, for the establishment of independent union organisations in Eastern Europe.

Based on the model developed by Huzzard in Chapter 2 (Figure 2.1), the prospects and implications of unions' strategic decisions taken during the transition from a centrally planned economy to a market-based economy are examined. The first order union choices on mission, ideology and identity (Level 1), were primarily affected by the existing systems of industrial relations in 1989, economic context and the social expectation of their members (Rusu, 2002; Clarke *et al.*, 2003; Lado and Vaughan-Whitehead, 2003; Stanojevic and Gradev, 2003). As trade unions were the largest mass organisation, and in countries such as Poland, unions (e.g. Solidarity) were the initiators of the politico-economic change, they were expected to support the change towards a more efficient economic system that would (hopefully) improve workers' conditions in the long term. In countries such as Romania, where unions were not involved in the political change, they could be easily labelled as relics of the communist regime (Martin, 1999; Pollert, 1999). In this context, by and large, unions acted as social movements and they supported the transformation process (prevalent dancing approach), although restructuring led to massive declines in trade union membership.

The first order strategic choices shaped the second order choices concerning the scope of their activities and which relationships to enter into (Level 2 – Figure 2.1). The choice to support the transformation process, gave unions the opportunity to be involved in shaping the emerging industrial relations systems, to participate in the social policy formulation and sometimes even in the economic policies (see Clarke *et al.*, 2003; Kohl and Platzer, 2003; Lado and Vaughan-Whitehead, 2003). Additionally, the process of accession to the EU, particularly the requirements regarding the transposition of the social chapter into the national legal framework, represented an opportunity for unions to be involved in policy formulation (see Rusu, 2002; Kohl and Platzer, 2003; Lado and Vaughan-Whitehead, 2003). However, the union role has diminished with the progress in economic restructuring and the finalisation of transposition of the social chapter into national legislation (see Lado and Vaughan-Whitehead, 2003).

As indicated previously, by 2003 Romanian unions were stronger and more involved in the tripartite bodies at the national level than unions in countries where reforms were more advanced, such as Hungary and Poland. Evidence suggests that Romanian unions mobilised more intensively than their counterparts in other CEECs to achieve a relatively supportive legislative foundation for the defence of union recognition by employers and collective bargaining (Martin, 1999; Kideckel, 2002; Clarke *et al.*, 2003). Nevertheless, as in other CEECs, most unions' activities are related to the transition process. Hence, unions would have to redefine and anticipate the needs of their members in order to maintain (at least) their influence in the decision-making process. Also, an obvious choice would be to attempt recruiting members in the growing number of small- and medium-sized companies, where there is usually no union representation. However, unions' second order choices are constrained by the third and fourth order choices, as will be shown below.

The third type of strategic choices refers to key choices on ways of relating to employers, members, other unions and civil society (Level 3 – Figure 2.1). Evidence suggests that since 1989, Romanian trade unions, similarly to those from the other CEECs, faced problems of survival and legitimisation, and they focused more on the political field than on workplace representation (Martin, 1999; Pollert, 1999). Unions participated in national public policy formulation via tripartite bodies or individual positions in the government (Rusu, 2002). Their political participation only partially solved the problem of survival and this did not solve the problems of internal legitimisation. Hence, unions had a degree of influence in shaping the new labour legislation. However, the economic recession, the massive reduction of personnel and unions' inherited legacies resulted in a decentralised and fragmented union movement, with weak influence at the company level.

Throughout Eastern Europe, unions generally did not manage to preserve labour's purchasing power and employees' jobs (see Galgoczi and Mermet, 2003).

Despite a long-term commitment to partnership (dancing), real wages had been lagging substantially behind labour productivity in most countries (Galgoczi and Mermet, 2003: 50). Nevertheless, the Petromidia case study indicates that genuine partnership with a positive outcome for both labour and capital may be achieved even in the uncertain transition context. Therefore, evidence suggests that elements of both dancing and boxing have been developed together during the transition period in Eastern Europe, but their effectiveness for labour, in terms of maintaining at least the quality of working life, has usually been reduced (Clarke *et al.*, 2003; Kohl and Platzer, 2003; Lado and Vaughan-Whitehead, 2003). This is primarily a result of the weak development of the social partners along with a politico-economic context that favoured neo-liberal policies.

The case of Romania indicates that fourth order strategic choices which refer to internal union structures (see Chapter 2) had also affected union choices and their degree of influence in setting terms and conditions of employment at all levels. A precondition for unions to have strategic choices is to be established as autonomous organisations from the management. As indicated above, union choices to have a company based membership resulted in no representation in the newly established companies as well as a debatable independence from the company management in many companies. Furthermore, there is rivalry between old reformed unions and the newly established organisations (Pollert, 1999). Nevertheless, an attempt by union federations to establish an individual membership base may result in a sharp decline in union membership, since there is no such tradition in Eastern Europe. Moreover, trade union officials from the construction and chemical federations in Romania revealed that company unions oppose the establishment of such structures. The weak establishment of intermediary structures is common across Eastern Europe, not least because the company unions have had the power to choose to remain the most important layer in the union hierarchies (Clarke *et al.*, 2003; Kohl and Platzer, 2003; Lado and Vaughan-Whitehead, 2003).

In order to become a social partner that has strategic choices in relation to (organised or unorganised) employers, unions need to be well established (in terms of representation, internal coherence and legitimacy) and independent organisations at all levels. The Petromidia case study revealed that a genuine partnership approach (dancing) as well as collective bargaining (boxing) requires strong and autonomous partners. Research findings suggest that trade unions in Eastern Europe are still learning how to acquire resources to be able to have choices of dancing and/or boxing with the employers. Although this chapter emphasises the common opportunities and constraints faced by unions in Eastern Europe based on the Romanian case study, it is acknowledged that there is great variation in the industrial relations systems across and within CEECs (see Trif, 2000; Kohl and Platzer, 2003).

Conclusion: learning to dance

Trade unions in CEECs have been subjected to dramatic changes in their role and strategies as these countries have undergone a period of fundamental change. The shift from centrally planned economies to market economic models has presented trade unions with crucial strategic choices in relation to their roles as industrial relations actors. This chapter has focused on the strategic choices of trade unions in Romania during this period of intense economic transformation; in particular it assessed the trade union propensities towards boxing or dancing relationships with employers.

Adversarial and partnership scenarios between trade unions and employers take place at national, sectoral and workplace levels. In the national arena the social partners are mostly out of step, some co-operation takes place through institutional arrangements such as the social pact but collective bargaining at national level manifests itself as conflictual. Union gains have been modest, as the central issues of pay and employment have been dominated by employers and government failure to uphold labour codes. Social partnership at the national level has been characterised by a distinct lack of a stable co-operative model.

On the other hand, at sectoral level the establishment of a dance floor has given the social partners the opportunity to practice the intricacies of boxing and dancing. As has been argued formal frameworks, the Consultative Commissions of Social Dialogue, for example, have provided a forum where trade union federations, employers' associations and government representation can engage in dialogue on a range of pertinent issues. Although Romania has in this respect more advanced arrangements than other CEECs, research has revealed that the tripartite forums have a low effectiveness. A central problem is the weakness of the employers' associations in Romania; trade unions are faced with a dancing partner incapable of deciding on what kind of dance they wish to engage in. Collective bargaining at sectoral level provides an opportunity for the trade unions to box, but conflicts, particularly in the public sector, have decreased due to the poor economic performance of Romania and the decline of union membership. Research findings show that strategic choice at this level, by the central actors in the trade unions, has gravitated towards co-operative choices rather than overt strikes.

However, the major strategic choice by the trade unions in Romania and the CEECs has been to retain their company based membership to support their traditional institutional monopoly. The configuration of boxing and dancing at company level is complex and varied because of reform measures which on the one hand have allowed participation in decision-making processes by the unions; the Petromidia case study illustrated this during the restructuring and privatisation programme of the company. On the other hand, rationalisation processes leading to redundancies are clearly in the boxing ring. Formal participation rights enshrined in Labour Codes are on present evidence no guarantee that effective dance floor rules will evolve. The general conclusion is that trade unions have limited strategic choices at company level; but there is a spectrum determined partly by the stage of transformation of individual Eastern European countries and partly by the structure and nature of companies. Petromidia, for example, had developed autonomous trade unions that were able to genuinely choose between boxing and/or dancing with the employer. However, the case study company was atypical of Romanian experience and the social partners primarily danced because their common aim was to sustain the economic viability of the company during the difficult transition period.

Social partnership in the Western pluralist and democratic sense is a new phenomenon in Romania; it is easily masked by the pre-1989 contours of socialist co-operation. The trade unions' initial strategic choice was to support the transformation of the centrally planned economy to a market-based economy, but the unions were confronted, and still are, with the vestiges of the communist legacies. Their strong involvement in tripartite bodies at national level is a determined attempt to influence and create an acceptable dance floor. The unions did have a measure of success in shaping the post-1989 labour legislation, but it was dancing with faltering and uncertain steps because the legitimisation of the unions remains a significant issue. The evidence from Romania is that unions are still in the process of acquiring legitimacy, of having to resolve internal tensions, of becoming autonomous representative organisations and of convincing employers of the value of the social partnership model. The case study leads us to the conclusion that where partnership has developed between management and trade unions, dancing and boxing had clear benefits for both parties. The overall picture in the Romanian story, however, suggests that the actors in the industrial relations system are still learning to dance.

Notes

1. The study is based on 107 semi-structured interviews conducted in 2000–01, with trade union officials (six respondents), employers' association officials (five respondents) and state representatives (five respondents), plus company union officials, shop stewards, human resource managers and employees (91 respondents) from 20 companies from different industrial sectors.
2. For instance, not to pay taxes or to get raw materials – see Petromidia case study.
3. They are also called representative confederations, because they fulfil the minimal membership condition that at least 5% of the entire labour force is needed, to be allowed to negotiate collective agreements at national level.
4. The reliability of data may be questionable. Data is provided by the Centre for Trade Union Resources, being based on a survey conducted in 2000.
5. Compiled from Stefanescu 1999, pp. 528–30 and *Codul Muncii*, 1999: 127–8.
6. Formally, company unions should be independent from the management, hence in contrast with 'yellow unions', but in practice they are frequently co-opted by the management.

7. A document provided by the state official interviewed indicated that the sectoral commission from the chemical sector met 12 times during the first half of 2001.
8. The legislation requires that provisions of the national agreement should apply to all companies.
9. For example Confederatia Sindicatelor Miniere din Romania.
10. The Social Democrat Petre Roman's Government.
11. For example 30% of the total labour force in Petromidia case study.
12. The Gross Domestic Product in 2001 was 83.5% as compared to 1989 in Romania (United Nations Economic Commission for Europe, 2002: 150).

References

Burloiu, P. (1997) *Managementul resurselor umane – Tratare globala interdisciplinara*. Bucharest: Lumina Lex.

Centrul de Resurse Pentru Sindicate (2000) *Starea sindicatelor in Romania*. Bucharest: Centrul de Resurse Pentru Sindicate.

Clarke, L., Cremers, J. and Janssen, J. (2003) *EU Enlargement – Construction Labour Relations as a Pilot*. London: Reed Business Information.

Codul muncii – Contractul colectiv de munca unic la nivel national, pe anul 1999–2000 (1999) Bucharest: Lumina Lex.

Croucher, R. (1998) *Economic Development and Trade Unions in a Transitional Context: The Romanian Case*. London: Labour and Society International – Discussion Paper, No. 4, March.

Draus, F. (2001) *Social Dialog in the Candidate Countries – Synthesis Report* [online]. Study commissioned by the European Social Partners ETUC, UNICE–UEAPME and CEEP, Available from: http://www.etuc.org/events/Romania_En.cfm [Accessed 21 Mar. 2002].

Galgoczi, B. and Mermet, E. (2003) 'Wage Developments in Candidate Countries', *Transfer: European Review of Labour and Research (ETUI)* 9(1): 50–64.

Hethy, L. (1991) 'Industrial Relations in Eastern Europe: Recent Developments and Trends' in Adams, R. J. (ed.) *Comparative Industrial Relations: Contemporary Research and Theory*. London: Harper Collins Academic.

Hethy, L. (2001) *Social Dialog in the Expanding World. The Decade of Tripartism in Hungary and Central and Eastern Europe 1988–1999*. Report 70, Brussels: ETUI.

Kideckel, D. A. (2002) 'Winning the Battles, Losing the War: Contradictions of Romanian Labour in Postcommunist Transformation' in Crowley, S. and Ost, D. (eds) *Workers After Workers' States – Labour and Politics in Postcommunist Eastern Europe*. Oxford: Rowman and Littlefield Publishers.

Kohl, H. and Platzer, H. W. (2003) 'Transformation, EU Membership and Labour Relations in Central and Eastern Europe: Poland – Czech Republic – Hungary – Slovenia' in *Transfer-Enlargement as a Trade Union Issue (ETUI)* 9(1): 11–30.

Kollonay-Lehoczky, C. (1997) 'The Emergence of New Forms of Workers' Participation in Central and East European Countries' in Markey, R. and Monat, J. (eds) *Innovation and Employee Participation through Works Councils: International Case Studies*. Aldershot: Avebury.

Kornai, J. (1992) *The Socialist System – The Political Economy of Communism*. Oxford: Clarendon Press.

Lado, M. (2002) *Industrial Relations in the Candidate Countries* [online]. Available from: http://www.eiro.eurofound.ie/2002/07/feature/TN0207102F.html

Lado, M. and Vaughan-Whitehead, D. (2003) 'Social Dialogue in Candidate Countries: What For? *Transfer: European Review of Labour and Research (ETUI)* 9(1): 65–87.

Martin, R. (1999) *Transforming Management in Central and Eastern Europe*. Oxford: University Press.

Martin, R. and Cristesco-Martin, A. (1999) 'Industrial Relations in Transformation: Central and Eastern Europe in 1998', *Industrial Relations Journal* 30(4): 373–87.

Martin, R. and Cristesco-Martin, A. (2002) 'Employment Relations in Central and Eastern Europe in 2001', *Industrial Relations Journal* 33(5): 523–36.

Mihes, C. and Casale, G. (1999) 'Industrial Relations in Romania' in Casale, G. (ed.) *Social Dialog in Central and Eastern Europe*. Budapest: ILO-CEET.

Moarcas, A. (1999) *Sindicatele componente fundamentale ale societatii civile*. Bucharest: Tribuna Economica.

Nelson, D. N. (1986) 'The Politics of Romanian Trade Unions' in Pravda, A. and Ruble, B. A. (eds) *Trade Unions in Communist States*. London: Allen and Unwin.

Ost, D. (2000) 'Illusory Corporatism in Eastern Europe: Neoliberal Tripartism and Postcommunist Class' *Politics and Society* 28 (4) December.

Pert, S. and Vasile, V. (1995) 'Romania: Introducing Wage Bargaining in a Monopolistic Context' in Vaughan-Whitehead, D. (eds) *Reforming Wage Policy in Central and Eastern Europe*. Budapest: EU and ILO.

Pollert, A. (1999) *Transformation at Work in the New Market Economies of Central Eastern Europe*. London: Sage.

Rusu, M. S. (2002) *Romania's Planned Accession to the European Union and the Country's Trade Unions*. M.Phil Dissertation, Cambridge University.

Stanojevic, M. and Gradev, G. (2003) 'Workers' Representation at Company Level in CEE Countries', *Transfer: European Review of Labour and Research (ETUI)* 9(1): 31–49.

Stefanescu, I. T. (1999) *Tratat elementar de drept al muncii*. Bucharest: Lumina Lex.

Thirkell, J. E. M. and Vickerstaff, S. (2002) 'Trade Unions and the Politics of Transformation in Central and East Europe', Rainnie, A., Smith, A. and Swain, A. (eds) *Work, Employment and Transition: Restructuring Livelihoods in Post-Communism*. London: Routledge.

Trif, A. (2000) 'The Transformation of Industrial Relations in Romania at the Micro-level', *South-East Europe Review for Labour and Social Affairs* 3(4): 139–59.

United Nations Economic Commission for Europe (2002) *Economic Survey of Europe* [online], No. 2. Available from: http://www.unece.org/ead/survey.htm

Vidinova, A. (1997) 'The Transformation of Industrial Relations in Bulgaria and the Role of the State', in Brady, J. (ed.) *Central and Eastern Europe – Industrial Relations and the Market Economy*. Dublin: Oak Tree Press.

11
Private Dancer: Boxing and Dancing in the US
Steven Deutsch

Introduction

While the US is not within the European Community, two powerful factors makes its relevance felt in this discussion. First, American multinational corporations are major players within Europe with substantial capital investment, employment facilities and a European workforce. Regardless of whether local workplace managers are European or American nationals, the enterprise must operate within European Union (EU) guidelines, social directives and in an industrial relations climate that is European. Second, the globalised economy makes transnational labour relations ever more relevant. Just as employers have traded information, trade unions are ever more actively involved in multinational labour relations and collaborative engagement with union counterparts across the ocean. This makes the US experience an appropriate part of this volume that focuses on management partnerships within the EU.

For many years the American trade union movement resisted a European approach to partnerships. Emphasis was squarely on negotiated agreements within a broad framework of employer and union rights. Throughout the 1970s and 1980s, while many in Europe promoted worker participation and work democratisation, the American labour movement, with few exceptions, declined to push in that direction. This has changed, dramatically so since the change in national labour federation leadership in the mid-1990s. 'Management is too important to leave to management' became the new call and pro active, union driven strategies for partnerships have been developed.

At the same time there have been sceptics and critics and some outright opposition to changing the pattern of labour–management relations. This is hardly surprising given the split in the management community, which has practitioners who espouse co-operation and others who are actively hostile to unions and worker rights. Overall the pattern seems to suggest a continuing split or divergence in the labour relations arena within the US.

The most innovative union driven and strategic labour approaches to partnering are what have sparked the most interest in many quarters. What follows is an examination of some of these developments and what they may portend for the future. Two cases are highlighted with more detail in the Appendix. But before we can explore labour management partnerships some contextual overview is needed.

A brief note on the US industrial relations context

A brief overview of the US brings more of a challenge than is true for many of the small, highly centralised, and more homogeneous industrial nations in Europe. A nation of 285 million, covering a territory the size of Europe, makes sweeping generalisations difficult due to the highly diverse and heterogeneous population, the tradition of decentralisation and local variation, and the contradictory trends in economic activity and industrial relations that exist.

Diversity of race, language and cultural tradition is a critical feature of the landscape in the US and will help to shape all of its institutions in the decades to come. The current population mix is multicultural and will become much more so in the decades ahead. Those of European descent constitute three-quarters of the population at present, but this is changing rapidly and by the middle of this century non-European Americans will become a majority. Immigration and natural population increase makes the US ever more multicultural, multiracial and multilingual.

The legacy of British labour–management relations shaped the character of the US from the beginning of the nation at the end of the eighteenth century. While some features of the more traditional adversarial labour–management relations are shared with Britain, there is also a strong decentralist tendency in the US. The modern era of industrial relations stems from the 1935 National Labour Relations Act which is a federal framework law. But, in practice, the emphasis is upon a highly voluntaristic pattern of relationships between employers and their employees with considerable emphasis on the local work site. As a result, close to 200 000 individual collectively negotiated contracts are in place. The overall industrial relations system emphasises voluntary engagement and places primary focus on the collective bargaining process and the formal system of negotiated agreements covering wages, hours and conditions of work.

While a federal constitution and legal framework and labour legislation exists covering many features of work life and labour–management responsibilities, there is also a parallel tradition of legislation at the level of the 50 states covering workplace and worker protection, minimum wages, and laws on the right of public sector employees to collectively negotiate and the right to have a union shop. Some of the features of the federal labour law are rather unique, for example, the absence of a ban on employers hiring replacement workers when the long-standing workforce is out on a strike. This has been a weapon used quite regularly in recent years by employers intent on breaking the union and having a 'union-free' workforce.

In contrast to the centralised industrial relations systems of many countries, in the US the employers and unions are quite decentralised. Most unions are affiliated with the AFL-CIO, although some have remained unaffiliated. Negotiations are not with employer's associations but typically with individual employers and one company, and occasional co-ordinated industry bargaining, even though a particular workplace may have multiple unions representing the workforce. In short, it is a more decentralised system with more focus at the individual workplace than is true in many industrialised countries.

Introducing the boxing and dancing styles in the US

Having already emphasised the contradictory character of the overall US labour–management scene, the following represents the contrasting style of labour relations that is characterized as 'boxing' versus 'dancing' in this analysis.

At the national level   there are some partnership agreements in place today, illustrating *the 'dancing' relationship*, which follow the national agreements pioneered by the Autoworkers (UAW) and General Motors in 1973; and the Communications Workers (CWA) and AT&T in 1980. An exceptional case is the Kaiser Permanente/AFL-CIO Union Partnership Agreement that is reviewed in an appended case study. For a large sector of the economy the traditional, adversarial relationships that rely on hard bargaining, or *the 'boxing' relationship*, continue to dominate. The prospects are that this split at the national level will continue, with boxing being more significant at the national level.

At the regional level   some public sector unions and regional employer bodies have evolved *a 'dancing' relationship*, such as state governments and the union or unions that represent the workforce. More commonly, however, the traditional *or 'boxing' relationship*, characterises the labour–management relationship. The likelihood is that this pattern will continue in the near future.

At the local level   more labour–management agreements operate at the local level, even with large, multi-site employers. Hence, the largest number of partnership agreements exists at this level. The *'dancing' relationship* with some form of employee participation is common and might even exist in some form at one-half of local workplaces. That, of course, means that the *'boxing' relationship* best describes the other one-half of local workplaces in the US. The prospects continue for such a split, although there are some possibilities of enhanced 'dancing' with evidence of the practical and mutual benefits of such labour–management relationships in terms of quality of service and production, efficiency, and cost savings. Illustrations will follow to help illuminate this; a full summary of boxing and dancing in the US is set out in Table 11.1.

Table 11.1   Boxing and dancing in the US: a classification

Level	Boxing	Dancing	Prospects
Global/ international	Traditional bargaining dominates.	Few successful partnering arrangements across national boundaries, some links with Canada.	Efforts by some unions to exert more influence with multinational employers, join with other national union efforts and international trade secretariats.
National	Most bargaining arrangements are traditional and adversarial.	Substantial growth in labour–management partnerships.	Partnerships will continue to expand but traditional bargaining likely to dominate.
Sectoral/ regional	Most labour– management relationships are traditional, adversarial or 'boxing'.	Some partnerships, notably in regional/sector public sector work organisations, have developed.	While some labour–management partnerships will grow, traditional bargaining relationships are likely to dominate.
Local workplace	Most workplaces have traditional labour– management relations.	Here is where there is the largest growth of labour– management partnerships across all sectors.	Traditional relationships will dominate, but a large proportion of work sites will have some form of employee participation.

Employee involvement and workplace change in the 1970s and 1980s

There is a long history of industrial democracy in the US, but until recent decades this was typically equated with collective bargaining. American unionists and employers were vaguely aware of workplace reforms and innovations in the 1960s, and by 1973 the national Work in America Commission published a report highlighting such workplace change within the US and worker participation schemes in Europe. That same year saw the pioneering agreement between General Motors and the United Automobile Workers union (UAW). The decade of the 1970s saw an explosion of interest in work reform and increasing negotiated agreements establishing worker participation structures (Deutsch and Albrecht, 1983). In auto, steel, aerospace, telecommunications and other industries, the 1970s ushered in a new era of mutual gains in which employers and unions approached best uses of technology and systems of work organisation so as to increase quality and production efficiency for the benefit of all parties. Enlightened employers and thoughtful unionists took the position that traditional adversarial labour–management relations, based on old-style Tayloristic principles with sharply divided functions and hierarchical structures, were inadequate to meet the challenges of global competition and new technologies which called for flexibility, creativity, problem solving, and best forms of work. Such a view assumes that workers and their organisations are necessary and important partners and stakeholders in the work organisation must be drawn in and involved (Kelley and Harrison, 1992; Kochan and Osterman, 1994).

The US Congress passed the 'Labour–Management Co-operation Act of 1978' and the Federal Mediation and Conciliation Service continues a programme to this day providing grants for joint labour–management efforts to promote employee involvement and workplace change. However, the formerly more active federal government role in nurturing labour–management partnership has been subdued under recent political administrations in Washington.

In the US the lack of a tradition of labour participation in economic decision-making and the absence of consensus building and tripartite bodies that have been important in many other national systems is a critical reality. The reliance upon 'free collective bargaining' within a context of hostility to unions in both private management and public policy, has been critical for shaping labour's agenda (Deutsch, 1994).

The shift in American labour union perspectives

For many years the American labour movement has been resistant, or at least ambivalent, to accepting the assumptions of a joint labour–management work restructuring and participative work organisation model. In point of fact the typical scenario was that 'management acts, labour reacts'. In February 1994 the AFL-CIO issued a new call, *The New American Workplace: A Labour Perspective* (AFL-CIO, 1994). A proactive and union-driven approach to changing technology and work organisation was endorsed with a challenge for unions to move rapidly in this direction. This may not appear as a major leap in the context of other nations, but for the US it had significance. The Australian Council of Trade Unions has had years of experience with such an approach: adopting a strategy of work restructuring as the foundation for the implementation of labour's goals on affirmative action and equity, skills formation and opportunities for worker education, worker-centred approaches to the best uses of new technology, and concern over occupational health and safety or work environment improvement (Ogden, 1993; Mathews, 1994). This approach has been highlighted in recent reports and crucial publications in the US that have attempted to gain labour commitment to work reform and proactive strategies to promote employee involvement (Baugh, 1994; Herzenberg, 2001).

A myriad of management writings in the late 1980s and 1990s underscored the failure of US firms and the economy to adapt well to a changing economy and the need to alter management practices for the future. The parallel within union structures was to move towards a union agenda for workplace change (Deutsch, 1994). A national AFL-CIO Technology Committee was created for the first time. The George Meany Center for Labour Studies, the AFL-CIO labour college, developed a curriculum around unions and technology and work organisation, total quality management and labour, and related issues. The training arm of the AFL-CIO, Working for America Institute, has promoted training of workers for leadership on workplace change (Baugh, 1994; AFL-CIO Working for America Institute, 2002). Various unions that pioneered technology training, such as the Machinists, have elaborated this work sharing their curriculum and experience with other unions (Deutsch, 1986). Union linked groups and members of the United Association for Labor Education have been active in building curricula, offering educational programmes for unions and in some cases joint labour–management programmes, and in assisting unions and employers in making changes in work organisation towards mutual gains (Cohen-Rosenthal and Burton, 1993).

It certainly would be premature to suggest a total change in direction, but it is correct to observe an important turn in the road in the US, particularly in the union adoption of a proactive posture on the matter of workplace change (Strauss, 1992; Rubenstein and Kochan, 2001). Moving from a limited past involvement which concentrated on collective negotiations on matters of technology, occupational health and safety, and features of work organisation, activity in the past couple of years has taken a more omnibus approach to work restructuring. By the late 1990s the AFL-CIO established the Center for Workplace Democracy and promoted aggressive union strategy development around employee involvement and workplace change.

However, within the US, a lack of unity amongst trade unions and the traditional reliance upon local arrangements both mitigated against a national policy, or consistent and strategic approaches by unions. In contrast, in Australia, the Australian Council of Trade Unions evolved a union-driven and proactive approach to worker/union participation and work restructuring. This came from an international appraisal and conclusion that labour needed to be a driver and not merely a reactor to management in the work organisation and economy (ACTU, 1987).

Developments in the 1990s

The rapid changes of the 1980s and 1990s promoted significant shifts as employers and unions alike recognised the need for greater mutual participation in matters of technology design and application so as to extract maximum gain in efficiency and quality. Increasingly, employers and unions came to appreciate that ergonomic intervention, through joint labour–management approaches, would reduce such injuries and illnesses, save money, and achieve a 'win–win' for both employers and employees with improvements in the work environment (Deutsch, 1991; Askenazy, 2001). Again the argument for a mutual gains approach was strongly presented by both labour and management and some important collective bargaining models were developed with joint technology committees addressing issues of design, training, work environment/ergonomic factors, and other considerations. The key principle learned is that few areas better represent the potential for effective worker involvement than technology, with benefits accruing to employers and their workforce alike (Deutsch, 1994, 1996; Haddad, 2002).

While many managers and union leaders have taken a proactive stance concerning joint labour–management involvement in restructuring work organisations, many traditional attitudes remain. They range from anti-union views and those resistant to power sharing, to those who are locked into Tayloristic concepts and outmoded styles of industrial relations. There is urgency in the views of many concerning the need to reverse and alter some management and union views so as to best move towards work organisations and work relationships that maximise efficiency, quality and benefits to all parties. The challenge to Fordism or Toyota-ism and lean production in the minds of many is to create a viable pattern of participation which is authentic, builds mutual gains for labour and management, and is good for the economy (Kochan and Osterman, 1994; Rubenstein and Kochan, 2001).

Americans tend to be pragmatists rather than ideologues (Adams, 1995). The fact is that the practice of industrial relations, much management practice, and some union practice no longer work well to accomplish the goals that are articulated. Unions have increasingly sought to move from the model of servicing members to actively engaging and empowering them in an organising mode (Banks and Metzgar, 1989). Many in the management community have come to appreciate that human resources are vital for the success of an enterprise and that moving from old style adversarial relationships to mutually engaged and joint labour–management posturing is good for the organisation as well as all of its participants. Policy-makers in the US are more confused and divided perhaps and seem to be pulling in different and contradictory directions. However, one segment is persuaded of the need for concerted action with greater consensus and participation by government, management, and labour in the making of economic policy affecting trade, workforce skills development, work environment improvement, new technology, and many other key areas of policy and practice.

The fact is that in most nations, even Sweden with its high union density rate, the majority of initiatives come from employers, and unions react. The AFL-CIO position tilts in the direction of the Australian Council of Trade Unions that has led the industrial world in conceptualising a proactive, union-driven approach to workplace change. Such a strategic unionism (Ogden, 1993) would be a real change in the US and the AFL-CIO new Center for Workplace Democracy and Center for Corporate Affairs may well portend significant changes in the near future. Workplace reform is more developed in Australia, in part because the unions have actively promoted such change. The government has consciously supported the effort and provided education and technical consultation to employers and unions (Mathews, 1994). While there are important historical differences in the system of industrial relations between Australia and the US, both having roots in the British system, enough similarities have sparked interest in each other's experiences. Australian strategic unionism has interested many in the US, while more US style enterprise bargaining has taken place in Australia.

Earlier the pragmatic emphasis in US industrial relations was explained. This is prominent for gaining an insight into the adoption of new labour relations approaches. In brief, the evidence suggests that an approach that will solve problems at the point of production, in manufacturing or office environments, is worth looking into. Since negotiated agreements are collectively bargained only every three years or so, there is a lot of time in-between for working out problems. Increasingly interest-based bargaining approaches have been adopted, joined with ongoing processes for joint labour–management problem solving (Kochan and Osterman, 1994; Walton, 2000). In contrast to the Scandinavian or German models that have legislated works councils, employee representatives on company boards, and mandated means of employee participation in enterprise decisions, in the US there are no such mandates. All participation is by voluntary manager action in unorganised workplaces, or by jointly negotiated agreements between employers and unions representing the workforce. Employers in non-union settings adopt participative practices both to obtain higher levels of employee commitment, better production and quality, and also to enhance employee loyalty and hence reduce their desire to join a union and have collective bargaining protection. Employers in organised workplaces are similarly motivated, but fewer choose participative management as a means to weaken unions or even eliminate them. But, the antipathy to unions remains within a segment of the American management community and some have adopted employee involvement schemes to keep unions out.

Labour–Management partnerships in the public sector

While private sector employment in the US, as in many nations, has decreased, the union density in the public sector has increased, where it is 37%, versus 9% organised in private employment. It is in the public sector that some of the most innovative labour–management efforts have been developed, with the same dynamic of economic crisis, tax cuts for public services, pressure on management to save costs, and concerns by unions and workers to protect jobs, improve health and safety, and improve quality (Gallagher, 1992).

In the 1990s there was an especial effort in the governmental sector to achieve reorganisation to increase efficiencies and improve quality. This was nurtured by the federal government, which convened conferences, published best case reports, and provided funding for labour–management partnerships in the public sector (US Department of Labor, 1996). The last is a national programme for private and public sector partnerships, operated by the Federal Mediation and Conciliation Service, under the Labor–Management Co-operation Act of 1978. While there are three million national government employees, more than five times that number work at the level of state and local government, and it is there where most labour–management innovations have been played out. What follows are some illustrations, and two appended case studies.

Portland, Oregon, which is a metropolitan area of about two million people is a typical case. The City has seen increasing pressure to save costs and deliver better service more efficiently and with fewer resources. Out of necessity, not just management enlightenment, the City felt compelled to search for new arrangements to enlist the workforce to accomplish these goals. The several public employee unions representing the full range of the city workforce of more than 5000 had been in some co-ordinated bargaining, with each retained their own contracts. The multi-union leadership moved to become more proactive on issues of workplace change in the face of budget constraints and threats to employment, and the worsening conditions at work with greater demands and less staff. The result was to establish a multi-union structure with management, obtaining City funding, with a grant from the Federal Mediation and Conciliation Service, to work on enhancing an effective partnership to improve public service and meet joint labour and management goals.

The process led to considerable increases in internal union education, member mobilisation, new efforts in organising, and more involvement in work environment issues. Many hundreds of union activists received capacity building training on labour–management partnering, strategic unionism and committee effectiveness. A small number were also trained to be trainers of rank and file members. The net effect was to upgrade capacity in the unions and to see higher levels of member union involvement. This has seen parallel results in other cities. For example, in June 2002, the City of Eugene had an outside bid of $66 000 for alterations at the Performing Arts Center. The workforce, members of the American Federation of State, County and Municipal Employees, accepted the challenge and found solutions costing $6000. Such cost savings came at a time of contracting city budgets threatening workers' jobs, and hence is a solid example of 'win-win' in partnering.

At the same time, in Portland, there were distinct limits set by city management and some disenchantment set in. When management unilaterally withdrew from the partnership, things reverted back to bargaining strategies, going from 'dancing' to 'boxing'. The story sounds very familiar as one reads the case reports (Gallagher 1992; US Department of Labor, 1996) and compares such local and state government labour–management partnerships. Few are long sustained, but most are successful in generating measurable cost savings and quality improvements and strengthening local unions.

Across the country there are demonstrable successes in helping workers in low wage jobs, private as well as public, succeed through labour–management partnerships efforts (Working for America, 2002). More important, it is clear that partnerships become significant components of strategic planning by forward-looking unions and enlightened management. There is considerable momentum around the country that promotes labour–management partnerships in the governmental sector, and the contextual realities, including fiscal pressures, assure that this is likely to continue and perhaps increase.

Our experience in the US suggests that there is an eagerness within the public sector to learn best principles and action plans for workplace change (Gallagher, 1992). An emphasis is growing within public sector unions upon adopting workplace change practice to obtaining quality and also efficiency in light of fiscal pressures (US Department of Labor, 1996). The proportion of requests for technical assistance and educational programmes around employee involvement in workplace change coming from the public sector unions and agencies has been increasing in my experience and those of my colleagues who work in this area. In some instances the projects are as far ranging as they are in manufacturing where in 2003 a major forest products company asked the union to figure out a plan to increase output relative to costs if a plant was to be kept open. In short, get the workforce to assess the system of production, the technology, and make a determination of how to increase efficiency.

Illustrations of some private sector Labour–Management innovations

Similarly comparable challenges are occurring in the service sector; for example, telecommunications. Microelectronic technology has profoundly affected this industry with a myriad of problems. Competitive and market-driven pressures, along with productivity-increasing technology have led to significant redundancies. Firms that pioneered early quality of working life agreements and co-operative labour–management relationships have been prominent in 'downsizing' and handing out layoff notices. Widespread use of electronic workplace monitoring has been demonstrated to be associated with higher rates of workplace stress and muscular-skeletal illness. This environment cries out for a new approach to addressing the challenges in the work environment within the present economic climate.

Some description of cases will help to illustrate the move towards the triangulation of technology and the work environment to work reorganisation. They are meant only to suggest in briefest terms how change processes have linked these factors, as practical approaches to partnering for effective problem solving.

Health care is a burgeoning sector in all industrial economies, reflecting an aging population and ever-rising expectations of health and quality of life. As a result serious cost efficiency considerations are widely employed in hospital projects. At the Oregon Health Sciences University we have been involved in a project designed to train labour and management representatives in each working unit to problem-solve, thus reducing grievances and the strain on the formal labour–management system, and moving to efficiently resolve issues where they emerge. Linked to that a programme of skills formation and educational upgrading has built greater competencies and, thereby, working efficiencies. These issues connect directly to the technologies in health care and the high incidence of work-related injury and illness. A needs assessment among dental hygienists at the Kaiser Permanente clinics in Oregon revealed 83% with work-related pain, mostly in the upper extremities, while nurses' back injury from inappropriate patient lifting is a major human and cost problem for the Kaiser hospitals. A joint labour–management ergonomics/risk reduction committee was negotiated to attempt to reduce injuries and costs. Work environment considerations not only included equipment and tools and technological features but work organisation concerns. In short, technology, work environment and work organisation factors all come into play. This fits within a much broader innovative, multi-union/Kaiser Partnership (see case study in Appendix).

In manufacturing, the initial concerns which generated some change programmes have been technology. Cascade Steel is a mini-mill with state-of-the-art technology. It became immediately apparent that the workforce skills were out of synchronisation with the technology and the capabilities of how the work could be organised. A major training programme was launched to upgrade skills and to build higher levels of competency, flexibility, and hence different kinds of decision-making structures. At a Fort James Corporation plant in Oregon the advanced technology in recycling and producing paper products compelled a new approach to work organisation, which, in turn, emphasised the need for workforce skills training and a new labour–management relationship. A similar sequence at the Roseburg Lumber Company emerged with a major workforce skills training effort that engaged the union in a new way with management to best utilise technological change and new work organisation to achieve greater efficiency and productivity and, thereby, job security. Occupational health and safety factors were linked into each of these cases.

In the case of the Potlatch Corporation Idaho lumber mills the sequence was quite different. The company received major governmental penalties for safety violations and part of the negotiated settlement with the union was to develop a training and intervention programme to reduce risk. There we initiated joint labour–management health and safety training and, of course, explored technology issues and how the work was organised. In one of the mills management asked the union directly to offer a plan for production which would better meet the competitive market pressures. The experience of engagement in work environment improvement and the threat of job loss, unless new ways to organise work could be achieved, energised the union. This was parallel to the case of Qwest telecommunications, which experienced creative new approaches to market and products when management turned the challenge over to the two unions representing the workforce. Job design teams expanded their agendas to look at technology, consumer markets and products. The union also actively engaged in work environment improvement efforts, particularly through ergonomics training and linking technology and health factors to work organisation issues.

To be sure, these are only brief capsules and not meant to communicate in-depth stories of labour–management partnerships and workplace change projects. What they do suggest is that while there may be different avenues of entry, the issues of technology and work environment are logically connected with work organisation and all based on a foundation of empowering workers through participation and education.

International influences in the US

At the same time there are profound international influences and developments within the European Union, which are helping to shape labour–management partnerships within the US. European Union directives, most notably the June 2001 Directive on Employee Consultation, compel all employers to conform. Hence, US employers, while perhaps wishing to take their ideology and practice concerning unilateral managerial prerogatives into EU settings, are obliged to act differently and are propelled into social partnership arrangements. This is likely to have spillover back into the US context. Starting 30 years ago reports of industrial democracy innovations in Europe had some influence on labour and management within the US, but a system of voluntary or 'free' collective bargaining has been maintained. Nevertheless, practical realities have propelled major labour–management partnerships. The significant developments within the EU are likely to help indirectly influence the US climate as well.

No single blueprint holds, but some principles obtain and are likely apply in most sectors and in most societies, with accommodation given the framework labour legislation and mandates as well as practice of worker and union participation in decision-making at work (EIRO Observer 2003; Gillan and Patmore, 2003). The evidence is clear that national managements are quite capable of altering their practice when put under mandate to do so. American multinational corporations demonstrate different management practices across the border in Canada and in Mexico, in both cases reflecting what those nations require of management and what the local labour union milieu is.

The European Union directives as well as national statutes will help move labour and management into partnering arrangements which help transcend ideological gaps and compel moving towards pragmatic solutions to best achieve those goals which labour and management hold in common, including organisation economic well-being, employment security, workforce skills development, improved work environment, and enhancements in quality of production and services.

While there are strong traditional managerial objections to extending greater influence to workers and their unions, pragmatic considerations and affirmative innovations and examples all work to push for more labour–management partnerships in the US as well as in other nations. More important, it is clear that partnerships become significant components of strategic planning by forward-looking unions and enlightened management. There is considerable momentum around the country that promotes labour–management partnerships in the governmental sector, and the contextual realities, including fiscal pressures, assure that this is likely to continue and perhaps increase.

Strategic unionism

The US is a crisis-driven society. Change comes about not because of an inherent forward-looking and planning mentality; quite the opposite. The crisis which global economics, technological change, and corporate and workplace restructuring has introduced, raised new challenges in terms of employment security, skills development, workplace health, and quality of work. These issues have also driven a great deal of the worker participation and workplace change agenda (Melman, 2001; Poole *et al.*, 2001). Unions have been seriously challenged to address changing worker needs and an altered environment.

This comes at a time when the haemorrhaging of union density has slowed, but the statistics are staggering. In 1948 there were over 13.5 million private sector workers in unions; by 2000 that figure was only 9.1 million. Public sector employees in unions went from 680 000 in 1948 to 7.1 million in the year 2000. As a result the total number organised increased, but the percentage drop is enormous. That 16.3 million is 13.5% of the workforce organised. It is critical to note that only 9% in the private sector are organised and 37% in the public sector. This is all a fundamental challenge for unions to survive, grow and remain a central force in the US economy and society (Herzenberg, 2001; Turner *et al.*, 2001).

Considerable change in organised labour is likely (Osterman *et.al.*, 2002). Major new organising efforts to unionise sectors of the workforce are growing, such as health care, hospitality and related services, computers and allied high technology jobs. Renewed efforts to organise women, minorities, immigrant workers as well as professionals, is to be expected. The promotion of a union-driven approach to workplace change, use of technology, workforce skills training, and employee participation to achieve high performance work organisations will be an important agenda (Wheeler, 2002). This may well lead to a more centralized role of labour than has heretofore been true in the US bringing the AFL-CIO closer to the labour federations in Europe. Collective bargaining and industry-wide bargaining may not be altered, but other more central activities, including the promotion of union amalgamations will likely continue.

Unions have developed a host of strategies for effecting workplace change and altered patterns of worker and union participation (Nissen, 1997; Rubenstein, 2001; Rubenstein and Kochan, 2001; Yates *et al.*, 2001). What is most critical is the shift towards strategic planning and placing mutual gains or labour management partnering efforts within a broader union agenda (McKersie, 2001). And that agenda needs to accommodate the significant shifts in worker attitudes. A 2000 study shows a major change across generations in attitudes towards work and life integration. 'This gender shift is of major proportions. It promises to have significant effects on how work and family life are organised' (Rayman, 2001: 169). Males are much more likely today to value family and private life and want arrangements at work to reflect that. It is not merely a gender issue reflecting women workers' needs; but is generic. For that reason many unions have focused on work/family issues in bargaining, in strategies for union participation and internal member mobilisation, and how work is structured and issues at work resolved.

The European Industrial Relations Observatory in 2002 surveyed work/family issues in the EU and chronicled how various partnership agreements (e.g. Irish and Dutch agreements) have emerged and dealt with the issues around work and family time and care (European Foundation, 2002). The point is that this is a good illustration of how union-driven agendas are shaping the labour–management partnership agreements and not simply a reflection of management initiatives with only a workplace or productivity focus.

The build-up of national labour federation units and staff focusing on corporate affairs and workplace democracy has helped in strategic thinking. Much union and university labour education centres training in recent years have addressed skill building in strategic and active unionism, with a growing curriculum and publications. A key reality in all of this is that the training of union leadership involves new challenges. In the US there has been an important and continuing discussion about the organising model versus the servicing union model. Union staff and leaders accustomed to the approach that left the union as an organisation primarily engaged providing services for workers as needed, such as handling workplace grievances, experienced new challenges with the shift towards a mobilization and organising approach (Nissen, 2003).

Boxing and dancing – challenges for union leaderships

This new way of addressing union activism very directly entered the arena of worker participation (Banks and Metzgar, 1989). Furthermore, the competing roles for union leadership became increasingly clear. The traditional role of contract negotiation and enforcement continued, while the new challenges of a system of labour–management partnerships were raised. Individual union leaders were, indeed, expected to know how to 'box' with managers in the old adversarial role, and expected as well to be able to 'dance' with some of the same managers in a newly developed partnership arrangement.

The adversarial posture, long established in American labour relations, has the advantage of building worker solidarity and strengthening worker will in times of conflict with 'the bosses'. These issues cut across the US, Canada, and the UK as Nesbit found (Nesbit, 2003). The new partnerships posed dilemmas, as Paul Clark explains:

> This culture, however, created problems as unions began to enter into co-operation programmes in the 1980s and 1990s. Increasingly some union leaders and management officials began talking about common interest and shared values. Instead of the enemy the employer increasingly became a partner. Unions began signalling to their members that the employer could be trusted. All of this, of course, was in conflict with the prevailing union culture, which often said exactly the opposite.

> Some union leaders, while endorsing the exploration of a co-operative relationship with the employer, simultaneously argued that the strong, adversarial culture had to stay in place to keep the employer honest. Not surprisingly, many members were confused by these conflicting signals. *This suggests the need for a union's culture and its actions to be consistent. It also suggests that if a union desires to make significant changes in policy and strategy, it must make sure that the organization's culture changes as well* (emphasis added) (Clark, 2000: 161).

All of us who have been involved in workplace partnering schemes and in doing the union training for such participation will recognize the dilemma that Clark talks about. In some cases there have been major splits within a local union and elections for officers have been turned into referenda on whether the rank and file wishes to 'box' or 'dance'. The reality is that a large portion of workplaces now has some sort of employee involvement and participation structure. The real challenge of union leadership is to build a strategic approach to carrying out the union agenda and placing such worker participation efforts within that plan. And for most union leaders there will be movement back and forth between the roles of working co-operatively on mutual goals and the need to struggle against unilateral management power and pursue legitimate grievances and bargaining issues. What that translates into is a recognition that union leadership capacity building and training must help identify skills in both roles and how to develop ease of moving fluidly between them and knowing when and how to do so. This theme is taken up further in the concluding chapter of this volume.

Lessons for unions from the US experience

- There are strong advantages for a centralised system of labour relations, as in Northern Europe, whereby labour can consolidate more power. The decentralised, or enterprise bargaining system, as in the US, typically weakens labour.
- In the absence of legislated mandates for employee participation, negotiated agreements are critical.
- Co-ordinated partnerships, such as the Kaiser Permanente case, enhance labour's ability to work with large, multi-site employers.
- For many reasons, the public sector continues to be much more highly organised and therefore labour has greater leverage and ability to gain influence.
- Unions must approach work restructuring and labour–management partnerships from a strategic perspective. This means that how such efforts fit into the larger union agenda is critical.
- Training for changing union leadership roles, making union leaders more adept at the 'dancing' as well as 'boxing' roles is vital. Unions must push for training within partnership agreements, meaning paid release time and support for training.

References

Adams, R. J. (1995) *Industrial Relations Under Liberal Democracy: North American Comparative Perspective*. Columbia: University of South Carolina Press.

AFL-CIO (1994) *The New American Workplace: A Labor Perspective*. Washington, DC: AFL-CIO.

AFL-CIO (2002) *Helping Low Wage Workers Succeed Through Innovative Union Partnerships*. Washington: AFL-CIO.

Askenazy, P. (2001) 'Innovative Workplace Practices and Occupational Illness in the United States, *Economic and Industrial Democracy* 22: 485–516.

Australian Council of Trade Unions (ACTU)/Trade Development Council (1987) *Australia Reconstructed*. Canberra: AGPS.

Banks, A. and Metzgar, J. (1989) 'Participating in Management: Union Organizing on a New Terrain', *Labor Research Review* 14: 1–55.

Baugh, B. (1994) *Changing Work: A Union Guide to Workplace Change*. Washington: AFL-CIO.

Clark, P. (2000). *Building More Effective Unions*. Ithaca: Cornell University Press.

Cohen-Rosenthal, E. and Burton, C. (1993) *Mutual Gains*. Ithaca: ILR Press.

Deutsch, S. (1986) 'Technology, Union Strategies and Worker Participation', *Economic and Industrial Democracy* 7: 529–39.

Deutsch, S. (1991) 'Democracy and Worker Health: Strategies for Intervention', in Johnson, J. and Johansson, G. (eds) *The Psychosocial Work Environment: Work Organization, Democratization and Health*. Amityville, NY: Baywood Pub. Co.

Deutsch, S. (1994) 'Union Initiatives on Technological Change and Work Organization', in Deutsch, S. and Broomhill, R. (eds), *Recent Developments in US Trade Union Strategies*. Adelaide: University of Adelaide Centre for Labour Studies.

Deutsch, S. and Albrecht, S. (1983) 'Worker Participation in the United States', *Labour and Society* 8: 241–69.

European Foundation for the Improvement of Living and Working Conditions (2002) *Quality of Women's Work and Employment: Tools for Change*. Dublin.

European Foundation for the Improvement of Living and Working Conditions (2003) 'Corporate Governance Systems and the Nature of Industrial Restructuring', *EIRO Observer* 1. Dublin.

European Industrial Relations Observatory (2002) *EIRO Annual Report 2001*. Dublin: European Foundation for the Improvement of Living and Working Conditions.

Gallagher, J. (ed.) (1992) *Restructuring the American Workplace: Implications for the Public Sector*. Eugene: University of Oregon Labor Education and Research Center.

Gillan,P. and Patmore, G. (eds) (2003) *Partnership at Work – The Challenge of Employee Democracy*. Sydney: Pluto Press.

Haddad, C. (2002) *Managing Technological Change: A Strategic Partnership Approach*. Thousand Oaks, CA: Sage.

Herzenberg, S. (2001) 'The US Labour Movement: Inventing Postindustrial Prosperity – A Progress Report', in Jose, A. V. (ed.), *Organized Labour in the 21st Century*. Geneva: International Institute of Labour Studies.

Kelley, M. and Harrison, B. (1992) 'Unions, Technology and Labor-Management Co-operation', in Mishel, L. and Voss, P. (eds), *Unions and Economic Competitiveness*. New York: ME Sharpe.

Kochan, T. A. and Osterman, P. (1994) *The Mutual Gains Enterprise: Forging a Winning Partnership Among Labor, Management, and Government*. Boston: Harvard Business School Press.

Mathews, J. (1994) *Catching the Wave: Workplace Reform in Australia*. St. Leonards, NSW: Allen & Unwin.

McKersie, R. B. (2001) 'Labor's Voice At the Strategic Level of the Firm', *Transfer: European Review of Labour and Research (ETUI)* 7, Autumn: 480–93.

Melman, S. (2001) *After Capitalism: From Managerialism to Workplace Democracy*. New York: Alfred Knopf.

Nesbit, T. (2003) 'Learning for Change: Staff Training, Leadership Development, and Union Transformation', *Labor Studies Journal* 28: 109–32.

Nissen, B. (ed.) (1997) *Unions and Workplace Reorganization*. Detroit: Wayne State University Press.

Nissen, B. (2003) 'Alternative Strategic Directions for the US Labor Movement', *Labor Studies Journal* 28: 133–55.

Ogden, M. (1993) *Towards Best Practice Unionism: Strategies for Renewal*. Sydney: Pluto Press.

Osterman, P., Kochan, T. A., Locke, R. M. and Piore, M. J. (2002) *Working in America* Cambridge, MA: MIT Press.

Poole, M., Lansbury, R. and Wailes. N. (2001) 'A Comparative Analysis of Developments in Industrial Democracy', *Industrial Relations* 40: 490–525.

Rayman, P. (2001) *Beyond the Bottom Line – The Search for Dignity at Work*. New York: Palgrave/St. Martin's Press.

Rubenstein, S. A. (2001) 'A Different Kind of Union – Balancing Co-Management and Representation', *Industrial Relations* 40: 163–203.

Rubenstein, S. A. and Kochan, T. A. (2001) *Learning From Saturn*. Ithaca: Cornell University Press.

Strauss, G. (1992) 'The United States', in Szell, G. (ed.) *Concise Encyclopedia of Participation and Co-Management*. Berlin: Walter de Gruyer.

Turner, L., Katz, H. C. and Hurd, R. W. (eds) (2001) *Rekindling the Movement: Labor's Quest for Relevance in the 21st Century*. Ithaca: Cornell University Press.

US Department of Labor (1996) *Working Together for Public Service: Report of the Task Force on Excellence in State Government Through Labor-Management Co-operation*. Washington: US Government Printing Office.

Walton, R. E., McKersie, R. B. and Cutcher-Gershenfeld, J. E. (1994) *Strategic Negotiations: A Theory of Change in Labor Management Relations*. Boston: Harvard University Press.

Wheeler, H. N. (2002a) *The Future of the American Labor Movement*. Cambridge: Cambridge University Press.

Wheeler, J. (2002b) 'Employee Involvement in Action: Reviewing Swedish Codetermination', *Labor Studies Journal* 26: 71–97.

Working for America Institute (2002) *Helping Low Wage Workers Succeed Through Innovative Union Partnerships*. Washington, DC: AFL-CIO.

Yates, C., Lewchuck, W. and Stewart, P. (2001) 'Empowerment as a Trojan Horse – New Systems of Work Organization in the North American Automobile Industry', *Economic and Industrial Democracy* 22: 517–41.

Further reading

Deutsch, S. (2001a) 'The United States: An Economic Leader Seeks Answers for the Future', in Szell, G. (ed.) *European Labor Relations Vol. II Selected Country Studies*. Aldershot: Gower Publishing Co.

Deutsch, S. (2001b) 'Innovative Union Driven Partnerships with Management Within the USA', *Concepts and Transformation* 6: 219–26.

12

Dance, Dance, Wherever you May be? Partnership in Comparative Perspective

Tony Huzzard[1]

Strategic choice and the dynamics of boxing and dancing

In this chapter we attempt to integrate our findings on 'the dance' with a view to making some general observations on international experiences as a possible 'new' strategic response to the challenges faced by unions, albeit from different starting points and often very different notions of what the term partnership actually means. In particular, we suggest that discussions of strategic choice can be usefully assisted by reference to the 'policy space' in which strategic choices can be made. Indeed, we show how in certain instances unions can act so as to increase the policy space in which such choices can be made.

Our primary motivation for focusing on strategic choice both for assessing social partnership and debating union renewal has been to emphasise that union futures are not necessarily dependent on systemic factors (cf. Dunlop, 1958). As we stated in Chapter 2, unions have potentials and responsibilities for their own renewal in an increasingly unstable environment which in many instances can also be seen as hostile. However, we do not pretend to cover the entire spectrum of strategic choices for unions as identified in Chapter 2, indeed, we would certainly accept criticism that we have not focused on Level 2 strategies in relation to recruiting new members or seeking new ways of relating to existing members, for example, women, young employees or ethnic minorities. Such matters must await further research. Nevertheless, although many aspects of union environments are changing, it seems likely that dealing with employers in the joint regulation of the labour process will remain a core union activity, hence our focus on the strategic choices of boxing and dancing.

It is perhaps fruitful here to recap on our usage of the concept of strategic choice. Following Kessler and Purcell's conceptualisation of strategic choice in the public services in the UK (Kessler and Purcell, 1996), we see strategic choice for unions as similarly multilayered. Such choices start from basic positions of ideology and identity that are often deeply institutionalised historically, for example, in rulebooks. From such a platform unions decide which relationships with members they wish to enter into – choices that naturally lead to further choices on relationships with employers. Having established such relationships, unions will then seek to develop such relationships in terms of adversarialism or co-operation – boxing or dancing. Such relationships may need bolstering by additional relationships with other unions or key actors in civil society. Finally, the implications of choices to box or dance may have implications for how unions design structures and processes internally – and their overall capacities to learn, change and develop.

A further distinction also needs to be made between boxing and dancing as strategic choices and boxing and dancing as tactical choices. Strategic choices by their very nature involve the long-term alignment of an organisation with its environment. It is generally accepted in the strategy literature that for new strategies to be sustainable some sort of cognitive shift is required throughout the organisation and that this is consistent with the newly selected alignment – in essence this amounts to shifts in organisational culture (Peters and Waterman, 1982), new paradigms (Johnson, 1987) or a new strategy as perspective (Mintzberg, 1987). In Chapter 2 we identify this phenomenon as the cultural dimension of boxing and dancing – that of the collective mindset governing the parties in the employment relationship. This is not something that changes from day-to-day; on the other hand, there will rarely if ever be a situation of either full conflict or full co-operation in the employment relationship (Haynes and Allen, 2001). As pointed out in Chapter 1, it seems useful to point out that choices therefore also exist on boxing or dancing at the tactical or day-to-day level within either a predominantly boxing or predominantly dancing mindset: there is prolonged engagement at the dance academy as well as one-off visits to the disco.

The distinction between strategic and tactical choices on boxing and dancing suggests the need for a nuanced view of boxing and dancing dynamics as set out in Figure 12.1. Here the vertical axis represents the strategic choices of boxing and dancing as practices embedded in contrasting industrial relations dispositions or cultures, whereas the horizontal axis represents day-to-day to practices of boxing and dancing. As we will argue later in the chapter, there appears to be some evidence that longer term strategic choices on whether to box or dance can have a cyclical tendency (see also Kelly, 1998) – this is represented in the figure by the two larger arrows. On the other hand, within each culture there will be tactical choices to oscillate between both activities (as depicted by the smaller arrows) – but one will tend to dominate, hence the broken lines in both the upper and lower parts of the diagram that are intended to signify the less likely movement from boxing to dancing in the former and dancing to boxing in the latter.

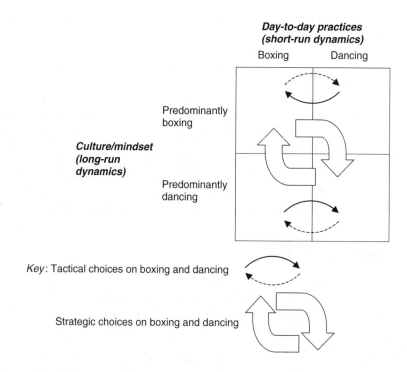

Day-to-day practices
(short-run dynamics)

Boxing   Dancing

Predominantly
boxing

Culture/mindset
(long-run
dynamics)

Predominantly
dancing

Key: Tactical choices on boxing and dancing

Strategic choices on boxing and dancing

Figure 12.1   To box or to dance – strategic and tactical choices.

As stated in the discussion on union strategic choices in Chapter 2, such choices will be constrained by a number of factors. The various constraints identified therein, however, will impact differently according to the context a union finds itself in. In some contexts unions will have little choice at all; in others unions will be able to choose from a number of different options. We believe it is useful to talk in terms of strategic choices being made within a certain space or freedom of action – what we will call here 'policy space'. There is a strong parallel between the concept of 'policy space' and that of 'design space', used in the 1980s debate concerning workers' influence on technology and organisation (Bessant, 1983; Deutsch, 1986, 1994; Sandberg *et al.*, 1992). In that debate it was recognised that certain labour processes had more scope for job redesign than others, not least because of the nature of the work involved and/or the technology. In the same way, unions with a stronger power base will usually have greater policy space than those with weaker power bases.

There seems to be greater policy space associated with the strategic choice to dance in contexts of expanding product markets or market share than where these are on the decline and employers are engaged in rationalisation or restructuring (Kelly, 2004). Steadily expanding product markets, relatively immune to cyclical swings, seem to support the endurance of partnerships in the pharmaceutical and chemical sectors (see the Astra Zeneca and Italian chemical sector cases). In the contrasting situations of expanding and contracting product markets, the policy space for unions is opened up and closed down respectively by the strategic choices of employers. Yet some of the cases in this book also show that unions themselves can help shape their policy space. For example, in the Industristion case the FNV officials tried to compensate for their weak power base by offensively using the dance floor to embarrass and seduce their counterparts. The new opportunities to box and thereby make distributional gains can usefully be seen as the outcome of an increase in the 'policy space' opened up by the strategic choice to dance. The strategic choice to dance, too, can open policy spaces by means of allowing unions *earlier* influence on company decision-making as at Astra Zeneca.

The politics of the dance

Throughout this book we have resisted taking an absolute ideological position on social partnership or making value judgements on boxing versus dancing as strategic choices underpinning union renewal. Indeed, as we elaborate below, partnership in any event is a complex phenomenon, deeply embedded in its contexts, and not a subject for grand narratives. Rather, we see this book as evaluative of a diverse range of experiences of partnership in practice as seen by practitioners.

Nevertheless, we approached this project as pluralists with a critical posture towards the unitarist project of human resource management (HRM) that marginalises unions or at least downplays the ongoing conflict of interest at the core of the labour process (Thompson, 1989). We are thus deeply sceptical of social partnership conceived of as a natural extension or even a new language for HRM. In any event, the empirical evidence that HRM is some sort of best practice philosophy that can guarantee superior organisational performance is far from clear-cut. In reality, the evidence is very uneven, notwithstanding the difficulties of conceptual precision in research to date. Many researchers have argued that intervening variables such as quality and leanness have a key impact on outcomes and that it is premature for managers or others to embrace HRM, let alone see social partnership as the natural extension of an HRM ideology (see Wood, 1999 for a review of the literature). Moreover, there is little evidence that HRM has led to any noteworthy change to core institutions; as a philosophy (and even a distinct academic field) it is largely restricted to the English speaking world.

We would, however, go further than pluralism. The demise of certain labour processes such as assembly lines has not diminished the asymmetry in power relations at the workplace. Moreover, in many instances, new forms of work organisation such as lean production in manufacturing or the 'electronic sweatshops' of call centres can be understood as a continuation of Taylorism (Smith and Thompson, 1998) and many claims with regard to increased empowerment are decidedly questionable (Willmott, 1993). Accordingly, while we acknowledge the plurality of the employment relationship, questions of power remain fundamental. With regard to partnership, the issue is thus whether or not it empowers unions: to the extent that it does empower them, even through the obtaining of better and earlier information, it can be said to add value to unions provided that union independence is not sacrificed. Clearly, empowerment will be greater still where partnership enhances union capacities to shape decision-making in firms or public sector organisations.

In our view it is misleading to attach political labels to the choices to box or dance, not least because of the diversity of contexts in which industrial relations processes are embedded; it is more helpful we believe to assess partnerships in terms of a comprehensive range of outcomes, hence the application of the social partnership matrix to our case studies (see below). Moreover, we have argued in Chapter 2 that theoretically, social partnership is quite distinct from business unionism. Whether such an argument is sustainable is a matter for empirical investigation – a task we hope to have undertaken in this book and will reflect on in the remainder of this chapter. Before drawing up conclusions on the evidence, however, it is necessary to explore and unpack the complexities of social partnership.

The varieties of the dance[2]

The various country chapters and cases in this book underscore difficulties associated with the concept of social partnership not least because it means different things in different contexts and is generally value-laden. However our use of the dancing metaphor as a generic term for co-operative industrial relations has enabled us to develop dialogues that have cut across the obvious conceptual problems of 'partnership'. But rather than sidestep partnership altogether we believe it is nevertheless fruitful to unpack the concept by identifying a number of key dimensions along which partnership can be analysed and understood arising from our empirical material. We believe that such understanding can be enhanced by identifying six distinct dimensions as illustrated in Figure 12.2: union power base, scope, nature, level, leadership and outcome. These will be elaborated below.

The first dimension of dancing is that of the power base underpinning the union approach. A clear distinction in the cases exists between partnerships that are motivated by unions seeking to make advances on well-defined agendas on developmental issues such as work organisation from a position of a relatively strong power base. This, for example, is associated with the recent strategic choices exercised by blue-collar unions in Sweden and Germany. Many of the choices to dance elsewhere, however, appear to have

Union power base:	Weak	←---→	Strong	
Scope:	Narrow (time/issue)	←---→	Comprehensive	
Nature:	Informal	←---→	Formal/ codified	
Level:	Workplace/ organisational	Sectoral/ regional	National	Transnational
Leadership:	Reactive	←---→	Proactive	
Outcome:	Soft (process and culture)	←---→	Hard (audited measures)	

Figure 12.2   The social partnership matrix – mapping out the dance floor.

been made in contexts where unions have a relatively weak power base. Here union strategic choices can be seen in terms of an attempt to regain legitimacy or even presence at a workplace – as in the TUC's (Trades Union Congress) policy in the mid-to late 1990s in the UK as well as cases reported on in this volume such as Vertex, the US cases and Industrishion. We use the terms *strong* and *weak* respectively to distinguish between these two contrasting power bases.

The second dimension is *scope*. This covers both the *narrowness* and *comprehensiveness* of the issues covered within a partnership arrangement as well as the timescale over which such an arrangement is in force. In some situations a 'fully blown' partnership agreement might encompass the entire range of issues covered within the regulation of the employment relationship, including distributional issues (where they are not 'boxed'), and have the ambition of enduring indefinitely (Claydon, 1998); in other situations the aim might be more restricted around a single issue and within the definite timescale of a project. Most of the cases presented in this book fall into the former category; we feel it of analytical value, however, to point out the limited nature of some partnership formations such as the Industrishion case and as identified in research elsewhere, for example, work organisation development projects in Scandinavia (see e.g. Huzzard, 2000 Chapters 10 and 11).

Third, there appears to be some variation in whether or not the partnership arrangements are codified, both in terms of an actual agreement and/or in some form of written minute under what we call *formal* partnership. However, to obtain legitimacy for change, and secure quality information from the union side at the point of production, the employers may be prepared to withhold from exerting some of their power and thereby grant the local union a high degree of influence. This alternative, *informal* partnership, implies that the parties reach agreement, but this is not codified and, rather, is acknowledged through a 'handshake' or 'gentleman's agreement'. If social partnership is arranged formally, the minutes are in some contexts legally equivalent to a negotiated agreement, as in Sweden. In dual systems the situation is more complex. A number of partnerships have started in the Netherlands, for example, in a (rather) unformalised way, at sector and/or regional level (see Chapter 6). In some projects, for example, the Industribution case, processes were formalised because power was handed over to Works Councils that made use of their statutory rights. Sometimes this is consciously pursued by the unions, sometimes 'it just happens'. Yet, formalisation could be used to reinforce workers' positions that were otherwise hard to maintain.

Fourth, partnerships can operate at different levels of industrial relations processes. The significance of this can clearly be appreciated by reference to the 'boxing and dancing matrix' included in each of the country chapters in this volume. Partnerships can exist at the *workplace* or *organisational* levels, *sectoral or regional* levels, *national* levels and even the *transnational* level if European Works Councils (EWCs) and global agreements can reasonably be understood as predominantly an arena for dancing. There appears to be wide variation in which levels can most plausibly be designated as the site of the dance. In some cases dance floors at one level are connected to dance floors at other levels (e.g. in the white-collar process agreements in Sweden); in others there may be tensions between a harmonious dance at one level and a vigorous boxing match at others.

Fifth, it seems quite clear that there is some variation about who is leading the dance and who is following. For example, in the cases of the Swedish teachers and Industribution, the unions concerned both saw opportunities for making advances by inviting the employers to dance. In contrast, the unions at Astra Zeneca and Kaiser Permanente appear to have accepted the invitation to dance offered by the employer. In other cases, a different type of dance is discernible where the decision to dance has been a joint effort and it is harder to single out a distinct leader (Vertex, Seattle, Jury's Hotels). In some cases, moreover, the identity of the dance leader appears to have shifted over time (Anglian Water). To distinguish the leadership of the dance we use here the terms *proactive* and *reactive* to denote the two opposite poles of a continuum whereby the union or the employer is leading the dance respectively.

Finally, it seems significant to draw distinctions in partnership arrangements in terms of *outcomes*. Clearly, all partnerships will aspire to deliver mutual gains, by definition. But these may vary from *soft* aspects of workplace development to *hard*, quantifiable elements (Legge, 1995). Mutual gains can certainly be conceived in terms of a new workplace organisational culture that has the appearance of encouraging co-operation, learning, shared values and so on. On the other hand, the parties may seek to assess partnership outcomes according to more tangible factors be they essentially distributional in nature or developmental. It may even be the case that some trade union innovation should be seen as being based on a new model of hard social partnership agreements, whereas traditional socio-political solidarity and corporate industrial relations cultures should be seen as nothing new at all.

The wide diversity of the dance in practice is illustrated by a summary of our case studies of partnership in Table 12.1.[3] The figure considers the six varieties or dimensions of the dance identified above for each of the cases in the book. This analysis shows a complex picture whereby partnership is highly contextually dependent. For example, the degree to which partnerships are formalised will vary according to the legal underpinnings of national industrial relations context. There are long traditions in industrial relations that distinguish countries with legislated or mandated employee involvement schemes (Sweden, Germany) and those which historically have relied upon voluntary negotiated agreements between employers and employees and their unions (the UK, Ireland, the US). Some nations have hybrid systems in-between these (e.g. The Netherlands, Italy). However, what we conclude is that regardless of the level of nationally legislated systems, mainstream union strategy is to go beyond informal partnerships and to seek formalised agreements at the workplace. This, of course, is especially true in settings where mandated systems of labour participation are absent. Clearly, however, the evidence suggests that partnerships have a better chance of enduring in contexts where there is statutory underpinning as in Sweden or Germany (see also Terry, 2003). A multitude of more localised factors also appear to influence strategic choices; accordingly it is extremely difficult to make generalisations about partnership.

Our national chapters and case studies also show unions' new boxing and dancing strategies to be highly influenced (and sometimes even directed) by a number of general developments in working life internationally. These can be summarised under a number of headings.

Privatisation and/or the decentralisation of public services. Privatisation, for example, has profoundly changed conditions in former public utilities and state firms. An upshot of this has been that unions are weakened in a context of more competition in product markets (Anglian Water and Petromidia). This is a particular feature of Eastern European economies where the Petromidia case in Romania has shown how the union has made strategic choices initially to shift from an incorporated form of unionism under communism. Initially the union moved to boxing and then changed to dancing as a number of shared interests opened up, not least to ensure company survival in an increasingly competitive context. Such a context also appears to have been a key factor in shaping union strategic choices at Anglian Water. Elsewhere, activities have remained in the public sector but appear to be characterised by market testing and often localisation, generally with an aim of bringing service provision closer to 'customers' at the local level. The need for skills development to support interactive service work has generally been recognised by both employers (Swedish Teachers,

Table 12.1 The dance in comparative perspective

Case	Union power base	Nature	Scope and issues	Level	Leadership	Outcome	Comments
Anglian Water	Relatively strong 60% of the workforce unionised	Voluntary agreement in parallel with conventional collective bargaining	Comprehensive: strategic development of company and impact on employment relations	Company level with divisional and business unit forums and application	Proactive	Hard: mitigation of outsourcing strategy, extension of TUPE	Broadening of joint problem solving; more effective collective bargaining process.
Vertex	Relatively weak less than 50% of the workforce unionised	Voluntary agreement linked with recognition and restoration of collective bargaining	Comprehensive: based on joint problem solving	Company level and site specific	Joint leadership of the dance	Hard-developed key employment relations policies and agreed changes to work organisation	Has explored areas of the employment relations terrain untouched by orthodox collective bargaining. Credibility of partnership severely stretched by threat of outsourcing.
Astra Zeneca	Strong	Formal (Co-determination)	Comprehensive, for example, pay and conditions	Organisation but bound by sector level bargaining	Reactive	Hard	More boxing on blue-collar side. Expanding product markets. Knowledge-intensive firm
Swedish Teachers Agreement	Strong	Formal – linked to state level process agreement	Workplace development and an associated new salary agreement	National but with local application	Proactive	Hard	Expanded union role and new professional identities for teachers.

Table 12.1 (Continued)

Case	Union power base	Nature	Scope and issues	Level	Leadership	Outcome	Comments
Dutch Railways	Strong	Formal	Comprehensive: Jobs and conditions.	Organisational/ sectoral	Reactive	Too soon to say: fragile	Even monopolies are fragile. Cyclical nature of B and D trade off. Trust building.
Industri-bution	Weak	Formal via various collective agreements. State endorsement	Narrow – limited to labour supply issues, for example, training and labour pools.	Sectoral/ regional (value) added logistics)	Proactive	Hard – new agreements on activities and jobs	Prompted by FNV Region in an area of non-unionism. New union role as a contributor to regional social capital.
Germany (group work)	Strong (but under pressure)	Formal (esta-blishment agreements) and informal	Comprehensive: work organisa-tion and related matters.	Workplace but with sectoral initiative (early 1990s)	Proactive; more recently proactive/ reactive	Hard: working conditions, co-determination rights, wage increases	Forms and outcomes varied between work-places and firms.
Italian chemical sector	Strong	Formal: joint commissions and observa-tories	Comprehensive – Production pros-pects, research, employment trends, technology, work organisation, training.	Sector	Proactive	Hard and soft	Apparently stable climate for consensual IR and a 'dancing' culture has consolidated over time. Many SMEs not covered.

	Strength	Formality	Scope	Level	Orientation	Hard/soft	Context
Italian engineering sector	Strong	Formal: joint commissions and observatories	Narrow – training, safety, work environment and equal opportunities	Sector with local applications	Reactive – following national unions	Hard on soft items	Dancing and concertation grinding to a halt. CGIL returning to the boxing ring.
Jury's Hotel Group	Relatively strong	Formal	Narrow – Employee input into workplace decision making	Organisation with local application	Joint leadership of the dance in response to invite from third party (ADAPT)	Hard. Considerable input into work environment and organisation	Seen as a 'best practice' partnership agreement in Irish context: rolling out to other sectors.
Petrimidia	Relatively strong	Formal: annually renegotiated company agreement	Narrow – areas of common interest with company in obtaining resources from the state. Training, work organisation	Organisational within a sector agreement	Reactive – partnership seen as only alternative to closure	Hard. New (improved) agreements and advances on work organisation and QWL	Unions seeking new role in post-communist context. Privatisation of firm in 2000.
Seattle City	Weak	Formal labour contracts	Comprehensive – 'any issue' including pay and conditions	Organisation master agreement, but with local applications	Reactive	Hard agreements. Organising successes for unions	Mutual gains registered in many areas. Survived crisis in 2003.
Kaiser Permanente	Strong	Formal labour contracts	Comprehensive: quality, job design, business planning and strategy	Organisation master agreement, but with local applications	Proactive	Hard and soft: Many local agreements but also cognitive shifts by management	Private sector health. Explicit aim of power sharing in wide ranging settlement after experiences of boxing.

Seattle City, Dutch Railways) and unions. New opportunities have opened for unions in such situations to support such skills development. Interactive services appear to involve ongoing relationship building and high trust – both key characteristics of the dance.

Private sector services. As with services in the public sector, firms engaged in private sector services also see the need for HR strategies that build on trust and stable employment conditions to underpin interactive service work. What appears to be a strategic choice by employers to engage in the dance has been taken up by unions at Kaiser Permanente, Jury's Hotels and Vertex. In particular, the need for training is seen as a site of shared interest. Greater influence and increased policy space appear to be strategic outcomes of the dance in these cases.

Major changes in labour regulation, especially on the future of collective bargaining. In some countries at the macro level there appear to be threats to the legislative bases of existing regimes of joint regulation, notably in Germany and the Netherlands. Reunification and the pressure for structural reform have posed the German unions, in particular IG Metall, with a considerable challenge. Likewise, threats to the Mandatory Extension system in the Netherlands are putting unions under pressure. In Italy there is a de facto de-legitimisation of the existing system of collective bargaining with an increasing shift towards company regulation locally. In response to these problems and in anticipation of their effects, unions in these countries are seeking new sites of legitimacy on local level dance floors that hold out the prospect of new policy spaces.

New union products for workforce differentiation, diversity and individualisation. An increasing diversity among union members and potential members is prompting unions to rethink Level 2 strategic choices both in terms of appealing to new groups of members and delivering new products. A clear example of strategic choice to recruit in new areas has been Industribution, whereas the cases of the Swedish Teachers Union, the Swedish RUD project and the experience of the German unions on work organisation exemplify well the attempts of unions to move onto developmental agendas and offer new services and expertise on change competences. The Dutch Career Services case shows an example of a union strategy both to appeal to new members and to offer new services – what we call a diversification strategy. These Level 2 choices, often on process rather than zero-sum issues, seem to be associated with the Level 3 choice to dance – at least in the first instance, although such a choice can open up subsequent opportunities to engage in new boxing rings (Industribution case).

New economic activities, industry clusters and international outsourcing. One consequence of the globalisation of operations and product markets is that core activities are being outsourced; call centres are the latest in a line of outsourced activities. This is putting unions under pressure and severely limiting the scope and possibilities for boxing. Clearly, unions, as at Vertex, are seeking to look for novel ways of 'adding value' to firms to retain jobs that would otherwise be lost to lower cost economies. A further example of union responses to restructuring can be seen in the Industribution case: here, new regional clustering activities around logistics chains have not only resulted in union strategic choices to dance, but these in turn have opened up new possibilities to box that otherwise would not have materialised.

Rise of knowledge organisations. The evidence suggests that workers' representatives can develop new roles as 'knowledge brokers' more easily in knowledge intensive activities than in more traditional organisations. This has been a particular feature in the Swedish Astra Zeneca case where the strategic choice to dance has opened up policy spaces for union influence on salary discussions and managerial appointments, as well as being a significant player in discussions on corporate strategy in terms of a major merger. Knowledge management also appears to be a factor on which unions have sought leverage at Kaiser Permanente.

The need for new union capacity building. The Level 3 strategic choice to dance, often shaped by Level 2 choices to appeal to new members, deliver new products or both, has clearly been feeding through to shape Level 4 choices on union capacity building. This has been evident in a number of the cases reported in this volume, most notably the Swedish RUD project case, the Dutch Industribution case, the Dutch Career Services case and the US City of Seattle case. Expertise on laws and agreements appears to be insufficient as a skill base for union full timers. New individual competencies appear to be required for officers and even activists in new roles as change agents. In turn, this may imply new Level 1 choices for unions to reconstruct their role and identity to become knowledge organisations (see discussion in final chapter).

The analysis here suggests that the strategic choice to dance is being prompted by a multitude of factors. On the other hand, there is no evidence from any of the cases in this book that partnership is superseding collective bargaining. In some cases, the dance has begun to cover distributional issues and is considerably reducing the tendency to box, as at Astra Zeneca. But even here collective bargaining retains a role, particularly on the blue-collar side. In other cases, the boxing and dancing configuration is more evenly balanced.

The processes of the dance

There is little evidence across the countries covered in this book to suggest that the pursuit of the dance, whether this entails leading it as in proactive partnership or following it as in reactive partnership, is resulting in any new end state or convergent industrial relations dancing paradigm. Rather, many cases show dynamic shifts between modes of industrial relations engagement that are predominantly boxing or predominantly dancing. Such dynamics, in our view, are better understood as the outcomes of strategic choices shaping long-run movements back and forth along a continuum from one mode to the other. Strategic choices can be made to dance, either leading it or following the steps of the employer, as a means for pursuing developmental agendas from a high power base (the Swedish teachers case) or, to regain union influence, from a weak power base (Vertex, Industribution).

But the dance can disappoint; in such circumstances the strategic choice is made to leave the dance floor and return to the boxing ring either due to a collapse of mutual trust or a misalignment of partnership outcomes with expectations. In Italy, for example, there is evidence that the dancing activities of the CGIL unions at the sectoral level originating in the 1990s are now being succeeded by a strategic choice to return to the boxing ring; there are signs that other unions could be following suit. In the UK, too, successive elections of new union leaderships in 2002 and 2003 openly critical of partnership appear to have presaged a similar development. Alternatively, unions may make the strategic choice to seek gains in the boxing ring when they sense an increased capacity to mobilise resulting from shrewd activity on the dance floor, as was seen with FNV in the Industribution case. Other cases suggest a rather constant position on the continuum (Astra Zeneca) or movement from one steady position to another (Petromidia, Kaiser Permanente) or even movement of a more cyclical nature (Dutch Railways).

A further complexity in understanding the dynamics of boxing and dancing is that in many cases those dynamic forces involve an interplay of parallel processes operating at different levels in an industrial relations system. We have already pointed out the significance of different levels of partnership in our mapping out of the dance floor earlier in the chapter. These have also been illustrated empirically in the 'boxing and dancing matrices' in the country chapters. In the case of the CGIL engineering unions, an increasingly boxing mindset at the sector level seems to coexist with a greater tendency, in part, to engage in more dancing locally. The opposite appears to be evident in the Industribution case. In Sweden, Sif at Astra Zeneca appears to be predominantly dancing both at the sector level and the workplace, whereas its blue-collar counterpart is characterised by a more traditional boxing mindset. Elsewhere, for example, in the UK and the US, the national and sector levels seem to have less significance.

The issue of parallel industrial relations processes at different levels will almost certainly be mirrored by parallel internal political processes within trade unions. Where similar approaches are taken to boxing or dancing at different levels this may not be a matter of controversy within unions or indeed a matter of great research interest. On the other hand, where the boxing and dancing configuration differs, the matter of combining the various interests and power bases at stake into an attractive strategy for union members and a coherent strategic change process may be a particularly challenging organisational task. The issue may be complicated further by the fact that some unions may be more 'loosely coupled' than others, that is, in some unions local organisations enjoy considerable autonomy whereas in others control is tighter. We feel, however, that such issues are beyond the scope of this book, but well worthy of future research.

Our cases indicate not only that the dynamics of strategic choices to box or dance show a tendency to move along a continuum, but also the significance of varied power bases as relatively independent variables impacting on union strategic choices. To some extent the power base is determined by national industrial relations cultures, traditions and institutional arrangements. But this does not appear to be the entire story. There also appear to be variations within countries as well as between them (cf. Hyman, 2001). For example, in Italy basic ideologies that caused the original separation between CGIL and CISL still appear to be a factor underscoring current Level 3 choices on whether to box or dance. Such historical differences, too, between the white-collar and blue-collar unions in Sweden are clear in the Astra Zeneca case.

Accordingly, the attempt by Hyman to analyse union movements through a country-by-country categorisation seems to vastly oversimplify the international scene. Such complexity, in our view, defies any such categorisation and can be illustrated by Figure 12.3. This plots the cases in the volume in relation to just two of the dimensions previously identified for mapping out the dance: union power base (vertical axis) and leadership (horizontal axis).

The point should also be made that the duration of movements along the boxing and dancing continuum will vary. We would also reiterate the

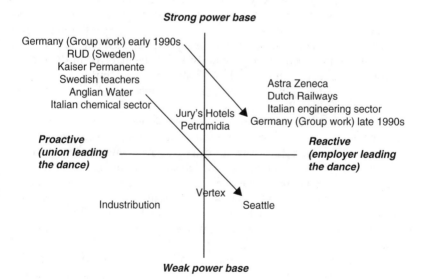

Figure 12.3 Proactivity, reactivity and power – the diversity of the dance.

point that the boxing rings and dance floors depicted here are those of the long-run dynamics identified in Figure 12.1. The mindset and practices of either boxing or dancing will tend to predominate over the other at any particular point in time. At the tactical level, however, effective unions will need to skilfully combine both activities which should be seen as mutually supportive and not comprising a trade-off. Naturally, too, there is more to strategic change in unions than the simple formulation and adoption of a 'strategic choice'. Change is often a messy political process involving interest legitimation and shifting coalitions of actors.

The outcomes of the dance

There is evidence in the literature to support the view that different sectors will show different characteristics in terms of partnership and its dynamic relationship with collective bargaining (Oxenbridge and Brown, 2002). Our cases support this assessment as well as illustrating the differences between countries. In some cases it is durable (as at Astra Zeneca) and adds value to unions, in others it is highly fragile. In terms of outcomes for the unions, there does appear to be evidence from our case study audits that partnership can deliver benefits for unions without falling into the trap of compromising union independence.

Clearly, the policy space is much greater during early phases of production decision-making than during later ones. Early interventions from the employees' side, with good insight on design parameters, has mostly proved to be more effective than late efforts to influence the design of technology and organisation. In parallel, in later phases of policy development it is much more difficult to realise workers' interests against employers' or state interests, or to realise specific union goals. On the other hand, pure boxing strategies can also be effective during later stages of industrial relations processes, be it only to correct or counterbalance management or state decisions. To be involved in the process of decision-making itself, however, more policy space and time is necessary.

The Dutch experience in particular suggests that in a number of projects 'policy space' was partly realised because a certain distance was kept from core trade union activities. This made it possible to develop longer term strategies, somewhat separately from day-to-day unionism. This appeared to be a key success factor for the unions. Accordingly, we believe such experiences highlight the need for a certain amount of policy or design space within union strategies for results to be obtained in new fields or at new levels of trade union organisation.

The evidence, however, is too patchy for us to draw overall generalisations about the durability and benefits of social partnership, although the statutory underpinning of participation rights clearly appears to be a facilitating factor. Yet even *within* countries the dance expresses itself in a variety of forms with different implications for the dance partners. It does seem clear, however, that where new partnership forms have become established they complement rather than supplant collective bargaining: good dance partners also need to hone their skills in the boxing ring.

The success of the dance?

As argued elsewhere in the literature (e.g. Kochan and Osterman, 1994), the issue of mutual trust appears to be a central factor behind the enduring of successful partnerships (see also Cohen-Rosenthal and Burton, 1993). The factors that contribute to trust building include statutory underpinning (as in Sweden and Germany). Yet there appears to be a crucial contradiction in the logic of social partnership that may well be a key reason why certain partnerships do not endure and strategic choices are made to return to the boxing ring. The logic of joint-problem solving at the core of partnership practices is generally motivated by the need to operate in a context of the increasingly turbulent environments of firms. In many sectors restructuring has become the norm rather than the exception forcing unions and works councils into a more intense engagement with business issues. These thus assume a more prominent position on trade union agendas. Yet these changes also act as external shocks that undermine the very trust on which partnership is built. Trust cannot be taken for granted even in industrial relations cultures that are normally considered to be underpinned by relatively high trust. The starting point for the dance cannot usually be trust – trust has to be built-up gradually not over a series of dance steps but over an ongoing engagement at the dance academy.

A clear lesson from the UK cases is that dancing is a high maintenance activity. Partnerships are fragile and certainly not an industrial relations quick fix. Our evidence has also highlighted that there appears to be a further contradiction in the dance. Partnership appears to require some degree of formalisation to endure. A difficulty is that the leading architects of a partnership on either side may well be succeeded by individuals who are less disposed to the dance. A codified, formal arrangement, however, will make it harder for them to leave the dance floor. Yet at the same time a formal agreement establishes an institutional constraint that can impede the dance if the rules governing the dance steps are too unwieldy. The experience of partnership agreements thus indicates that whilst desirable, they should be 'framework agreements' that codify but do not specify. The need to be conscious of the right degree and type of commitment by unions to the dance is also demonstrated by the Dutch experience whereby the most successful partnerships were projects that were not easily hampered by other union activities, including collective bargaining.

What can we conclude about the attitudes and role of management as a prerequisite for successful partnerships? In our view, the dance will be more likely to endure when management recognises that the basic conflict between buyers and sellers of labour will continue during the dance. Such a conflict of interest may not necessarily be something dysfunctional that requires managerial action to suppress through top-down unitarist cultural control or even coercion. Indeed, the tensions between divergent stakeholder interests may, on the contrary, be a source of creativity and innovation. The extent to which this is the case may, however, be dependent on the relative significance of human resources in the value-adding activities of the organisation concerned and how closely related these are to organisational strategy (Barney, 1991). This appears to be a key prerequisite for the dance, for example, in the Astra Zeneca case where the white-collar union representing knowledge workers was able to benefit from partnership and where its blue-collar partner has declined the strategic choice to dance. An acknowledgement of the key role of human resources as a source of added value is also a feature of the Kaiser Permanente case.[4]

The management position at Astra Zeneca is that of pragmatically seeing the added value of a partnership approach (and the value of retaining union independence) rather than that of an HRM-based ideology. Such a view from the management side appears to be an important success factor. Clearly, partnership can be of value to managers in reducing uncertainty in change situations: it is not just the union side that benefits from the earlier exchange of information. In effect this is quintessential knowledge management. The difficulty, however, is whether managers are prepared to accept a change of culture from the low road of command and control or leanness (Womack *et al.*, 1990) to the culture of the high road that foregrounds spaces for dialogue, creativity learning and innovation (Hague *et al.*, 2003). The dance academy not only requires a different mindset by unions, it also requires a similar transformation in management circles.

Concluding comments

To sum up, it can be seen that collective bargaining and partnership can be mutually supportive rather than mutually exclusive regimes for joint regulation. If unions are increasingly adopting qualitative agendas (Rigby *et al.*, 1999), it would suggest that greater significance will be placed on the processual aspects of union–employer interaction. If this is true, then collective bargaining and partnership are potentially interdependent components in industrial relations processes – in this sense we can talk in terms of the *dynamic dualism of boxing and dancing*.

Clearly, different unions in different countries will be approaching the issue of social partnership (or indeed disavowing it) from varying positions of strength and weakness. We might thus expect to find activity on dance floors pursued as a means to consolidate union positions through advancing on qualitative agendas or as a means to recover lost ground. The latter can involve seeking out a new role at the workplace, boosting legitimacy in the eyes of employers and potential members, perhaps with a view to re-establishing boxing rings.

Our conclusions on partnership can be summarised thus:

- There is little evidence that social partnership constitutes some new form of convergent industrial relations settlement.
- The prospects for enduring partnerships that deliver mutual gains appear to be greater in contexts of expanding product markets or market share.
- Partnerships are fragile in contexts of rationalisation and restructuring as mutual trust is undermined.

- Established partnerships can allow unions earlier influence on company decision-making and better quality information disclosure.
- Partnership prospects are highly dependent on context; in particular, statutory underpinning of participation rights is an important facilitator.
- The advantages of formal agreements that codify partnership without specifying are generally acknowledged by unions.
- There is no evidence that partnership is superseding collective bargaining, although in some cases dialogues are held within partnerships on distributional issues.
- In only two of our cases was there any evidence that partnership was being seen to compromise union independence.

Notes

1. I am grateful for the comments of all the 'New Trade Union' network members on earlier drafts of this chapter.
2. The various interpretations of the cases in this and later sections have been undertaken by the case study and country chapter authors and cannot in general be seen as 'negotiated outcomes' between the researchers and practitioners in the field.
3. Two cases, Dutch Employability and the Swedish RUD Project, focus on union renewal efforts rather than partnership practices per se. For this reason they are not included within this analysis.
4. The point being that human resources, capabilities and knowledge are seen as the primary source of value creation rather than the 'right' moves being made in product markets.

References

Barney, J. (1991) 'Firm Resources and Sustained Competitive Advantage', *Journal of Management* 17(1): 99–120.

Bessant, J. (1983) 'Management and Manufacturing Innovation: The Case of Information Technology', in Winch, G. (ed.) *Information Technology in Manufacturing Process: Case Studies in Technological Change*. London: Rossendale.

Claydon, T. (1998) 'Problematising Partnership: the Prospects for a Co-operative Bargaining Agenda', in Sparrow, P. and Marchington, M. (eds) *Human Resource Management: The New Agenda*. London: Financial Times/Pitman.

Cohen-Rosenthal, E. and Burton, C. (1993) *Mutual Gains*. Ithaca: ILR Press.

Deutsch, S. (1986) 'New Technology, Union Strategies and Worker Participation', *Economic and Industrial Democracy* 7: 529–39.

Deutsch, S. (1994) 'New Union Initiatives on Technological Change and Work Organization', in Deutsch, S. and Broomhill, R. (eds) *Recent Developments in US Trade Union Strategies*. Adelaide: University of Adelaide Centre for Labour Studies.

Dunlop, J. T. (1958) *Industrial Relations Systems*. New York: Holt.

Hague, J., Den Hertog, F., Huzzard, T. and Totterdill, P. (2003) *The Convergence of QWL and Competitiveness in Europe*. Report for EU Commission (Innoflex Project).

Haynes, P. and Allen, M. (2001) 'Partnership as Union Strategy: A Preliminary Evaluation', *Employee Relations* 23(2): 164–93.

Huzzard, T. (2000) *Labouring to Learn: Union Renewal in Swedish Manufacturing*. Umeå: Boréa.

Hyman, R. (2001) *Understanding European Trade Unionism: Between Market, Class and Society*. London: Sage.

Johnson, G. (1987) *Strategic Change and the Management Process*. Oxford: Blackwells.

Kelly, J. (1998) *Rethinking Industrial Relations: Mobilisation, Collectivism and Long Waves*. London: Routledge.

Kelly, J. (2004) 'Social Partnership Agreements in Britain: Labor Co-operation and Compliance', *Industrial Relations* 43(1): 267–92.

Kessler, I. and Purcell, J. (1996) 'Strategic Choice and New Forms of Employment Relations in the Public Service Sector: Developing an Analytical Framework', *International Journal of Human Resource Management* 7(1): 206–29.

Kochan, T. A. and Osterman, P. (1994) *The Mutual Gains Enterprise: Forging a Winning Partnership Among Labor, Management, and Government*. Boston: Harvard Business School Press.

Legge, K. (1995) 'HRM: Rhetoric, Reality and Hidden Agendas', in Storey, J. (ed.) *Human Resource Management – A Critical Text*. London: Routledge.

Martin, A. and Ross, G. (eds) (1999) *The Brave New World of European Labor*. New York: Berghahn Books.

Mintzberg, H. (1987) 'The Strategy Concept: Five Ps for Strategy', *California Management Review*. Fall: 11–24.

Olney, S. L. (1996) Unions in a Changing World. Geneva: International Labour Office.

Oxenbridge, S. and Brown, W. (2002) 'The Two Faces of Partnership? An Assessment of Partnership and Co-operative Employer/Trade Union Relationships', *Employee Relations* 24(3): 262–76.

Peters, T. and Waterman, R. (1982) *In Search of Excellence*. New York: Harper and Row.

Rigby, M., Smith, R. and Lawlor, T. (eds) (1999) *European Trade Unions: Change and Response*. London: Routledge.

Sandberg, Å., Broms, G., Grip, A., Sundström, L., Steen, J. and Ullmark, P. (1992) *Technological Change and Co-determination in Sweden*. Philadelphia: Temple University Press.

Smith, C. and Thompson, P. (1998) 'Re-evaluating the Labour Process Debate', *Economic and Industrial Democracy* 19(4): 551–77.

Terry, M. (2003) 'Partnership and the Future of trade unions in the UK', *Economic and Industrial Democracy* 24(4): 485–508.

Thompson, P. (1989) *The Nature of Work: an Introduction to Debates on the Labour Process*. Basingstoke: Macmillan.

Willmott, H. (1993) 'Strength is Ignorance, Slavery is Freedom: Managing Culture in Modern Organizations', *Journal of Management Studies* 30(4): 515–52.

Womack, J. P., Jones, D. T. and Roos, D. (1990) *The Machine that Changed the World*. New York: Harper Perennial.

Wood, S. (1999) 'Human Resource Management and Performance', *International Journal of Management Reviews* 1(4): 367–413.

13
Lessons and Futures
Denis Gregory, Tony Huzzard, Regan Scott and Steven Deutsch

Partnership and union renewal

As we start the third millennium there is little disagreement that unions internationally are facing changing environments that are posing new and difficult challenges (Martin and Ross, 1999; Rigby *et al.*, 1999; Waddington and Hoffmann, 2000; Hyman, 2001a). Accordingly, there is an urgent need for unions to develop and adapt new strategies, especially as various long-term processes are operating that have profound implications for union organising. Trade unions in Europe and the US have always been able to exercise strategic choices to box or dance in various combinations. But in the environments that unions find themselves in today what combinations appear to be viable? Is a new globalised and 'post-Fordist' world inviting a new trade union logic around partnership as the central union strategy?

Purely boxing strategies appear to be encountering great difficulties in coming to grips with long-term changes as capital is increasingly able to transfer production facilities and jobs to low cost countries. The differentiations in the workforce of the highly industrialised countries and the serious problems unions face in keeping up membership density and maintaining 'visible' achievements vis-à-vis these changes make the necessity to develop new union strategies only more demanding. The growing economies of scale in trade union organisation, moreover, are also adding new demands and complexities to this strategic challenge.

In this final chapter we aim to draw out some conclusions on the lessons of partnership for unions from our cases and country accounts. We also discuss some of the implications of the strategic choice to dance for union renewal, in particular on the issue of skill and capacity building. Continuing the themes discussed in Chapter 3, we conclude with a discussion on industrial relations futures for the European Union (EU).

Towards union renewal

The strategic choice that unions make to box or dance is fundamentally bound up in calculations of the likely impact which either activity may have on their power and influence. These calculations, whilst generally complex and frequently constrained by information and time, have always been at the heart of the industrial relations engagement. For the reasons elaborated elsewhere in this book (decentralisation, globalisation and the need to mobilise knowledge at the workplace), the frequency with which unions are confronted by such calculations appear to be growing at all levels of trade union activity. The implications for union renewal to be discerned in this trend are many and various. Where an increase in dialogue based engagement is readily seen to confer an increase in power and influence, then it is reasonable to assume that this will translate into the potential for renewing and advancing general interest and support for the union concerned. On the other hand, where dialogue based approaches are either hidden from the membership's view or are palpably failing to deliver, then a return to the boxing ring can equally serve to revive interest in the union simply by raising its profile.

The question for union strategists concerns the risks associated with either choice and their ability to factor these into their decision-making processes. Moreover, as we have sought to elaborate elsewhere in this book, the actions of boxing and dancing are inextricably interwoven to form the DNA strings (the 'dynamic dualism') of modern labour relations. We are not, then, looking at 'either or' choices regarding boxing and dancing as much as when, where and how much? Answering these latter questions is critical to the effective application of trade union power. Equally apparent is the impact such answers have on the perceptions that employees hold regarding trade unions. In the UK, for example, it was plainly the case that the removal of tripartite consultative forums carried out by the Conservative administration shortly after its election to power in 1979, effectively and visibly reduced the influence of trade unions on macro-economic policy formation. Whilst trade unions were losing power and influence at national level, a raft of new restrictive legislation was equally constraining union activity at the workplace. The conclusion drawn was that unions in the UK were finding it hard to box or dance. Similarly, in France in the 1980s and 1990s the General Confederation of Unions (CGT) progressively lost influence in key sectors as it opted to stay out of the dance. The point to be made here is that the potential for union renewal is dependent upon the visibility and perceived effectiveness of the union strategy.

This simple conclusion is of course difficult to put into practice. On the one hand, union members want unions to be strong and independent in defending and advancing their interests as, for example, in collective bargaining. On the other, they want their unions to be in a continuous dialogue with employers and governments to ensure that a whole range of employment policies and practices are developed and applied. Union renewal depends upon balancing both of these needs. The extent to which the formalisation of dancing, as in systems of co-determination, makes unions better able to achieve this balance is a question of some interest particularly to those nations who have hitherto relied more upon voluntarism to configure their industrial relations system.

In the UK, Terry (2003), concluded that for partnership approaches to survive they would need a legal underpin. At the same time, experience from both Germany and France has demonstrated that favourable legislation has not stopped the decline in union density or influence in those countries in recent years. This would suggest that employee rights and employer obligations to carry out an industrial relations dialogue do not, of themselves, guarantee union renewal. Since co-determination confers employee rights, unions have to gain recognition and win support in order to be the agency by which these rights are exercised. This in turn, depends upon the perception employees have of the union and how convincing the union can be. Some years ago, a prominent trade union leader in the UK observed that with high levels of unemployment and aggressive management strategies being increasingly used at that time 'people should be queuing up to join trade unions'. They were not and membership levels continued to spiral down.

Latterly, union renewal in terms of gains in membership (as in the UK) and the emergence of more militant attitudes and leaders appears to be associated with the return of union 'leverage' consequent on falling levels of unemployment rather than any sudden upsurge in constructive dialogue. It is notable of course that in these changed labour market circumstances employers may be much more supportive of the 'dance'. Insofar as the spread and sustainability of partnership is concerned, we may be about to discover that employers' attitudes hold the key.

The point should also be made that the traditional distributional union role will in all likelihood continue. Although there is some evidence of unions seeking to explore greater moments of consensus in this, notably in Sweden, we nevertheless see it as inevitable that boxing will continue as a core union activity. But in some cases, the strategic choice to dance can be seen as a way for unions to create new legitimacy or even power to enter new boxing rings. Alternatively, the choice can entail obtaining resources, for example, knowledge, to strengthen the hands of union or works council negotiators in boxing rings where they are already active. The danger to unions is whether the employers see partnership simply as a device for ensuring smoother and less costly change management: the dance can simply be a device that legitimises restructuring efforts.

Our case evidence shows that partnership can lead to earlier information disclosure and that this can enhance the potential for union influence. Moreover, such potential implies that new strategic options can be formulated at an earlier stage, a benefit that opens up the degree of 'policy space' that trade unions may have. This is a transferable experience from various national contexts and cases. As already indicated in Chapter 2, unions acting strategically are generally considered to engage in activities of forecasting employment changes and production trends. This, in turn, can enlarge their forecasting capacities. 'Early warning systems' may be very fruitful here on the union side.

Implications for unions

There is no theoretical mechanism whereby union renewal is an outcome of partnership per se (Kelly, 2004). On the other hand, if unions do make (Level 2) choices to engage in new areas (e.g. to extend union activities from distributional to developmental issues), then this may necessitate a co-operative approach in terms of Level 3 choices (dancing), as the Swedish evidence makes clear. On the other hand, if a union sees its mission in purely distributional terms, or has little choice but to box because of employer strategic choices to do so, then there will be little to be gained from dancing. In essence, therefore, the question of whether partnership is a route to union renewal or even revitalisation is that of 'What Should Unions Do?' Naturally, this is a question that only unions themselves and their members can answer.

Irrespective of whether unions choose primarily to box or to dance, their memberships appear to be diversifying. In many respects there is evidence that unions are beginning to cater for individual needs as exemplified by the à la carte approach to pay and conditions in the Netherlands and interactive market research efforts in Sweden. Yet we would be hesitant about describing this as a move away from collectivism towards individualism. Rather, it is better understood as a means of bringing more diversity into collective services. Nevertheless as the Dutch experience in particular suggests, unions in contexts of 'organising deserts' may have little alternative but to combine sensitive approaches to a diverse membership with skilful pursuit of the dance. Perhaps the same could be said for unions working in hostile political environments: there are certainly grounds for questioning how viable a pure boxing trade unionism can be in the twin contexts of EU enlargement and subsidiarity.

One way of understanding the benefits of social partnership from the perspective of management is that in allowing earlier and better quality exchanges with unions there are possibilities for reducing uncertainties on the human resource implications of business decisions. As the Astra Zeneca case demonstrates, quality is also enhanced as information through union channels can be less politically distorted than that coming through line management. If these propositions hold, then it suggests that partnership can be seen in effect as an arena and process of knowledge management. The logic is clear: decisions are better road-tested. But developing partnerships in such a way, even presuming that they are viable, implies an enormous cultural challenge to management. In terms of unions, this may even imply them to rethink Level 1 choices on missions and identities so as to become knowledge organisations. In this sense, enduring partnerships – the 'dance academy' – can become an institutional sphere of competence or 'learning space' (Fulop and Rifkin, 1997).

Clearly, the dialogue of partnership is a different type of engagement than the negotiation of collective bargaining or for that matter the debate of internal union representative structures. The specific qualities of dialogue require distinct skills that not all prospective dance partners possess. Inadequate skills at dialogue, on either side, can undermine the effectiveness of partnership. A further difficulty is that it is generally difficult for union representatives to disconnect themselves from representative structures, yet business decisions often have to be made quickly by management. They cannot always wait for discussion at the next union branch meeting. Within a partnership, therefore, there are often differences in the speed of decision-making on the union side and the management side. The resultant strains from this suggest the need for considerable degrees of trust, both between unions and management as well as between the administrative and representative spheres of union organisation (Child *et al.*, 1973).

Social partnership is no automatic route to union renewal, and it is not the intention of this book to argue such a case. Where, however, unions see that a more co-operative approach is deemed necessary to achieve certain goals and objectives, a number of points seem clear:

- Unions should be prepared to put demands to management in a partnership situation.
- Co-operative approaches seem inevitable if unions seek to pursue workplace development agendas.
- Unions may need to accept practices of direct democracy as well as representative democracy, although this is likely to lead to a difficult balancing act.
- Union leaders will require attenuated skills on dialogic forms of communication, trust, business strategy and decision-making.
- Union structures will need to be more decentralised to serve local actor needs.
- The role of full-time officers will be that of coaching, tracking, sharing good practice and knowledge brokerage.

It will be recalled from the discussion on 'the diversity of the dance' in Chapter 12 that our cases could be plotted on a 2×2 matrix bound by the two axes of union power base (strong versus weak) and dance leadership (union proactive versus union reactive). This suggests that unions on the dance floor can be typologised into four behavioural types as depicted in Figure 13.1. We call these here 'innovators' (strong power base and proactive),

DANCE LEADERSHIP

		UNION PROACTIVE	UNION REACTIVE

		Innovators		**Exploiters**
STRONG	Motive to dance	Level 2 choices to advance on developmental agendas or seek more influence. Generation of new knowledge bases.	Motive to dance	Mutual gains based on existing knowledge bases from strong positions.
	Role of boxing	Traditional bargaining on distributional issues supported by generation of new knowledge gained from the dance floor.	Role of boxing	Traditional bargaining on dancing outcomes.
		Explorers		**Followers**
WEAK	Motive to dance	Level 2 choices to organise in new areas.	Motive to dance	Consolidation around existing (fragile) position but largely on management terms. Vulnerability to incorporation.
	Role of boxing	Potential outcome of skilful dancing.	Role of boxing	Traditional bargaining from weak position (where recognised).

UNION POWER BASE

Figure 13.1 A typology of union behaviours – combining boxing and dancing.

'explorers' (weak power base and proactive), 'exploiters' (strong power base and reactive) and 'followers' (weak power base and reactive). For each of these, boxing and dancing will have different interdependencies according to the context a union finds itself in. In most cases, however, unions will organise or potentially organise in a wide variety of settings and debates around renewal will thus need to revolve around combining many if not all of the behavioural ideal types proposed here. Clearly, however, there may be cases where union renewal does not entail dancing at all: in situations where unions have a strong presence and there is little scope for developmental unionism, then renewal debates have to centre around classical boxing in what we term the Level 2 choice of mobilisation (see Chapter 2).

Transnational union leadership skill building

We have argued that a lesson from the cases appears to be that the dance requires individual officer skills that are quite distinct from those of collective bargaining – yet unions and union leaders will need to combine the skills of both. One further dimension of skill building is also that of competences and expertise to advance member interests in the increasingly transnational context of trade unionism.

There is little doubt that the challenges for union leaders will become ever greater as corporate ownership changes, there is international mobility among managers, and as the European Union adopts more Directives and hence mandates employee involvement and information sharing, universal standards of conduct, and an altered environment for labour–management relationships.

The differences in the industrial world may be diminishing in some regards, and there certainly is a transnational flow of ideas and practice in labour relations, which parallels international capital flow and multinational corporate ownership. The resistance to authentic power sharing is strong in the US. In Europe the union density rate varies considerably, but collective agreements cover 70–90% of the labour force and 'in Europe ... the objective is to ensure that there are institutions in place that allow all working people to influence their conditions of work', while in the US, by contrast, ' ... the large majority of working people are excluded from enterprise decision making' (Adams, 2001: 531). In Canada, too, while union leaders place high priority on strategies for partnering to enhance worker participation, employers are resistant to effect major change (Kumar and Murray, 2002). Even in Sweden, with mandated co-determination and high union density, there has been a growing trend towards enterprise and decentralised bargaining and limited gains by unions to reach high-level enterprise decision-making (Wheeler, 2002). The point is that the contests for power will continue to be upfront and central on labour's agenda, albeit the push for partnerships may gain some real advance, including those achieved by EU legislated mandates.

Some of the parameters appear clearer, such as the need for international union co-operation and strategic mobilisation responding to the globalised environment (Gordon and Turner, 2000; Nissen, 2002). Some of the future developments within the EU are less certain. Some see a move towards a more decentralised bargaining model within Europe, something typical within the US, while at the same time seeing more transnational trends and pacts (Boeri *et al.*, 2001). The growth of social directives certainly will alter the local work organisation milieu so far as partnering is concerned (Hyman, 2001).

After more than 30 years of debate, the EU saw the adoption of the 'Regulation on the European Company Statute' and the accompanying Directive on Worker Involvement in European Companies ... and the adoption of the (proposed) Directive Establishing a General Framework for Informing and Consulting Employees, in the EC ... (EIRO, 2002: 43). Companies will have three years to comply, with a longer time for smaller firms in countries without statutory employee involvement provisions (UK, Ireland). But that means that union leaders as well as managers need to develop skills in working in new ways along with the traditional approaches that may be retained (Andersen and Mailand, 2002; Kjaergaard and Westphalen, 2002). But what, exactly will this new labour relations environment look like?

Most analysts see greater integration within the EU (Martin and Ross, 2000) and some have explored and initiated training of union leaders for this new climate (Miller, 2002). There is little question that a more strategic and big-picture posture will be required for unions to operate without too much risk, and a social unionism, going beyond the old wage focus is needed (Munck and Waterman, 1999). There may be more European centralised bargaining, sectoral bargaining or the opposite. The real point is that there are unknowns and they pose risks for labour (Waddington, 2001). Will European Works Councils build-up and will they strengthen or weaken national unions (Martin and Ross, 1999)? Up until now most EU Directives and social protocols have not been that far-reaching, and it remains to be seen where the most recent Directive goes. All of this uncertainty makes the road for labour dangerous. As Martin and Ross state: 'The new situation will not be "win–win" for most unions; rather "lose perhaps to win later". This means pressing for employment security, labour market and training policies in the face of new technology and flexibilisation. They need to find new ways to structure new decentralization and flexibility so that it does not destroy their own capacities and turn their supporters' lives into nightmares' (Martin and Ross, 1999: 396). Not a sanguine vision. But never before has there been a situation like the present and near-term future, and labour must be clever and tough, seeking realistic and appropriate strategies for partnering while aggressively pursuing fundamental rights for workers. That is a recipe calling for agile, well-trained union leadership and the skills in performing myriad and sometimes contradictory roles of 'boxing' and 'dancing'. The hope and expectation is that labour will share experiences and learn internationally and transnationally.

Has Europe run out of dance tunes?

A key finding from this book is that political and economic context is an important factor in determining partnership endurance and capacity to deliver. Statutory underpinning is a fundamental aspect of this. It will be recalled that a central argument of the 1997 Green Paper was that a common European trajectory could be possible – but what were the implications of this in terms of statutory underpinning at the European level, and what happened? And what are the future prospects for such underpinning now?

Our project has been based on a 'sense of Europe', drawn from policy and academic literature as well as our practitioners' experience. Our view, however, is that almost ten years after the Green Paper on Work Organisation, Europe has failed to find instruments and purchase in what it has increasingly defined as the strategic area for European industrial relations, namely, economic modernisation and global competitiveness.

The Delors' settlement, establishing monetary orthodoxy through wage restraint in return for a substantial social programme and empowerment of social partners, pushed global social settlement best practice to a new high. Not only was the European social space the best such space globally, but it was also developing and advancing in its own right. Few commentators would therefore dispute that there has been a substantial industrial relations 'thickening' across most levels of European industrial relations, as Hyman has called it (Hyman, 2001b) as a result of the complex range of supports offered to national systems by the European social programmes. Delors was a process and a period of what might be called the European rescue of national industrial relations (Milward, 1992). But we have a strong sense that an end of period was reached with, in effect, the blockage of the Green Paper agenda.

Accordingly, in the late 1990s, meta-trends in political economy, social structures and especially labour market status seemed to be relentlessly corroding well tried and trusted industrial relations institutions at nation state level, while countervailing European regulation of labour markets and industrial relations supports were insufficient. The required scale of European socio-political co-ordination and resourcing to boost growth rates, create plentiful jobs and generate sufficient economic surpluses to continue to fund post-War welfare settlements has not emerged. The neo-liberal trend has come about both as a matter of high governmental politics and as a matter of employer and maybe even social politics turning against unions – in most countries – in a period when these same authorities seemed to be searching for instruments of industrial mobilisation to achieve broader economic goals.

While the substantial achievements of the European Union's social 'acquis' has limited and qualified a full 'market state' trajectory for the

European Community, many key member states embraced this neo-liberal doctrine, putting road blocks in the path of deeper Social Europe development. To use the language of the European Trades Union Congress (TUC), 'the high road to European modernisation and innovation' seemed to be a sensible path forwards, but it looks more like a sketch on a map than a realisable strategy, while the map shows cumulative and threatening topographical movements. To the extent that all practical industrial relationships are journeys, the union travellers, and maybe even some employers, have been experiencing an official Europe either not prepared to, or unable to, put its resources behind a high-trust, high value-added road, despite a powerful, embedded tradition of social partnership in its own arenas and substantial if varied traditions in most of its member states. Even if there had been a will to develop the appropriate levels and instruments of European industrial relations, major questions remain about actual mechanisms and powers.

One starting point for mapping out futures is the Supiot Report's chronicle of impressive dynamism in boxing relations (Supiot, 1999). But this has been at national, sectoral and leading company levels within an overall pattern of atrophy of traditional labour market status and bargaining coverage. There has been little in the way of collective bargaining at European level, despite some interesting experimental projects. And even where there has been bargaining about European Works Councils (EWC) procedures, or labour market directives, it has taken on, arguably, a special character, a specific form of political enactment through quasi-bargaining under the shadow of minimum legal fall backs.

The development of EWCs has been substantial, but they remain a complementary system to primary bargaining relationships in member states, and have suffered setbacks at the hard edge of industrial co-operation when dramatic restructuring imperatives have undermined soft processes of information exchange and consultative dialogue, without much outcome in the way of altered managerial decisions (see Huzzard and Docherty, 2004 for Swedish case evidence).

Moreover, the high hopes of sectoral social dialogue appear to have been undermined by a general legal problem in that bargaining decentralisation has resulted in the effective demise of many European level employer groups. As to the unions, while they have seen sectoral social dialogue as a kind of political enactment or quasi-bargaining, there has been limited union innovation in seeking mandates for European level agreement making, even in cases where employers have been equipped and willing to negotiate.

The problem remains that if Europe wishes to proceed collectively with a common industrial relations agenda – that this would be through intentionally co-operative means goes without saying – employers can simply withhold their involvement. It can therefore be argued that nothing has changed. On the other hand, maybe the Fundamental Human Rights

Charter might re-open fundamental matters, not the least of which remains Clause 6 of Article 137 of the Social Chapter.

One of many conceivable corollaries of the problematic legal terrain is that unions who wish to innovate by making strategic choices on co-operative industrial relations expressed through dancing processes and mutual gains agreements may need to refresh their boxing skills. There is a likely lengthy period ahead during which Europe both needs to consolidate a full legal basis for its industrial relations and looks unlikely to find political support from its dominant governments. That does not mean that dancing skills need necessarily be set aside in social dialogue, macro-economic policy, in consultation procedures within works councils or in trying to settle the terms of the few directive reviews and future labour market directives on the table. But it would be foolish to think that disconnecting boxing from dancing will make the dance more successful, and indeed, in areas of cross-border activity unions would do well to develop strategies and mechanisms to employ their boxing skills to seek mutual gains in agreements and solidarities in defence of common interest and standards. To adapt a classical phrase, if unions want to dance, at home and in Europe, maybe they should prepare more fully for boxing.

As for innovation, it is worth recalling that the creation of the European TUC itself was a massive innovation, for solidarity, and against the debilitating dualisms of the Cold War and especially the American dominated ICFTU. It had a genetic determinant in the Schuman Plan and the Coal and Steel Community, but it was never exclusively Communitaire and embraced European Free Trade Area (EFTA) countries from the first day. Maybe today's trade union innovations in an enlarged Europe need to be as bold: perhaps they might consist of rebalancing boxing and dancing practices to cope with a world that is both harsher and, in some cases, perhaps also able to hold out realistic prospects of generating bigger mutual gains at the level of both enterprises and macro-political exchange.

References

Adams, R. J. (2001) 'Choice or Voice? Rethinking American Labor Policy in Light of the International Human Rights Consensus', *Employee Rights and Employment Policy Journal* 5: 521–48.

Andersen, S. K. and Mailand, M. (2002) *The Role of Employers and Trade Unions in Multipartite Social Relationships*. Copenhagen: The Copenhagen Centre.

Boeri, T., Brugiavini, A. and Calmfors, L. (eds) (2001) *The Role of Unions in the Twenty-First Century*. Oxford: Oxford University Press.

Brown L. D. (1983) *Managing Conflict at Organizational Interfaces*. London: Addison Wesley.

Child, J., Loveridge, R. and Warner, M. (1973) 'Towards an Organizational Study of Trade Unions', *Sociology* 7(1): 71–91.

Gordon, M. E. and Turner, L. (eds) (2000) *Transnational Cooperation Among Labor Unions*. Ithaca: Cornell University Press.

European Industrial Relations Observatory (EIRO) (2002) *EIRO Annual Report 2001*. Dublin: European Foundation for the Improvement of Living and Working Conditions.

Fulop L. and Rifkin, W. (1997) 'Representing Fear in Learning in Organizations', *Management Learning* 28(1): 45–63.

Huzzard, T. and Docherty, P. (2004) *Between Global and Local: Eight European Works Councils in Retrospect and Prospect*' Paper presented at the 22nd International Labour Process Conference, University of Amsterdam, 5–7 April.

Hyman, R. (2001a) *Understanding European Trade Unionism*. London: Sage.

Hyman, R. (2001b) 'The Europeanisation – or Erosion – of Industrial Relations?' *Industrial Relations Journal* 32(4): 280–94.

Kelly, J. (2004) 'Social Partnership Agreements in Britain: Labor Cooperation and Compliance', *Industrial Relations* 43(1): 267–92.

Kjaergaard, C. and Westphalen, S.-A. (eds) (2002) *New Roles of the Social Partners in Europe*. Copenhagen: The Copenhagen Centre.

Kumar, P. and Murray, G. (2002) 'Canadian Union Strategies in the Context of Change', *Labor Studies Journal* 26: 1–28.

Martin, A. and Ross, G. (eds) (1999) *The Brave New World of European Labor*. New York: Berghahn Books.

Martin, A. and Ross, G. (2000) 'European Integration and the Europeanization of Laborí, in Gordon, M. E. and Turner, L. (eds) *Transnational Cooperation Among Labor Unions*. Ithaca: Cornell University Press.

Miller, D. (2002) 'Training Transnational Worker Representatives: The European Works Councils', in Spencer, B. (ed.) *Unions and Learning in a Global Economy*. Toronto: Thompson Educational Publishing, Inc.

Milward, A. S. (1992) *The European Rescue of the Nation State*. London: Routledge.

Munck, R. and Waterman, P. (eds) (1999) *Labour Worldwide in the Era of Globalizations: Alternative Union Models in the New World Order*. New York: St. Martin's Press.

Nissen, B. (ed.) (2002) *Unions in a Globalized Environment: Changing Borders, Organizational Boundaries, and Social Roles*. Armonk, NY: M.E. Sharpe.

Rigby, M., Smith, R. and Lawlor, T. (eds) (1999) *European Trade Unions: Change and Response*. London, Routledge.

Supiot, A. (1999) *Beyond Employment: Changes in Work and the Future of Labour Law in Europe*. Brussels: European Commission.

Terry, M. (2003) 'Partnership and the Future of trade unions in the UK', *Economic and Industrial Democracy* 24(4): 485–508.

Waddington, J. (2001) 'Articulating Trade Union Organization for the New Europe', *Industrial Relations Journal* 32: 449–63.

Waddington, J. and Hoffman, R. (eds) (2000) *Trade Unions in Europe: Facing Challenges and Searching for Solutions*. Brussels: European Trade Union Institute (ETUI).

Walton, R. E., McKersie, R. B. and Cutcher-Gershenfeld, J. E. (1994) *Strategic Negotiations: A Theory of Change in Labor Management Relations*. Boston: Harvard University Press.

Wheeler, H. N. (2002) *The Future of the American Labor Movement*. Cambridge: Cambridge University Press.

Appendices: Case Studies

Engineering, Chemicals and Pharmaceuticals

Appendix A1
War Dancing: the Difficult Trade Union Relationships in the Italian Metalworking Sector
Aldo Marchetti

Introduction

This case looks at industrial relations in the Italian metalworking and steel sector. During the 1990s, the prevailing climate of co-operation between governments and social actors allowed a small amount of dancing to start. But the sector has always been dominated by conflict, and currently we are seeing the dancing and concertation grinding to a halt. The dance hall of the biggest company in the sector, Fiat, is closed and no one knows when it will be re-opened. In some big companies and many medium sized ones, however, concertation is moving forward.

The metalworking sector

This sector comprises car workers, steelworkers, shipbuilding, electrical and computer engineering and small metal product workers. This varied composition of products and manufacturing is reflected in company size and types of company. The sector includes small firms and large holdings, monopoly companies and many companies operating in highly competitive markets. There are a total of 107,600 production units and 1,700,000 employees, excluding small artisan companies. The average number of employees per company is 16. Turnover in the sector is slightly higher than 40% of total turnover for manufacturing as a whole.

There are at least three main models of company negotiation:

- FIAT style 'unilateral decisions'.
- Social partnership as in companies like Electrolux, Olivetti and Merloni.
- In most other unionised companies, there is informal partnership covering issues such as working hours, employee categorisation and salaries. The employers' organisations in different provinces tend to have different approaches according to local traditions and the density and type of company. Most companies are in the north of Italy and 42% companies are in the Lombardy region.

Differences are also discernable in membership figures for the trade unions from the three main confederations, as shown in Table A1.1. Moreover, the three trade unions in the sector exhibit different approaches to social partnership, mainly reflecting the national organisations they are affiliated to.

Table A1.1 Trade union membership in the metalworking sector

Union federation	1997	1998
FIOM-CGIL	365 698	365 942
FIM-CISL	179 573	183 446
UILM-UIL	100 453	100 534

This case study was carried out through semi-structured interviews with members of the FIM-CISL and the FIOM-CGIL, national members of the FIM responsible for large companies including FIAT and regional secretaries of the FIOM, FIM and UILM in Lombardy. We also used proceedings from the most recent congresses of trade union federations, national contract agreements from the last ten years and national metalworking sector Observatory publications.

Boxing and dancing in the metalworking sector

In recent times this sector has been a typical example of boxing. As shown by the high number of strikes, there have been high levels of conflict and large numbers of workers involved on the occasion of contract renewal and company downsizing. Recently the number of strikes has declined but the rate of strike incidence is still higher than in other sectors.

Our analysis looks at the opportunities there have been for social partnership in the sector. Collaboration has tended to follow input from industrial relations nationally. The aim of social partnership in the experimental phase of the early 1990s was mainly the securing of better and earlier information. The following instruments were used:

- A national bilateral commission, responsible for collecting data on the economic trends in the sector. This commission subsequently became the 'National Observatory of the Metalworking Industry'.
- Joint national and local commissions on equal opportunities and vocational training.

The experimental phase ended in 1999 when in the opening section of the national agreement the sides recognised the validity of social partnership as carried out by the national observatory as well as in local and large companies. The model (see Table A1.2) is decentralised and complex compared to that in the chemicals sector as set out in Appendix A2.

The national observatory consists of six representatives of the national employers' association (Federmeccanica of the national CONFINDUSTRIA) and the same number of union representatives. It started activities in the mid-1990s and regularly publishes surveys of trends over the whole sector. It was established that joint activity was to be carried out in local commissions but this has yet to be implemented because of a low level of interest shown by employers' associations and a lack of initiative on both sides.

But some joint commissions have started functioning regularly. The vocational training commissions have been the most active and have set up general training programmes and permanent training activities. In Milan, for example, the three trade unions and the employers' organisation have set up a training consortium that has provided numerous courses. The commission in Milan, similar to those in other

Table A1.2 Dancing institutions in the metalworking sector

	National	Local	Large companies with 3000 plus employees
Joint observatories	National metalworking observatory	Regional metalworking observatory	Company observatory
Joint commissions	Commissions of working parties on Mezzogiorno (Southern Italy) Performance related pay awards Vocational training Equal opportunities	Regional commission on vocational training Local commission on equal opportunities	Company commissions on Vocational training Equal opportunities Performance related pay awards

provinces, is organised as follows: (1) the local vocational training commission is set up and identifies problem areas; (2) trade union and employers' representatives meet separately and draw up proposals together with the RSU (company worker representatives) and company management; (3) after this initial phase, the whole commission meets to discuss both sides' proposals and reach agreement; (4) the decisions are publicised and implemented; (5) lastly, training programmes are agreed with training institutes.

This clearly shows social partnership at work and that training does not follow the usual lines of negotiating, that is, collective bargaining. Issues that would otherwise be part of negotiations are dealt with collaboratively and thus are not fought out in boxing rings. Trade union members of the commission are members of the province executive but act autonomously and are entirely responsible for their actions.

Significant results have been achieved by some of the Equal Opportunities Commissions, especially in the field of training. Training courses have been organised nationally for women members of EO Commissions in large companies and some of these commissions have been successful. Many companies have also been the site of successful implementation of commission work on performance related pay awards. Overall, however, the results are partial and there is widespread uncertainty regarding the growing divergences between the trade unions and the Federmeccanica, who do not appear to have a clearly defined approach.

The practice of trying out a new model in one company or area and then extending it nationally if it is successful is part of the tradition of trade unionism in Italy. A bottom-up phase, from company to national negotiations, is followed by a top-down phase where there is progression from national negotiations down to other individual companies.

The same process is currently evident regarding flexibility. The unions are interested in two cases in particular; Merloni, an electrical consumer goods manufacturer in Central Italy, and ZF, a medium-sized multinational company in the north-east which makes gears for ship engines. Merloni is a family business at the first instance in the continental market, quoted on the stock exchange, but the family owners and its roots in the local area are very important. The dancing in industrial relations goes back to the 1970s, and was very helpful in aiding the complex rationalisation of the period. This helped propel the company to enjoy the highest market in the sector throughout Europe. Flexibility is regulated by a joint commission that has worked intensely to find solutions acceptable to workers and management. ZF is a medium-sized company with about 450 employees. Ten years ago management and unions reached an agreement on working hours, which was rejected almost unanimously by workers. This serious failure led to both sides finding new methods involving increased concertation. A permanent mixed commission was set up to study solutions for flexibility taking into account management and worker requirements. Both Merloni and ZF thus constitute interesting examples of dancing. They are in fact widely studied in training courses and union meetings all over Italy. On the other hand, they cannot be seen as representative of the sector. In most cases, a boxing culture persists and if there is any movement towards the dance academy, it is tentative and slow, albeit with elements of tactical choices to dance at the day-to-day-level that supplements collective bargaining.

The unions have different strategies among themselves, but so too do the employers. The Federmeccanica has remained united but there are divergent opinions among its members. For example, the employers' association in Brescia, the third most important industrial province in Italy, has shown itself unfavourable to social partnership on several occasions.

The different attitudes of collective actors towards sector economic problems have encouraged strategies oriented towards conflict. There were 12 hours of strikes over agreement renewal in 1996 (a two-year economic period review) and 40 hours in 1999 over the renewal of the terms and conditions. In 2000–01, for the review of another two-year period, 16 hours of strikes were called. In 2002 the renewal of terms and conditions was agreed without strikes by the FIM and the UILM, but the FIOM continued the negotiations and called numerous strikes. The rupture between the three unions had negative effects on the workings of the joint commissions and the development of the whole concertation model.

Conclusions

Recent developments have made it rather difficult to make a final assessment of social partnership in this sector. In some areas social partnership has not got past an experimental phase, although it appears to be working for issues such as safety and the work environment, equal opportunities and vocational training. Joint commissions are working in all these areas in an atmosphere of dancing. At the same time, boxing prevails on questions of salaries, working hours and job classification. The coexistence of boxing with dancing can be explained because the questions for concertation are those of immediate common interest for the two sides. There is more conflict on issues where there is more divergence between the sides. This coexistence is leading to a continuous adaptation by which union officials take part in commissions and also take part in bargaining. So the same people dance or box according to the context. Table A1.3 summarises the situation.

This very complex mix of boxing and dancing is an enormous challenge for the unions. Elements of the challenge are the deeply rooted tradition of conflict, the divisions between the union federations, the divisions among the employers as well as local differences. So no clear overall pattern of the impact of national concertation on social partnership in the sector and the company is discernable. In the 1990s, unions played a central role in public policy through concertation and this widened the national dance floor, opening up new opportunities for dancing at sector and company level. In those companies where it has evolved, however, concertation has had important consequences.

Table A1.3 Boxing and dancing in the Italian metalworking sector

Level	Boxing	Dancing	Trend
Sector	Hourly rates of pay, classification	Vocational training, safety and the environment, equal opportunities	From repeated and consolidated dancing towards paralysis
Large companies	Many companies see boxing on hourly rates of pay and classification. Other companies see a combination of boxing and dancing.	Partnership in many companies over professional training, safety and the environment, equal opportunities	A new combination of dance floors and new boxing rings. Varies from firm to firm.
Small and medium enterprises	In many companies boxing prevails over the most important issues	In many companies informal dancing over working hours, rates of pay, staff training	Combination of boxing and dancing

Trade unions can draw several lessons from the metalworking sector in Italy:

- It is difficult for dancing to advance without favourable government policy. But as we saw in our overview of Italy (see Chapter 8), the present government has not expressed a clear position on the issue.
- Italian trade unions are traditionally hostile to legislation that seeks to regulate labour, but many union officials think that legislation encouraging participation would help it to diffuse among companies. The trade unions are currently watching European directives in this field (e.g. the directives on European companies and CAE – European companies' worker representatives) with a great deal of interest.
- Concertation has had more success in medium or medium-large sized companies than in very large ones like Fiat. Unions are currently considering this aspect: it may be that the joint commission system needs to be reviewed especially in large companies where there are perhaps too many commissions.
- At a time of rapid and continuous technological and organisational innovation and market uncertainty, concertation appears to be the best way of conducting industrial relations in that it allows for more elastic procedures and for problems to be dealt with as soon as they arise. (See the examples of Aer-Macchi and Merloni.)
- Concertation allows for more frequent contact between the sides and means that more efficient and better solutions can be found than when decisions are taken unilaterally or decided by boxing. (See the examples of Aer-Macchi and ZF.)
- Concertation requires adjustments from unions and RSU members in terms of skills and know-how in interpreting company management information. This means that greater commitment from union officials and more training resources within the whole union organisation are needed.

Audit criteria for innovation partnership agreements

Gains in information and consultation rights and procedures.   Information and consultation rights have been improved and extended. Procedures for discussion between sides have been improved through bipartite commissions, even though these have been only partially implemented, and through extended participation of the RSU in discussing performance related benefits.

Structural improvement in trade unionism.   Concertation agreements improve the structure and representative function of trade unions in that they require union officials and RSU members to develop their skills and increase their knowledge of company organisation. Negotiating structures become more elastic with concertation – problems can be discussed immediately rather than being passed on to the negotiation rounds every four years. It is difficult to say if concertation improves union capacity for representation. FIM officials say that concertation means the current membership levels can be maintained in spite of company rationalisation and reductions in employee numbers.

Gains in joint problem solving.   Concertation helps joint problem solving. Meetings between the sides are more frequent, the number of agreements increases both where the union has to defend its position and where it puts forward new demands.

Advances in the substance of collective agreements.   The favourable climate in the 1990s meant that the issues dealt with by concertation were increased to include individual rights, hours banks, vocational training, equal opportunities and flexibility. At the same time, agreements became more effective because concertation allows for a constant check on their implementation.

Measurability of gains.   It is difficult to say whether concertation has made gains more measurable. In general concertation procedures mean that there is more direct awareness of company dynamics and financial results, and this helps unions to assess the relationship between wages and company profits. This is particularly clear as far as performance related benefits are concerned, as these are fixed by bipartite commissions.

Improvements in target setting and aspiration management.   The procedural clauses in dancing allow for an improvement in target setting as problems are brought out into the open before they become too serious. Company management is thus able to plan better and also adapt rapidly to continual variations in output caused by market instability.

Preservation of union independence.   FIOM and FIM make opposing assessments of union independence. The FIOM believes that concertation can modify and weaken the negotiating role of the union, and it can become largely ineffective. But the FIM thinks concertation is the only viable way of representing worker interests in a world where production is continuously subject to change.

Advances in the quality of working life or work organisation. Participation appears to be the best way of improving the quality of working life and work organisation in companies that have to make continuous and rapid adaptations to the market. It is more immediate. Working life and work organisation may improve in various respects: vocational training, flexibility in return for fewer working hours, professional development necessitated by mobility or changing duties are often decided by concertation. Currently the danger is not so much that these achievements will be reversed as that they will not be extended to the whole sector.

Appendix A2
Dancing Classes: Industrial Relations in the Italian Chemical Sector

Aldo Marchetti

Introduction

This case looks at the evolution of the negotiating culture in a capital-intensive sector. It is a sector where structural characteristics have encouraged the replacement of boxing by dancing. The move from the boxing ring to the dance floor was led from above with collective national actors, sector trade unions and employers' associations acting as disc jockeys and dancers. The sound track encouraged different types of dance on different dance floors and the boxing ring became gradually smaller. We ask whether the national social partnership started by the associations has encouraged individual companies to start dancing too. This is the problem currently being faced by social actors.

The chemical sector

The chemicals sector in Italy includes drugs companies, plastics manufacturers, energy and pottery but it mainly consists of basic chemicals. It is thus closely linked with both the national economy and international energy prices. In the past, state ownership of larger companies was another feature; only in recent years has the sector been largely privatised. Because of its strategic importance, high capital concentration, safety problems and high environmental impact, state owners and employee organisations have always based industrial relations on advanced information, transparency and collaboration. This model has become stronger in spite of the repeated crises in the sector and finally influenced the private sector too, so much so that even today the Employers' Association in the chemical sector is to a certain extent independent of the Confindustria (General Confederation of Industry, the national employers' association). 'Dancing' rather than 'boxing' appears to have been more common in other EU member states too (see also Astra Zeneca case in this volume). In December 2002 a European agreement between the Employers' Association and the European Trade Union Federation of Chemical Workers opened social dialogue at the sector level. The agreement laid down information and consultation procedures for this and agreed bipartite plans for development.

Of a total number of employees in the sector of 449,186 (figures from the late 1990s), 72% are concentrated in Northern Italy. Company size varies considerably: 86% of companies have fewer than 100 employees and only 2.5% of companies have more than 500 employees. These large companies however account for 60% of employees in the sector.

Our case study used semi-structured and individual interviews carried out in the spring of 2002. We interviewed the national secretaries of the two largest trade unions, FILCEA CGIL and FEMCA CISL, the Lombardy regional secretaries of these two unions and delegates of the RSU at Eni in Milan. We also examined documents from the most recent national congresses of the CGIL, the CISL and the UIL, the national agreements of the last 12 years and recent company agreements from some of the largest companies in the sector.

The system of 'social partnership' in the chemical sector

The strategic choice of concertation or 'dancing' is traditional to the chemical sector. In recent years, moreover, it has become institutionalised rather than being simply widespread practice. There is a bipartite 'National Observatory' for the sector, the only one of its kind to be recognised by government law decree – this occurred in 1997. Our analysis focuses on this observatory and its workings (see Table A2.1).

The national observatory consists of three representatives from the sector national employers' association and three representatives from each of the three main sector unions, FILCEA affiliated to the CGIL, FEMCA affiliated to the CISL and CEM affiliated to the UIL. These are full-time officials on the national executives of their respective union organisations. The observatory is a joint organisation and meets at least biannually. It publishes the most important information and data on the sector twice a year. It sets up temporary working parties or commissions that study and make proposals on separate issues. The commissions consider problems at all levels: national, regional, local and company.

The high membership level of the observatory shows that both sides consider it important. Its activities have moved from being information and consultation as at its

Table A2.1 Workings of the 'Chemicals Sector National Observatory'

Level	Main subjects of discussion
Nationwide	Market trends, work organisation, training programmes, the labour market, relations with government bodies, national insurance and accident insurance/prevention.
Regional and provincial	Production and employment prospects, work organisation, youth and female employment.
Groups and plants with 1,000 plus employees	Production prospects, spending on research, employment, technological innovations and their impact on work organisation, trends of female employment, apprenticeship training programmes, new training initiatives.

inception towards co-determination superimposed onto traditional negotiating. In other words, not only does 'dancing' take place but in part it has replaced the more traditional 'boxing'. An example is the Observatory's recent commission on working hours and flexibility: (1) the observatory sets up a commission and in the preliminary phase defines the problem and discusses possible solutions; (2) union side and management sides meet for separate discussion and there is consultation between the RSU (company worker representatives) and management in larger companies. Different proposals are drawn up; (3) there is joint discussion of the two proposals; (4) agreement is reached.

In this case the 2000 national commission looked at improving flexibility, a system for banking hours, shift work and annualised hours. Its decisions became a point of reference for the whole sector and were automatically incorporated into the national contract agreement of 2002. The process was entirely without industrial action and the final signing of the agreement was a mere formality after the real process of concertation.

There are other examples of this practice in the sector, and one of its consequences is that it is no longer necessary to wait for a contract to expire in order to look for solutions to problems, as is the case in other sectors. Problems can be discussed during the four years period between one national sector contract and its renewal, and agreements negotiated along the way can be incorporated into the new contract. We can see this in the case of flexibility where the issue was taken care of by concertation or dancing. Working hours are a notorious problem when they are negotiated for contract renewal and the issue often leads to conflict. But here they were dealt with by partnership and the problem solved by dancing.

Problem solving by the commissions means there is a gradual reduction in occasions of industrial conflict. Strikes in fact tend to focus on circumscribed aims such as wage demands on national contract renewal. But the boxing ring is getting smaller, and the dance floor getting larger as more issues are taken over by the joint commissions. Agreements signed by the national commission are moreover fully legitimised by the fact that both union and management members are the same people responsible for contract negotiations. As both 'directors' and 'actors' in the consultation process they are autonomous and their only responsibility is towards their membership. They first consult the workers' representatives of the largest companies and union executives which in theory could delegitimise the commission if they disagreed. But as a national sector secretary remarks:

> If this has never yet happened it is because in the big companies concertation has always prevailed and because social partnerhip is not a recent invention but a historical fact.

But the unions are not starting from scratch. There are numerous examples of harmonious dancing in companies. An interesting example is 'Bracco', a Milan drugs company where some years ago during a financial crisis the management decided to shift to sweet manufacture. The union strongly opposed this, the production manager was replaced and the company went back on its decision. Shortly afterwards, the research department at Bracco made a discovery important for the diagnosis instruments they manufactured, which rapidly conquered the world market. The company had to increase production facilities. The development was governed by joint working groups. On the basis of this positive experience, the RSU asked for representation, without the right to vote, on the company board, along the lines of the German model. But the company refused, one reason for the refusal being the opposition of the national employers' federation. It was feared that in Italy it would have set a dangerous precedent from the companies' point of view. But other companies too have become real dance academies. In the multinationals Bayer, Roche and Boeringher Inghelheim, all important company problems are discussed by joint commissions. These problems include safety and the environment, work organisation and personnel training. Performance related benefits, an important item in the variable part of the wage packet, are measured jointly every year. This is common practice in many companies in the chemicals sector and it allows the RSU to be informed of company trends.

So social partnership is a practice that has consolidated over time. But it is also an explicit policy agreed by the biggest unions. The closing motion at the Lombardy regional congress of the FEMCA–CISL expressed the strategy clearly.

Congress reaffirms the validity of a participatory model of trade unionism which does not rule out industrial action and which takes as central the individual with his or her moral and material requirements. (Proceeds of Regional FEMCA–CISL Congress, 10–11 May 2001)

In the same year the FILCEA–CGIL of Lombardy approved a similar motion:

The workings of a company and the improvement of qualitative and organisational standards are increasingly linked to the involvement and participation of workers. (Proceeds of the Regional FILCEA–CGIL Congress, 28–29 November 2001)

The evolution of the chemicals unions towards social partnership has brought several difficult challenges. The first was the periodical reorganisation of the sector. Plant closures and continuous redundancies led part of the sector towards boxing, even though the government always intervened with measures to guarantee the protection of redundant workers and employers have also tried to make the effects of plant closures as untraumatic as possible. Another challenge was that the traditional culture of boxing had to be modified, and that dancing implied new skills and know-how for both management and RSU members. So sector organisations have organised full-time intensive training for union officials with the aim of improving participation. A regional secretary of the Lombardy FEMCA notes:

We have had to take account of the fact that in concertation and in negotiation, the RSU and company management discuss different issues in different ways. In the light of this we have revised our training programmes.

A third challenge, perhaps the greatest, is still being faced. One of the limits of 'social partnership' in the sector is its national centralisation, which means that there are significant differences in behaviour between central and peripheral structures. The model of participation at higher levels means that there are few decentralised dance floors, and observatories and joint commissions need to be more fully extended to the periphery. The current aim of the trade unions is to overcome this problem.

Conclusions

Industrial Relations are currently in a phase where partnership and dancing is seeing constant development. At the moment, as we have seen, the bipartite commissions which make decisions and direct the sector work only nationally. To this extent it is a nationally centralised model. But commissions are spreading locally and inside companies, and it may be that over the next few years concertation will become the model of the whole sector. The other strength of concertation is its flexibility. Commissions or working parties are formed to discuss a specific issue and are then dissolved. For these reasons the 'dancing' model in the chemicals sector is now a point of reference for new national contract agreements for other workers such as electrical and telecommunications workers, who until now have been included in other sectors.

Concertation has lowered the overall level of conflict in the sector. Of course, the strike trend does not depend solely on the observatory, but the number of strikes over the renewal of national contracts fell steadily during the 1990s. In 1994 there were 13 hours of strike per worker, in 1998 eight hours and in 2002 no hours at all. Union officials agree that this is due to improvements in relationships between the two sides and that bi-partite organisations have played an important role in this. A decline in industrial action appears to be the consequence of participation rather than a necessary condition. But industrial action, as we have seen, is still frequent in smaller companies. A summary of boxing and dancing in the sector is set out in Table A2.2.

Trade unions can draw several lessons from the chemicals sector in Italy:

- Even in a situation like Italy where there is widespread and deep-rooted experience of boxing, dancing is possible if the two sides are explicitly oriented towards it and there is mutual trust between the sides because of this. But it is an extremely slow process and difficult to spread to the whole sector.
- Participation appears to be a particularly promising way of solving problems of organisational innovation and solving problems of a high capital and research-intensive sector. This is shown by the examples of Bracco and Varese.
- An over-centralised model of social partnership may prevent worker participation and generate excessive differences in behaviour between national and decentralised levels.

Table A2.2   Boxing and dancing in the Italian chemical sector

Level	Boxing	Dancing	Trend
Sector	Conflict remains over distributional aspects of national contract.	Dancing over developmental aspects	Towards dancing, although boxing has not entirely disappeared.
Large companies	In many large companies there is industrial action over distribution and for defence of rights and jobs.	In some companies there is dancing over all aspects including distribution of productivity bonuses.	Towards dancing for distribution and developmental aspects.
Small and medium companies	Boxing over many aspects and for defence of rights and jobs.	Difficult for dancing to start in many small and medium companies.	Towards dancing on condition that sides increase participation.

- The spread of concertation depends on union officials at plant level and local and regional management being adequately trained for it. Concertation requires better organisation of the union structure, dedication and professionalism from union officials.
- Concertation lessens but does not completely eliminate industrial conflict. And conflict may come and go according to the economic trend of the sector.
- Concertation may take place not only on developmental objectives but also on distributional ones. This is shown by concertation agreements on performance related benefits.

The model has developed thanks to the prevalence of certain historical and social conditions. Chemicals is a capital-intensive sector, the trade unions are not in competition with one another, the work force is mainly skilled and the state traditionally had a role in management. The tradition of co-operation has consolidated over time. In other sectors we do not find such a harmonious orchestra and such good music for dancing.

Audit criteria for innovation partnership agreements

Gains in information and consultation rights and procedures. Through the National Observatory information rights were guaranteed nationally, locally and at large and small company level, and they were extended to include issues of company management. In the same way consultation rights are guaranteed by the national company but are not always applied in small and medium companies.

Structural improvements in trade unionism. Nationally and in large companies, concertation brought big changes in the role and responsibilities of trade unions. Analysis of company management became more important and required new skills on the part of trade unionists. And the whole structure of representation is laid down and much more organised. It is difficult to say whether concertation has improved the representative capacity of the unions. Membership rates have been about 35% for a long time. But union officials agree that social partnership allows them, in the words of a Lombardy official, to 'stay close to workers especially during the most difficult stages of rationalisation, so that union membership is maintained if not increased'.

Gains in joint problem solving. The national agreement explicitly encourages sides towards concertation and in most large companies the procedures for information and meetings are laid down. The National Observatory is moreover a good example of concertation for the whole sector.

Advances in the substance of collective agreements. The national agreement has extended its scope in recent years to include individual rights, equal opportunities, vocational training, flexibility, social security policy. And the clauses on checking that concertation agreements are carried out in large companies guarantee that negotiation is more efficient. But many small and medium-sized companies are not covered by the agreement, and many of them have no company contract.

Measurability of gains.   Concertation sometimes gives more opportunity to assess results. This is the case with performance related benefits, where union officials have to be informed of company performance figures.

Improvements in target setting and aspirationmanagement.   Social partnership allows individual companies to plan output more efficiently in that it reduces industrial unrest. But over a local area too, development can be better predicted and planned when sector problems are confronted jointly. We can see this in the case of Varese.

Preservation of union independence.   Both the FEMCA–CISL and the FILCEA–CGIL agree that participation does no harm to union autonomy in the chemical sector. This is a different picture from that in the metalwork sector. In the chemical sector, industrial unrest has decreased nationally, but it has not completely disappeared and can sometimes flare up to high levels.

Advances in the quality of working life and work organisation.   It is not possible to say whether dancing brings more improvements to working life than boxing. For both, the results appear to be positive. But the most widespread opinion among unionists is that 'without concertation we would perhaps not have achieved such good results on issues like individual rights, flexibility and working hours'.

Appendix A3
Acceptance and Decline: Two Tales of the Knowledge-intensive Dance
Tony Huzzard

Astra Zeneca: case background

The current structure of the Astra Zeneca group arose out of a merger in 1999 between the Swedish firm Astra and Zeneca, formerly a subsidiary of the British pharmaceutical firm ICI. The newly formed group is a pharmaceutical multinational that has production facilities at 30 plants in 19 countries and sells its medicinal products globally. Group sales amounted to 150 billion Swedish Kronor (SEK) in 2000. The group has some 50,000 employees worldwide, 10,000 of whom are based in Sweden (Astra Zeneca, 2000). The mission is stated as being 'to find good medicines that prevent human suffering' (ibid.) and key competencies are identified as being in the discovery, development and marketing of innovative drugs for treatment in areas with important medicinal needs. Astra Zeneca has a number of therapeutic areas and in these it is the world market leader in stomach and intestine drugs, the leader in anaesthetic drugs and second in cancer relief medicines (Astra Zeneca, 2001).

The case was conducted at the subsidiary Astra Zeneca AB in Södertälje where around 7,000 staff are employed in marketing, production, and R & D facilities. The firm has a central business concept of being 'first for innovation and value', seeing the latter from a diverse stakeholder perspective. The centrality of research in the business renders it a definitive knowledge-based firm having strategic partnerships with academics and commercial partners.

Case method and union organisation at the plant

The Astra Zeneca employees at Södertälje are represented by four unions. As well as SIF (The Swedish Union of Clerical and Technical Workers in Industry) and the IWU (Swedish Industrial Workers Union), managerial staff are represented by the Swedish Association for Professional and Managerial Staff (Ledarna), and graduate engineers are represented by the Swedish Association of Graduate Engineers (CF). Company and union documents were collected and interviews were conducted with the head of human resources, and representatives of the largest unions SIF and the IWU. In all, union density at Astra Zeneca AB is 64% (blue-collar staff) and 67% (white-collar staff).

At the time of the case study interviews the (white-collar) SIF club had 2,100 members and is organisationally divided into a number of sections that parallel the divisional structure of the company into different functional activities. Each section has a number of representatives who are responsible for day-to-day contact with the members. Apart from aggregate meetings arranged in connection with salary reviews, most communication with members occurs through regular newsletters and electronic mail-shots. The (blue-collar) IWU club had 1,800 members and is organisationally split into six sections, each representing different factories and each having its own chair, secretary and officers. A recent innovation of the clubs is that of working together in a joint inter-union reference group in order to create a common front in discussions vis à vis the employer and elect union representatives for the company board.

Boxing and dancing in practice

Industrial relations at the Södertälje site have been underpinned by the written policy dating from 1983 that sought to codify the Swedish co-determination act in the then Astra. Those interviewed from SIF, however, stated that they did not in practice need to fall back on the provisions of the agreement to make partnership work. The approach to bargaining at Astra Zeneca was process-based and illustrated by the SIF club leaders by reference to the issue of salaries. The salary system dates from the merger in 1999 when the new company made a strategic choice to move from (collective) profit sharing to an (individual) bonus system. This was generally supported by the SIF respondents, despite being a clear departure from the traditional union ideology of collective solidarity.

As a first step, the HR Director and unions enter into a dialogue and establish joint criteria for laying down affordability on distributional issues. This dialogue is based on a common view of affordability in the context of common understanding about the developmental trajectory of the business. Such dialogue typically includes identifying changes in the labour market, focusing on special groups as well as analyses of salary statistics. The HR Director described this as follows:

> We almost don't talk about the salary levels. We talk about what do we have to emphasise this time – is there any group whose salary structure is out of line? Is there anything in the market that we haven't adjusted for? Are there things that people are concerned about? We also study the internal structures – the statistics there.

According to a SIF interviewee, this process is generally consensual and can reasonably be said to comprise a dancing activity. This results in a written agreement on the aims and direction of the salary round without specifying figures. This step is clearly a new feature of the salary setting process; yet it is not underpinned by any change to the 1983 agreement that lays down the specific rights and responsibilities for both sides on collective bargaining, dispute negotiations and co-determination issues.

Thereafter, line managers set individual salaries based on the previous year's individual planning and development dialogue with all white-collar employees (step 1). An individual dialogue then takes place between this manager and the individual on the proposed salary (step 4 – white-collar staff only) and then a formal negotiation on the individual salary proposal is conducted with the union (step 5). Guided by the previous steps and objective performance measures, the salary is then confirmed and implemented at step 6 and subsequently evaluated at step 7. As far as union involvement in the process is concerned, step 1 can reasonably be described as dancing, and step 5 as boxing. The process is illustrated in Figure A3.1.

Step	White-collar process		Blue-collar process	
	Activity	Actors	Activity	Actors
1	Planning and development dialogue	Line manager and individual employee	Planning and development dialogue	Line manager and individual employee
2	Dialogue on issues of importance in the salary round. Produces written document.	HR managers and local union leaders (DANCING)	Negotiation on basic rate at company level. Produces written document. Parallel negotiation at sector level	HR managers and company union leaders (BOXING)
3	Individual salary setting: performance based pay at company, functional and individual levels	Line manager	Individual bonus setting: performance based pay at company, functional and individual levels	Line manager
4	Salary dialogue	Line manager and individual white-collar employee	↓	↓
5	Formal negotiation (only if disagreement at step 4)	HR managers and local union leaders (BOXING but rare in practice)	Negotiation (only if disagreement at step 3)	HR manager
6	Confirmation and implementation	HR manager	Confirmation and implementation	HR managers and local union leaders (BOXING)
7	Evaluation	HR manager	Evaluation	HR manager

Figure A3.1 The salary setting process – Astra Zeneca AB (source: adapted from company documents and interviews).

The SIF interviewees were of the opinion that in recent years more time and effort has been devoted to the preparatory work associated with step 1 and that this had tended to simplify step 5 and shorten its duration, a view shared by the HR Director. The former SIF chair, with experience from developing the early partnership approaches in the 1980s, was of the view that:

> The actual negotiations today are more of a formality – if we're fully involved in the preparatory work then one really only needs to document the proposals at the end. If we commit ourselves properly to dancing then the boxing becomes quicker and kinder.

And, in describing how the process is played out, he stated:

> We are agreed on the process over the course of the year, how it should work, how everything should hang together. We have a joint responsibility on this – if we didn't, the process wouldn't work. On the other hand, the process [dancing] doesn't always fully settle our differences. It never does that; but that's the challenge. I mean we never arrive at exactly the same figures in terms of krona – then we get

to boxing. But we agree over the size if not the distribution ... and then sometimes the negotiation can conclude that there is nothing to distribute.

The point should also be made that the company shifted to a system of performance related pay after the merger in 1999 and has agreed objective measures for determining bonuses at the company and functional levels. This, together with the absence of any general cost of living element in the pay structure, has reduced the scope for distributional conflict in the pay round.

The IWU club had not pursued a proactive agenda on work organisation issues but felt the need that workplace development was something that should be taken up as the blue-collar labour process largely consisted of relatively undeveloped teams working on production lines. But the club chair said that the limited discussions they have with the management on such issues resembled dancing:

I think I would call it dancing. The thing is you couldn't box them into something. If you present them with some idea, they have to like it. It's the company that would save all the money from it. You have to present it and dance it in in that way.

On the other hand, the club chair stated that on co-determination issues the tendency to box or dance varied according to issue, the personalities of the actors involved as well as by factory according to their history and industrial relations culture.

Although the IWU club is a party to the 1983 agreement, a rather different picture is evident of the salary setting process. This is illustrated in Figure A3.1. By contrast with the process for white-collar staff, a basic rate continues to play a central role in the blue-collar salary structure and negotiations on this have continued to remain a boxing activity.

The motivations, outcomes and benefits of dancing: SIF

A primary motive cited by the SIF interviewees for pursuing a partnership-based approach was that of early influence. The attempts at gaining such influence through dancing on salary negotiations involved entering dialogue on developmental aspects of the business, at least at the operational level, that extended the range of union competencies and influence beyond that of traditional bargaining. The goal of securing early influence on company decisions is something that SIF nationally has sought. The logic of this was expressed by a SIF national official in the following way:

Personally, I think that if one can break down the boxing culture clubs will benefit from it. Because then you can come in earlier – and have more than you have in the formal arena. The formal influence SIF has is really very limited ... without partnership thinking we have very little to give.

It was argued by both club interviewees that early influence helps head off decision makers in the company from taking entrenched positions from which they cannot easily escape and is thus a useful means of conflict avoidance. Defending a decision, even if it was ill-informed, becomes a matter of prestige and a power struggle ensues. Moreover, the mandate of union representatives legitimises the voice of union leaders in partnership discussions. The club leaders expressed this thus:

Our democracy has been a way of gaining acceptance from the company's side when we meet and has helped us succeed with seeking early influence. We thus obtain an entry ticket to be in on the major decisions and influence at an earlier stage. We have to be involved as early as possible so as to avoid it becoming a matter of prestige.

In other words, dancing in the form of earlier involvement in change processes buys informal influence.

The club leaders also stated that they could supply, on the dance floor, unique knowledge to the company particularly in relation to the individual characteristics and needs that helped inform subsequent salary discussions. This helped boost the status of the club as a legitimate actor. Knowledge from the line managers tended to be distorted by considerations of self-interest: the union was thus seen as a more reliable source. The former club chair went so far as to claim that the salary developments secured by the club had been better than elsewhere in SIF companies. He said:

in terms of salary development we come out better than the rest of SIF, we do ... and this comes from working with dancing. And that we dare. It was we who from the employee side who suggested we should work this way. In salary negotiations at the individual level we said that we know more about the individual than the company – and knowledge is power.

The leaders also saw dancing as an opportunity for the company and the club to act together as allies against other stakeholders. The merger of 1999 was cited as an example of this in that both the union and the Astra management supported the move whereas many shareholders opposed. Union support, in the form of a jointly authored debate article in a national newspaper, was seen as crucial in securing the deal against initial shareholder opposition. A further input that they saw as helping add value to the company was in the form of quality assurance: they saw the club as an aid to correct company decision-making on matters such as managerial appointments. On the other hand, those interviewed felt that they had little input into the business at the strategic level.

The motivations, outcomes and benefits of dancing: the IWU

Despite being party to the 1983 agreement, the blue-collar club did not see the relationship so clearly in partnership terms. Indeed, the club chair was of the view that since the merger there has been less of a co-operative relationship with the company as decision-making was seen as moving away from Sweden. This had led to less union influence at the strategic level. In his words:

We have been talking about the Anglo-Saxon way of doing things – and I think it has been affecting us. Before we were dancing more with the company. We were more into discussions earlier. They told us that before something went out on the market we would get advance information – we were more into the questions. Now we get told the same things as those in the market at the same time. Before we were influencing the company earlier on.

On the other hand, he stated that on operational issues fruitful dialogue was evident in certain factories:

At some places there have been a lot of good changes ... the company has started to talk to the union in a better way and started to see the union as a resource rather than something that has to be fought and boxed with and won over.

The motivations, outcomes and benefits of dancing: the company

As to the company, the main motivations to dance were cited by the HR Director as being a belief that joint agreements last longer than decisions made by only one party. The desirability for conflict avoidance was also mentioned. For example he argued that:

> sometimes it could be seen as weak leadership or something like that. But then again if you reach your targets at the same speed as you would have done by shouting and making one-sided decisions then why fight? There is no value in fighting in itself.

And:

> I usually say don't fight over things that aren't worth fighting over. Save your bullets for when they're needed. If you live like that you normally don't need the bullets. What you get from that is quite a smooth way of making changes, because that's what it's all about.

The importance of union influence and involvement in shaping decisions was recognised in managerial circles. The HR Director admitted that:

> we feel positively about the experience of the union representatives. They have a lot of common sense, they have a lot of knowledge about the organisation, they know what people think, often more than the managers do, so we can both gain from having an open dialogue with union representatives. They know they get the correct information and they also know when to diffuse it. This also means that the message from the company to the employees comes from two channels meaning that if we have a message from the company on say organisational change and it only comes from the company channel there is a chance that it will be misunderstood or maybe there would be more concern about the reason behind it. In most cases we have the same message from the unions and that means that the total message is received as being trustworthy.

In terms of contributing to company performance, however, it is extremely difficult to establish causal connections between a particular form of industrial relations arrangements and key performance indicators. Nevertheless, since the merger in 1999 there has been an increase in the Astra Zeneca AB payroll of 1,600 and in increase in investment of some 6 billion SEK as product markets have evolved. Perhaps more importantly, actors from both sides *see* partnership as having been of positive mutual benefit. More critically, however, we can question whether the salary agreements are effective. Although evaluation is an explicit part of the annual cycles, the company admits that salary setting is no science and, on the white-collar side, is generally based on judgements by individual managers. This subjectivity in salary setting was admitted to by the SIF respondents.

Conclusion

The Astra Zeneca case was selected for study on the basis of claims made by SIF nationally that it illustrated how partnership arrangements can work. As such, it is presented here as an example of 'good practice'. The case confirms the existence of something that might be deemed partnership in the case of the white-collar union club at the company as well as perceived benefits for both sides. On the other hand, there is also clear evidence that a more adversarial relationship exists between the blue-collar union club and the Astra Zeneca management. Why, then, is there an apparent difference between the two clubs despite them both being party to the same general agreement?

Our view is that it is no coincidence that the case volunteered to us by SIF at the national level is that of a knowledge-intensive firm. Clearly, the market for knowledge workers is highly competitive giving employees considerable leverage on employers and their unions considerable scope to exert influence at the workplace. Such workers, described by Robert Reich as 'symbolic analysts' have been predicted as being able to enjoy increasing rewards from work compared to other groups (Reich, 1991). Research and development in knowledge-intensive firms is a site of high added value stressing the strategic importance of the HR function.

It is far from the case, however, that all work undertaken in a knowledge intensive firm is knowledge work. The blue-collar work in the factories at Astra Zeneca is seen by the chair of the IWU club as Tayloristic and not characterised by high knowledge. In the absence of a high profile developmental agenda by the blue-collar union at the plant, it is no coincidence that something more closely resembling a 'boxing' culture prevails. The strategic choice to dance on work organisation issues, advocated by the IWU centrally, is being declined at Södertälje where the local leadership has clearly taken a disliking to the music. Such a view, however, needs to be qualified by the fact that there appear to be differences between factories and the attitudes of key actors can also have a decisive impact on the regulative culture locally.

Audit criteria for partnership agreement (since 1983)

Gains in information and consultation rights and procedures.   Occurred in 1983 on the codification of co-determination at Astra. Gains still in place despite merger with Zeneca in 1999.

Structural improvements in trade unionism.   New forms of inter-union collaboration, but links to partnership unclear.

Gains (and scope) in joint problem solving.   Yes, but blue-collar union is somewhat reactive on work organisation issues.

Advances in substance of collective agreements.   Yes – but clearer on the white-collar side.

Measurability of gains.   Yes, in particular on new payments systems.

Improvements in target setting and aspiration management.   Not clear from case data.

Preservation of union independence.   Yes. No evidence that co-determination has led to incorporation.

Advances in the quality of working life and/or work organisation.   Yes on QWL and work environment. Some early advances on teamwork, but IWU reluctant to push for further advance on blue-collar side.

References

Astra Zeneca (2000) *Annual Report.*
Astra Zeneca (2001) internet http://www.astrazeneca.se/iSverige/kortafakta.asp : 19.5.2001.
Reich, R. B. (1991) *The Work of Nations – Capitalism in the 21st Century.* New York: A. A. Knopf.

Appendices: Case studies

Private Sector Services

Appendix A4
The Dutch Industribution Project – Boxing and Dancing in a 'Union Desert'

Maarten van Klaveren and Wim Sprenger

Introduction

This contribution reports on the 'Industribution Project' of the Dutch FNV union confederation. Confronted with rapid employment growth in a 'union desert' where various economic activities interrelated, the confederation and four affiliated unions felt forced to follow unusual ways to establish a union presence. The confederation pursued dancing strategies by using research, tracing employer interests that might be areas for compromise with the affiliates, and by bringing various union levels and union competencies into action – essential conditions for the development of a permanent dance floor and boxing ring.

We first have to explain the odd term 'industribution'. It is a conflation of (manufacturing) 'industry' and 'distribution'. Industribution activities have been developing where industrial, logistics and servicing activities meet. These activities are part of what is internationally known as VAL (Value Added Logistics). VAL can be described as adding services to physical distribution activities, both non-physical (like invoicing) and physical (like packing, assembling and labelling). The additional physical services can be defined as 'industribution'; such services include assembly of laser printers, disk drives and so on, pre-assembly of car parts, reconditioning of shoes, reconditioning of clothing, adding certificates, testing and quality control of monitors, laptops, and others assembly of software packages, repacking and conditioning of medical products, assembling 'action articles' for retailers.

A number of these activities had already appeared in the course of the 1980s. American multinationals profited from the strength of the Dutch transit economy, with the Rotterdam port and Schiphol airport as 'gateways to Europe'. Hewlett Packard, Nike and other US companies established their European Distribution Centres (EDCs) in the Netherlands, followed by Japanese and European companies. At the same time, containerisation reached maturity and stimulated shifts in employment, away from the port quays to 'low wage zones' just outside classical union strongholds and further, towards the hinterland. In 1996, Statistics Netherlands estimated that VAL and industribution activities employed about 160,000 people. Dutch ministries as well as employer pressure groups predicted the creation of 80,000 new jobs in these activities until 2000. Later, these figures turned out to be heavily overestimated: in 2003, total employment may be about 200,000. Moreover, these predictions neglected any social context. The industribution project leader of FNV Bondgenoten assessed the situation in 1995 (cit. in Van Klaveren, 2001):

> It was a sub-sector without collective agreements, with low wages and bad working conditions, without any vocational training system, and with hardly any Works Councils. After all, at the time union density was depressingly low: a white spot in union country.

In this appendix we explore the FNV efforts to strengthen the union presence in this 'white spot' or 'union desert'. This strengthening aimed at recruiting more members as well as creating a social infrastructure in which the unions should play a structural role. We concentrate on questions of strategic unionism related to the boxing and dancing issue. Our main sources are research projects based on surveys and interviews (especially Bouwman *et al.*, 1998) and on documents and interviews (Van Klaveren, 2001, 2002).

The early history: 1990–95

Logistics problems of the port of Rotterdam laid the foundations for the FNV industribution project. The port unions traditionally held a strong position, with a union density in the mid-1980s of 80%. Since 1985, the regional organisations of FNV and CNV, the Transport Union FNV on the one hand and the port employers federation SVZ on the other had developed a 'social dialogue', oriented towards the economic and social assessment of new technologies. Thus, they created a common dance floor. In 1990 the Rotterdam Port Authority (GHR) started the RIL (Rotterdam Internal Logistics) project, meant to combat the congestion of container traffic to and from the hinterland. It was quite logical that the RIL project developed in a tripartite way, with a steering group made up from GHR, FNV and SVZ.

However, management consultants divided RIL into a number of pilot projects, mainly pleasing employers (concerning driving at night and numerical flexibility). The regional officer of the FNV confederation, noting this, asked for more backing from his Amsterdam headquarters. Consequently, FNV decided to integrate its representation in RIL in project activities of its own. The confederation gave an assignment to STZ consultancy and research to assess the social consequences of the RIL pilots and other port-related logistic plans. Interviews with many stakeholders and a number of union training meetings led to growing insights into:

- the development of logistics corridors, especially the growth of the west–east-corridor from the Rotterdam port through North Brabant to Venlo and further east-bound, to the German and East European hinterland;
- the growth of VAL and industribution activities along these corridors in 'low-wage areas' just outside the Rotterdam port collective agreement area (Bouwman, 1993, 1994).

The research results sharpened the notion among the FNV leadership that new logistics chains were putting traditional collective bargaining structures under heavy pressure. Against this background, the FNV Transport Union initiated talks with the FNV Industry Union and the FNV Service Workers about an 'FNV-wide' approach to industribution. Yet, many tensions remained between these unions, mainly because of the potential membership gains in industribution.

Interviewed seven years later, board members of the three FNV unions point to an FNV conference of June 1994 in the Dutch Railway Museum in Utrecht as a landmark. Here, they agreed upon a joint effort. They suggested to start pilots in three regions in the west–east corridor: in and near Rotterdam, in the North Brabant province (Tilburg, Eindhoven), and in the Venlo region in the Limburg province. The process accelerated in Autumn 1995, with the Food Workers FNV joining the preparatory committee.

The project: 1996–2000

From 1996 on, the FNV industribution project developed in close co-operation between union officials and researchers/employees consultants. As we explain in the national chapter in this volume, the Dutch union movement is weak at company and workplace level, where the union groups lack a legal status. On the other hand, the unions are rather strong at regional level. This especially held true for the regional organisation of the FNV confederation, FNV Regiowerk. There about 20 paid officers represented the confederation in many networks, varying from regional chambers of commerce to the official labour supply agencies. Thus, it was rational for the unions to seek the support of national and regional authorities and to try and create common dance floors in the regions. The FNV confederation and the four unions installed a national Steering Group, chaired by a Transport Union officer. An STZ consultant was appointed project manager – a role created to formalise and subsidise project activities. Over half of the project costs had to be covered by external resources. The unions asked FNV Regiowerk to chair and coach the three regional working groups. In the years previously, Regiowerk officers had taken a number of initiatives for union, bipartite and tripartite projects. These projects led to the (re)discovery of regional policy space or, in Dutch terms, of a 'regional consultation economy'.

Research was used as a strategic crowbar to persuade authorities and employers of the need for joint action. To underpin the industribution project, STZ developed a major research project, covering 80 companies through in-depth interviews. In 1996, the project manager succeeded in persuading the four interested national ministries to fund this research, a public relations campaign and (re)training activities. While the external conditions developed favourably, the internal conditions were lagging behind. Workable co-operation patterns between the national and regional union levels were difficult to put into practice, as the regional pilots showed (see next paragraph).

On 6 March 1997, the official launching conference of the FNV industribution project took place. Central features were presentations of a videotape and a brochure, based on the research results. On the one hand, the brochure was highly critical about the flexibilisation of the workforce and about working conditions. Moreover, experienced workers complained about the very high work pressure during peak business periods (cit. in Bouwman and Scheepmaker, 1997):

> In this business of fashion reconditioning we've got spring and summer peaks with extreme pressure. Then, it's a complete madhouse here in Oldenzaal (female production worker at Bleckmann)
>
> The agreements with large customers are razor-sharp. At the end of each month we are all stressed (male transport planner at Frans Maas Logistics)

On the other hand, the booklet read as an invitation to dance. It recommended a number of joint initiatives by unions, government bodies and employers: labour pools and training programmes; a joint inventory of problems in working conditions, and frequent union–employer consultations. Industribution will only be able to develop into a stable pillar of the Dutch economy as a regulated sector, striving for 'quality', the brochure argued. In his conference speech, Ad Melkert, the Minister of Social Affairs and Employment from the Social Democrat ranks, supported this vision.

Shortly after the conference, the four FNV unions announced their goal to amalgamate in 'FNV Bondgenoten' ('FNV Allies'). Although judged positively in general at the time, the new union planned to abolish the existing regional structures of the four unions. The FNV was to remain the only connection between all FNV-affiliated unionists active at regional level. On 29 January 1998, the founding congress of FNV Bondgenoten was convened and the individual unions were disbanded. Within a year the new Bondgenoten project leader pointed out that the abolition of the regional structures caused serious problems. She concluded that the project was not 'translated' well towards union activists and (potential) members. She announced a new impetus: a number of spearhead sub-sectors and companies were selected, and paid and unpaid officials alike should focus on developing internal union networks, on setting up works councils, and raising union density in these spearheads.

In January 1999, Bondgenoten organised a major conference, its input being the final STZ research report (Bouwman *et al.*, 1998). The project leader linked the future of industribution activities in the Netherlands with immediate union needs. The headlines of her interview with FNV Magazine, published on conference day, could not be mistaken: 'Working hard, earning little. Industribution is crying for a collective agreement.' In her conference speech, she emphasised that many industribution companies were still not covered by any such agreements. After her, the Minister of Economic Affairs, Ms Annamarie Jorritsma, affirmed:

In social respects, something has to be done.

Moreover, Jorritsma, from the ranks of the right-wing Liberal Party, praised FNV Bondgenoten. She pointed to the training facilities for all-round warehouse workers in Venlo and Tilburg:

These people get a view on challenging and better work, while the employers get motivated and flexible staff.

In July 1999, the Bondgenoten project leader could report much more positively than nine months earlier. The spearhead goals had largely been met. Within a year, the number of companies carrying out industribution activities under collective agreements grew from 37 to 68: 60% of the spearhead companies. The number of union activists doubled, membership grew by 600 to 1800 (and to 2400 in July 2000). In these terms, co-operation between works councils and union officers yielded good results, especially among migrant workers. The Bondgenoten board allowed the project an extra (fourth) year. Yet, already in the course of 1999 the boards of FNV and FNV Bondgenoten decided to phase out the role of FNV Regiowerk. Some Regiowerk officers had mixed feelings about this, as they judged three years too short to embed results of the project in the organisation and policies of the FNV confederation. In the next three years, they were proved to be right.

Dancing in the regions?

Developments in the three pilot regions showed a diverging pattern, mainly depending on whether dancing patterns developed. After 1991, the 'social dialogue' in the

Rotterdam region faded away. It came to an end in 1995. Then, the negotiation tasks of the local employers' federation SVZ were taken over by AWVN, a national employers' service institute. Rotterdam now lacked a dance floor. Under these conditions a transfer mechanism between union strongholds like the Rotterdam port and 'union deserts' could not be created.

Yet, the negative consequences of this lack of transfer remained limited. The pilot groups for the provinces North Brabant and Limburg both made astute use of the fact that the authorities of these provinces were keen on the growth of industrustion activities. In the Venlo region of the province of Limburg in particular, these activities, often characterised by production fluctuations, were hampered by shortages in jobs like fork-lift truck drivers at peak production levels. The STZ research proved that the 'normal' employers' solution, hiring workers from temp agencies at random, caused problems of loyalty, reliability, costs and performance. Confronted with this outcome, the authorities and the regional employers' organisations accepted joint labour pools as an alternative.

In the Venlo region, the regional FNV officer took the initiative to create an Industrustion Foundation, that developed training programmes for all-round ware-house jobs. She chaired the tripartite board and succeeded in keeping the initiative. The unions succeeded in bringing special scales for these jobs into the collective agreements of Venlo-based transport companies. This development was regarded in the Dutch union movement as trendsetting for regional labour market constructions and was widely copied. In the Tilburg region FNV Regiowerk took the initiative too, although it proved quite difficult to keep it: temp agencies like Randstad and Adecco aggressively tried to claim the new labour pool business for themselves. Yet, in the end, the Venlo and Tilburg developments stimulated labour supply arrangements for logistics staff (and broader categories) elsewhere in the Netherlands with structural roles for the unions. In doing so they helped create many new dancing opportunities in the labour supply field in 2000–02.

Conclusions and lessons for the unions

If we look at its external effects, the industrustion project has been rather successful:

- the basis for a social infrastructure was created, in which the unions involved gained access to company and sub-sector information;
- the unions gained credibility as competent partners in problem solving especially on labour supply;
- collective agreements became better geared towards specific (industrustion) activities and jobs, and covered substantially more companies and workers;
- a number of companies started moving in the direction of quality-oriented production, with some improvements in the quality of working life such as lower workloads in peak periods.

These outcomes were helped by the boom in the Dutch economy between 1994 and 2001. Yet, the project also created momentums of its own, especially caused by astute dancing practices. It can be called innovative, looking at how confederation and individual union officers integrated project work in their daily activities. This was done rather flexibly, directed towards the creation of networks, and by looking for win–win situations without losing focus on short-term policy efficiency.

These positive outcomes of the project cannot mask its slow and uneasy internal development. We suggest two main causes. First, its strong external dependence. The dancing practices needed for finding funding and support from the authorities absorbed much time and energy. Moreover, these practices were sometimes at odds with boxing practices needed to put unwilling employers under pressure. Second, the development of the project was hampered by the problematic relationship between the regional FNV organisation and the FNV unions. The co-ordinating role of FNV Regiowerk was undermined by the merger of the unions. Moreover, the new union created a vacuum in the regions by abolishing regional structures. At the same time, the FNV confederation board chosen for Regiowerk left the industribution project. This retreat was at the cost of learning effects. Here a critical assessment of the project seems justified. New ways of union work and related learning effects have been rather limited to individual regional officers; organisational learning was virtually absent. Transfer of positive regional experiences to the national policy level remained scarce. We could hardly trace new instruments for competence development of officials and activists and only minor alterations in ways of working at confederation level inspired by the industribution project.

Finally, a number of lessons for trade unions can be drawn from this case:

- For a union movement that is weak at company and workplace levels, creating dance floors at regional levels and using formal representation combined with informal networks at that level can deliver a solid base for more company and member-oriented activities.
- Research commissioned and guided by the unions can be used as a strategic crowbar in order to persuade authorities and employers in a 'union desert' of the need for joint action.
- Unions can create solid positions as competent partners in problem solving at regional and sub-sector levels by integrating paid officers' knowledge and company information, gathered officially and by members.
- Attaining the conditions for these strategic interventions (creating dance floors, commissioning and guiding research, developing positions, integrating knowledge) normally cannot be realised in daily union work without creating structured projects.
- Such projects should last at least four to five years, and must be guided by strong and authoritative project management.

Audit criteria applied to industribution case

Gains in information and consultation rights and procedures.   No

Structural improvements in trade unionism.   Rapid growth of number of activists and membership, although from a very low level

Gains (and scope) in joint problem solving.   Gains in joint management of labour supply arrangements

Advances in substance of collective agreements.   More and better agreements

Measurability of gains.   Yes, concerning agreements, activists, membership

Improvements in target setting and aspiration management.   Not at national level, maybe within union at industry level

Preservation of union independence. Yes
Advances in the quality of working life and/or work organisation. Too early to judge

References

Bouwman, T. (1993) *Containers, logistiek en arbeid. Kansen en bedreigingen van Rotterdams Interne Logistiek voor werknemers.* Amsterdam: FNV.

Bouwman, T. (1994) *Snel weg. Goederenvervoer, arbeid en milieu.* Amsterdam: FNV.

Bouwman, T. and Scheepmaker, M. (1997) *In-dus-tri-bu-tie. Een wereld te winnen.* Amsterdam: FNV Pers.

Bouwman, T., Van de Camp, A. and Van Halem, A. (1998) *Sociale aspecten van indistributie. Eindrapport.* Eindhoven/Utrecht: STZ/FNV Bondgenoten.

Van Klaveren, M. (2001) *De FNV en de regionale overlegeconomie.* Eindhoven: STZ.

Van Klaveren, M. (2002) 'The FNV "Industribution" Project. Trade Union learning in the Netherlands' *Concepts and Transformation* 7(2): 203–24.

Appendix A5
AFL-CIO Multi-Union/Kaiser Permanente Partnership, US
Steven Deutsch

Background and context in the health care sector

The US is the only industrial nation that has no public health care system. While there are many public health institutions, the system remains a market-driven and privatised one. This may sound like such a strong qualifier that no conclusions might be drawn for application within other countries, but that obscures what are, in fact, generalisable points. In short, this is a private sector case analysis and it can serve as a useful model for other private sector organisations and labour–management partnerships.

Health care is large, with over ten million employed, and more than 15% of the GNP, with a growth of 8.7% in the year 2001 (Pear, 2003). There continues to be a significant growth of this sector, with internal shifts that are similar in all other industrial nations. These include the ageing population and more geriatric health needs, the lessened use of hospitals and acute care centres and more outpatient resources, the application of new technologies – including telemedicine, less invasive surgical procedures and information processing.

The lack of a national health care system means that while over 41 million Americans, almost 15% of the nation (Pear, 2002), have no health insurance – a catastrophic challenge in itself, most citizens have health insurance obtained through their places of employment. That means, for example, that each auto maker adds more than $1000 to price of a vehicle to pay for the negotiated health insurance coverage for workers, which obviously affects competitiveness in a world market. The upward spiralling of costs of health care, taking an ever-larger share of the GNP, has also been a huge challenge. This has led to great pressures on hospital administrators and managements to cut costs. That has led to hospital closings, contraction of the work force, moving work down within professional categories to less-paid professionals – with related concerns about quality of patient care. In short, it is a massive system in great crisis.

Among other factors, a nursing shortage has developed, leading to a major increase in workload (Abelson, 2002). As a result there have been rising rates of stress, ergonomic injury and illness, and a growing focus by nurses on workload issues. At Oregon Health Sciences University a strike was barely averted in 2002 over key issues on giving nurses more say in the workplace. In California politicians approached mandated staffing levels in hospitals as a public policy, while journalists headlined articles such as 'Health Care Crisis Grows As Political Will Wanes.' All of this bears heavily on the labour–management environment and will likely do so in the foreseeable future.

The US is a crisis-driven society which has aversions to planning and social engineering, a strong national psyche in contradiction to many European nations, which in this century have well-developed philosophies and institutional arrangements for doing national planning at all levels and in all sectors. Unions in the US have in recent years understood the critical need for forward-looking, proactive and strategic planning, but mostly they have operated in response to crises.

Innovative labour–management partnerships and the Kaiser case experience

In health care this has led to some of the most creative new labour–management arrangements. Some are at the local level with a particular hospital, such as the agreement between the Oregon Nurses Association and Sacred Heart General Hospital in Eugene which gives the nurses' union a new role with management in staffing decisions. Others are by state-wide organisations and employers, for example the California Nurses Association which has an agreement with Kaiser Permanente, the largest health organisation in the nation, that a nurse will be released in each hospital to work with management on patient quality assurance. Each of these break new ground and hold potential as models.

The report that follows is based on some years of observation, interviews, and an action research effort involving training and change evaluation.

Kaiser Permanente is the largest and most unionised health care organisation in the nation, with 90,000 employees in 12 states and Washington, DC. It is a highly diverse workforce. After many years of difficult labour relations and lack of co-ordination among the several unions, a new initiative was launched engaging 8 national and 26 local unions representing 90% of the organised 62,000 employees (Kaiser Permanente, 2001). This agreement came after a time of tumultuous labour relations, some strikes, strongly contested closings of hospitals and layoffs, serious economic challenges for management, and concerns over patient quality care. Into this milieu came a creative approach, led by the national labour federation, AFL-CIO, to bring all of the unions together into a co-ordinated effort which would not only work on traditional bargaining, but would push for a new approach to labour–management relations. Over several years a large working group from each union and from locations around the country came together with employer representatives to work out mutual understandings of what was being sought and strategies which would not only forge a partnership but lay out concrete mechanisms to achieve mutual goals such as employment security, improved work environment, assured quality of patient care, economic efficiency, and a host of other objectives that both management and unions had.

The scope of the initial agreement was monumental and included as legitimate matters for the labour–management partnership to address items around quality and business planning – ranging from quality standards and improvement, to budgeting, re-engineering, and acquisitions and closings. It included skill standards, job design, job assignments and technology, all as part of the decision-making where union representatives would share power with management. In short, to best accomplish the meeting of mutual goals, a huge leap was to be made in giving worker representatives a say. Nothing was more innovative than the sharing of power to make staffing decisions, a key in the current agreement. Ninety-two per cent of union employees supported the initial Partnership Agreement.

Assessment of achievements and transferability to others

While the agreement is new enough to have minimal assessments completed, the evidence already suggests that the process has altered thinking among some of the more traditional management people. Prior to the agreement they had joint labour–management committees, for example on ergonomics for dental hygienists, which allowed the union to utilise consultants to help demonstrate the need for work reorganisation. This effort was important in reducing work-place illness and hence saved costs and protected workers. But such efforts were constrained in scope, not part of a total package of partnering, and hence limited in application.

The current agreement has unleashed a rippling process of employee training and skills building, internal union education to build capacity for shared decision-making with management, and, most importantly, nurtured a process of union strategic thinking and action planning for labour–management partnering. This has helped significantly in union organising. The Oregon Federation of Nurses and Health Professionals has seen a growth of more than 30% in new members in the last year with considerable enthusiasm to join a union that is going well beyond traditional bargaining agendas and is pushing for a significant voice in all decision-making at the workplace to best advance interests of workers and their union, while at the same time helping to achieve management goals of growth, economic expansion, cost containment and quality improvement.

Now in the sixth year, the Kaiser Partnership has accomplished some significant advances. As of 2003 a major joint labour–management initiative on work environment improvement has shown excellent results with reduced injury and illness reports and costs savings. This injury-reduction programme builds on a commitment by labour and management to work from the bottom-up and engage employees in hazard awareness and training to intervention and abatement practices, including work organisational change. The goal is to train 25% of the workforce each year over the next four years, which would be a major achievement and has gained a large financial commitment for paid-released time for training. A March 2003 report suggests a ripple effect with good results (Partnership Progress Notes, 19 March 2003).

Beyond the master partnership agreement, it is clear that the local agreements have become much shorter than previously due to the problem-solving partnership approach. Staffing is a short section because it reflects a joint labour–management means. It remains a major issue in disputes and strikes and a critical area for partnership efforts in more tranquil times.

The skills training around partnership is a critical component. The substantive areas such as occupational health are further along than capacity building for partnership committee participation. For labour one of the on-going issues is that there are too few persons carrying too much responsibility. There is ample evidence that local union staff representatives and local leaders are very much caught in the 'boxing and dancing' dilemma, and need skills training to be better able to navigate in these conflicting waters (Eaton, 2003).

Interestingly enough, labour leadership in the overall national partnership is considerably more stable over the five years than is true for management. Both top management and union leaders agree that the biggest stumbling block is management co-operation at the lowest level. First-line supervisors have been less integrated into the partnership and are less 'on board'. Labour has been more successful in inter-union and organisational communications, and universal awareness of and engagement with the Partnership Agreement and thrust. Most agree that more education of managers is absolutely key for the continued operation and success of the effort.

As of year six in the agreement, there are renewed feelings of 'cautious optimism'. The CEO has given strong evidence of commitment to the Partnership Agreement and the chief management negotiator who had left the organisation in 2002, to the consternation of union leadership, was brought back by the new CEO as part of the renewed effort.

Finally, the assessment demonstrates that some significant success in union involvement in marketing has been obtained. This is important in terms of market share, competitiveness and the financial success of the company, and thereby the ability to sustain employment security and many of the basic provisions of the Partnership Agreement. The union role in marketing, as well as in cost savings around health and safety and worker compensation payments, is seen as critical. Many managers have altered their scepticism in the face of demonstrable achievements ranging from productivity increases to reduction in grievances (Eaton, 2003).

The biggest challenge perceived by union leadership is to accelerate the pace of change, and to move the effective top-level labour–management partnering to the local work sites where some managers continue to operate in more traditional styles. This is such a common reality amongst most approaches to workplace change by innovative labour–management partnering, that it would be surprising if it were not true, even in this affirmative case.

In sum, this innovative partnership has revitalised labour at each level. The national federation, AFL-CIO, took an extraordinary role in leadership and has demonstrated some creative approaches with a large, multi-union employer in the private sector. Affiliated unions, the largest is the Service Employees, have seen this approach reinvigorate their organising efforts and there is a ripple effect in other parts of the union. Local unions, such as those in Portland, San Francisco and elsewhere have seen major growth in organising, in rank-and-file participation, and internal union skills building and education. At the same time this may well help the employer stop some cost haemorrhaging, preserve jobs and gain clientele and business. It holds considerable potential as a win for both labour and management.

Another notable by-product of this multi-union collaborative partnership has been witnessed by six labour organisations in Oregon jointly working to introduce state legislation which will improve patient care and workplace safety. In this instance it moved into another level of partnering in the arena of public policy, and hence widened the net of social partners. Partnering on public policy became an added goal in the 2003 national agreement.

Finally, it is critical to point out that this partnership moves into a direction opposite to the trend which for years has seen managerial pressure to move collective agreements and bargaining to the local enterprise level (Mills, 2001). American multi-national corporations have also pushed enterprise bargaining in Australia and in European countries where there have been strong national patterns of labour relations. Here is a significant case where all of the worksites, local unions and national labour organisations came together and partnered with national corporate management to promote best practice and outcomes which were of economic benefit to management, gained in quality and improved working conditions for the workforce. For good reason this case has captured significant interest in other industries and many see it as having considerable potential for being transferable and applied elsewhere.

To summarise the achievements from this partnership for the unions has been: employment security obtained; extraordinarily broad scope of coverage in the agreement with union participation in virtually all facets of the organisation; success in union organising linked to the agreement; achievement of concrete goals such as enhanced training, improvement in the work environment, and higher levels of worker and union participation in workplace decision-making.

Concluding lessons from the case for trade unions

- Health care is privatised in the US, hence the case has transferability to the private sector, and to multi-site and multi-union settings as well.
- Health care is a large sector in the economy, many parts are heavily gendered (male/female occupations), in serious economic crisis, with quality, work environment and other issues. Hence unions need to target issues such as gender equity and work environment to build union member commitment and gain advances through the partnership.
- In an unusual move, the national labour federation played a leadership role in this case, bringing many unions together with a large national employer, to achieve a national labour–management partnership agreement that is path-breaking in its inclusion for what the unions now have as areas of decision-making – virtually nothing is excluded. Central labour bodies might explore such assistance, in the wake of pressures for decentralised, enterprise bargaining.
- Substantial successes have been achieved in training, developing joint worksite committees, making progress in work environment improvement and quality measures. This helped union organising and activism. Skill building and training for union leadership must be a key part of any partnership.
- This agreement has lasted for five years, the limit for most such efforts, boding well for the future and the potential this agreement and case has. Unions must work to sustain partnerships, utilising on-going feedback and evaluation to problem-solve and sustain the process.
- It is vital for the union to place the labour–management agreement within the scope of the larger union agenda and to develop a strategic approach to the partnership.
- Top leadership commitment is vital, but there must be institutionalised participation that goes beyond particular leaders, so that the process is maintained in the face of leadership change.

Audit criteria for partnership agreements

Gains in information and consultation rights and procedures.   Major information, sharing and enhanced levels of union and worker participation in workplace decision-making has been a key result of the partnership. The scope of the partnership agreement is a model of information sharing, and worker and union rights to participate in virtually all critical decisions affecting the work organisation and workforce.

Structural improvements in trade unionism.   Some significant new worker organising has been gained, directly linked to the partnership agreement.

Gains (and scope) in joint problem solving.   An extraordinarily broad scope of coverage has been obtained with union participation in virtually all facets of the organisation.

Advances in substance of collective agreements. Gains in employment security have been a key achievement in the partnership. Significant gains in employee training rights and opportunities have been achieved.

Measurability of gains. A number of critical elements have been measured that show achievements, including reduction of injury and illness and improvement in the work environment.

Improvements in target setting and aspiration management. No clear evidence in the case study data.

Preservation of union independence. The partnership built new recognition and respect for the unions involved, with a major shift of authority and power-sharing in decision-making.

Advances in the quality of working life and/or work organisation. The partnership has led to improvements in many aspects of the quality of working life, with tangible work environment gains.

References

Abelson, R. (2002) 'With Nurses in Short Supply, Patient Load Becomes a Big Issue', *New York Times,* 6 May.

Eaton, S. C. (2003) *The Kaiser Permanente Labor Management Partnership: the First Five Years.* Boston: MIT Sloan School of Management (January).

Kaiser Permanente and Kaiser Permanente Unions AFL-CIO (2001) *National Agreement 2001.*

Kaiser Permanente and the Coalition of Kaiser Permanente Unions AFL-CIO (2003) 'Partnership Progress Notes', March.

Mills, N. (2001) 'New Strategies for Union Survival and Renewal', *Journal of Labor Research* 22: 599–613.

Pear, R. (2002) 'After Decline, the Number of Uninsured Rose in 2001', *New York Times,* 29 September.

Pear, R. (2003) 'Spending on Health Care Soars in 2001', *New York Times,* 8 January.

Appendix A6
On the Hotel Dance Floor – Social Partnership at Jury's Doyle Hotel Group

Kevin O'Kelly

Introduction

The approach to partnership at Jury's Doyle Hotels provided an important competitive advantage for the Hotel Group in its response to the problems experienced in the industry following 11 September 2001, the outbreak of Foot and Mouth Disease in 2002 and the SARS scare in 2003. It has enabled the Group to respond with greater flexibility to the developing crisis and ensured that the need for the strategies and actions undertaken were widely understood and supported by the staff. Important developments at Jurys Doyle include the development of a more innovative culture among employees, the mainstreaming and diffusion of partnership as an approach to change and the approach to sharing gains within the Group.

The Company

Jurys Doyle Hotel Group is Ireland's leading hotel group. It employs approximately 4,000 people in 32 hotels throughout Ireland, the UK and the US. A further five hotels are under construction in the UK and US. Sixteen of the hotels are located in Ireland, employing approximately 2,600 people. The Company operates in city centre locations, and is primarily focused on the corporate market. The organisation has undergone significant change and expansion in the last 10–15 years, including the development of the highly successful Jurys Inns concept in 1993 and the acquisition of the Doyle Hotel Group (including such top of the range hotels as the Westbury, Berkeley Court and Burlington Hotels in Dublin) in 1999.

The partnership context

The Group's competitive advantage is derived from its ability to respond rapidly to customer needs and its business is a people-oriented one. With the rapid expansion in the Irish economy from the mid-1990s, and the expansion of the Group itself, both management and unions recognised that changes needed to be implemented which would enhance the input of employees and the competitiveness of the organisation. This was reinforced by the effects on the industry of the Gulf War, which resulted in a dramatic reduction in visitor numbers, with a consequent impact on business. It led to a realisation that a range of work practices which did not necessarily promote flexibility and responsiveness to customer needs had to be changed. These customs and practices applied as much to management's approach as they did to the unions. It was also widely recognised that in order for any change initiative to have credibility within the organisation, it needed to be strongly supported by the main union, SIPTU.

The structures

In 1998, such an opportunity arose. SIPTU received support from the European Commission, under the ADAPT programme, to examine the issue of workplace partnership and to pilot some initiatives. The Jurys Doyle Group was approached to participate and nominated its flagship Jurys Ballsbridge Hotel to participate. At this time, the hotel employed a workforce of approximately 500. The hotel was 100% unionised and all employees were represented by SIPTU. A partnership steering committee was formed, consisting of five management and five union representatives and an independent facilitator was employed to support the process. The role of the facilitator became less important as the process developed momentum. It was challenging at times to maintain the momentum when the steering committee members changed, as new members needed to be brought up to speed on the process. An important element in the success of the project was that the steering committee included senior managerial representatives, including the general manager. The committee also included key union personnel who could clearly be identified as champions of the process.

The activity

In the initial stages the steering committee focused on team dynamics and building trust. Formal and informal training in decision-making and communication skills facilitated this process. Also, union representatives received training to assist them in understanding financial information, for example, so they could make meaningful contributions once they fully understood the company's financial position. All outstanding industrial relations issues were 'ringfenced' and dealt with through the normal collective bargaining structures. The objective was that future issues of conflict would be dealt with through the partnership process.

The importance of communication was recognised as a key requirement for success and the steering group briefed all employees in the hotel on the partnership group and its function. Minutes of all meetings were put on the appropriate notice boards and sent to all employees with their payslips. Department-level partnership committees were established in areas such as banqueting, accommodation, reception and the kitchens to actually carry out the detailed work.

All parties agreed that a series of 'quick-wins' were required to give the process credibility. The practical work carried out by the department committees was significant. For example, a pilot job-sharing initiative was introduced in the accommodation and reservations sections of the hotel, and was sufficiently successful for it to be introduced on a permanent basis after the pilot period. Employees began to have greater input into decisions affecting their work. Housekeeping personnel were consulted at the design stage when rooms were re-designed and this enabled the introduction of very practical changes and for issues of concern to bedroom staff to be addressed. Reception staff was involved in the re-design of the hotel reception area and all those with a capacity to advise on the best way of achieving the objective were involved.

A key issue of conflict was that of rostering arrangements, in particular for the house-keeping and reception areas, where staff were 95% female. This potential source of conflict was addressed by the introduction of job-sharing and a greater emphasis on 'family-friendly' policies and, for housekeeping staff, shorter working hours.

Productivity deals were also addressed using the partnership mechanism, including one that involved gainsharing for front desk personnel in return for a reduction in staff levels. The actual way of conducting business within the hotel itself began to change, and the relationship between management and unions began to change as trust was established at all levels. A SAYE (Save As You Earn) scheme was introduced in 2000 and extended to staff in the other hotels in the Group in Ireland. These have resulted in additional earnings and better working conditions.

With the challenges the sector has faced in recent years, the existence of the part-nership committee has provided a forum for both sides to address together the impact on the business and to work to develop acceptable strategies needed to survive.

Outcomes and benefits

The organisation's partnership approach helped it to compete well against its rivals during this extremely difficult period for the industry. The Group recognised the value of this approach, and two of the union members on the steering committee were seconded for a period to brief the other hotels within the group on the approach. This offered an excellent opportunity for the other hotels to raise issues that were of concern to them and, as a result, the sick pay scheme has been standardised. The process has been extended to the Berkeley Court Hotel where department meetings have been established and the communications process within the hotel has improved significantly.

The process, like any formal structures, needs to be constantly monitored and reviewed. The original steering committee structure is constantly updated, as are the compositions of the local partnership committees and their activities. A significant amount of the partnership approach has been mainstreamed into the way the hotel does its business on a daily basis and, at present, structures are being reviewed so that they remain relevant to meet the challenges of the industry.

The main benefits of the partnership process have included:

- An enhanced capacity to respond to market changes, through appropriate organi-sational change. The steering committee and local partnership committees have tackled difficult issues and resolved them through a partnership approach. In a fast-changing customer-oriented business environment, this is a significant achievement of the partnership process.
- Higher levels of trust between management and unions. The spin-off benefits of this are evidenced in the relationship between the two on an on-going basis.
- The development of a more pragmatic approach to problem solving. Better qual-ity solutions are now devised as a result of involving all key stakeholders in the development of a solution.
- The identification and delivery of shared benefits. The process has delivered more cost-competitive and flexible working arrangements for the organisation, and has provided employees with an opportunity to influence decisions that affect their work and with the possibility of financial reward as a result of certain initiatives.

Audit criteria for partnership agreements

Gains in information and consultation rights and procedures. Information-sharing and proactive union participation in organisational decision-making has been a key result of the partnership arrangements.

Structural improvements in trade unionism. SIPTU has had to change its way of working with management within the hotel and, as part of the review of the process, the union is examining how it can get closer to the members, while still remaining supportive of the partnership process.

Gains (and scope) in joint problem solving. Productivity aspects of the process have resulted in additional income for staff, shorter working hours in some sections, family-friendly policies and employee share ownership schemes for employees who availed of the offer of share options.

Advances in substance of collective agreements. The partnership process supplements, at a micro level, the agreements on National Programmes at the macro level.

Measurability of gains. The Group has a greater ability to compete in a very difficult business environment, thus securing good quality jobs for the staff of the hotel.

Improvements in target setting and aspiration management. Partnership has allowed the union to have a significant influence on the strategic decision-making and the development of policies which might have an impact on employment.

Preservation of union independence. While continuing to be committed to the partnership process, SIPTU insists it remains independent of management and is working to remain relevant to the concerns of its members and to continue its representative role.

Advances in the quality of working life and/or work organisation. The partnership process has resulted in improvements in the quality of working life, such as employment security, working conditions, the work environment and investment in training.

Appendix A7
Take Your Partners for a Quick Step ... Social Partnership at Vertex

Denis Gregory

Case background

Vertex Data Sciences is a wholly owned subsidiary of United Utilities (UU) one of the biggest utility companies in the UK. United Utilities was formed in January 1996 as a result of a merger between North West Water (NWW) and North West Electricity (NORWEB). Both companies having previously been privatised in 1989 and 1990. Vertex was established primarily to provide 'call centre' services to UU but also with an eye to the emerging markets for outsourced services.

By the time the partnership agreement was signed, Vertex had successfully begun to penetrate the outsourcing market. Within two years, the company had gained a range of contracts within the UK in both the utility and local authority sectors. This had doubled its employee base and enabled the company to become one of the main players in the outsourcing market for call centres and other customer service functions. By 2003, Vertex had become one of the leading payers in the UK outsourcing market and a global operator with capacity in Canada and India.

Employment relations at Vertex

The UK utilities sector has traditionally been highly organised from a trade union perspective. When public ownership predominated, union density was frequently close to 90% of the workforce. Privatisation in 1989 and 1990 led to density falling typically to around 60%. All the unions involved campaigned actively against privatisation. For much the same reasons, they were all strongly against the practice of outsourcing which became a feature of the post-privatised environment. Consequently, many of the senior managers at UU had experienced some bruising times at the hands of the unions both before and after privatisation. Influenced by this, the management strategy at Vertex was to ensure a 'break with the past' insofar as employment relations were concerned. The objective was to create a clear and different non-utility identity at Vertex. Whilst not explicitly anti-trade union, the company's initial plan was to move staff (many of whom had been transferred from elsewhere in UU) on to personal contracts. This was calculated to pre-empt the need for collective bargaining and to undermine the basis for trade union recognition and influence. A basic pay increase and the lure of bonus pay was sufficient to gain 95% support from within the staff for the personal contracts on offer. Not surprisingly, UNISON, the main trade union at Vertex was opposed to this strategy.

As part of the culture change programme initiated by Vertex in its first year of operation, a company-wide forum was elected by secret ballot to promote employee consultation. Some union representatives were elected to this (as employee representatives) and, as a result of discussions between national union officials and the UU board, seats were allocated for regional officials of the unions involved. Thus, whilst formal recognition of the unions for bargaining purposes was not offered, a degree of union involvement was, nevertheless, assured.

Hard dancing

At the start of the partnership the strategic and organisational changes facing both management and workforce at Vertex concerned the need for Vertex to expand its business base in order to become independent of UU and be able to meet the needs of city financial institutions – the ruthless 'boys in braces'. In order to meet these challenges, management stressed that new contracts would be subject to stringent cost analysis and tough benchmarking, that existing contracts required continuous improvement if they were to be retained and the outsourcing market in general would be looking for cost reductions in the order of 30% when contracts were up for tender.

At the same time, management recognised a further challenge namely that living with the concept of privatisation and adapting to the practice of outsourcing were going to be difficult for trade unions who had battled hard to minimise the use of such strategies.

Why dance?

Given the determination of management at Vertex to break with the past, the question naturally arises as to why a partnership approach involving the restoration of collective bargaining and the formal recognition of UNISON was considered at all. Three factors have been identified as being crucial here. First of all, management soon recognised that operating a personalised contract system was a high-cost strategy. In the second place, was the realisation that trade unionism remained a reality inside Vertex and was a potential benefit with some potential customers. Finally, it was evident the unions had begun to recognise that Vertex was shaping up as a good employer. As a result, informal contacts with union representatives grew through 1998. This involved intensive consultation about pay, with a general conclusion that the outcome that year was better for the trade union involvement. UNISON was also involved in assisting the company in framing and making bids for contracts in the public sector. This latter activity saw the conclusion of an agreement covering Local Authority Business which gave formal recognition to UNISON and began to set out the beginnings of a partnership approach.

In the wake of collective bargaining being established in its local authority contract and in Field Services, pressure began to mount on Vertex for collective bargaining to be implemented at their biggest call centre in Bolton. Following joint presentations, a consultative ballot was held in November 1999 which resulted in a 9 : 1 vote in favour of collective bargaining (on a 75% turn out) for staff at the Bolton call centre.

In order to avoid a rapid return to the past though, collective bargaining at Bolton was to be embedded within a partnership framework. This was designed to promote social dialogue and joint problem solving as an alternative to the more adversarial approaches frequently produced by traditional forms of collective bargaining. The agreement reached with UNISON at Bolton was influenced by the emphasis on partnership that had emerged in the Government's recently published 'Fairness at Work' White Paper. Key managers at Vertex felt the language of that White paper reflected a new employment relations vocabulary and signalled an orientation they were happy to follow. Linked to this was the growing realisation that potential clients of Vertex, at least in the public sector, were likely to be supportive of an organisation which, with the full support of a trade union like UNISON, practised this 'progressive' form of employee relations.

From UNISON's perspective the emergence of a partnership approach, whilst something of an unknown quantity for the local UNISON representatives, echoed developments elsewhere in the utility sector, for example at Scottish Power, Welsh Water, Southern Water and Transco. Thus, the UNISON national officers involved had some useful experience to draw upon. Moreover, as the agreement itself made clear, the intention initially was to frame something that was 'enabling rather than prescriptive and detailed' with the expectation that the agreement would be developed '... over time ...' In the meantime, UNISON had realised two strategic objectives: recognition and the restoration of collective bargaining for their members at Bolton.

Objectives and orientation of the partnership

The partnership agreement between Vertex and UNISON signed on 25 January 2000 was prefaced with eight guidelines.

- The business and the trade unions share a commitment to achieve and maintain an industrial relations climate of mutual trust and co-operation.
- We also share a common interest in the success of the business.
- We all recognise the need for both managers and staff to be flexible in their outlook and receptive to change.
- The business recognises the right of staff to belong to a trade union and the right of the union to represent their members.
- The union recognises the right of management to manage the business in an effective and efficient manner.
- Representatives within the employment relations structure recognise their responsibility to reflect the views of all staff not just trade union members or a particular group of interests.
- There is a common understanding that the objective of this agreement is to look forward not backwards. We start from where we are and aim to improve.
- It is jointly recognised that there is a place for both a consultative and a negotiating framework. The business recognises the need to strengthen the existing consultative framework to ensure both forums are fully effective.

The structure of the partnership at Vertex

The coverage of the partnership agreement was limited to the 1,000 employees working at the Bolton call centre. Staff here were, amongst other things, responsible for delivering the core contract between Vertex, and their parent company UU. It is fair to say that the Bolton call centre, when the agreement was signed, was the centrepiece of the Vertex operation. The agreement covered all staff (both permanent and temporary contracts) in the main operative grades, that is, Customer Services Agents (CSA) and Customer Services Representatives (CSR) plus some specialist roles. Specifically excluded were: managers, team leaders, senior professional, agency or other non-Vertex employees.

To implement and develop the partnership approach, the agreement established: a *consultative* forum with a wide-ranging remit to consider business performance and business opportunities affecting staff. The forum would act as 'sounding board' on all business issues. Where relevant, the views of the consultative forum would be referred to the *negotiating forum*. The responsibility of this body was to review and negotiate changes to contractual terms and conditions of employment, consider, when necessary, specific issues concerned with redundancy, transfer of undertakings and protection of employment (TUPE) and working time arrangements and generally engage on any matters of a collective nature that affected employees across the business as a whole. Whilst the forum was to consider the local application of Vertex policy and procedures, for example, discipline and grievance, the agreement was careful to specify that the forum would not, act as an arbitration panel. Moreover, collective issues of a purely local nature would be resolved by local trade union representatives and local managers with the involvement of the full-time official of the union where appropriate.

Representation on these forums was differentiated to reflect the fact that UNISON had won support in a workplace ballot for the restoration of collective bargaining. Thus, the employee representatives on the negotiation forum were appointed by UNISON solely from within their membership. By contrast, the employee members of the consultative forum were elected every two years by the call centre staff, although two additional seats were reserved for trade union members elected from the negotiating forum. In all, the consultative forum comprised 22 members representing 8 sections of the business using a formula of approximately 1 representative for every 50 employees. Part-time employees were also represented with 1 seat on the forum.

The negotiating forum comprised 6 trade union representatives and up to 6 management representatives. The full time UNISON officer responsible for Vertex also had a seat on the forum. Since the trade union representatives on the negotiating forum are recognised as the relevant individuals to deal with local employment relations issues, the union is required to ensure that representatives are drawn from appropriate parts of the business.

Relations between the dance floor and the boxing ring

The fact that the consultative forum was designed to ensure that non-union employees were represented alongside the unionised areas of the business might have been seen as a threat by UNISON. However, given that union density at the Bolton site was somewhere between 40% and 50% it was clear that for the consultative forum to be representative of the whole workforce some degree of non-union representation was inevitable. Acceptance off this by the local UNISON representatives was probably made possible by the fact that the employee side of the negotiating forum – which for many was where the real power and influence lay – was made up of UNISON representatives.

It was clear that both management and union representatives recognised that the consultative forum would struggle to raise its profile and legitimacy against the more orthodox role and format of the negotiating forum. There was, moreover, the possibility of role confusion where some individuals sat on both forums. In effect, both management and unions needed to explore the ramifications of what had been agreed here. In addition, they both had to address the fact that neither managers nor trade union representatives locally had any real experience with a dialogue-based, joint problem-solving approach called 'partnership'. In these circumstances, the need for training and a chance to develop some 'partnering' skills was compelling.

Dancing lessons

UNISON and Vertex management secured DTI Partnership fund support for a six-month training programme aimed at developing partnership skills and competencies. A series of two-day joint workshops attended by trade union representatives and senior and middle managers were held to implement the programme. The training facilitators used the real-life business and social issues facing the company as the substance of these workshops. This enabled some frankly sceptical managers to witness at first-hand the quality and effectiveness of trade union thinking. Equally, it gave trade union representatives the chance to see the 'bigger picture' and to get at detailed information. For both parties it afforded the opportunity of working together at problem solving in a 'safe' (i.e. a training) environment. The second part of the training extended this approach by setting up three sub-groups to examine some particularly difficult employment relations issues with a view to reporting back to the partnership forums. The results were, by popular consent, impressive. Perhaps most significant was the 60-page guide to raise awareness about the cultural diversity amongst the ethnically mixed workforce in the Bolton call centre. It was recognised that such a guide would never have been produced by orthodox collective bargaining engagement: 'we just would not have gone there' was the common conclusion. Equally, the other two groups came up with sound proposals for improving the flexibility of the workforce (crucial in a 24 hour, 7 days a week, 365 days per year business) and came up with a means of boosting the recruitment and retention of employees (high attrition rates are a feature of many call centres) by improving the pay opportunities of new starters.

By the end of the training programme Vertex were confident enough to roll out the 'Bolton model' in their other call centres in the North West of England. The partnership approach became an integral part of their bids for new outsourcing contracts and UNISON stood squarely alongside them as advocates of this form of industrial relations engagement. Their joint efforts were recognised by the Chartered Institute of Personal Development (CIPD) who awarded Vertex the prestigious 'people management of the year' award.

Conclusion: growing pains and increasingly complex strategic choices

By conventional business measures, Vertex has been a notable success in a highly competitive market. The partnership approach with UNISON has been spread across virtually all of the new contracts the company has subsequently obtained. It is fair to say that this process has not always been easy or enthusiastically received by local management and trade union leaders. The realisation that the universality of the Bolton model could not be relied upon ('one size does not fit all') has been painfully recognised. Nonetheless, the senior management at both Vertex and UNISON have, to date, been unstinting in their commitment and efforts to find ways to adapt the partnership approach to the prevailing local conditions.

Two notable challenges have tested the partnership in recent years. The first has been the management's desire to produce a harmonised pay and conditions structure to cover all the various workplaces that Vertex has acquired. A wide-ranging dialogue was set up with UNISON and the other unions involved and a series of joint 'problem solving' workshops were held to finalise an agreement. The second, emerged partly from the Enron debacle and partly from the rapid rise of India as an 'offshore' call centre location. One of Vertex's key contracts was to deliver call centre and billing services to Eastern Electricity owned by TXU. TXU sold Eastern in the wake of Enron and the new owners made it clear to Vertex that they were looking for cost savings. At about this time Vertex acquired call centre capacity in India where labour costs are a fraction of those in the UK.

These developments have altered the economic dynamics and have posed a significant challenge to the partnership. At the time of writing, the dialogue is still going on how best to deal with the 'global' dance represented by India. The idea of 'formation dancing' with a harmonised pay structure has been partially achieved, although the difficulties experienced in trying to finalise pay negotiations in 2003 demonstrated that at that time this was one dance too far as unions balloted their members and some contemplated industrial action.

Audit criteria for partnership agreements

Gains in information and consultation rights and procedures. The partnership agreement brought substantial increases in both the scale and significance of the information disclosed to the trade unions. New procedures were put in place for both bargaining and consultation.

Structural improvements in trade unionism. UNISON was able to represent members at the Bolton call centre more effectively in both the consultative and bargaining forums. The extension of the Bolton 'model' to other call centre sites generally brought with it similar structural improvements. This was not universally acknowledged however. There were two call centre locations where the partnership approach was seen by local UNISON representatives to be more problematic insofar as structural improvements were concerned.

Gains (and scope) in joint problem solving. The partnership procedures rapidly extended joint problem solving (initially at Bolton but later in other sites) into issues that would not normally have been touched by conventional collective bargaining. The drawing up of the guide to cultural diversity within the workplace was a good example of this.

Advances in substance of collective agreements. Considerable efforts were put into developing a collective agreement that would realign terms and conditions of employment across the company's sites within a common framework. Improvements in flexibility at the workplace were agreed by the partnership process.

Measurability of gains. Both managers and union representatives were keen to develop meaningful measures of effectiveness. Commonplace here was the impact that joint decision-making had on the rate of attrition in the business. It was also widely agreed that decisions on a range of employment issues had, on the whole, been reached more rapidly.

Improvements in target setting and aspiration management.   Call centre operations are inherently target driven. What the partnership dialogue achieved was a much wider knowledge of the target-setting process and the significance of missed targets in terms of contractual penalties incurred. The success of the Bolton model certainly lifted the aspirations of both managers and trade union representatives to extend the coverage of joint decision-making elsewhere in Vertex's operations

Preservation of union independence.   The need to preserve union independence was much debated. The fact that pay negotiations in 2003 resulted in disagreement and consultative ballots run by the UNISON was evidence that unions could still operate independently of the joint processes of partnership.

Advances in the quality of working life and/or work organisation.   Some of the changes suggested by the unions to achieve greater flexibility at the Bolton site resulted in improved start and finish times for groups of workers. Improvements in the pay and prospects of new starters obviously boosted their quality of life in and out of work.

Appendices: Case Studies

Privatised Organisations

Appendix A8
It's a Knock-out: Social Partnership at Anglian Water

Denis Gregory

Introduction

The privatisation in 1989 and subsequent restructuring of the UK's Water industry, in the 1990s, confronted trade unions with some uncomfortable strategic choices. First, there was the need to deal with the initial threat and then reality of privatisation. Second, came the challenge of how to adjust in the immediate post-privatisation period. Lastly, and more recently, unions have needed to come to terms with the consequences of tougher regulatory pressures and the restructuring and further fragmentation of the Water industry as the ownership of companies has changed and new corporate strategies have developed.

This case study looks at the strategic choices made by the trade unions at one of the privatised water companies, Anglian Water Services (AWS), over the period 1996–2003. In particular, it attempts to evaluate the partnership strategy developed by the unions and the company to deal with the consequences of the post-privatisation business environment.

Methodology

The case study is mostly drawn from the author's first-hand experience and observations as a consultant to the social partners at Anglian Water. In the first instance, this involved facilitating a series of workshops to explore the concept and produce a design for a partnership structure and process. Thereafter, it led to facilitating various trade union meetings and workshops to review the operation of the partnership process at the company. The author was also centrally involved in delivering a training programme aimed at developing partnership skills for trade unionists and managers involved in the partnership at Anglian Water. Finally, the case study draws upon an interview-based research project that looked at the awareness of partnership at the company. This contact was spread over a period of seven years from 1996 to 2003 which enabled the partnership to be observed through its launch and early development to its current position.

Background to the company and trade unions

In terms of geographical area covered, AWS, is one of the largest of the UK's regional water companies supplying some five million customers in an area spanning 27,500 square kilometres. Following privatisation, the Directors of Anglian Water have pursued an expansionist corporate strategy which has seen the formation of an ultimate parent company: Anglian Water Group (AWG) to oversee and co-ordinate the activity of the traditional water and waste water business (AWS) with the emerging and acquired businesses such as the group's overseas activity (Anglian Water International) and its move into construction and civil engineering. Most recently (2002), AWG has completed a major restructuring which has in essence *demarcated* AWS which operates under licence and is *separated* from the 'non-regulated' businesses that form the rest of the group.

Anglian Water during the period under review recognised and negotiated with four trade unions namely, UNISON, GMB, AMICUS and the TGWU. As is frequently the case in large UK companies, the unions involved were, to an extent, competing with each other for membership. Broadly speaking, UNISON had the biggest membership covering field operatives, administrative, technical and clerical staff, the GMB were next in size covering field operatives, AMICUS represented skilled craft workers such as engineers and electricians and had some supervisory staff in membership whilst the TGWU had a relatively small presence covering transport staff. All the unions involved had campaigned vigorously and vociferously against privatisation.

Industrial relations at Anglian Water

Under public ownership, the Water industry was not known as a militant or particularly dispute-prone sector. It could be more accurately characterised as a relatively trouble-free industry where union membership density was high and stable. Terms and conditions of employment in the Water industry were regulated by a national collective bargaining agreement.

After privatisation, the individual water companies all set up company-level negotiations. In most cases these arrangements continued to recognise the unions who had traditionally been involved in collective bargaining. In one or two instances, however, trade unions were de-recognised insofar as collective bargaining was concerned as management sought to break away from past practice and develop alternative approaches. Anglian Water was not one of these breakaway companies. What Anglian did was to seek a 'better way' to carry out the processes of industrial relations by modifying the existing relationship it had with the four trade unions. This led eventually to the setting up of a 'Company Council' charged with developing and implementing a partnership approach to industrial relations.

Given the vehement opposition of the Unions, it was hardly surprising that industrial relations at Anglian went through a period of deterioration in the aftermath of privatisation. As unions adjusted to the reality of privatisation at the political level, they were confronted by management bent on reorganising the company to meet the twin sets of pressures from shareholders and the Office of Water Regulation (OFWAT). This prompted new management strategies targeting 'costly staffing levels' and 'inefficient working practices'. This set the scene for industrial relations unrest.

Certainly, the final agreements that were achieved in the sector as a whole during the first few years after privatisation were in line with or above the 'going rate' across the labour market. In Anglia's case, however, the time it took to reach agreement became steadily longer – to the frustration of all concerned.

New dances: the emergence of management's strategy

The introduction of a range of Human Resources Management (HRM) initiatives by the company in the early 1990s was also influential in creating uncertainty and industrial relations turbulence. As with the majority of the UK's privatised utility companies, Anglian wasted little time in beginning a process of rationalisation aimed at reducing 'headcount', de-layering management and promoting teamwork.

The strategic choices facing management at this point ranged from de-recognising the trade unions and replacing them with a form of company-based representation to keeping faith with the unions but radically re-designing the existing industrial relations system. The arrival of a high profile Director of Human Resources (HR) confirmed that the company had chosen the latter course. In a presentation to the unions in 1995, setting out their business agenda for 1995/96, the company also proposed a new consultative machinery to help deliver change in HR practices. The company envisaged a consultative structure that would have three operational joint committees: Customer Services, Production, and Engineering and Support. In addition, there would be a joint consultative committee at company level. The latter was formally constituted as the Anglian Water Company Council and held its inaugural meeting in June 1995. The function of the Council was to: '...negotiate and consult on collective terms and conditions, to resolve any collective disputes or grievances arising from them and to address any matter that either party has a legitimate concern about'. Meetings were to be quarterly or more frequently if the business required it and the chair and vice chair positions would alternate annually between the two sides.

The strategic choice for the unions at Anglian Water: boxing or dancing?

It is perhaps worth recalling that a primary strategic choice made by the unions, namely to oppose and campaign against privatisation, had been a failure. This is not to criticise the unions who were bound ideologically, politically and constitutionally to oppose any proposals to end the public ownership of the Water industry. The strength of their opposition did however raise doubts whether they could operate effectively in an environment and with a form of ownership they so plainly rejected. The notion that unions would be willing partners in the prosecution of change at Anglian could not be assumed – a point quickly brought home to management in the first few years after privatisation. At the same time, there were enough realists in key union positions who recognised that being overly defensive and constrained by their distaste for privatisation was not going to be in the best interests of their members.

A paper written by the trade union side chair of the Company Council in 1996 acknowledged that: 'it is no longer sufficient simply to react to whatever the employers propose'. On the contrary, he argued: 'The Trade Union Side need to seize the initiative and set the agenda.' Amongst the issues that the paper highlighted as being crucial to such an objective was the need to consider a dialogue-based 'partnership' approach to manage change at the company. At first glance this looks to be the trade union chair deciding strategically that it was time to 'dance'. Note, however, the aggressive way in which the decision was phrased: the trade unions need to 'seize the initiative and set the agenda'. In other words, the trade unions were signalling their intent to take over the 'dance floor' and install a union disc jockey. Implied in this was the potential for future 'skirmishes' on the dance floor.

Shortly after the unions had completed their review of the first year of partnership, the same trade union official submitted a paper to the Company Council in which he summarised the concerns identified by the trade unions. The primary criticism was, '...management were, in essence, hijacking the agenda and using partnership to drive the issues forward'. In essence, the unions' evaluation of the first year of the Council showed the consultation process (the dance) was in of danger of becoming a means for the company to force through a range of difficult changes based on a shared understanding of the 'business case' for restructuring and reorganisation. Put another way, the unions found themselves dancing almost exclusively to the company's tune. The disappointment of the unions was evident: the hoped for 'win–win' outcomes were seen to be unbalanced – big wins for the company (downsizing and the beginning of outsourcing, for example) against some very small improvements in the issues the unions were pressing.

Nonetheless, after their review the union side decided to continue with the dance. Their strategy at this point was to seek changes in the structure and functions of the Company Council and the three operational joint committees which had, by this stage, been renamed as 'Process Tables'. In effect, the unions wanted to re-configure the dance floor and the type of dancing that could be expected to take place. The changes they proposed were aimed at clarifying the role and functions of both the Council and the Process Tables and dealing with some representational issues that had emerged. In an echo of their earlier paper (seizing the agenda), the unions also set out seven key issues for the Councils' immediate agenda and five objectives for the medium and long term.

Why dance?

The broader, evaluative question arising here concerns the other options confronting the unions at this stage in the development of the partnership at Anglian. Could the unions walk away from the partnership process? Would they be better off returning to a more traditional conflictual (boxing) form of industrial relations engagement? First of all, it should be noted that despite the criticism and disappointment of the key trade union participants, the option of walking away was not put forward during or after the initial review. Even the most critical shop stewards accepted that partnership remained the best option. This may have been because they recognised that one year was too short a period upon which to make such a judgement. It may also have reflected the fact that fellow trade unionists at the benchmark Company Welsh Water had emphasised that it took some time to get the partnership process right.

In the second place, there was the risk that in leaving the partnership the unions would lose the potential to challenge and mitigate at an early stage any plans for re-structuring. Thirdly, the absence of a history of militancy at the company together with the commonly held view that Anglian, despite the uncertain future, was a 'good company to work for' meant there could be no guarantees that the membership would have supported the return to a more traditional, defensive form of industrial relations engagement. Finally, the dialogue at the Company Council had begun to signal the increasing pressures Anglian faced from the Water industry regulator. Moreover, it was also clear that UK water companies had become prime targets for takeover and that Anglian was thought to be vulnerable. Against this backdrop it is perhaps not surprising that the unions chose to give dancing another go.

Reeling and rocking

In the years that followed, the structure the unions had called for following their review was largely put in place. The Company Council became the Company Collective with an expanded brief which included discussing issues of a 'corporate/strategic nature' and 'working to become a strategic business partner' resolving issues and coming to decisions based on 'mutual best interests'. At the same time, the number of Process Tables grew as the company restructured. A major training programme aimed at providing 'partnering' skills to union representatives and management alike was designed and implemented and the partnership at Anglian began to be the subject of external interest. Pay negotiations were settled amicably and on time. Notwithstanding these developments, the partnership was, by common consent, stretched to the limits between 1997 and 2003. What tested the partnership to the extreme was the combination of some unresolved 'trust' issues and the increasingly fraught and complex corporate strategies adopted by the Anglian Board.

It is worth noting that a low level of trust between the partners was identified in the early exploratory workshops at Anglian as the most important constraint to the development of partnership. Linked to this was the issue of poor communications within the company which, it was argued, served to reinforce low trust levels. From the outset it was clear that some participants, both unionists and managers, were uncomfortable with the open dialogue approach which underpinned the partnership. To put it bluntly, they were adherents to the 'management proposes and unions oppose' school of thought. For them, sharing information and reaching consensus-based decisions was a time-consuming exercise which challenged management prerogative and potentially compromised trade union independence. A dual strategy was adopted by the proponents of partnership to deal with this. On the one hand, peer group pressure was applied through very clear messages of support for partnership from the very top of the management hierarchy. On the other, they ensured that the doubters were trained in the techniques and practice of joint problem solving. Both elements in this strategy worked to an extent. However, the trust that was built up was fragile to say the least.

The linked issues of corporate restructuring and outsourcing have both dominated and dictated much of the work of the Company Collective. As Anglian moved from being a regional, publicly owned water business and re-invented itself as an international, business to business, whole infrastructure and asset management company (such went the jargon) there were bound to be difficult industrial relations consequences and casualties. Like the other privatised water companies, Anglian has struggled to appease the regulatory authority's demands for greater efficiency and lower prices whilst keeping shareholders happy and fulfilling the EU's requirements for major investment in infrastructure. The dominant employment relations consequences have been repeated programmes of 'downsizing' and a constant search for higher productivity and lower labour costs. That the partnership process has, to date, survived is a testimony to the efforts of those involved and reflects the strength and value of the dialogue systems that have been developed.

So, how was the dance?

The partnership structures described here have delivered a dialogue which has enabled the workers' voice to be heard both in terms of day-to-day labour relations management issues at the Process Tables and as regards longer term strategic planning and general oversight of the company at the Company Collective. This has both broadened and improved the scope of joint problem solving. One obvious example has been in the efficiency of the collective bargaining process. In recent years, agreement on pay has been reached amicably and on time – something that generally had not been achieved by the previous system. Similarly, the partnership has enabled the scope and substance of agreements to move beyond dealing with the normal terms and conditions of employment. Notable here was the success the partnership had in negotiating a 'TUPE plus' deal (TUPE in the UK stands for Transfer of Undertakings Protection of Employment. It is the UK's transposition of the EU's Acquired Rights Directive) which extended for Anglian employees the coverage of TUPE to embrace the protection of their pension rights if and when they were transferred to another employer. Such pension protection is not covered by the TUPE legislation.

Improvements in the efficiency of pay bargaining and the conclusion of the TUPE plus deal were directly attributable to the partnership process and were measurable. On the other hand, the partnership process did not appear to have made much impression on the ordinary workforce. A survey carried out by members of the Company Collective revealed that five years into the partnership nearly a third of the 200 staff they interviewed had no knowledge of the partnership. Paradoxically, whilst recognition of the Company Collective was high, more than half of those questioned had no knowledge of the Process Tables. The survey showed that staff were inclined to agree that the partnership had made the management of change easier for the company but they rejected the idea that it was also easier for the individual employee. There was overwhelming endorsement for the view that not enough time was given to the views and advice of the workforce when change was taking place at the workplace. Significantly too, the survey participants identified 'ensuring that employees were not under too much work pressure' as the leading priority for partnership action. This latter point suggests that the partnership had struggled to preserve the quality of working life against the backcloth of continuous change. Although it should be said that it is equally difficult to conceive a more orthodox industrial relations approach being any more effective in this context.

Conclusion

Looking back over the period since the partnership process began in 1996, it is easy to conclude that the gains were unequally shared. On the face of it, management downsized the workforce and re-structured the business without much opposition from the trade unions. For their part, the unions preserved collective bargaining, maintained pay levels and (until very recently) achieved an impressive extension of the TUPE regulations. The partnership also led to better inter-union relationships. Moving behind these stark 'headlines' we see that neither side had much room for manoeuvre once the post-privatisation honeymoon period ended and regulatory pressures and predatory competitors began to emerge. In this context, the dialogue-based approach to change was plainly the option favoured by both unions and management. Whether a more traditional confrontational approach would have been any more effective from the union's point of view is impossible to say. It would have been a higher risk option that is for certain and it would appear that the union leadership at Anglian decided that it would not necessarily have delivered commensurate rewards.

Audit criteria for partnership agreements

Gains in information and consultation rights and procedures.   Significant gains in information disclosure and consultation procedures. Workers' voice heard in day-to-day labour relations issues at the Process Tables and on longer term strategic planning.

Structural improvements in trade unionism.   Bargaining rights preserved and enhanced – no threat of de-recognition, but no significant improvements in membership density. Some inter-union tension on poaching members.

Gains (and scope) in joint problem solving. Process Tables and the Company Collective have both broadened and improved the scope of joint problem solving.

Advances in substance of collective agreements. Scope and substance of agreements have moved beyond dealing with the normal terms and conditions of employment, for example, the TUPE agreement.

Measurability of gains. Improvements in the efficiency of pay bargaining and the conclusion of the TUPE plus deal directly attributable to the partnership process and were measurable. But partnership process had little impression on the ordinary workforce.

Improvements in target setting and aspiration management. Survey of staff showed they agreed that partnership had made change management easier for the company but rejected the idea that it was also easier for the individual employee.

Preservation of union independence. Union representatives on occasions plainly did feel compromised, but partnership was seen as allowing room for disagreement. Earlier involvement in decision shaping and greater access to detailed company information both felt to be important strategic gains that on balance enhanced the unions' ability to represent their members effectively.

Advances in the quality of working life and/or work organisation. Partnership struggled to preserve the quality of working life against the backcloth of continuous change. But would a more orthodox industrial relations approach have been any more effective?

Appendix A9
Cautious 'Dancing' in a Privatised Romanian Manufacturing Company

Aurora Trif and Karl Koch

Petromidia: case background

Set up in the late 1970s, Petromidia is the most recently established among the four petrochemical complexes operating in Romania. It was a state-owned company until 2000, when the Rompetrol Group bought 70% of its shares (see Table A9.1). Petromidia comprises a petrochemical plant and a refinery with a processing capacity of around 4.8 million tonnes of oil per year (*The Romanian Oil Sector – Consolidations in the Pipeline*, 2002). After an investment of US$50 million between 1991 and 1994, the company has a globally competitive technology (Florescu, 1996: 18). In 2000, its production of petrol and diesel covered around 4% of the Romanian market, while more than 80% of petrol and 66% of diesel were exported, primarily to Moldavia, Bulgaria and Turkey (Petromidia, 2000). However, the company did not work at full capacity before privatization,[1] due to a shortage of raw materials and a lack of markets for its products. These market distortions were consequences of Romania's oil processing over-capacity (more than three times national demand) as well as a refining capacity that was almost double the size of demand on the domestic market (*The Romanian Oil Sector – Consolidations in the Pipeline*, 2002). As production declined, the company reduced its number of employees from 5,300 in 1989 to 3,668 in 2001, of whom 77% are blue-collar workers (see Table A9.1). Hence, Petromidia represents a case of a large manufacturing company demonstrating difficulties surviving during the transition period due to pre-1989 market distortions.

Table A9.1 Profile of Petromidia (in 2001)

Ownership (% of the main shareholder)	Industry	Exports	Number of employees	Of these, blue-collar workers	Jobs lost since 1989 (% of total in 1989)	Trade union density	Profitable in 2001
Private (70)	Petro-chemical	80%	3,668	77%	30	97%	Yes

Source: Petromidia Human Resource Department.

The study is based on a total of 18 one-to-one semi-structured interviews conducted in June 2001. The sample consisted of seven managers (three senior managers, two human resource managers and two line managers), three trade union representatives and eight employees (two foremen, two white-collar employees and four blue-collar employees).

'Dancing' and 'boxing' at Petromidia

Before exploring industrial relations at Petromidia, the characteristics of the main parties involved are briefly summarised:

- The trade union had begun to play a role in protecting workers' interests only after 1989. There was a company trade union[2] before 1989, but it had insignificant role in the communist context (interviewees). The old union was dissolved in 1989 and a new organisation was established in 1990 by a group of blue-collar workers. It covered 97% of the labour force in 2001. The trade union was divided into a number of sections corresponding to the divisional structure of the company. Each section had an elected representative employed in that particular division, who was responsible for day-to-day contact with union members (interviewees). The company union was affiliated to the Lazar Edeleanu Federation, which belonged to the largest Romanian confederation, called the National Free Trade Union Confederation of Romania – Fratia.
- As regards the employer, the state was the owner of the company until 2000. Before 1989, it established the terms and conditions of employment. After 1989, it had a major role in re-structuring the company, by managing the privatisation process as well as by (not) enforcing financial discipline, which affected job security and other terms and conditions of employment (e.g. wages). Between 1990 and 2000, the company was represented by the largest employers' association from the chemical sector, called Elpega, which negotiated the sectoral collective agreement. Nevertheless, this agreement represented only the minimal framework for the company collective agreement, which has been annually negotiated between the trade union and the company's management team (interviewees). After privatisation the 'new' employer opted out from the employers' association because services provided by the Elpega were considered inadequate. However, the company collective agreement included terms and conditions of employment far better for employees than the sectoral collective agreement, according to the respondents (interviewees).

Therefore, Petromidia had a strong trade union after 1989, which had to deal with the company's management as well as the state that played, at the same time, the role of 'partner' (as employer) and 'referee' (as legislator) during the 1990s.

The approach to industrial relations in Petromidia is examined considering the four dimensions of 'boxing' and 'dancing' identified by Huzzard in Figure 2.7 (Chapter 2). Their synthesis is presented in Table A9.2.

As regards the *action dimension*, which refers to the mode of engagement between the parties, partnership between trade union and management had generally been the strategic choice at Petromidia (Table A9.2). Before privatisation in 2000, trade union and the management had shared interests to get raw materials from the national state agency (the sole authorised distributor), to operate at full capacity to ensure that employees would receive their entire wages.[3] As the company could refine only imported crude oil,[4] it suffered a shortage of raw materials because the state tried to

Table A9.2 Boxing and dancing at Petromidia

Dimensions of interaction	Boxing	Dancing
(a) *Action dimension* (mode of engagement between parties)	*Before privatisation:* Negotiation between trade union alongside management and state over resources, particularly to get crude oil *Since privatisation:* Collective bargaining	*Before privatisation:* Management and trade union shared interests to receive from state as many resources as possible *Since privatisation:* Shared interests to make the company profitable
(b) *Spatial dimension* (arenas of engagement between parties)	*Before privatisation:* • Trade union and management 'boxing' with the state to keep the company operating • Limited company collective bargaining (wages, health and safety etc.) *Since privatisation:* Collective bargaining (wages, investment, training, health and safety, private insurance, job security etc.)	*Before privatisation:* • Management and trade union shared interests to get subsidies for the company to survive • Management and workers learn together to operate the sophisticated technology *Since privatisation:* Commitment of the labour force to the company, training, dialogue concerning organisation changes
(c) *Cultural dimension* (mindset governing engagement between parties)	*Before privatisation:* No boxing culture at company level (high trust) *Since privatisation:* Degree of suspicion between the parties (medium trust)	*Before privatisation:* • Commitment of the union to the firm and training, employee participation, and job security by management • Management and workers belong to the same community outside the workplace *Since privatisation:* • Commitment of the union to the firm and encouragement of employee participation, empowerment and job security by employer
(d) *Identity dimension* (roles of the parties)	*Before privatisation:* Protect employees rights against the state *Since privatisation:* Protect employees rights against employer	*Before privatisation:* • Generally, value-adding partners (trade union and management team) • Social gap between management and employees has increased *Since privatisation:* • Value-adding partners

reduce imports to a minimum to pay back its debts during the 1980s. This shortage had become even worse during the 1990s after the embargo against Iraq (which was supposed to pay back its debts to Romania in crude oil) due to the Gulf War. Additionally, trade union and the management had a common interest in maintaining the company operation despite its huge debts towards the state during the 1990s. As a result, the trade union and the management team were partners performing on the same dance floor, while boxing together against the state, to get resources to keep the company operating.

After privatisation, the trade union chose a partnership approach with the new employer. Since Petromidia had struggled to survive during the 1990s, trade union alongside management supported the privatisation of the company, being considered by respondents as the only way to make the company profitable (interviewees). Furthermore, the employer's strategy has been to build on the existing partnership. Collective bargaining had taken place, but the employer fulfilled almost fully trade union demands, including job security and the highest wages in the local area (interviewees). Therefore, as regards the action dimension, dancing and boxing co-exist at Petromidia, but evidence shows that dancing had been the dominant approach.

With regard to the *spatial dimension,* which refers to arenas of engagement between the parties (Figure 2.7), findings indicate that at the company level the parties engaged more on the dance floor than in the boxing ring. Nonetheless, the relationship between the newly established trade union and the management team started with a 'boxing match' in 1990. The elected trade union leaders required that employees through secret vote should (also) endorse managers (interviewees). Employees generally validated the management team, apart from the general manager, who left the company following the 'low trust' vote.

Subsequently, there was genuine collaboration ('dancing') between the management team and the company trade union, and decisions regarding the labour force were taken jointly (interviewees). A union official revealed that union representatives have had a consultative role and are invited to all meetings of the management board regarding production. They are also consulted on redundancies, training and investment (interviewees). The partnership approach was confirmed in 1997, when the government decided that Petromidia should be closed down due to the fact that it was making huge losses. Trade union officials initiated a meeting with the Prime Minister Ciorbea, where, together with the Chief Executive, they convinced the government that it was state intervention in the price of fuel as well as the exchange rate (which was kept very low) which made the company non-profitable (respondent participant in the meeting).

Additionally, the union was involved in the privatisation process. The union negotiated with the buyer the level of investment as well as securing the jobs of the 3,577 employees for five years (*Rompetrol Magazine,* 2000: 6). According to a senior manager from the Rompetrol group:

> ... at Petromidia there was a trade union which had a company attached not a company with a trade union. In the privatisation contract, union representatives achieved a clause to keep the number of jobs for five years and to retain certain managerial prerogatives, such as to be part of a mixed commission which takes any employment decision. The contract also stipulated that trade union should be allowed to participate in individual bargaining as well as to be informed about individual wages, which are supposed to be confidential.

This gives the impression that the 'new' employer is willing to change some of these clauses in the near future. Therefore, the 'partnership' approach at company level has proved to be a viable solution for the company to win its 'boxing match' with the state in order to survive, but 'cautious' dancing with the new employer appears to have taken place since privatisation.

With regard to the *cultural dimension*, there was virtually no boxing culture at company level before privatisation. Petromidia was built on the Black Sea coast to have easy access to imported oil, but there was no specialised labour force in the area, since it was the first chemical company in the Dobrogea region. In order to attract and retain employees from areas with tradition in the chemical industry, such as Ploiesti and Petrosani, the management team offered them a 'package' comprising a flat, a gas cylinder and the job for the 'wife' (interviewees). As a result, apart from few senior managers, most employees, both managers and workers, had begun to work with Petromidia at the same time (for many it was their first job), lived in similar flats and created a community that has became a town (Navodari). Furthermore, managers and workers learned together how to operate the chemical installations (which were the most advanced in Romania), while the opportunity to change jobs was very limited even after 1989 (interviewees). In this context, the union was committed to the firm, while the management encouraged high trust relationships (interviewees).

Since privatisation, the trade union and the new management team have worked together to maintain the high trust relationships, but some suspicions from both parties have remained. Despite the agreement that the company would secure the existing number of jobs, employees feared that they might lose their jobs as well as the fact that trade union leaders might become co-opted by management (interviewees). From the employer side, certain senior managers considered that the trade union has had too many rights (as indicated by the extract presented earlier). Another issue pointed out by respondents was the limited communication and transparency, which promoted distrust between management and employees (interviewees). Therefore, overall, there has been a long-term 'partnership approach' ('dancing'), but certain suspicions about possible 'boxing' or 'sleeping together' between the dancing partners have occurred since privatisation.

As to the *identity dimension,* which refers to the role of the parties, evidence suggests that the strategic choice of the trade union has been to act as value-adding partners. The choice of the union was to adopt a partnership approach, since the union had the fundamental shared interest with the management maintaining operation of the company during the difficult transition period to keep employees' jobs (interviewees). However, the social gap between managers and workers has been increasing, particularly since privatisation (interviewees), as managers' salaries have become far higher than workers' wages. Nevertheless, union representatives considered the partnership approach as the best way to protect members' interests even after privatisation, to make the company profitable, as otherwise everybody would be in a losing position (interviewees). Hence, the roles of the parties and their social position have become more distinctive, but they still act as value-adding partners.

Summing up, the trade union and management have not always been partners on the dance floor even if there have been occasions where they have danced separately. However, evidence indicates that partnership has dominated their relationship concerning all four dimensions identified in the theoretical framework. Hence, Petromidia illustrates a case where the strategic choice of both trade union and the management team has been to develop a partnership 'dance' approach to industrial relations at the company level, which resulted in a win–win situation for both parties.

Conclusion

This case study explores industrial relations in a recently privatised petrochemical company (Petromidia). Evidence indicates that partnership between top management and the trade union had developed during the 1990s as the only strategy to keep the company operating. Following a fierce 'boxing match' between the trade union and the state in 1997 when the company was supposed to be closed down, the company was privatised in 2000. The strategic choice of both trade union and the new management team was to build on the existent partnership approach. Despite an unfavourable external context, the company managed to make considerable profits in 2001, which resulted in an improvement of the quality of working life of the labour force (e.g. to secure jobs, high wages, training etc.).[5] Nevertheless, evidence suggested cautious 'dancing' between trade union and the new employer in 2001, when the research was conducted. The gains made during the 1990s in consultation procedures and the scope of joint problem solving may begin to diminish if the trade union cannot preserve its independence as well as respond to, or even anticipate, the needs of its members in dealing with the private employer. Although very limited research concerning industrial relations has been conducted in Romania, this case study appears to be an atypical example of an (uncertain) successful partnership at the company level.

Audit criteria for partnership agreements

Gains in information and consultation rights and procedures. Information sharing and proactive union participation in organisational decision-making has been a key result of the partnership before privatisation. Enhanced employee participation (information and consultation) in the workplace decision-making initiated by management after privatisation.

Structural improvements in trade unionism. It is difficult to say whether partnership determined structural improvements, as a very high union density is typical for very large companies in Romania.

Gains (and scope) in joint problem solving. A very broad scope of coverage has been obtained with union participation in virtually all matters concerning the organisation. However, the scope of joint problem solving appeared to diminish after privatisation.

Advances in substance of collective agreements. Gains in employment security and wages have been key achievements in the partnership. Important gains in employee training rights and opportunities have been achieved.

Measurability of gains. Measurable achievements are the preservation of the existing number of jobs for five years (2000–05) after privatisation, a high level of wages and improvement in the work environment.

Improvements in target setting and aspiration management. Partnership has allowed the union to be consulted in the privatisation process, including in setting the level of investment for the period 2000–05.

Preservation of union independence. The outcomes of the partnership increased the internal legitimacy of the union. However, since privatisation the union has begun to lose its power as well as its independence from the management according to some respondents.

Advances in the quality of working life and/or work organisation. The partnership has led to improvements in many aspects of the quality of working life, such as employment security, work environment and training.

Notes

1. For example in 1999, Petromidia was inactive for eight months and operated at 20% capacity; it had sales of US$167 million, but net profits were minus US$ 32.4 million (*The Romanian Oil Sector – Looking Back in Anger,* 2001: 14).
2. In Romania, as in other Eastern European countries, the basic unit of the union hierarchy is the company (Clarke *et al.*, 2003).
3. Even before 1989 employees only used to receive between 60% and 80% of their monthly wages due to the fact that the 'plan' was not fulfilled (interviewees).
4. Domestic crude oil has too high a sulphur content for its technology.
5. It is acknowledged that apart from the partnership approach, Petromidia had particular features, which helped it survive and to have a positive outcome in 2001 (e.g. it was bought by an investor which had considerable resources, had a globally competitive technology etc.).

References

Clarke, L. Cremers, J. and Janssen, J. (2003) *EU Enlargement – Construction Labour Relations as a Pilot.* London: Reed Business Information.

Facts and Figures [online], December 2001. Available from: htpp://www.rompetrol.ro/about/facts.asp [Accessed 23 Jan. 2003].

Florescu, M. (1996) *Este eficienta petrochimia?* Bucharest: Chiminform Data S.A.

Petromidia (2000) *Raportul pentru privatizare [Privatisation Report]* (unpublished).

Rompetrol Magazine, November 2000, Bucharest: Rompetrol Publication.

The Romanian Oil Sector – *Consolidations in the Pipeline* [online], 2002. Available from: http://www.majorcompanies.ro/digest/business.htm [Accessed 25 Jan. 2002].

The Romanian Oil Sector – Looking Back in Anger [online], 2001. Available from: htpp://www.majorcompanies.ro [Accessed 14 Nov. 2001].

Appendix A10
Dutch Railways: From Dancing to Boxing – And Back
Maarten van Klaveren and Wim Sprenger

Introduction

It was a horrible week for users of the Dutch railway network, that first week of December 2001. Performance according to the timetable and production schedules, heavily contested by many workers of Nederlandse Spoorwegen (NS, Dutch Railways), reached an all-time low. Only 68% of Dutch trains officially arrived on time (within three minutes of scheduled time). At the same time, the sickness rates of the NS workforce went up to historic records. A typical headline from front-page journal articles included: 'Social climate at NS at zero level' (De Volkskrant, 2001). Distrust seemed omnipresent, not only between management and the workforce, but also between various 'blood groups' among the workers. NS staff were described as 'demoralised', travellers as 'utterly discouraged' (cf. Van Walsem, 2002).

Yet at the same time, hidden from the general public, hopeful developments were taking place inside NS. A major initiator was the works council. The council invested much time and energy in developing a new production model – a major condition for restoring trust at all levels. The acceptance of this model by a new generation of more partnership-oriented managers has indeed opened up new perspectives for NS. New combinations of dancing and boxing seem to be developing, although the actual trust levels are still fragile.

In this appendix, we will describe and analyse the development of labour relations at Dutch Railways: from old-style dancing to boxing – and back. We first go into the plans for privatisation and splitting up of the railway system, a major external constraint in the last decade. Then, we consider the debate about the contested 'trip-around-the-church'.

Privatisation

In the early 1990s, a process of privatisation of the Dutch railways system started. By 1992, the government had already agreed with the principle that NS had to be self-sufficient and competitive towards outsiders. Three years later, under the first 'purple' coalition in The Hague, a parliamentary majority voted for self-sufficiency for NS, appeased by weak promises concerning the responsibility of the government for maintaining adequate service levels.

Railway workers, their unions and the NS works council felt the threat of job losses and lower wage levels as the most probable results of the announced outsourcing of large parts of the railway network to cheaper newcomers. NS developed into an autonomous company, with the perspective of a stock exchange quotation and with the state, remaining the main shareholder, 'at arms length'. Anticipating EU railway traffic deregulation, the government split up the company into divisions. However, a legal basis for privatisation was still lacking.

In this insecure situation, the NS Passengers management postponed investments in new trains until after 2002, and cut maintenance costs by €50 million. From 2000 on, in particular, service levels and customer satisfaction figures for Dutch Railways went down dramatically. NS lost its top position on punctuality among the European railway systems. In summer 2001, NS CEO Hans Huisinga recognised (Huibregtsen, 2001):

> To be honest, we have already been cutting back expenditures since the early 1990s. This means that we are a long way behind on service and quality.

Under growing opposition, outsourcing only happened in the North East and the outer Southern regions. By mid-2001, the responsible minister, Netelenbos, declared the privatisation process of NS Passengers dead and buried. She re-negotiated a performance contract with NS, agreeing upon 80% punctuality in one-quarter as the bottom line instead of the former 88%. When this average in the last quarter of 2001 turned out to be 79.9%, the minister dismissed Huisinga as CEO. The directors, supporting Huisinga, resigned. The minister replaced them by top government officials. In his first press conference Karel Noordzij, the new interim-CEO, made the new orientation clear: NS would no longer be made ready for a stock exchange quotation and sold 'in pieces'.

Yet, in between, the privatisation process had been the driver of fundamental changes in the most important relations in and concerning NS:

- the former hierarchical relations between NS and the state transformed into contractual and conflictual relations. Boxing dominated the negotiations between the company and the Ministry of Transport and Public Works about ticket prices, levels of service and punctuality, and necessary long-term investments – negotiations that lasted for over five years;
- a new and predominantly boxing relation developed between NS and Rover, the association of travellers/customers;
- the relations between management and workers', representatives, formerly characterised by 'dancing' and strong feelings for 'the big railways family', gradually developed into distrust – partly because both parties were losing focus on conditions for sustainable development of NS, partly as a result of new, more antagonistic managerial strategies, willing to combat the so-called bureaucratic public services culture.

The 'trip-around-the-church'

Before the recognition by the NS CEO that cost cuts were the main factor behind the service level decline, the NS board had focused on the efficiency of the train crews. In May 1999, they launched a strategic plan with a new production model as its core. In this model, shifts and personnel logistics were restructured in order to diminish disruption to the heavily challenged time schedules. The majority of train crews were to be restricted to a small number of lines. Soon, this model for 'process simplification' was condemned by growing numbers of NS workers and typified as the 'trip-around-the-church' model. First, they perceived the plan as another attack on their autonomy at work. This was understandable. NS directors made clear in interviews that the plan could be instrumental in breaking down the comradely ties of engine drivers and conductors, seen as a main force behind wildcat strikes (Breedeveld, 1999). Second, many NS workers saw more job-related disadvantages in the model: more monotonous work might lead to less safety, and the risks to be traced and recognised by aggressive customers were thought to be quite large.

Last but not least, many were afraid of the new plan as a way of preparing less productive or profitable lines for further outsourcing. A deep trust gap became clear. The state was no longer safeguarding the position of NS 'having parked the company in nowhere land, somewhere between market and state', as an old unionist put it (Strating, 2002). The alternating boxing and dancing strategies of the management side also had a high price. Distrust seemed to prevail everywhere. Moreover, the poor performance of NS made 'railways bashing' a national sport in the Netherlands, with detrimental effects on the self-esteem and motivation of many NS workers from all ranks.

How, then, were perspectives changed? In summer 1999, the main negotiator of the largest union at NS, FNV Bondgenoten, decided to accept a model for 'process simplification' as such, when the NS management guaranteed a minimum of variety in drivers' and conductors' jobs. In this, he was followed by colleagues from four other unions, including the VVMC, a young non-confederation union of NS drivers. Both negotiators stated their conviction that NS had to go through a thorough change process and that the damage would be enormous if this process were blocked. However, a majority of the rank-and-file of both unions voted against the 'agreement in principle'.

When in April 2000, the FNV members again voted against the agreement, the FNV negotiator quit his job. All unions signed the agreement, also the VVMC, because they had no legal possibilities to withdraw. As a reaction, the first 'workers' collectives', most of whom were instantly formed during the negotiation rounds, showed their presence. In June 2000 they organised the first, rather small wildcat strike against the new production model. Militant VVMC and FNV activists were among the organisers, but the unions were bound to the agreement and could not support them. At the same time, the new FNV negotiator, Andries van den Berg, tried to use strike threats in arguing that the 'trip-around-the-church' agreement had no future because it lacked rank-and-file support. His effort failed. Two years later, Van den Berg reflected on the positions of management and workforce alike (Wessels, 2003: 87):

> I came from manufacturing industry and had negotiated with Shell and Akzo [...]. In 'normal' manufacturing companies, an agreement doesn't count if there is no support among the workforce [...] The workforce too took a position different than I was wont to. In manufacturing, everybody, from top to bottom, is convinced of the necessity of the continuity of the company. Even when boxing, they keep this in mind. At NS, this is different. Workers here cannot imagine a future without Railways.

The next strike, organised by 15 collectives, took place in December 2000. The FNV union used this workers' pressure to initiate 'peace talks', including representatives of the collectives and chaired by former FNV union officer Han Noten. VVMC preferred the boxing route and walked away, whereas FNV and the small CNV union negotiated some improvements for the workers in the process schemes. Yet, the majority of FNV members vetoed the new agreement. On 8 March 2001, Van den Berg took a quite unusual and 'unpolderlike' step: he unilaterally cancelled the agreement of April 2000. His FNV union board accepted the risk of a huge NS claim. The collectives felt strengthened and announced the next strike.

Minister Netelenbos reacted in polder model terms: she started an arbitration procedure. Arbitrators were Johan Stekelenburg, former FNV chairman, and Hans Blankert, former chairman of the main employers' association. The dominant issue was the possibility of postponing the 'process simplification' before the new NS timetable started, on 10 June. The CEO of NS neglected the advice of the arbitrators, arguing that such postponement was impossible. From then on, the conflict escalated rapidly. In April 2001, FNV Bondgenoten and VVMC, competing for the favours of the more militant section of the rank-and-file, proclaimed in various ways three 1-day strikes. The FNV confederation came under pressure from angry members and passengers.

A new round of negotiations followed. The results as of 23 April did not differ that much from earlier agreements, except the clause that the works council should make a new process model, to be accepted by the NS management or at least subject to arbitration. Although fewer than 7% of FNV Bondgenoten membership at NS voted, a majority of these were against the new agreement. Bondgenoten leaders seemed to position themselves on the sidelines. The union board gambled on the works council, with 9 out of the 17 members belonging to the FNV faction. The works council decided to carry out the 23 April accord.

The introduction of the 'trip-around-the-church' in June was no success. Traffic control had to resort to an emergency summer schedule, withdrawing some 300 trains. The works council hired an external adviser, Prof. Chris Peeters, but he undermined trust relations by starting to work for the NS management as well. In November 2001, near the all-time low point in labour relations, the works council hired Basis & Beleid, employee consultants, and the Ortec technical bureau to support the development of the alternative process model. A broad consultation process was started up, by gathering ideas and bottlenecks among the staff; deepening these in working conferences; condensing them into a small number of models; testing these models; choosing a few models, and testing these again. A monitoring committee with external 'heavyweights', mainly retired unionists, had to keep all parties involved together (Nordbeck, 2002).

The works council project started in a situation of distrust between the various factions among the workers. This gradually changed. It certainly helped that in the meantime NS management had been replaced. Some more partnership-friendly managers came in, notably the new personnel director, Han Noten. He stressed the importance of good labour relations from the outset. Noten chose to stay passive on the works council project. In the short run, this continued insecurity on the council's side, but it may have strengthened its members' self-confidence. Moreover, Noordzij, Huisinga's successor, gained popularity by his 'listening and talking everywhere' efforts to restore trust relations.

On 22 May 2002, the works council handed over their advice to the NS Passengers board. The central message was: 'Replace the "trip-around-the-church" by the alternative production model: "Sharing the fun and the trouble".' The board decided to accept the latter model and to introduce it, with some minor alterations, in the 2003 timetable.

Unions, works council and collectives

The FNV Bondgenoten union found itself during the heyday of the 'trip-around-the-church' conflict in a difficult position. Its railway group, the result of a merger with a non-confederation railway union two years earlier, was being torn between three poles:

1. radical defensive claims brought forward by train crews, rather uncompromisingly supported by a rising non-confederation union and the workers' collectives;

2. the general public, partly joined by other FNV unions, broadly condemning the strikes as boxing actions too extreme considering the nature of the conflict;
3. NS top management, trying to break down boxing and dancing practices within the company based on its public character, sometimes suggesting to dance themselves and then sticking to boxing.

The main negotiator of FNV Bondgenoten until April 2000 tried to maintain a dancing dominated strategy, however, not keeping enough contact with the boxing arena and with the boxing attitudes of his membership. His successor oriented the union towards boxing again, but he played an ace of trumps: the works council. Although this was a gamble, the council's investment in the production model project resulted in the restoration of minimal trust levels and a basis for partnering. The changes in the union landscape were thorough. Bondgenoten installed a completely new full-time officers team, operating in a much more decentralised manner than before. Most workers' collectives had already been disbanded by spring 2002.

Yet, the restored trust levels are still fragile. It remains to be seen how they hold under renewed outside pressure. In the words of Noordzij and Noten: 'The system is still quite unstable' (Bouma, 2002). Recently a Minister of Traffic was upset by the poor state of maintenance, especially of railway infrastructure. The spare train capacity of NS is very low compared to international standards. There will be major financial constraints as well. Moreover, in 2002 the parliament voted for auctioning 22 'unprofitable' railway lines.

Finally, a number of lessons for trade unions can be drawn from this case:

- A union strategy of dancing and boxing activities, based on a stable model of industrial relations in the public sector, can be vulnerable if the environment changes drastically. In this case privatisation and new forms of competition, more antagonistic management strategies and lack of clarity about future developments undermined the effectiveness of the dancing arena.
- Restoring trust as a precondition for successful dancing strategies is a process that needs intense commitment from the different parties and players: at NS the different trade unions, the works council, management, arbitrators – and at arms length government and the passengers.
- Abstaining from dancing and returning to the boxing arena may seem less difficult, but cannot solve complex problems related to work organisation and employee commitment.
- Unions trying to combine boxing and dancing strategies face a huge challenge to 'organise' the trade-off between boxing and dancing: bringing together the different actors inside the unions, works councillors and public opinion. Making strategic choices is not enough: new competencies are needed to guide such processes, especially in turbulent environments.
- Unions and works councils can box and dance together effectively, under recognition of each others' strengths and weaknesses (that may vary over time).
- Differences between sectors and corporate cultures are highly relevant factors for success or failure of boxing and dancing strategies.

Audit criteria applied to Dutch Railways case

Gains in information and consultation rights and procedure. No.

Structural improvements in trade unionism. Stronger power base among activists and membership.

Gains (and scope) in joint problem solving. Gains in joint management of production model and shifts.

Advances in substance of collective agreements. Agreements include better working conditions and shift schemes.

Measurability of gains. Concerning new production model: yes.

Improvements in target setting and aspiration management. Too early to judge.

Preservation of union independence. Yes (but because of leading role of works council!).

Advances in the quality of working life and/or work organisation. Related to new production model: yes.

References

Breedeveld, M. (1999) 'Alles moet anders. De Nederlandse Spoorwegen reorganiseren', *NRC-Handelsblad*, 20 March.

Bouma, J.-D. (2002) 'Kaartjesknippen is geen verworven recht. NS-bestuurders Han Noten en Pamela Bouwmeester over de reorganisatie', *NRC-Handelsblad*, 12 April.

De Volkskrant, 'Sociaal klimaat bij NS op vriespeil', 6 December.

Dikker, A. (2002) 'Bedrijfsportret NS. Ontspoord', *Zeggenschap* No. 3: 22–8.

Huibregtsen, M. (2001) 'Het spoor bijster', *Management Scope* Summer 2001.

Nordbeck, H. (2002) *Het rijdend personeel laat van zich horen. Hoe het rondje om de kerk verdween.* Utrecht: OR NS Reizigers.

Strating, H. (2002) 'Falen van NS-directie is ook falen van de politiek', *De Volkskrant* 5 January.

Van Walsem, S. (2002) 'De treinreiziger is inmiddels volkomen ontmoedigd', *De Volkskrant* 4 January.

Wessels, K. (2003) *Verkeerd spoor. De crisis bij de NS.* Amsterdam/Antwerpen: L. J. Veen.

Appendices: Case Studies

Public Sector Services

Appendix A11
Multi-Union Partnership, City of Seattle, Washington, US

Steven Deutsch

Background

Municipal governments operate across the globe and constitute a large employer segment in each society. In the US, this sector has witnessed some of the more accomplished labour–management partnerships (see the full chapter on the US Chapter 11, in this volume). This case focuses on Seattle, Washington but there are obvious points of generalisability, which will be offered.

Seattle is a city located on the Pacific Northwest Coast. Historically the major industries that developed were wood products and aerospace. The city served as a major port on the Pacific and hence always had a strong internationally oriented economy. Boeing Aircraft extended that and the micro-electronic boom of recent decades spawned gigantic Microsoft and many other high-tech firms, which play a large part in the economy of the city and region.

The economic challenges, part precipitated by the 11 September 2001 tragedy, and the resultant stock market downturn and major impact on travel and aerospace, have been huge for Seattle. Pressures to improve city services while cutting costs and improving efficiency have been significant.

What follows comes from observation, interviews and action research – intervention training and evaluation.

The Seattle labour–management partnership experience

In the mid-1990s the first effort to create a structure led to the emergence of a city-wide union coalition leadership group of the 25 unions, which represent the city workforce. The 'Service Excellence Partnership' was born: 'The goal is improved services [to local citizens]; the method is to unleash the creativity of the entire workforce by giving it the authority and training to figure out how to work in better ways' (Kaboolian, 1999). The structure that was established recognised that while each City Department had considerable autonomy, it was critical to build a shared culture that permeated the entire city management and workforce. A City-wide Labor–Management Leadership Committee was created in 1995. By 1998, the labour agreement between the City and Coalition Unions established language for the Labor–Management Leadership Committee and the particular issues of employment security, which was a top union priority.

The city-wide structures have been critical to set the tone and build on-going labour–management trust and agreements. Yet the work happens at a lower level and Departmental Labor–Management Committees and local worksite Employee Involvement Committees are the operational structures to effect union and worker voice in work re-structuring and decision-making. As in all effective partnerships, training for committee effectiveness has been essential and a key part of the Seattle effort.

By 1999, the social partners did an assessment of accomplishments (*Results Book*, 1999), which documented real change. There was a dramatic decrease in grievances, a major drop in lost time due to injuries and illnesses, and many tangible cost savings. The continued Partnership seemed to deliver mutual gains results for labour and management alike. In 1991, a strong resolution on Work Force and Compensation Philosophy was adopted by the Mayor and City Council, which articulated a commitment to joint union– management decision-making, a culture of worker participation, and a joint approach to work place problem solving and change.

An election that brought in a new mayor was one of the intervening variables, something that often affects employee involvement efforts. One principle in labour-management partnering efforts is that a change in top leadership can be critical in altering the level of commitment, both in philosophy and critical resources, needed to sustain a partnering effort. This was exactly what the unions perceived to happen in Seattle, where there was a setback, which placed stress upon the labour–management relationship. Unions also recognised that the prior years' success had depended upon the strong commitment of the previous mayor. They also noted that unions had done an insufficient job of training union members as they newly came onto the labour–management committees, at each level. The recognition of this has renewed union commitment to internal training and linking union strategies to training (Douglas, 2003). This, again, is a key principle that runs through all successful labour–management efforts. Training of union participants is critical for the success of the effort, its link to over-all union strategies and goals, and to the building of the union.

By 2003, things had advanced again. The new mayor strengthened his recognition of the value of a good labour–management partnership to achieve the goals of improved service and reduced costs for the city doing its work – from utilities to transportation, parks and recreation to police, courts and libraries to housing, fire to convention centres and so on. The Coalition of City Unions has become stronger in strategic recognition of the role of the Partnership. The Labor–Management Leadership Committee union members meet monthly with the Mayor and City Council or staff to work on issues affecting labour. In short, there is a working and on-going relationship with partners committed to jointly working on shared goals and solving problems.

Another assessment was done which again documents many of the particular outcomes of the labour–management partnership (*Results Book*, 2003). Especially important are the 15 'lessons learned' which are articulated. Their importance is due to operating principles and their experience in identifying critical factors that will help to sustain the partnership. For example, 'having the right mix of technical and interpersonal skills, experience, and commitment among employee involvement committee members'. This fits well with general learnings from labour–management partnerships.

Early in 2003, the top leadership in the Partnership held a retreat to strengthen the labour–management relationship, particularly in light of fiscal pressures to reduce the workforce, contract work out of the bargaining unit to lower cost non-union private sector employers, hire temporary workers without benefits and at lesser pay rates and other such schemes antithetical to union interests. They adopted a statement on

'How City Work Gets Done', which was perceived to be a strong effort to reaffirm the commitment to working jointly in a partnering arrangement. The existing public document on the labour–management partnership not only discusses wages, hours, and terms and conditions of employment as within the scope of dialogue, but explicitly states, 'Any other issues ... may be brought to the discussion by either party, recognising that either party will have the right to choose not to enter into the discussion. However, in the spirit of engaging in this partnership relationship, all parties will do everything to honor the spirit of this agreement.' Having a wide scope of legitimacy for topics to be addressed by the partnership is a healthy indicator of authentic power sharing and commitment to working jointly.

Of course, the future of this public sector labour–management partnership remains to be seen. The life of most employee involvement efforts within the US does not exceed five years. Seattle has gone beyond that and the commitment by city management and leadership appears to be solid. More critical yet is the union leadership, which sees the partnership as an essential part of its strategic and proactive vision of the future (Douglas, 2003). Essential to the sustained effort in all partnerships is the continuing commitment and engagement by labour and management. The City of Seattle and Coalition of City Union has this in place. They both want to continue to 'dance' together.

Many of the success ingredients in the Seattle case were equally developed in the nearby city of Portland, Oregon. We turn briefly to that to highlight a key factor and lesson about the demise of a labour–management partnership.

A brief note about partnership success turned into demise

The chapter on US (Chapter 11) in this volume characterises the labour–management partnership in Portland, Oregon. As in Seattle, the partnership gained national recognition, was given a grant by the Federal Mediation and Conciliation Services and in the late 1990s made great progress. My involvement was considerable, including training of union leadership and union partnership personnel, and working with the union and management partnership leadership team.

A number of significant achievements are outlined in Chapter 11. These include demonstrable cost savings for the city, which meant employment security and prevention of contracting work outside of the union bargaining units (McIntosh, 2000). Other benefits for the union included higher levels of membership active participation in the union, decreased grievance filing, improvements in the work environment.

However, while the challenges continued all along, the arrangement came to a crashing end when management unilaterally chooses to terminate its participation in any partnership process. This is critical and typically a terminal act. While there might continue to be some employee involvement at local work sites, one cannot 'dance' in the usual mode without a dancing partner. A critical conclusion from this is that *it is absolutely essential to maintain commitment to partnering as a minimal prerequisite for potential good outcomes for both labor and management.* Unilateral withdrawal is tantamount to a 'kiss of death' and must be avoided.

While the change in top executive (Mayor) and some top management in Seattle posed challenges, there remained a continued commitment to search for common ground through a joint labour–management process. The lesson from Portland was well understood in Seattle.

Concluding lessons from the case for unions

- Top leadership in management and the union is vital, but authentic power-sharing arrangements must be institutionalised and not rely upon particular leaders who may be replaced.
- Capacity building and skills training for union leaders is vital and training must be a key component of a partnership agreement. The union needs constantly to build up its core of competent leaders to assure that the process works.
- The union must approach labour–management partnerships and worker participation schemes from a strategic perspective, assuring that the process and any agreement fits into the broader union agenda.
- Maintaining management commitment to a joint labour–management agreement is vital and any appropriate mechanisms to assure continuity and avoid unilateralism must be part of the union strategy.
- Because of the continuing fiscal crisis in the public sector, unions can anticipate permanent pressures in terms of cost containment, contracting out, reducing labour costs and employment security. This places labour–management partnerships in a chronic 'boxing' milieu, and compels unions to strategise how a 'dancing' approach might protect union interests while achieving mutual goals with management.

Audit criteria for partnership agreements

Gains in information and consultation rights and procedures. A greater voice for workers and the union in work organisation has been achieved.

Structural improvements in trade unionism. The partnership efforts have led to increased activism and participation by the union membership. There have also been some organising successes.

Gains (and scope) in joint problem solving. A greater voice for workers and the union in work organisation has been achieved.

Advances in substance of collective agreements. There have been advances in obtaining enhanced employment security.

Measurability of gains. There has been a reduction of grievances.

Improvements in target setting and aspiration management. No clear evidence from case data.

Preservation of union independence. No evidence of loss of independence in case data.

Advances in the quality of working life and/or work organisation. Notable improvements in the work environment have been achieved.

References

City of Seattle and Coalition of City Unions, Employee Involvement Committee (1999) *Results Book*. Seattle.

City of Seattle and Coalition of City Unions Employee Involvement Committee (2001) *Results Book*. Seattle.

Douglas, D. K. (2003) Union Representative, International Federation of Professional and Technical Engineers, Local 17, Seattle, Washington (conversations and communications).

Kaboolian, L. (1999) 'Municipal Government Positioned for the 21st Century: Labor–Management Cooperation in Seattle', Harvard University, Working Paper.

McIntosh, D. (2000) 'Portland Labor–Management Program Saving Tax Dollars', *Northwest Labor Press* (21 January).

Appendix A12
The Swedish Teachers Agreement: A Successful Date at the School Dance?

Erling Forsman

Case background and method

At the end of February 1996, the Swedish Union of Teachers and the National Union of Teachers in Sweden entered into an agreement implying a new way of thinking between the main parties in the industrial relations arena in the Swedish school sector.[1] Together with the employers, represented by the Swedish Federation of Municipalities and County Councils, it was agreed that school development, goal fulfilment and quality were a shared responsibility. From a union perspective, the agreement was a clear success: it contained concrete promises of higher salaries. During a five-year period, the teachers have been guaranteed 10% more than other groups within the municipal sector.

In December 2001, the parties entered into a new five-year school development agreement, built on the same basic idea of shared responsibility for a better education system and a salary system which would support school development. In this round, the salary development was guaranteed to be at least 20% over five years.

This is a case study of how the new agreements emerged. It is based on interviews with key actors at the central level from employers and unions as well as analysis of the main central agreements. The interview data collected also includes evaluative comments on the agreements and outcomes.

From conflict to dialogue

Before we enter into a closer presentation of the two 5-year teacher agreements, it is necessary to say something, briefly, about the prior history of the sector. The agreements, signalling a move towards co-operation, can be seen as a radical departure from the then existing trends in the Swedish public sector (Elvander, 2002). Why did this trend breach appear in the mid-1990s? During the latter part of the 1980s and the beginning of the 1990s, a process of decentralisation took place within the private sector from national agreements to agreements at the sector level. The same tendency was detectable at the municipal level, where municipalities and county councils wanted increased local influence on the setting of salaries. A more extensive use of salaries as an instrument of personnel policy was also desired. Marcus Gustafsson, Negotiation Director of the Swedish Federation of Municipalities, described the change thus:

> At the beginning of the 1980s the municipalities considered the then existing salary system as too rigid. More and more people were of the view that they wanted a system where the individual co-worker would be more visible. We had to be able to encourage and reward those who do a good job, it was said.

The central system for negotiations on teachers' salaries and conditions were thus under great pressure. At the same time, a transition from a tariff system[2] to individual salaries was in progress in the whole public sector.

On the eve of the 1996 salary negotiations, the teachers' associations faced a dilemma. It was estimated that it would not be possible to defend the centrally regulated systems and, simultaneously, reach the general goal of re-valuing the teaching profession. There was strong pressure from the members. The then chairperson of the Swedish Union of Teachers, Christer Romilson, expressed himself as follows:

> We had growing demands for salary adjustments. During the '80s we had fallen behind the private sector. At the beginning of the '90s the gaps increased. This led to intense pressure, sharp opposition. (Interview, Romilson, December 2001)

The question, then, was how the union could get out of a tight squeeze between the members and the employers. The answer was to enter discussions with the adversary on a school development agreement, where higher salaries became the central goal. At the same time, they were prepared to reconsider certain earlier standpoints. In interviews about the strategic assessments made from the union side, both Romilson and Johansson (Chairpersons of the Swedish Union of Teachers and the National Union of Teachers respectively at the time of the negotiations) stressed that a point was reached where they considered the traditional route of high salary demands supported by strike threats as being closed off. Romilson:

> We saw that there was an increased understanding in society about the role of education. The 'knowledge society' pointed towards school and the teacher's role. We can use an opinion like this, but only if we show that we take responsibility for school quality and development and not only talk about wanting more pay and shorter working-hours. (Interview, Romilson, December 2001)

Johansson pointed to the fact that the experience of other unions, for example the nurses' union, influenced their analysis:

> The Association changed its strategy at the beginning of the '90s. We had pursued a hard union struggle with poor results and had to find a new way. We also saw that those who had raised their salaries had not gone out on strike. (Interview, Johansson, December 2001)

The 1996 school development agreement

After more than a year's negotiating, the first school development agreement was signed at the end of January 1996. The negotiation process had been unique. For the first time, the parties exchanged no written demands. The agreement was, instead, developed over long discussions and dialogue – a clear trend breach in the industrial relations culture in the school arena.

The agreement begins with a short analysis of the importance of the school sector for Sweden's economic development. The chain of thought in short can be understood as follows: Sweden's potential for maintaining its internationally competitive position depended on its educational standards. Improvements in standards called for long-term development where both parties had responsibilities. The salary policy has been considered as a tool for raising quality (The Swedish Union of Teachers and the National Union of Teachers, 1996). The specific pot the teachers receive compared to other municipality employees, that is, 2% extra per year for five years, is directly connected to efforts concerning school development. According to the two teacher associations' written commentaries on the agreement, the extra 'salary space' is to be used as 'partly ... compensation for changes in the salary and working-hours system, partly for stimulating change and development work' (The Swedish Union of Teachers and the National Union of Teachers, 1998). In a supplement to the agreement, this is expressed more distinctly: 'Salary increases are in the first place to be distributed to those employees who in particular contribute to school development and renewal' (The Swedish Union of Teachers and the National Union of Teachers, 1996).

The agreement implies a change of system. The teachers are obliged to abandon their earlier tariff salary system with a central agreement laying down basic guarantees applying to individual salary setting. The latter has now been introduced. In the view of one of the unions at that time:

> The setting of salary rates is ... to be done consistently and is to be based on clear and distinct principles for salary rates, which are well known to the employees beforehand. The connections between salary developments and the development of work assignments and work performance must be made clear. (The Swedish Union of Teachers and the National Union of Teachers, 1996: 8)

Still more important, and more disputed, is the fact that the winding up of the regulation of working-hours has been initiated. This has existed for different teacher groups in the form of defined teaching duties. In its place the teachers now get the same working-hours per year as other full-time employees in municipalities and county councils.

The role of the parties

The central parties, the two teachers' associations and the Swedish Association of Municipalities, each expressly take mutual responsibility for the realisation of the intentions of the agreement. They see their role being changed from a normative to consultative one. For the first time, the agreement is presented at workplaces jointly by the representatives of the parties. The election of joint support teams has also been agreed. Their task, upon requests for help from the parties in a municipality, is to try to 'promote the local process concerning the development of work organisation, salary policy, local regulations of teachers' working-hours etc, and contribute to the solution of any disputes that may arise' (The Swedish Union of Teachers and the National Union of Teachers, 1996: 41). The local parties are also recommended to form working groups with the task of supporting the local process around the renewal of an individual school.

What happened?

In effect, the 1996 agreement ushered in something of a cultural revolution for schools. In five years, they were to move from a strongly centralised system to a situation where most questions of salaries and working conditions were decided at the local level, at the same time as co-operative partnerships on school development were set up. That problems would arise, however, was unavoidable. In interviews with employers and union representatives, some problems were pointed out as being more important than others:

- The agreement was launched parallel to substantial economies being affected within the public sector to address an accelerating budget deficit. This led many teachers to look at the agreement not as a development agreement but as a rationalisation agreement, where they were expected to do more with fewer resources. In particular, this was the case concerning working-hours.
- Difficulties arose in bringing about local responsibility for the development process anticipated by the central agreement. Johansson expressed this as follows:

  > Local agreements meant a cultural revolution. Many teachers became worn out and considered it was easier with central regulation: the daily problems took over. We did not have the strength to debate *why* we did this. (Interview, Johansson, December 2001)

In many places, it took the full agreement period, five years, to reach local agreements. Still, the dominant impression is that the parties are satisfied. The employers got their eagerly longed-for system change and thus a possibility for individual salary setting within the whole municipality. Above all, the teachers were awarded a substantial salary raise, 27–28% over five years. As inflation during this period had been around 2% per year, it is probably the best development in real salaries the teachers have ever had during an agreement period. For the first time in many a year, the teachers have enjoyed salary development equivalent to, or better than, the private sector. The agreement also seems to have given the teachers increased influence over school development. In a survey in 1999 of a random selection of 5000 members carried out at the request of the two teachers' associations, three quarters of those who answered said that they had participated in discussions on school development, connected to the agreement, on many or a few occasions (Stibra School consultants, 1999).

The year 2000 school development agreement

An effort is now being made in the current five-year agreement, signed in December 2000 and operative from 1 April 2000 to 31 March 2005, to find solutions to some of the problems identified by the parties during the first five-year agreement. This has included setting a clear deadline for when the local agreements must be ready. Already after five months, the parties must locally have made agreements which ' ... guarantee the employee's participation in the formation of his/her own work situation as well as in the work for change and development during the agreement period' (The Co-operation Council of the Swedish Union of Teachers and the National Union of Teachers, 2001). It also includes a declaration up front in its main clause against an exploitation of teachers: ' ... it (is) important that work organisation and job content are formulated so that teachers are not exposed to physical or psychic strain that can cause ill health' (The Co-operation Council of the Swedish Union of Teachers and the National Union of Teachers, 2001).

The salary section of the agreement departed somewhat from its predecessor. A guaranteed outcome, a minimum of a 4% or 2% raise respectively, only exists during the first two agreement years. Instead of also defining an outcome for the final three years, the parties state that they agree on a 20% outcome at the national level after five years. The basic principle is also now individual salary setting, as well as trust in the connection between salary and school development. One must create a ' ... process where the employee's results and salary development are tied together so that the positive connection between salaries, motivation and results is reached' (The Co-operation Council of the Swedish Union of Teachers and the National Union of Teachers, 2001). The agreement also defines how salaries are to be reviewed.

In an evaluation conducted by the Swedish Union of Teachers when half of the agreement period had passed, it was stated that the goal, a minimum 20% raise over five years, seems to be on its way to being fulfilled. Seven municipalities out of ten stated that it is certain or quite probable that they will reach the goal. Salaries seem so far to have increased by 4.5% to 5% a year on average, but the variations are considerable.

From salary struggle to professional co-operation partner

Several factors were decisive in the union's change of strategy from boxing to dancing at the beginning of the 1990s. Some of them seem, however, to have been more decisive than others in shaping the choice of direction.

External factors:

- The prevailing political discourse and a common view on the increasing role of education in economic growth were putting the education system and its improvement into focus. Here a strategic possibility could be found to exploit a willingness to invest in education.
- The increasing decentralisation of the Swedish school system. The goals of the national curriculum gave a wide berth for local adjustment on the road towards reaching these goals. It created a situation where the teachers as a collective as well as individually are given an increased opportunity to influence the formation of education. In one sense, the employer was becoming more dependent on the teachers for realising the educational mission. This dependency could be used for advancing union agendas.

Internal factors:

- An increased connection between professional positions and union strategy. The teachers were trying to use their knowledge of the school system to become strong actors in the school development process and to use participation as an argument for higher salaries.
- Even higher costs and fewer gains from the strike weapon were discerned by the unions. The experience of the 1980s was that strikes were expensive, not least from a public relations point of view, and only yielded some tenth of a per cent more in salary increases.

After seven years of school development agreements, it is also possible to see how a new union structure, new priorities and new working methods become a necessary condition for using the possibilities of the new agreement in a successful way. At all levels, this has led to needs for new competencies and a change in the distribution of resources. The meaning of membership and the role the member plays in the union has also changed. Here I will briefly point to some shifts in the centre of gravity for union work and union roles at different levels.

Central level

- Besides being a negotiator and a supervisor of the agreements, the mission of the union at the national level has transformed into an introducing, supporting and evaluating one. Co-operation and contact with the counterpart is also stressed after the negotiation process. Mutual support and evaluation is a part of the agreement.
- Training on internal union matters has received an increased focus in the union representatives' new mission.
- The new role of the individual member has created an increased necessity for information materials as well as for training on agreements and negotiation tactics as opposed to the union officers and representatives previously having this skill.

Local level (municipalities)

- The demand for local agreements in the school agreement has caused the union representatives to change from being mainly negotiators to also becoming agreement developers.
- The direct negotiations are complemented by negotiation support being given to individual members. The demand for local education of the members is accordingly growing.
- The need for extensive local networks (workplace representatives) has become greater. Co-ordination and supervision of these has become increasingly important.
- Active participation in school development calls for greater discussion of ideas: what does one want to achieve?

The individual member

- Is granted greater responsibility for salary development as well as participation in the forms of influence created through the agreement. His or her role is changing from being a democratic confirmer of the actions of the union representatives towards engaging in active cooperation at the workplace.

Audit criteria for partnership agreements

Gains in information and consultation rights and procedures.   New union role as participant in local development processes has opened up new channels of information disclosure and arenas for participation.

Structural improvements in trade unionism.   New horizontal structures emerging especially at the local level to facilitate exchanges of experience and learning.

Gains (and scope) in joint problem solving.   New union role as 'school developer' necessitates new joint dialogue both on problem solving and long-term issues.

Advances in substance of collective agreements. Various aspects of development work and job content are explicitly covered in the agreements. New participation rights also codified.

Measurability of gains. Surveys reveal that 75% of teachers have been involved in school development activities. Significant real salary increases in line with or better than the private sector.

Improvements in target setting and aspiration management. Three-year agreements with explicit targets in terms of salary levels.

Preservation of union independence. No evidence of concessions to employers that amount to incorporation.

Advances in the quality of working life and/or work organisation. Three quarters of union members have experienced job enrichment through being engaged in school and curriculum development. New participation practices and voice mechanisms have emerged at workplaces.

Notes

1. The Swedish Union of Teachers (Lärarförbundet, LF) has approximately 176 000 active members, most of whom work as teachers in compulsory primary and secondary schools, in upper secondary schools and as pre-school teachers and leisure-time pedagogues. The Swedish Union of Teachers is affiliated to the Swedish Confederation of Professional Employees (TCO). The National Union of Teachers in Sweden (Lärarnas riksförbund, LR) has around 55 000 active members. They principally work in the compulsory schools and upper secondary schools. The National Union of Teachers is affiliated to the Swedish Confederation of Professional Associations (SACO). Together the two associations organise more than 90% of teachers in Sweden.
2. The tariff arrangement comprised a central agreement with salary steps according to one's position and years of service.

References

Elvander, N. (2002) 'Industriavtalet och Saltsjöbadsavtalet – en Jämförelse', *Arbetsmarknad och Arbetsliv* 8(3): 191–204.

Lärarförbundet och Lärarnas Riksförbund (1996) *Avtal 2000*.

Lärarförbundet och Lärarnas Riksförbund (1998) *Gemensamt kommentarmaterial Avtal 2000*.

Lärarförbundets och Lärarnas Riksförbunds Samverkansråd (2001) *ÖLA 00*.

STIBRA Skolkonsult (1999) *Uppföljning av avtal 2000 – U3*.

Appendices: Case Studies

'New' Union Issues

Appendix A13
Work Organisation in Germany: A Case Study of Boxing and Dancing
Martin Kuhlmann

Case background

As in most other countries, work organisation has not been a major issue for German unions over the years. Although work organisation has always been relevant for unions because of its impact on occupational health, wages or working time, work organisation was not directly on the agenda of union policies and even most works councils began to work on the development of work organisation in a systematic way only recently. There have also been differences between sectors and unions: the most active in the field of work organisation has been IG Metall. Overall, work organisation is not a consolidated area for union policy and works council activities (Düll and Bechtle, 1988). Legally, the influence of the works council is only indirect. Co-determination rights exist only where work organisation affects wage systems, working times or safety issues.

Work organisation in Germany had been the domain of management, while wages and working times have been the most important union issues from the very beginnings of the industrial relations system. Even during the 'golden age' (see Chapter 7), unions used their bargaining power mainly to maximise benefits and to extend workers' social rights. The logic of collective bargaining in itself drew unions towards higher wages and shorter working times because demanding this could be generalised more easily than policies on work organisation. Finally, work organisation was not a major issue for a long period for unions because the German labour movement mostly had a positive view about rationalisation because of its productivity-oriented policy. Only in the field of industrial engineering where the unions have been integrated into associations like Refa (work-study) or the MTM-Foundation were there any connections to be found between issues of workload and wages in relation to work organisation.

A new policy field emerges for unions

In the 1970s, this situation started to change. In the wake of rising labour unrest since the late 1960s and the on-going discussions about rising problems at work (Schumann *et al.*, 1971), IG Metall not only struggled for a reduction in overall working time, but also reached an agreement which included five minutes extra rest time each hour for workers on assembly lines and other workers with repetitive work. Even this path-breaking agreement, reached in the region of Nordwürttemberg/Nordbaden, did not provide unions with direct influence on work organisation, which remained a core managerial prerogative. But it nevertheless did open up a new field for union policy (Schauer *et al.*, 1984). Backed by state-run action programmes and research initiatives around quality-of-work-life (QWL) issues, work organisation became an increasingly relevant issue for union activists. New legislation on co-determination and the new works constitution act were enacted that gave worker representatives stronger rights in the 1970s.

The central union federation DGB then started consulting works councils about technology and work through a network of technology offices ('Technologieberatung-sstellen') during the 1980s. So the issue of work organisation gradually became more important. In more and more firms, works councils backed by the unions tried to influence management decisions on work organisation. IG Metall in particular tried to establish a conceptual framework for getting more influence on planning decisions in the field of work organisation (IG Metall, 1984).

Within the broad framework of work organisation, group work is the type of organi-sation that has been discussed most. The first examples were already introduced in the late 1970s during the QWL-programme financed by government. In the beginning, both unions and management were sceptical, but – to cut a long history short – in the 1980s more and more union people and works councils came to favour group working which basically meant more qualified work, task integration/job enrichment and group self-organisation. These processes involved electing spokespeople, the self-organisation of group meetings and some degrees of self-organisation in daily work patterns. Elected spokespersons in particular were initially opposed from unions and works councils. Both learned only gradually, however, that such spokespersons do not erode their power rep-resenting employees but give them even more influence as long as they are subject to democratic elections. After the lean production-shock, which came in 1992–93 (AKNA, 1993), when German managers for the first time realised that what were often still Tayloristic forms of work organisation in their firms were being outperformed by other production systems, firms increasingly began to modernise their work organisation. In the car industry, for example, almost every company started with some form of group work, reinforcing this through plant/establishment agreements ('Betriebsvereinba-rungen') between management and the works councils (Sperling, 1994).

Boxing and dancing for work organisation choices

Both boxing and dancing emerged in an interesting way in the field of work organi-sation. The first results in this area, the agreement on additional rest times, were reached by the union in a more or less traditional way (boxing) ending in a collective agreement. But during the 1980s, there were also some arrangements which included a high level of co-operation (dancing) when management and works councils, backed by the union, worked together on introducing new forms of work organisation in high-tech production areas. In some cases, the works council together with union experts were successful in persuading management to try less Tayloristic forms of work organisation. Formally, management would have been able to introduce their pre-ferred form of work organisation unilaterally, so it was a mixture of good arguments, soft pressures and internal coalition building, which finally led to the forms of work organisation originally favoured by the unions.

Gradually, at least in some leading firms, a climate and a practice evolved where the works council became much more systematically involved in the development of work organisation. However, a tendency towards new forms of work organisation in line with union principles about group work was visible only where management introduced new technologies. With the introduction of new technology, management tried to win support from the works councils, and more and more firms realised that while non-Tayloristic forms of work organisation might well lead to higher wages, they also enabled higher productivity with a good payoff.

Works councils provide dance instructors for the arrival of lean production

When the idea of lean production came to Germany, it arrived in a situation where a discussion on the modernisation of work organisation was already in place. The German debate at that time was very much about getting away from Taylorism, and therefore, lean production was perceived as anti-Tayloristic and more or less in line with what unions were asking for over the years. More qualified work, less hierarchy, group work, employee involvement all looked possible. Based on this consensus, which broke down later on, the first half of the 1990s saw a couple of joint initiatives between management, works councils and unions to introduce new forms of work organisation based on the principle of mutual gains. Even more important for the tendency towards dancing which was obvious at that time was that companies used members of the works council as experts on work organisation and as partners in the daily work of convincing (and pressuring) middle managers during the process of reorganisation, as well as getting the workforce on its side. When significant advances towards a group-based work organisation and a better work situation were made, this was often because knowledgeable works council members were actively involved in the reorganisation of work. Often far-reaching forms of co-operation between labour and management evolved with work council members taking on virtual managerial roles during the introduction of the new work organisation.

Effects on works councils and the dual system

How did these developments affect the roles and practices of unions and works councils? Did they change the way the dual system worked at the company level? According to case studies on the introduction of group work and interviews made with union officials and members of works councils that were involved into the development of work organisation there were significant changes in their roles. But these changes did not mean that the specific, established style of antagonistic co-operation broke down. Members of works councils stressed that their job still consisted of boxing *and* dancing. Most stated that they were now much more, and more frequently, for the first time officially, involved in planning decisions and the daily management activities of driving and reviewing the reorganisation process. Moreover, this had not meant that the different roles became blurred. Often it was pointed out that it is important to accentuate clearly the different perspectives when explaining the reorganisation to the workforce, the works council's original claims, and what the negotiations with management finally delivered.

Since group work at that time was already an official union policy, there was no split between a union point of view and the policy of the works council. Often the works council used union resources to inform the workforce and sometimes to train spokespeople. Although works council members made it clear that a new form of co-operation was evolving and that much could be gained by exchanging ideas about work organisation, there was no doubt, that (good) results also depended on bargaining. More than that: negotiations about work organisation needed to be backed up with independent legal power and a willingness to take actions if necessary. The importance of boxing is still valid because of lasting differences in the interests of employees and management. But, because of mutual gains that could be reached by group work and other forms of non-Tayloristic work organisation, dancing had a growing importance. Most union people and works council members stressed that boxing and dancing worked hand in hand in the field of work organisation.

Dancing alongside the boxing rings

Although the mutual gains policy on work organisation had a strong focus on dancing, boxing was at that time still important, for several reasons. Works councils used both close co-operation *and* their bargaining power to influence decisions around work organisation. At the same time there were other issues where boxing was basically still in place – although in the German way of always blending it with a willingness to reach a compromise when feasible. In the field of wages and working times, the more adversarial type of action was more or less in place, and the general climate between labour and management became rougher during the 1990s, with several examples of concession bargaining both at the sectoral and the company level. A wave of work stoppages took place when a number of companies announced that they intended to cut sick leave compensation after the conservative government made this possible by changing the law in 1996.

Looking at general developments since the early 1990s, it is obvious that the joint initiatives of introducing group work or other innovations in work organisation were often in parallel with tough bargaining on employment pacts. Managers at many workplaces asked, for example, for work on three shifts instead of two, or working on Saturdays (and sometimes Sundays, too). At the same time, most companies tried to reverse the wage drift of the 'golden age'. More than that, since the second half of the 1990s, conflicts have arisen in several companies even in the area of work organisation when management tried to revert to more restricted forms of work organisation. In the car industry in particular there are examples where there was not only a roll-back of cycle times (Jürgens, 1997), but where at least some actors inside management tried to introduce more elements of the Toyota Production System. Examples included management attempts to appoint team leaders instead of elected spokespeople, others where managers tried to get away from group meetings organised by the group itself.

In some firms, management renegotiated the group work agreements from the early 1990s (OPEL), in other cases management stepped back from their initial plans of a far-reaching break with the existing work policy after resistance from the works council. Sometimes a new phase of close co-operation involving both boxing and dancing was started which led to a further development of new work organisation according to its initial principles (Dörre, 2002). Although there are many initiatives at the local level and the issue of 'good work' is much more on the agenda today (Peters and Schmitthenner, 2003), IG Metall (and German unions in general) nowadays has lost much of its determination and capacity, from the late 1980s and early 1990s, to influence work organisation.

Compared to the work of Manfred Muster from the late 1980s, there is no straightforward concept of good work nowadays. Often the policy on work organisation is simply defensive, and other problems or the debate on the future of collective bargaining are very much in the forefront. Works councils on the other hand are often still active in trying to influence work organisation since this issue is of major importance for many employees. Often, they complain that they get less support and assistance from their union in these areas, particularly when they nowadays have the additional burden of dealing much more with traditional issues like wages, working times or employment security. Depending on the positions adopted by management, there are a range of policies which works councils can and do follow today. In a multi-industry study on innovative work policy (Kuhlmann *et al.*, 2004) we have found all kinds of strategies: these range from close co-operation and active involvement in reorganisation projects within a mutual gains perspective to conflict-oriented bargaining for extra rest times where management have left the mutual gains approach. An overall case audit from the German experience is not possible, however, an audit of the experience at Mercedes Benz is presented here as being illustrative.

Audit criteria for Mercedes Benz work organisation case

Gains in information and consultation rights and procedures. Works councils/ unions became much more involved in strategic (conceptual) and day-to-day (implementation) management tasks. In several plants innovations in work organisation became a joint initiative. Some agreements extended co-determination rights which have been rather weak in the field of work organisation.

Structural improvements in trade unionism. Yes. Since work organisation became the target of union policies and works councils and unions worked much more in detail and concretely with issues related to daily work, the relationship between workers and unions/works councils became much closer. Unions/works councils proved competencies and a willingness to work for employees in a much more direct way than in traditional collective bargaining. Examples of an integration of direct (work groups) and institutionalised (works council/union) representation.

Gains (and scope) in joint problem solving. Employees were able to make gains (better work organisation, good work, working conditions) although the overall economic situation did not allow for major wage increases or other benefits.

Advances in substance of collective agreements. Both on material aspects ('good work'/work enrichment, better working conditions, institutionalisation of group self-organisation) and on procedural rights (co-determination on work organisation issues).

Measurability of gains. Working conditions, 'good work'; since wages are connected to tasks sometimes this policy even resulted in higher wages.

Improvements in target setting and aspiration management. Not clear.

Preservation of union independence. Both for unions and works councils: basically yes but, depending on concrete policy and how the policy was spelled out to the workers/members.

Advances in the quality of working life and/or work organisation. Work enrichment, good work, improvements in working conditions.

References

AKNA (ed.) (1993) *Teamarbeit in der Produktion*. München: Hanser.

Dörre, K. (2002) *Kampf um Beteiligung. Arbeit, Partizipation und industrielle Beziehungen im flexiblen Kapitalismus*. Wiesbaden: Westdeutscher Verlag.

Düll, K. and Bechtle, G. (1988) 'Die Krise des normierten Verhandlungssystems. Rationalisierungsstrategien und industrielle Beziehungen im Betrieb' in Bolte, K.M. (ed.) *Mensch, Arbeit und Betrieb. Beiträge zur Berufs- und Arbeitskräfteforschung*. Weinheim: VCH.

IG Metall (1984) *'Der Mensch muß bleiben'*. Frankfurt/Main: IG Metall.

IG Metall (ed.) (2001) *Flexible Standardisierung*. Frankfurt/Main: IG Metall.

Jürgens, U. (1997) 'Rolling Back Cycle Times: The Renaissance of the Classical Assembly Line in Final Assembly' in Shimokawa, K., Jürgens, U. and Fujimoto, T. (eds) *Transforming Automobile Assembly*. Berlin: Springer.

Kuhlmann, M., Sperling, H. J. and Balzert, S. (2004) *Konzepte innovativer Arbeitspolitik. Good-Practice-Beispiele aus dem Maschinenbau, der Automobil-, Elektro- und Chemischen Industrie*. Berlin: Ed. Sigma.

Peters, J. and Schmitthenner, H. (eds) (2003) *'Gute Arbeit'. Menschengerechte Arbeitsgestaltung als gewerkschaftliche Zukunftsaufgabe*. Hamburg: VSA.

Schumann, M., Gerlach, F., Geschlössl, A. and Milhoffer, P. (1971) *Am Beispiel der Septemberstreiks. Anfang der Rekonstruktionsperiode der Arbeiterklasse? Eine empirische Untersuchung*. Frankfurt/Main: EVA.

Sperling, H. J. (1994) *Innovative Arbeitsorganisation und intelligentes Partizipationsmanagement. Trend-Report Partizipation und Organisation*. Marburg: Schüren.

Appendix A14
Employability and Career Services: A Dutch Example of Combining Collective and Individual, Dancing and Boxing in Union Strategies

Wim Sprenger and Maarten van Klaveren

Introduction

This contribution examines (1) the 'discovery' on the union side that the collective results of boxing and dancing strategies concerning employability and job careers did not break patterns of societal inequality and left groups of individual members aside and (2) union efforts to close this gap by setting up their own services helping workers in making strategic choices about their careers. These efforts ask for new forms of dancing, taking individual interests into consideration within collective conditions.

Since the beginning of the 1980s, the social partners in the Netherlands have been promoting extra training facilities for workers and the unemployed. In various recommendations from SER- and STAR[1] to the bargaining partners, the union confederations and their employer counterparts had been arguing for structural incentives to raise the percentage of the skilled workforce. These recommendations can be characterised as merely dancing activities; however, they paved the way for achievements in boxing rings (collective bargaining in all kinds of sectors).

Following up this preparatory 'massage' at national level in a growing number of sectors special funds had been established to enlarge the number of training and retraining activities, and to refund individual employers for the loss of productivity and the absence of their workers during training sessions. These funds were based on agreements in collective contracts obliging every employer covered by the contract to raise money on an annual basis. When sending one or more workers to a training course, the fund would compensate for various costs incurred.

Nearly every training fund was to be governed jointly: unions and employer organisations in the sector established a governing body, a new dance floor developing out of the boxing agreements. The actors had to decide by consensus on amounts to be refunded to employers training their workforce, on the sort of training that could be financed and the institutions delivering it, and on special groups to be highlighted. Indeed, since 1980 the number of sectoral training funds and the percentage of the workforce to receive training rose quickly and persistently, to over 100 (sub)sectors. However, a number of problems arose, especially for the unions:

- In practice it turned out to be the single employer or the HRM department deciding whether and which workers were invited to training courses.

- Core workers proved to be over-represented among the users; women, older workers, migrants and low-skilled workers were significantly less trained, despite the financial opportunities.
- Employers' needs seemed to be dominant over workers' interests, despite the bipartite governing body of the funds.
- Employers' organisations (and sometimes also unions) blocked possibilities to use the funds for mobility training directed to other employment in the same or another sector – the 'sector money' should primarily be used for training in the existing job.

The collective dance floor turned out to be inadequate to really influence decision-making at the individual level: within the single firm in relation to the single worker. Over and again unions had to face the problem that the most vulnerable or 'needy' workers did not attend courses. Facilitating training in general could be organised, yet ensuring employability of as many workers as possible was much more difficult.

When employers and the European Union increasingly stressed the need for employability in order to cope with rapid changes in the labour market and at workplace level, the unions were hesitant (Veenis, 1998). Was this a management need only, or could employability be turned into a key issue from a workers' perspective?

A pilot with career services

In April 1998, the Dutch Confederation of Trade Unions (FNV) and its largest union, FNV Bondgenoten (manufacturing, services, food and transport) started an experimental training programme in career development for women and low-skilled members, as well as for non-union members. As a Level 2 strategic choice, the pilot could thus be considered as both service development and diversification (see Chapter 2). This pilot project was situated in Rotterdam, and partly financed by the Dutch government and the EU (ADAPT programme). The initiators designed a union training programme aimed at 'multisectoral' job orientation and job mobility. During the training modules, workers were invited to analyse their current job and labour market position, and to identify career steps inside and outside the industry they had been working in.

A year earlier, the Dutch Ministry of Economic Affairs had launched a national employability campaign, inviting various actors – including the trade unions – to promote labour market mobility and job rotation as a condition for competitive growth and empowerment (Ministerie van Economische Zaken, 1998). The FNV confederation took up the challenge, and decided on a proactive strategy on employability, providing workers with new chances and challenges in their professional careers. The Rotterdam pilot was one of the ways in which the union came to the fore within the emerging employability debates in the country (Slob, 2001). It soon turned out that many workers were interested. The pilot training scheme, aimed at 20 participants, had to be repeatedly held to satisfy many more within four months.

In addition, the union organised a survey on employability and career planning needs among its membership. More than half of the members expressed their interest. There was a strong feeling that the union was in a favourable position to offer a career service, considering its special 'knowledge of the labour market'. Moreover, GFK – the survey bureau – reported:

- Workers were considering career possibilities as an ever more important aspect of their working conditions (put in third place of top priorities, after employment and wages).

- Career consultancies were very orientated 'towards the moment': people express their needs only when special circumstances occur. Some of these needs can reflect external factors, such as reorganisation at work or unemployment threats; others are of a more internal character, such as personal ambitions, new work challenges and the wish for different working conditions.
- The interest in union career services was proportionally spread among full-timers and part-timers, men and women, higher and lower skilled workers.
- A potential 'market' for union career services could expand to about 100 000 workers per year, covering 1.5% of the workforce (and about 8% of FNV membership).
- The respondents did not immediately consider the union a serious career consultant. After an explanation by the GFK interviewer of which kind of services a future trade union career consultancy could provide, the idea of career consultancy was very positively received: the workers involved did not expect a union to offer the service, but were very much in favour of union expertise in this field.

Now, nearly five years later, a regular union career service has been developed. FNV Bondgenoten (485 000 members) and the public employees union ABVAKABO FNV (350 000 members) are closely working together in 'FNV Loopbaanadvies' (FNV Career Consultancy). The third large union, FNV Bouw (construction), joined in 2003. Together these unions cover around 85% of the total membership of FNV. Since the end of 2002, members can attend one of the three forms of career services structurally offered by these unions in all seven FNV regional centres:

1. A weekly individual consultation ('spreekuur', 45 minutes net), to discover the promoters of and barriers to labour market mobility.
2. Workshops on special themes for groups of interested workers (one or two half days).
3. Training schemes to assess one's competencies and take steps in the direction of job improvement or job change (6 half days during a course lasting 1–2 months).

One of the main union debates in 1999, when decision-making on how the pilot experiences would and could be implemented was at stake, was about *how* to offer a union career service. Some unionists opted for outsourcing of the service, career consulting being a too professional and risky union activity. They feared that the union would never be able to provide it on a large scale at the quality level needed. Others argued that the union should try to organise the service as close as possible to its core activities, such as collective agreements and member protection (Korte *et al.*, 1999). The pilot experience, which showed that qualified members could be found to offer their skills for a special union service, made these unionists believe a consultancy with professional standards could be developed inside the unions.

FNV Loopbaanadvies: a mature career service

After three years, these optimists now seem to have made their point. Gradually a service has been built up covering the whole country (Sprenger, 2002). Tuesday night is the national 'spreekuur' night. Workshops and training programmes are offered during the year. A group of 40 paid union officials is responsible for the regional organisation, for coaching their consultants and trainers, and for reporting the outcomes in terms of visits and employability questions. At the time of writing, 130 members have been running the service as visiting consultants ('spreekuur') or as a trainer

Table A14.1 Building up FNV Loopbaanadvies 2000–03

Year	Regional centre starting	Visitors 'spreekuur'	Workshops (and visitors)	Training sessions (and visitors)	Total number of visitors
2000	West, North West and Centre	182	—	10 (90)	272
2001	North, East	621	8 (84)	18 (200)	905
2002 (Estimation)	South East,	750	15 (185)	32 (330)	1 265
2003 (Estimation)	South West	1 200	21 (300)	42 (500)	2 000

(workshops and training sessions). All of them have been trained by the unions, and receive annual retraining to keep up with new developments. The growth of Loopbaanadvies is illustrated in Table A14.1.

Women are well represented among the visitors: almost 50%, whereas 29% of the FNV membership is female. Highly skilled members are well served. The lower skilled are somewhat under-represented compared to their share in FNV, although in the core category of visitors (members between 30 and 45 years, those 'in the middle' of a career path) they reasonably make use of the service. Nevertheless, it has been decided to reach more low skilled members with a targeted communication strategy.

Based on two recent surveys we may conclude that the visitors appreciate the new services and rate them quite high. One triggering outcome is that nearly half of the visitors do not immediately feel their expectations have been met. Yet, they rate the service amazingly positively. This outcome could be connected with one of the core values of FNV Loopbaanadvies: the union is not offering solutions or 'taking over' career questions. Instead it is offering a service supporting members to make their own decisions and choices, backed by expertise and process knowledge the consultants and trainers are providing. This is something of a paradigm shift in union services and union identity. Clearly, new level 2 strategic choices are feeding back to Level 1 choices. Empowerment of members, to be in charge of their lifetime decisions, is seen as the enduring form of union employability and career policy – complementing more traditional forms of (social) security and collective protection.

Asked whether the FNV Loopbaanadvies aims had been realised, respondents mentioned about 1.5 of their personal goals actually being realised as a result of visiting the service. A summary of the effects of FNV Loopbaanadvies as reported by visitors is set out in Table A14.2.

Those visitors reporting a conflict situation at work or having high career ambitions show positive results.

'Members for members'

One of the characteristics of FNV Loopbaanadvies is the use of the principle 'members for members'. Consultants and trainers are to be recruited from the membership. Of course, this raises questions such as: were enough well-qualified members available? What is the basis of their profession? Do they appreciate being active for the union in this field? Some 130 members were recruited without many problems. Attracting a

Table A14.2   Effects of FNV Loopbaanadvies as reported by visitors

Realised effect	Percentage of visitors mentioning a personal goal being realised by the service	Relative share of the answer as a percentage
Stimulated thinking about career possibilities	56.4	36.5
Clear view on possibilities and impossibilities in the labour market	43.2	27.9
Looking for new job or function	14.1	9.1
Higher self-consciousness or personal effectiveness	12.4	8.0
Achieved special knowledge	10.8	7.0
No direct effect	17.8	11.5
Total	154.8	100.0

much larger group of members-experts does not seem to be problematic. All seven regional centres have candidates available for enlarging the group. Two of the three consultants and trainers are 'new' union activists. They are relatively highly skilled. The largest group works in commercial and public services. A third is in Human Resources Management, nearly half of them have some management experience. Most combine a personal interest (developing oneself as a career consultant) with a union motive (helping other members in finding their way in their present job, in a new job, or in developing new competencies). For union officials working with this new group of highly motivated members with expert knowledge has proved to be a stimulating and challenging expansion of their own competencies. It appeals to coaching and empowering capacities, quite a new form of dancing within the union.

Based on the now existing regional infrastructure, an increasing number of tailor-made employability projects are now being run or are in the making. For example, all over the Netherlands truck drivers are offered a short workshop on career planning, one of the options being a change in professional life in this demanding and risky job.

A group of experienced metal workers has been assisted in making a career change into a part-time or full-time and certificated job as a teacher in preparatory vocational education for youngsters between 12 and 16 (the school system VMBO). For the members it means using their accumulated skills in a new configuration, often a long cherished dream to help children achieve a skilled job in the metal industry. In other words, the union acts as a facilitator helping its members enter regular vocational training by means of a short entrance trajectory, honouring the post-educational competencies they have achieved at work.

FNV Loopbaanadvies has provided new chances for combining individual services and collective bargaining. FNV recently analysed 219 leading collective agreements and found that 2 out of 3 workers now have the contractual right and facility to develop a personal development programme at company level in which the workers' competencies and preferences for future training and careers are outlined and evaluated (Pentenga, 2002). The individual career service enables unions to acquire first-hand knowledge and experience about employability needs and questions prioritised by the members. This is now to be valued in a better and more proactive employability policy in industries and enterprises. Organising special services, directly connected with collective boxing and dancing challenges, could well be a key for unions to turn themselves into specialists and real representatives of the workers covered by contracts and funds. Recently the newly established infrastructure has been used to help or consult special groups of members faced with job loss or future changes in their workplaces.

Conclusions and lessons for the unions

- For the last 20 years Dutch unions have claimed money and facilities in collective agreements (boxing) to improve training and employability facilities for workers and unemployed.
- In over 100 (sub)sectors bipartite training and employment funds have been established, providing for training costs and compensating employers' sending workers on training courses. Unions and employers together decide on budgets and their use (dancing).
- From 1998 on, the unions decided to be promoters of employability for workers: rapid changes in work organisation and on the labour market urged workers to gain new competencies during working life.
- The FNV confederation set up a career service project to support members in their orientation on the labour market. In this way collective arrangements (boxing and dancing) are connected with individual services (new forms of dancing), leading to empowerment of union members in their job and on the labour market.
- Most of the expertise in this project is provided by skilled union members, many from new member categories (women, higher skilled, service workers). Now unions are starting to make use of existing funds of knowledge and expertise within their membership, that were previously rarely applied for the benefit of members ('members for members'). Using the expertise which is 'at hand' in the union itself is one of the means to rebuild unions into learning organisations.

Audit criteria applied to Dutch career development case

Gains in information and consultation rights and procedures.   Not applicable.

Structural improvements in trade unionism.   Yes, new expertise and experiences conditional for better boxing and dancing on employability.

Gains (and scope) in joint problem solving.   Yes, at the individual level empowering workers.

Advances in substance of collective agreements.   Yes, more expertise on practical needs of workers and 'translation' into collective regulations.

Measurability of gains.   Yes for the service as it runs (members developing into consultants, visits and membership feedback), partly only for longer term results (career steps in response to the service, reactions employers).

Improvements in target setting and aspiration management. Only if collective, workplace-oriented services have been established (employability schemes in cases of mergers or closures, sectoral initiatives for truck drivers, 'cross-overs' from metalworking to the teaching profession).

Preservation of union independence. Yes: one of the 'quality aspects' users attach to this union initiative: unions seen as independent from employers, social security and market institutions.

Advances in the quality of working life and/or work organisation. Yes, certainly quality of working life is improved by members achieving more (em)power(ment) – incidentally it can lead to discussions and steps forward on work organisation.

Note

1. SER is the Social Economic Council, a tripartite national institution with employers, unions and experts advising the government; STAR is the Labour Foundation, a bipartite meeting place of national trade union and employers representatives, reporting to the government and to bargaining parties at sectoral or company level. For more details and backgrounds see Chapter 6.

References

FNV en ITS (2000) *Netwerkvorming, arbeidsmarkt en kwalificatie*, Amsterdam, FNV.

Heijden, B. I. J. M. van der and Thijssen, J. G. J. (eds.) (2003) 'HRD and Employability', *International Journal of Human Development and Management* 3(2).

ILO (2002) *National Initiatives Concerning Social Dialogue on Training – Netherlands.* Genève: ILO.

Korte, T. de, Singerling, E. and Schipper, E. (1999) *Ondernemingsplan Aanbod loopbaanservices FNV Bondgenoten.* Utrecht: Berenschot.

Ministerie van Economische Zaken (1998) *Employability, Verslag Employability Congres 8 October 1997.* Den Haag.

Naegele, G. *et al.* (2003) *A New Organisation of Time Over Working Life*, Dublin: European Foundation.

OECD (2002) *Review of Career Guidance Policies.* Paris: *The Netherlands, National Questionnaire.*

Pentenga, E. (2002) 'CAO-onderhandelingen 2002. Leren loont nog onvoldoende', in FNV, *Onderhandelen bij krimpende wind*, Amsterdam: FNV.

Ploegmakers, A. and Sars, S. (2002), 'Nog geen persoonlijke ontwikkelingsrekening. Een gemiste kans voor Employability', in FNV, *Onderhandelen bij krimpende wind*, Amsterdam: FNV.

Slob, E. (2001) Mobiliteit: werkgeverswens, of werknemersgeluk, in *Dansen over grenzen, Bij het afscheid van Wim Sprenger*, Amsterdam: FNV.

Sprenger, J. W. (2002) *Evaluatie Loopbaanadvisering*, Utrecht: FNV-Bondgenoten en ABVAKABO FNV.

Sprenger, W. (2003) 'Career Planning: A New Trade Union Policy in the Netherlands', in Naegele, G. *et al.* (eds) *A New Organisation of Time over Working Life*, p. 132. Dublin: European Foundation.

Veenis, J. (1998) 'Employability proves to be thorny issue in bargaining round', in *EIRO 1998/1*, Amsterdam: European Foundation, HSI.

Appendix A15
Preparing to Dance – A Development Project for Union Capacity Building at the Workplace

Tommy Nilsson

Introduction[1]

This case study describes a joint development project on competence development for union representatives. The purpose of the project was to strengthen their position at the workplace when dealing with work organisational issues. The text describes why the project started, how it was carried through and its outcomes. The partners in the project were the Swedish Trade Union Confederation, LO, and the National Institute for Working Life (NIWL). The latter is a state financed research institute for working life issues.

Until the 1980s, the main activities of the unions and employers mostly took place at the national level under a regime of 'societal corporatism' (Brulin and Nilsson, 1991). For many decades LO and the employers' top negotiating organisation, SAF (the Swedish Employers' Confederation) were the main actors on the labour market, and wage determination was mainly conducted at national level, albeit with some wage drift locally. Thus both the local union bodies and the employers played a certain role, mainly when dealing with piece rate issues and wage determination based on that system (Huzzard and Nilsson, 2003).

From the 1980s, the workplace became more important as an industrial relations arena. Increasingly, this level has come to play a more important role in wage formation. At the same time LO and its union members became more engaged on the issue of 'rewarding jobs'. Substantial critiques of the old Tayloristic work organisation identified serious health and safety problems and a low level of work motivation on the shop floor. In particular, the report on 'Good Work' published by the Metalworkers union in 1985 played an important role. During the 1990s, the LO unions focused more on organisational and business issues such as work organisation, competence development and productivity (Nilsson, 1999). The need for more co-operation – social partnership – has also been stressed. As one unionist has said: 'We cannot use the traditional negotiating practices to improve our members work organisational conditions, we have to co-operate with the employers to make advances in this field.'

But if union representatives are to dance with the employers at their workplaces and not just be used as pawns without a will of their own, then they have to improve their competencies in areas such as work organisation and productivity, particularly in the area of organisational change competencies. There has to be a change from reactivity to proactivity. The development project 'The Union Role in Workplace Development' – the 'RUD project' was a union response to that challenge, and it expressed a partly new way of thinking within LO.

Method

At the LO Congress in 1996 many speakers argued that local union bodies had to develop ways of exerting far more influence at the workplace on work organisational issues and wage formation systems, and that elected representatives should improve their competencies in these matters. At that time LO had realised that the union position in work organisational development was still pretty weak. The union demand for 'good work', which included horizontal and vertical integration of work tasks on the shop floor, had not progressed in a way that many unionists had hoped.

LO was thus commissioned by the Congress to start projects with the aim of pursuing this union agenda at workplaces. One of these projects was labelled 'Competence Development Directed towards Work Organisation and Wage Systems'. Its aim was to develop and introduce new working methods so that the unions 'could become a stronger participant in work organisational development at workplaces'.

LO proceeded by contacting the NIWL where an intensive action research project was set up. The researcher role became that of knowledge broker, process supporter, sounding board and financial administrator. Moreover, data was collected from the field on network processes as the project unfolded. At the end of the project a quantitative analysis was undertaken of a survey questionnaire of network participants.

Networking for competence development

The RUD project started in January 1998. The project idea was to support the introduction of cross-union networks in which elected unionists could develop their change competencies and competencies on work organisation and wage systems. The way to develop these competencies was through the exchange of workplace-based experiences within networks. The comprehensive goals of the programme were to contribute to the development of blue-collar work and to increase union influence at workplaces. The networks were seen as a complement to traditional union structures.

The learning logic was as follows: equipped with experiences from change processes and change projects at their workplaces, the 'networkers' meet in the networks to exchange experiences with each other, and reflect together on change activities at the workplaces. Equipped with the newly reflected knowledge of change processes, the networkers return to their workplaces where they perform new routines. Thereafter they take their newly acquired experiences back to the network for further discussion and reflection, and so on. With the correct preconditions, both at the workplace and in the network, this spiral-like learning process will improve the networkers change competencies. This competence development logic bears some resemblance to the experiential learning cycle of Kolb (1984).

But this is of course an idealistic learning process. In reality there are many obstacles. At the workplaces there can be a lack of consistent change activities, no participation in change activities from the union side and passive union activists who lack the competencies to take part in existing change projects. Problems found in the networks were that networkers were often absent due to a high degree of workload both for the employer and in the union, a lack of focus on the core change issues and the fact that discussions and reflections often led nowhere.

Project management

The RUD project ran from the beginning of 1998 until the end of 2001. The NIWL spent around 3.5 million SKr each year on the project. LO contributed around 1.5 million SKr. Most of the financial resources were spent on network meetings, covering travel costs, lodging and compensation for loss of earnings. Support for the co-ordinators was also costly (see below). The project was managed by a steering committee, consisting of seven members – two from NIWL (one of whom was the author of this text) and five representing LO. Each LO union selected a 'union contact person' for the project, and this group met the steering committee around four times a year for discussions.

At most, 25 networks were formed and they were spread geographically from the far south to the far north of Sweden. Almost all LO-unions were represented. Between 6 and 12 workplaces were represented in each network. More than 200 networkers were thus engaged in the project. By the end of 2001, 21 networks were still in operation. Most of them continued during 2002.

Each network was led by a 'co-ordinator', who was also a local union activist, and she or he was selected by the steering committee. This recruiting principle was quite new for the unions. Normally, union leaderships appoint the person to occupy posts in the various projects, committees and so on. In the RUD project the co-ordinators were chosen because of their specific qualifications: a high level of work organisation competence and knowledge of change processes at workplaces. The members of the networks were recruited by the co-ordinators. The members of the networks normally met 4–6 times a year, sometimes two days at a time. The union contact persons occasionally attended the three-day meetings for the network co-ordinators.

The 20 or so co-ordinators met together with the steering committee and the union contact persons twice a year, for three days, for discussion and reflection on change processes and work organisation: both successes and failures were reflected upon.

Each network was defined as a project and could spend around 90000 SKr each per year on meetings, costs for premises and compensation for loss of earnings. The network co-ordinators, together with the networkers, had to draw up a one-year plan of network activities and produce a report on the outcome of the activities. This report was to be delivered to the steering committee. The role of the committee, which had financial responsibility for the project, was to control the network projects, give support to the network members, especially the co-ordinators. The committee members also visited network meetings where they participated in seminars on work organisation development, change processes and wage setting principles. In several of the networks, employer representatives were invited to meetings for discussions and to listening to presentations, often given by representatives from the steering committee.

So what did the networkers do when they met at the network meetings? A common way of working was that one of the networkers invited the others to his/her workplace for one day. In the morning the work processes at a particular plant were shown to the networkers who then had the opportunity to discuss problems and solutions with the workers and their supervisors in the production process. In the afternoon, discussions took place between the networkers about the case that was seen in the morning. At these meetings workers and manager representatives could be present.

Another common type of network meeting consisted of a lecturer being invited to give a presentation on, for example, new types of pay systems. After that, joint reflections took place with the lecturer on how these systems could be implemented at the various workplaces. Sometimes employer representatives (often human resource managers) were invited to these presentations and the subsequent reflective meetings. However, sometimes the meetings did not work well. Instead of discussing matters associated with change in work organisation, discussions also ensued on why people were absent, general union matters, how to recruit new company members replacing those who had quit, and other irrelevant issues.

The outcomes of the project – the results of a survey

In December 2001, a survey of all 200 or so networkers in the project was conducted. Its aim was to see how the network concept of union learning had worked out. The results showed that the overwhelming majority of the networkers had learned considerably from the network meetings in connection with workplace experiences. They improved their capacity to understand work organisation processes as well as change processes and how to act in these processes. They improved their self-confidence, for example their arguing capacity, both in relation to management and to union members at the workplace. This is one important aspect of the concept of organisational change competence. As expected, the interaction between activists from the various unions increased and many new contacts were made both within unions and between them. A commonly held view was that inter-union networking helps activists 'avoid being blind to defects in their own house'. Another effect of the project was that LO leaders decided to support the development of various types of new union networks for competence development.

The survey also showed that some network members learned more than others. To put it another way, some networks had better preconditions for learning compared to others. In short, good preconditions for the type of learning we are talking about here are that the network, soon after setting up, develops a common goal or purpose for the network and that *the participants play an active role both in the network as well as in a change process at the workplaces*. It is also important that participants have considerable support not only from their fellow workers, but also from local managers. Surprisingly, the study showed that inter-union networking had no positive effects on learning. Improved knowledge on work organisation seems to be related to the quality of dialogue and network reflection rather than the networking in itself.

In general the union network participants had a very positive attitude towards the RUD project. The survey showed that over 80% of the networkers would gladly participate in further projects similar to RUD during 2002 or later. Almost nobody was of the view that RUD was unnecessary and that traditional union work was sufficient in the context of workplace change. Typical comments on benefits from the network included:

'... learning new things on general union work';
'... not being so afraid of discussing new union issues that require new ways of thinking';
'... easier to give convincing arguments [on change in work organisation]';
'... obtaining a new view, a holistic view, on rewards and work organisation issues';
'... acquiring more solid ground on which to make a stand';
'... becoming a better union representative'.

Summary and discussion

The conclusion of the RUD project is that exchanges of experience from workplace change in networks, could be a useful tool in the improvement of work organisational competencies for union activists. Inter-union networks for learning can thus function as an important complement to traditional union activities. Even though little actual change in work organisation occurred during the period of the network – the RUD project did not have an immediate effect on work organisation at workplaces – the participants nevertheless developed a capacity for potential action. Networking appears to improve the capacity of activists to be competent partners in work organisational change processes: they are better prepared as proactive partners when dancing with the employers.

Audit criteria for partnership agreements

Gains in information and consultation rights and procedures. None over and above the pre-existing underpinning of co-determination that is already supportive of joint development projects.

Structural improvements in trade unionism. Gains from informal networking within and across unions.

Gains (and scope) in joint problem solving. In the potential sense, increased change competencies have made union representatives more attractive as 'dance partners'.

Advances in substance of collective agreements. Not directly evident.

Measurability of gains. Not directly evident.

Improvements in target setting and aspiration management. Quantified improvements in individual change competencies, but uneven across the project.

Preservation of union independence. Not a joint union/management activity so independence not affected.

Advances in the quality of working life and/or work organisation. Potential improvements generated by increased competencies on work organisation and workplace change in line with union agendas on 'good work'.

Note

1. This text is based on the working paper 'Erfarenhetsutbyte i fackliga nätverk för ökad förändringskompetens', National Institute for Working Life, March 2002. Translated into English the title is: 'Exchange of workplace experiences in cross union networks: supporting change competence development.'

References

Brulin, G., Nilsson, T. (1991) 'From Societsal to Managerial Corporatism: New Forms of Work Organisation as a Transformation Vehicle', *Economic and Industrial Democracy* 12(3): 327–46.

Huzzard, T., Nilsson, T. (2003) 'Fackets nya roll – att dansa med arbetsgivare?' i Wilhelmsson, L. (ed.) *Förnyelse på svenska arbetsplatser: Balansakter och utvecklingsdynamik*. Stockholm: Arbetslivsinstitutet.

Kolb, D. A. (1984) *Experimental Learning; Experiences as the Sources of Learning and Development*. Engelwood Cliffs: Prentice Hall.

Nilsson, T. (1999) 'The Future Role of the Swedish Unions – Increased Local Cooperation for Production Development', *Economic and Industrial Democracy* 20(3): 461–82.

Index